interior Design

materials and specifications

interior Design

materials and specifications

Lisa Godsey

Fairchild Books, Inc.
NEW YORK

Director of Sales and Acquisitions	**Dana Meltzer-Berkowitz**
Executive Editor	**Olga T. Kontzias**
Senior Development Editor	**Jennifer Crane**
Development Editor	**Sylvia L. Weber**
Assistant Development Editors	**Robert Phelps and Blake Royer**
Art Director	**Adam B. Bohannon**
Photo Research	**Erin Fitzsimmons**
Production Manager	**Ginger Hillman**
Senior Production Editor	**Elizabeth Marotta**
Copyeditor	**Debra Kirkby**
Cover Design	**Adam B. Bohannon**
Text Design	**Dutton & Sherman Design**

Second Printing, 2008

Copyright © 2008 Fairchild Publications, Inc.
Fairchild Books, Inc.
A Division of Condé Nast Publications

Library of Congress Catalog Card Number: 2007923706
ISBN: 978-1-56367-487-7
GST R 133004424

Printed in the United States of America

CH12, TP13

CONTENTS

EXTENDED CONTENTS

PREFACE

The organization of this book and its accompanying CD-ROM was inspired by my students, who prefer a variety of ways to learn and appreciate an opportunity for a hands-on activity. The book is divided into three parts. Part One, Considerations Affecting Selections, introduces concepts such as budgets, codes, sustainability, and effects of materials on acoustics, all of which are applicable to many materials and are considerations for every project. Part Two, Materials, describes design materials and trade details in depth, including discussions of the physical and aesthetic properties of the materials, their uses in interiors, and considerations in specifying and installing them. Part Three, Constructions, Products, and Systems, deals with assemblies, which are the items made from more than one material, such as doors, electrical devices, and lighting systems. As in Part Two, the discussion covers the functional and aesthetic aspects of the assemblies, their use in residential and nonresidential spaces, and aspects of specification and installation.

About the CD-ROM

Practical application is the best way to retain knowledge. The CD-ROM accompanying this book, developed by Robert Hillery, is where the hands-on opportunity occurs, with a chance to make decisions, relay instructions, and consider the installation of materials to implement your design selections. You will assume the role of an interior designer whose client is a health club, one of several businesses participating in a larger reuse project, a health-care and wellness complex in a former shopping mall. Your client's space has already been designed, and you are responsible for specifying the materials and assemblies to be used in the project. This simulation will give you a chance to apply what you have learned from the text regarding the selection, care, and code compliance of interior design materials, as well as the characteristics and procedures associated with specific materials and constructions. The project will require you to choose materials that best suit the end use and to understand the reasons behind each material's choice.

Parts One, Two, and Three on the CD correspond to the parts of the text. For each chapter of the text, an activity on the CD relates the topic to the health club project. In Chapter 1, plans and elevations of the health club interiors introduce you to the design for the spaces in the health club so that you can familiarize yourself with the needs of the project. Chapter 2 includes videos featuring the design professionals in the field with whom interior designers interact. These are the people with whom you will communicate regarding your material selections for the health club. Activities for other chapters in Part One of the CD will show you where to look for materials and products that conform to your overall design for the health club.

Checklists in the chapters of Parts Two and Three on the CD will remind you of the myriad considerations that inform your decisions about each material or assembly you specify. These checklists will become good references for the real projects that you undertake both as a student and later in your career as an interior designer. Not only will they help you choose appropriate materials, but they will remind you of decisions you must make when you specify quantities and prepare instructions for installation. The CD also includes business forms that you can print and complete to provide instructions for fabricators and installers. As you complete the activities in each chapter, you will learn to coordinate the work of suppliers of both materials and labor, applying project management skills to the specific tasks of specifying materials. The fourth part of the CD is an extensive glossary with terms and definitions.

Acknowledgments

The organization and energy from Alana Clark at the zero hour helped pull the text through. Thanks to Fairchild Books, especially executive editor Olga Kontzias and acquisitions editor Joseph Miranda, for making it possible to share my approach to teaching about materials and specifications through publication of this text, and to my development editor, Sylvia Weber, who knit the whole thing seamlessly together, as if the entire disjointed, multifaceted industry could be one cohesive whole. My production editor, Elizabeth Marotta, guided me through the process of turning a manuscript into a printed book. Art director Adam Bohannon and photo researcher Erin Fitzsimmons provided support and advice in selecting the illustrations and photographs.

I am grateful to Robert Hillery of High Medium for the design and development of the CD-ROM. I appreciate the generosity of all those who volunteered to be taped to share their specialty with students.

I want to thank the following interior design educators, selected by the publisher, for their reviews and recommendations: Susan Ray Degges, North Dakota State University; Sandra Gibbons, Algonquin College; Harvey Levensohn, Newberry College; Kimberly Love, IADT, Orlando; and Jacque Mott, Harper College. Thanks to everyone who shared advice and lent encouragement, especially Gale, my sounding board and friend indeed.

part one

Considerations Affecting Selections

CHAPTER 1

Learning about materials for interiors

There is no shortage of information about materials and resources that we use in the course of our interior design work. Manufacturers are eager to dispense facts about their products and their proper use, installation, and care. People in the trades are constantly sharing their work experiences with us so we can make jobs go more smoothly. Despite all the information that is floating around on the topic of materials and resources, one important aspect is still missing: What exactly does it all mean for client jobs? This book and the accompanying CD-ROM are designed to assemble information about materials and the various construction trades from a very practical, project-focused angle. Through the use of a simulated interior design project, the book and CD-ROM will help you learn how to specify the appropriate materials for a job and how to communicate with vendors, installers, and clients about your material specifications.

Specifications in the Context of the Interior Design Business

The topic of specifications overlaps some aspects of project management and business, which are also addressed as necessary. Even though it intersects with codes, green design, and acoustics, this book is not intended to be a substitute for proper in-depth coverage of those topics. The content of this book exists only in the service of implementing design, but design itself is not dis-

cussed. The heart of this text is about making good selections for client jobs and communicating your intentions to suppliers and tradespeople. This goal is directly related to the specification of materials and labor. Designers are responsible for specifying both. The focus is on communicating for installation, rather than for legal "coverage" (as in protection from lawsuits). Occasionally, legal issues will warrant some mention, but the primary goal is to help you understand how work is communicated. Fortunately, the legal departments of design firms can easily add disclaimers to the essential communications on which we focus here.

Communications about Materials

Any of the topics presented here could easily be the subject of an entire textbook on its own. Therefore, each topic is covered only to the depth required to make you functional in that area. All the materials and items presented include information you should use as you make your selections and relay your intentions to those who will provide the materials and those who will install them. See the vocabulary lists on the CD for links to definitions for the technical terms in each chapter, because they can help you understand the jargon unique to each area. As you communicate with the tradespeople, you will want to speak their language, discussing lap marks with painters, abrash with rug dealers, and courses with masons. The vocabulary lists have also been culled to ensure they include only the most pertinent words in each topic. You will already be at the straining point when you complete your review of the discussion contained here, so let's avoid doing more than is necessary to cover the basics.

The Health Club Project Simulation

The book and CD present a project scenario that is used in a series of exercises. You will assume the role of the interior designer who is specifying materials for a health club, where several different spaces—a gym, a seminar room, a restaurant, and the manager's residence—require a variety of materials for each area. Apply the information in this book about the materials and products required for the project to complete the exercises on the CD. If you allow your imagination to flesh out the project as you do the exercises, this simulation should solidify your understanding of the subject matter. Imagine you are the project designer on this small commercial project and assume responsibility for understanding the issues, making good selections, and writing good specs.

CHAPTER 2

parties to the project

For simple construction jobs, the interior designer may be the one to perform all design tasks and prepare documentation for construction. For more involved jobs, there may also be an architect or engineer on the project. The chain of command for the project, the preparation of documents, and job observation responsibilities will vary depending on who is responsible for coordinating the construction project.

The Construction Process: From Contract Drawings to Building

Let's first consider the process within a scenario that does not require the services of an architect. We will look at the process from the point in time when the contract drawings are complete for bidding and then go forward from there.

The programming phase and concept drawings are completed and the contract documents have been produced. These documents describe the project in enough detail to obtain reliable pricing and define the contract. How the contract is to be executed will indicate just how much detail drawing is required. There are a few options defining the relationships involved in completing the construction.

Design–Bid–Build

The most commonly used basis for completing custom work is design-bid-build. The design professional prepares drawings and a project description in order to obtain bids. The bid process is

competitive, and the contractor will be selected on the basis of bid and qualifications. Additional drawings for clarifying details and additional selections for completing the material and equipment schedules often follow the bidding process.

The bidding process sometimes inspires changes to the plans. When the numbers come in (bids are received), adjustments are frequently made to the plans to bring the project more into line with the available funds. For this reason, the contract drawings are often developed only to the extent required for pricing and no further.

After the contract has been signed, the construction documents are produced. These include drawings, details, elaborated work lists, specifications, and other details to communicate every intention relating to project work and outcomes. These documents are produced with the intention that they will be fully self-explanatory, but that is never actually the case. The design professional must be available throughout the construction process to clarify issues and brainstorm about solutions for unforeseen situations.

Some contracts written between designers and owners limit the designer's participation in the construction process to accommodate a client's request for low fees. This arrangement can lead to misunderstandings if the client has no experience in the construction process. The client may assume that the drawings should be 100 percent complete and view every question from the contractor as a failure on the part of the designer.

It is a good idea to clarify the realities of the construction process in your contract. State that questions invariably arise on the job site and that you are available for consultation when they do. State the terms under which you will participate in such meetings; your terms will include your fees for participating in site visits if they are not already included in the client requests and in your compensation package.

Design–Negotiate–Build

The design-negotiate-build arrangement removes the bidding step and also affects the design work. Just as in the design-bid-build arrangement, the contract documents are produced, but they are usually less detailed for the design-negotiate-build approach. A contractor may be selected based on specialty, reputation, or previous relationship with the owner, rather than on price. The contractor is an active participant in the design process as the team designs the project in such a way as to manage costs and time schedules with the design decisions that they make. Because the contractor is a party to many of the planning sessions and is essentially part of the design team, there tends to be a little less documentation on these jobs. It is not inherently so; it just seems to work out that way.

Design–Build

The design-build arrangement is convenient for the client because a single entity is responsible for the entire process. Costs and time frames can be closely controlled. As the designer on a design-build project, you may have a partnership with a builder, you may be an employee of a design-build firm, or you may function as a construction manager-advisor. Your responsibilities will vary a little, depending on your relationship to the project. When you are the designer of the project, your responsibilities will be very similar to the designer's role in the design-bid-build and the design-negotiate-build structures. For a partner of the builder or for an employee of a design-build firm, the contract document phase may be diminished because the firm is hired before the design begins. Drawings will be produced to communicate

with subcontractors, who are providing specialty equipment or labor. A design process will be created that falls within a set price range for construction.

Owner-Build

If the owner has sufficient resources (time, money, and experience) to function as his or her own contractor, you may be hired to perform design tasks and produce construction drawings. This is another arrangement that often leads to the need for less documentation. This is not always the case, but it often works out that way. Under this kind of construction agreement, your presence on the job site is often less critical and while you are likely to make material recommendations, you may not be called upon to manage the specifications.

Construction Manager–Advisor

If you are functioning as a construction manager-advisor to the client, you will not perform the design work. You will be the "neutral party" on whom the client can rely to avoid conflicts of interest (e.g., if the designer and builder are the same entity). A client who has little expertise in construction projects may feel more comfortable with an objective advisor to review details, costs, punch lists, and so on. In this instance, you will not be responsible for any drawings or documentation but you may produce some anyway as a means of communicating with the design-build firm—the party ultimately responsible for them.

The Designer's Central Role

As a designer managing clients' projects, especially complex projects like the health club that involve many professionals and tradespeople, you are the most centrally positioned person in the flow of work related to your designs and specifications. You have defined the design program for the interiors from a functional and aesthetic standpoint, and you will be coordinating all work and details related to your specifications.

The designer has an awareness of the minute details of the completed installation that are not apparent to the architect or contractor. As an example, consider the location of the stackback for the drapery in the health club manager's apartment, which will project 4-6 inches from the wall and may interfere with the adjacent terrace door. An inside-mounted roller shade (mounted inside the window frame) could be planned, in which case the door will not interfere, but because the drapes that you have planned will project, you must be responsible for communicating the adjustments to the door swing or location required by your specification to both the architect and the contractor. The electrician does not know that the manager frequently gets up during the night and that the motion sensor for the step lights illuminating the path to the toilet must be positioned on the wall by the bed. The architect may know that a banquette is to be placed on the wall in the restaurant but is not as familiar as you are with the prescribed pitch of the back and the number of people to seat—all of which will affect the size and depth of the unit.

You must approach all jobs with a mind-set wherein you make yourself responsible for the success of every detail. You are kidding yourself if you think that it will be acceptable to your client for you to shrug your shoulders helplessly when the door smashes the drapery or won't stand in an open position. Your clients are smarter than that and will know that you have not taken good care of the details; they will now incur additional cost altering construction details or replacing product. In order to complete the job successfully, you will have to participate actively at every interface between planning and build-out, even if you are not acknowledged by contract (and compensation) for this role as the hub of the wheel. The job cannot be successfully completed without the interior designer's diligent attention.

Collaborating with Tradespeople and Professionals

Once your client has decided to proceed with the project, you may find yourself collaborating with varying combinations of tradespeople and professionals to complete the installation. Professionals with whom you interface may be architects, engineers, or other designers. The demarcation between designers and architects or structural engineers is legally drawn in all jurisdictions. The demarcation between the various arenas of design is more an issue of necessity than of governance. You must be honest with yourself about the limits of your expertise and suggest specialists to your client when appropriate. Lighting designers and acoustical designers handle complex needs and systems. IT (information technology) and AV (audio/video) designers are trained to design for and specify the equipment and controls that will be part of many of your projects. If you need a furniture or cabinet designer or an art consultant, it is a service to your client to be able to recommend one who is appropriate to the budget, style, and complexity of the project.

Many specialists include design service as part of the equipment, millwork, art, or furniture sale. Other design specialists can prepare documentation to be submitted for competitive bids. These designers will charge for their services directly.

The project may include some construction build-out, whether it requires the participation of an architect or not (refer to your local codes). The construction trades are organized into general contractors and subcontractors.

Who Does What?

Here are some of the players in the project and their responsibilities:

Client

- Communicate needs and desires for the project to the interior designer.
- Make payments as determined by contracts.
  - Progress payments.
  - Fees.
  - Assessments.
  - Permits (if these are not the contractor's responsibility under the contract).
- Voice concerns and communicate misgivings to the designer so they can be immediately addressed.
- Review plans, samples, and all transmittals immediately upon receipt and respond as requested.

- Make decisions in a timely manner and keep accounts current so as to keep the project on schedule.
- Review and understand all plans and specifications presented.
- Perform stain or other tests on material requested for that purpose.

Architect

- Perform design work related to structure and specifications of materials and workmanship for satisfactory completion of the project.
- Monitor the quality and progress of the work and confirm that it complies with contract documents.
- Represent the owner and the owner's interests (owner and contractor often communicate through the architect).
- Guard the owner against defects and deficiencies; reject, on the owner's behalf, construction work that's not in compliance.
- Observe tests performed by the contractor.
- Review samples prepared by the contractor.
- Confirm that conditions for progress payments outlined in the owner/contractor contract have been met; approve payments.
- Interpret requirements of contract documents in a manner consistent with the intent of the documents.
- Resolve disputes regarding the terms of the contract.
- Review product substitutions and deviations from the contract.
- Prepare modifications to the contract for approval and issuance by the owner and agreement by the contractor.

Architects must be licensed.

Interior Designer

- Develop plans, elevations, and material specs that adequately describe the job and are easily read. Nonstructural design tasks may be shared or divided between the architect and designer. Only the architect may perform design work related to structural configurations.
- Establish time and budget parameters with the client.

- Maintain current and accurate records of client and vendor accounts.
- Verify all dimensions; draft or review drawings prepared by others for accuracy of floor plans, elevations, millwork and cabinetry, soffits, and ceiling heights.
- Verify absolutely that what has been drawn can be built.
- Verify passage clearances and angles relative to installation and confirm that all plans conform to the intention of the project goals.
- Coordinate tradespeople, workrooms, and installers to complete the project within established parameters.
- Interface between the client and installers, workrooms, and other professionals.
- Work with client to make material selections on time in order to remain on schedule.
- Provide written specifications for all required products.
- Inspect construction; note any walls or ceilings out of plumb in addition to the quality of the finish work.
- Work only within the limits imposed by laws governing your practice. Assist client in locating and selecting other professionals as necessary.

Certification of interior designers is usually optional but always desirable. Licensing is required in some jurisdictions.

Other Design Professionals

Whether their participation is mandated by law (architects and engineers) or simply a good idea (acoustic, lighting, or structured wiring specialists), they will be responsible for the following:

- Understanding the intent of the work so recommendations match client needs.
- Communicating equipment needs for space, location, and relationship to other services.
- Working with the designer for convenient integration of recommended systems and constructions.

Certification is usually optional but always preferable.

General Contractor

- Schedule the work.
- Hire the subcontractors.
- Furnish the owner with a list of names of sub-contractors.
- Supervise job progress.
- Insure the client against claims; indemnify the owner against loses resulting from construction work.
  - Purchase and maintain liability insurance.
  - Furnish bonds required by the contract.
- Maintain a safe work environment.
- Work with the designer to keep the client on schedule with selections.
- Inspect the work by subcontractors.
- Keep records of all expenditures, changes, and additions.
- Manage all job costs.
- Adhere to the schedule of partial payment and pay subcontractors immediately upon receipt of payments.
- Proceed expeditiously with a sufficient work-force to complete the work on time.
- See to the production of samples required by the scope of work as the basis for the contract

General contractors must be licensed.

Demolition Crew

- Carefully remove all material and equipment without unnecessary damage to surrounding material and equipment that are to remain.
- Store items for reuse as directed.
- Dispose of items not required for new plans.
- Complete work safely and on time so as to not delay the schedule of following tradespeople.
- Call attention to any conditions uncovered that will affect the new plans.

A license is required for asbestos removal.

Electrician

- Review and verify compliance with code for all lighting and electrical plans.
- Review and verify total connected loads for all products specified.
- Physically locate and install all switches and outlets required by the approved plan and by code.
- Physically locate hook-ups for phone, fax, computer, appliances, TV, and fixtures, alerting the designer of any installation requirements that cannot be accommodated.
- Install all items as per contract.
- Perform all work on a timely basis and work with the designer to resolve all problems concerning compliance with all relevant codes.

Electricians must be licensed.

Plumber

- Review and verify all plumbing plans, including the hot water heating system if applicable, assuring compliance with code.
- Review all product specifications for plumbing requirements to assure compliance with code.
- Physically locate new stacks through to the exit of the building, if required.
- Alert the designer to any relevant details and collaborate with the designer to resolve all problems within requirements of code.
- Hook the plumbing fittings to the plumbing.

The plumber must be licensed.

Carpenter

- Review all dimensions and service locations (HVAC, plumbing, electrical, etc.) and verify compliance with code.
- Perform all work on a timely basis in accordance with code.
- Alert the designer to any relevant details and collaborate with the designer to resolve all problems.
- Interface with the designer, contractor, and other tradespeople about electrical, plumbing, and HVAC (heating, ventilation, and air conditioning) services to be installed by others within wall cavities relative to their space and support requirements, as well as coordination of timing.

The carpenter may have a certificate rather than a license in some jurisdictions.

How Will You Communicate with All Parties Collaborating on the Job?

Say it in writing. In the words of my favorite job-boss, Vince, "If you didn't write it down, you never said it." For example:

> "As per our meeting at the site on [date of meeting noted] the following approvals are confirmed . . . the following changes to the plans will be made . . . the following work will be omitted from the contract . . . the following substitution will be made . . ."

You get the idea. Copies of these written notices should go to the client, contractors (general and subs), the architect, and any other professionals involved in the project, *including* those in your own office, as necessary.

One other topic related to interfacing with the human resources on the job is responsibility. At the outset, define in writing who is to be responsible for what required work, preferably in written contracts. Architects, systems designers (music, theater, wiring), kitchen, lighting, and cabinet shops all have skills and duties that overlap with those of the interior designer. Clarifying roles in writing identifies the "go-to" person and is critical for managing the job and relationships on the job (which are inextricably connected).

To illustrate this, let's look at one example: Imagine you are designing custom cabinetry to scale for the health club project and sketching details for definitive drawing by others (the architect or cabinetmaker). While a commercial POS desk for the register can be designed and drafted with sufficient detail for construction in about 10 minutes, per-foot, totally custom, high-quality cabinetry requires anywhere from less than ten minutes to twenty minutes per foot to lay out and sketch details, including review of the drawings with the draftsperson. Complicated designs with specific requirements take longer to lay out and/or detail.

After the details are all defined, the drafting of the requisite dimensioned plans; elevations; sections; and enlarged details of raised panel profiles, pilasters, blocks, capitols, crowns and bases; interior fittings with detailed hardware specs (slides, hinges); lighting location and mounting with powering figured out and shown; and all material notes may take another hour per foot. The client's naive assurance that the architect will handle "all" the drawing really needs to be clarified because the architect may not have understood his or her responsibilities in exactly that way.

If the cabinet shop that wins the bid prepares its own shop drawings, you can meet with the draftsperson and later review the "shops" (shop drawings). If the winning bidder does not produce shop drawings, you will be the one responsible for answering all the open questions that can only be answered completely with drawings—at up to an hour per running foot. If you have not budgeted the time (or fees), you have a problem the minute the job has been awarded to a shop that needs drawings you expected would be produced by others.

You can see that the drafting of the simple and economical cabinetry for the cash register mentioned above cannot logically be produced by others, and you will be responsible for that drawing. The construction drawings for managing highly custom cabinet work are critical to production and are going to be time consuming to produce properly. If your understanding from a conversation with your client is that the drawings for 300 feet of cabinetry will be produced by others, this should be followed up in writing. If you do not document this understanding, you may have to give away $30,000 in fees, and your timetable for other work will suffer as you scramble to produce the drawings after the bid has been awarded and the shop is standing by. (Furthermore, the winning bidder was probably only $10,000 cheaper than the shop that makes its own shop drawings!)

To summarize, it is a good idea to meet with all parties on the job at the outset to define the procedural flow and timetable for the design work and to clarify the role of all persons developing details and specifications for the job.

CHAPTER 3

Budgets and Estimates

How do you manage all the project intersections? This includes the intersection between:

- Client desires and available funds
- Your client's needs and your plans and selections
- Your selections and the installation of your selection
- Plans and systems designed by others for incorporation into your plans.

Cost is constantly intermingling with process. We must design to a budget, even if a budget has not been established and the work at hand is to establish one. Even though formulating a budget seems like an extra and unnecessary step, the task always increases the efficiency of the project as long as it is carefully done. Once a reasonable budget has been drawn up, it serves as a guide to selections and design details as the project develops.

Early Requests for Estimates

Designers are often asked to set a likely budget, and the only appropriate way of presenting figures before you begin your design work is to present a high-low range based on whatever information you have at your disposal. Present a description of the general scope of work as you understand it along with your rough estimate, and describe the quality level that you have in mind for the project (based on the implications of

the building—a fine, stately interior space will be more costly than a modest retro one, and connoisseurs demand higher quality than style hounds).

Designers who specialize in a narrowly defined area of expertise are often able to come very close to the actual final cost in their estimates. Kitchen designers, for example, depend on their ability to make good guesses because they must proceed with the detailed design work after the contract has been executed (signed by the parties) with dollar amounts included.

One complaint that puts designers on the defensive from time to time is that we are always going over budget: Actually, this is very often the case. So what's happening? A common scenario is that the potential client is interviewing several designers and posing the "general budget" inquiry to each one: "How much will it take to do this project?" It's easy to suspect that the job may be awarded based partly on the general budget figure tossed out. If you want the job, you may be inclined to lowball the estimate, knowing that you can produce the work in that budget range (but also with full awareness that if you do so, the client will not be thrilled with the results of your work together). The process will usually straighten out the quality issue when clients reject the cheap options and—by their own choice—exceed the budget with better-quality selections.

What if you are honest and fairly accurate in your "general budget" estimate and your competition is low balling to get the job? You could lose the job. It will eventually come in around the figure that you quoted, but by then, it will be too late for you to win the contract because your competitor will have nearly completed the work. The switching costs (the costs to the client for switching to another designer in the middle of the process) are too high to end the relationship at that point, so the client keeps moving forward, complaining about how the designer went over budget.

When you are pressured into estimating the cost of work before it has begun, you might explain the dynamics of this situation and how posing the very question at the outset—before there is enough information to estimate—invites inaccuracy. Assure potential clients that you want to make their money go as far as it can. If you will help them make correct, value-driven decisions all along the way, you will have a more complete job to your credit. Be upfront with all pricing structures so they can relax (as much as possible) about the issue of cost. If you add a percentage to the cost of goods that you resell to them, tell them how that will be calculated. If some of your vendors give you a commission check on direct sales to your clients, tell them that this may happen on a case-by-case basis. Be transparent in your financial arrangement with your client and ethically adhere to the agreement. Never let it be said that you were underhanded and never apologize for your compensation. To do so would imply that the value of what you are providing is not reflected fairly in your fees. You enhance the quality of end users' experience in the space, for which you are being hired and paid fairly.

Remember that this is not Monopoly money; it's the real thing. So when you suggest a $25,000 net price conference table by a prominent local furniture designer, with all the data ports and outlets contained, be prepared to present the tangible *reasons* that make this a *reasonable* price. Not everyone is as buoyed by beauty as you are, and you must speak the *clients'* language in such matters. Always be an advocate for your clients, and always put their needs and the design program front and center of all your decisions. If the

approved design concept requires the expenditure, it is in their best interest to allocate the dollars. If your suggestion is over the projected budget price, figure out, before you go into the presentation, where in the project you can save funds to offset the additional cost.

Three Degrees of Exactness

So, what does all of this have to do with estimating? Despite all these reasons to avoid estimating too soon, you will have to evaluate the distribution of costs and estimate the job. The point in the process at which the request for an estimate arises will indicate the kind of estimate to be done. Generally speaking, there are three degrees of exactness with which you can respond to the request: ballpark, cost comparison, and actual costs for purchase.

Early in the selection phase, designers will frequently produce the rough estimates for furniture and soft goods. Designers will occasionally produce estimates that involve trade labor limited to the installation of a specific product or material. For very involved construction projects, designers typically do not estimate beyond the rough ballpark.

Ballpark Estimates

A ballpark estimate is delivered when a client is considering whether or not to pursue a particular design. It is logically delivered as a range and is based on past experience with similar projects. You may be able simply to tell your client that such-and-such a project is likely to cost $60-$90 per square foot for furnishing and soft goods, that a kitchen remodeling can be $100-$300 per square foot, etc. This may be enough information for your client to make a decision on whether to proceed with a project.

If you do not have personal experience that you can rely on because the project is not like anything that you have done before, you may be able to provide your client with information based on similar work by other professionals. Trade publications frequently include project costs, and while styles may vary, the location, function, and complexity may match your client's plans closely enough to allow you to rely on figures from other designers' projects. You may need a couple of days of research to come up with some usable figures for consideration, but if it leads you to winning a job, you will certainly be glad you made the effort. Share the sources of information referenced with your client.

Cost Comparisons

It may be that the client (or potential client) is already committed to doing the project but does not know how it will be configured and how it will look. You may make *cost comparisons* between material options to get the client headed in the right direction. You might suggest ceramic tile that may range from $5 to $25 per square foot or stone tile that costs from $12 to $35, with installation costs for stone that are twice as much as the installation costs for ceramic. You may know these figures off the top of your head after some experience, or you may have to research the costs. If you have to research, be prepared to spend two very organized days in order to provide this kind of comparison for a medium-sized job. Offer the service for pay if you can; otherwise, perform it as "charity work" in hopes of getting the job.

Life-cycle costs are typically considered at this level. *Life-cycle costing* includes the cost of the material and installation, plus maintenance costs over the expected life of the material, the cost of removal and disposal of the existing material, and eventually removing and disposing of the material currently under consideration.

Actual Costs for Purchase

When your client is ready to implement plans that you have produced and selections that you have made, you will produce contracts, proposals, work orders, specifications, requests for bids, or other documents that can eventually cause the work to occur. Unlike the two kinds of estimates that you provide, these documents of *actual costs for purchase* are legally binding. They must be very complete and precise. Once they have been agreed to, the work must be provided and paid for as stipulated in the document.

If your proposal to your client sells new carpet as "installed" but you have failed to include the cost of removing the existing carpet, you may still be obligated to cause the removal of the carpeting within the quoted figure. You will still have to pay for the removal, even though your client is not obligated to pay you, because the installed price that was agreed to is legally binding. If the contract is between your client and the installer, and you have failed to communicate the need for removing existing material in your communication to the installer, the installer is not obligated to provide the removal. You will have inconvenienced your client's budget management (the carpet must be removed and the removal must be paid for, now at an unexpected additional cost). In addition to the extra cost, your oversight may affect the timetable.

As a design professional estimating the cost of implementing your designs, at this stage, you will need complete and irrefutable communication with suppliers, installers, and your client in the form of complete written specifications and drawings (see Box 3.1).

BOX 3.1 | **A Cautionary Tale**

I once specified a fairly irregular (in thickness and dimensions) reclaimed terra-cotta tile salvaged from factory roofs in France. The contractor was opposed to it because it was irregular and would therefore require special and expensive installation techniques and sealants. All of this was known at the time I specified the material and was discussed until I was tired of defending the selection, which my client loved but the contractor did not.

The specification format that I was using included the material description and supplier for each material but no installation instructions. When the material arrived at the site, the installer saw it for the first time and informed all parties that the quoted price did not include the kind of installation required or the extra sealing. The client, general contractor, and designer were aware but the person doing the work was still in the dark, and his price had to increase by $3 per square foot to install properly—adding thousands of dollars to the cost of installation.

How Costs Are Measured

In each chapter in Part Two, you will find information about estimating quantity of materials. Materials sold (and therefore estimated) by the square foot include most surfacing material sold as field tiles, slabs, planks, and so on.

Wallcovering is typically sold by the roll or lineal yard. Carpet is currently sold to the trade by the square yard, although street sources selling to end users will price it by the square foot so its cost compares more favorably with the cost of other types of flooring, which are sold by the square foot. Room trims for base, case, crown, and other architectural trims are sold by the lineal foot. Items that are sold by the unit include trim tiles, plumbing and electrical fixtures and fittings, and assemblies (fireplaces, staircases). Fabric is sold by the lineal yard, and leather is sold by the hide (or half-hide).

Estimating for materials is covered by material type in Part Two. However, the math involved is quite simple.

To calculate square foot quantities, multiply the width of the area involved by the length of the

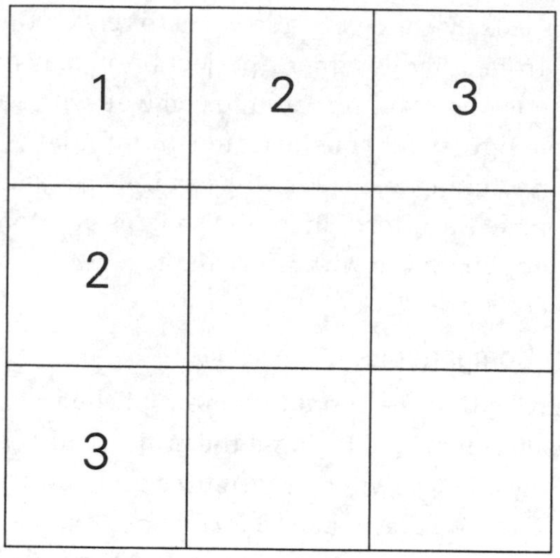

FIGURE 3.1   There are 9 squre feet in 1 square yard.

area. If your room is 15 feet by 20 feet, the floor area is 300 square feet.

To calculate square yard quantities, figure square feet as above, then divide by 9. It's all too easy to forget that there are 9 square feet in 1 square yard (Figure 3.1) because we are used to recalling that there are 3 feet in a yard and we want to divide by 3.

CHAPTER 4

codes pertaining to materials

All categories of materials that you specify will have inherent characteristics. These characteristics include "green-ness" of the material, how fire-resistant it is, and its acoustical properties, as well as its compliance with codes, including Americans with Disabilities Act (ADA) requirements. During production of building materials made from the material categories discussed in Part Two, these characteristics can be altered. For example, a combustible material such as wood can be treated to impart fire-resistant characteristics. A material that is not inherently green, such as carpet, can be made compliant with requirements for a green project through management of its components and production. A material with inherently poor acoustical properties can be installed in a construction that provides the required sound control defined by the design program. Each specified product and all the planned installation and construction details must be evaluated by the person responsible for the specification to ensure they satisfy the design program, which is unique to the project.

To study the impact of codes on material selections and specifications, we will reference the adaptive reuse project created for this course, a former department store that is to become a health club. As the specifying designer on the project, you will evaluate material selections and installation methods to fulfill the project requirements and satisfy the building code requirements for each material and its use in the project.

The Scope of Codes

Your project will be governed by local codes. Codes vary slightly from one jurisdiction to another, so you will want to get a copy of the local code for the project location. To determine which portions of the code pertain to your project, you will need to evaluate the building based on its use, building type, configuration, and size. Code books contain hundreds upon hundreds of pages, but the portions that pertain to your unique project will be limited and very manageable. Do not be daunted by the size of the publication. You comply only with those sections indicated by your project. The following information is general and does not eliminate the need to become familiar with actual local codes.

The purpose of building codes is to provide for what could be considered a minimum level of amenities and a minimum level of safety. Because the precise content of building codes varies from one jurisdiction to another, refer to local code when working in a new area. Basically, codes govern the same issues from one jurisdiction to the next. As might be expected, codes increase in strictness as one moves from private single-family residences through offices, mercantile spaces, and public spaces to schools, hospitals, and nursing homes, and on to hazardous environments. This list is not comprehensive. All occupancies are governed by codes. We will focus on codes as they pertain to materials, but be aware that codes also control quantity and location issues.

Building Fire-Safety Codes

Fire-safety codes stipulate resistance to flame. The stringency of the limitations depends on the location. Different requirements apply to an office from those that apply to an exit corridor in the same building. Flame spread resistance is rated as Class A, B, or C, with Class A being the most stringent in flame and smoke development and C being the least stringent. Smoke development is typically consistent because smoke can travel so easily from one location to another. Fire resistance and sanitation have the biggest impact on material selection for your project.

All building and surfacing materials are governed by codes. Building code, also referred to as life/safety code, includes among the items and surfaces that you specify doors, stairs, ramps, and interior surfacing and finishes.

Doors

Fire-rated doors provide resistance to fire for up to some specified length of time, depending on the specific code. One-hour and two-hour fire-rated doors are commonly required for public spaces. Door hardware for public doors must usually be able to be operated by a person who is unfamiliar with the door and, furthermore, who is standing in the dark. An exit door that requires a two-step operation to open is usually not allowed; for instance, a handle latch with a separate dead bolt is unlikely to be approved. Some classifications require panic hardware that opens the door when a person pushes against the hardware from the inside with a force not to exceed 15 pounds. If you select a revolving door, it counts as half of a door. Glazing is limited to maximum sizes, depending on location, and in fire-rated doors must often be made of wire-reinforced or other special heat-resistant glass that meets defined testing standards (depending on the size of the glazed area).

Stairs and Ramps

In addition to numerous restrictions on dimensions, load bearing, and configurations, stairs and ramps must meet material restrictions relative to fire resistance and slip resistance. Stairs in an exit stairwell must be of noncombustible materials. Handrails in public spaces must be continuously graspable along their entire length. Varying ratings are approved for different conditions and locations.

Interior Finishes

Interior finishes are tested to classify their flame resistance as Class A, B, or C. Classification of flame resistance and smoke development is governed by code. A variety of testing methods are used.

- The *methenamine pill test* tests a material's resistance to a burning object that falls on it. A pill is placed on the material and ignited. Seven out of eight samples must resist burning out from the center. Measured from the center to the edge of the burn, the flame must be extinguished in less than 8 inches.
- The *Steiner Tunnel test* involves a 25-foot chamber and gas jets. The material is adhered to the top of the chamber and the gas jets burn for ten minutes. The distance of burn indicates the rating from 0 to 200. Asbestos is 0, but oak flooring is 100, which is considered a moderate burn rate. Class A materials have a flame spread rating of 0 to 25; Class B, from 26 to 75; and Class C, from 76 to 200. Class D material ranges from 200 to 500 and is not permitted even in one- and two-family dwellings. Class D decorative paneling has been implicated in a number of fatal fires. Carpet manufacturers object to this test because the carpet is not tested in a manner imitating typical use (it is tested on the ceiling instead of the floor).

- The *chamber test* is similar to the Steiner Tunnel test, but the material is placed on the floor of the chamber. This rating system has only two classifications, B and C, so the scale is difficult to describe. Also, the relationship between the rating and fire spread has not been proven.
- The *radiant panel test* entails placing a sample of the material on the floor of the test chamber and heating it by a gas-fired panel mounted at an angle over it. The amount of energy required to sustain flame in the sample is measured and described as Critical Radiant Flux or CRF (here, flux refers to the flow of heat energy). The greater the energy required, the higher the number, which means greater resistance to flame, so low numbers indicated higher flammability. This test is usually used for flooring materials. Class I materials will have a CRF of 0.45 watts per square centimeter. Class II materials will have a CRF of 0.22 watts.

Materials can sometimes be altered to increase their rating, such as when they become part of an assembly or are treated in a way (for instance, with flame-retardant paints) that improves their performance. If the amount of flammable material is limited, it may be allowable as untreated material. Trims may have a Class C rating in A- or B-rated spaces if they do not exceed ten percent of the aggregate wall surface. The installation of a sprinkler system will often have impact on the limitations mandated by code.

Requirements vary by location, building type, and occupancy class. Typically, local codes require materials to be rated as follows in order to be compliant:

- Vertical exits: Class A
- Exit access: Class B
- Often, public corridors must meet the requirements for Class A and other public spaces must be rated Class B.
- Class C interior finishes are permitted in single-family residences.
- Individual apartments and private offices may be permitted to have a rating as low as Class C.
- Other occupancies typically must be rated Class A or B, with some occasional allowance for Class C.

ADA Codes

In addition to regulating space planning and clearances issues, the Americans with Disabilities Act governs product and material selection. The following are examples of how product selections that you will make to complete your project will be governed by ADA.

Lavatory Fixtures

Seat height of toilets must be 17-19 inches, and seats may not be sprung to return to lifted position. The maximum allowable height to the rim of a urinal is 17 inches. Paper dispensers that do not permit the continuous flow of toilet paper or that limit delivery are not permitted.

Faucets must be push or lever type or electronic, with no grasping or twisting required.

Lavatory waste and supply pipes must be protected against contact because a person with reduced sensitivity could be burned if the drain is full of hot water or bruised from bumping or pressing against the pipes.

Showers must have a seat, grab bars, controls that are lever- or push-operated, a 60-inch-long hose for a handheld shower head (unless vandalism is a possibility, then the showerhead may be permanently mounted at 48 inches Above Finished Floor (AFF).

Grab bars in shower and toilet stalls must be 1-¼ to 1-½ inches in diameter and resist 250 pounds of force without bending or breaking.

Wall Fixtures

Wall sconces and other wall-mounted items should be between 27 and 80 inches AFF and may protrude no more than 4 inches. If they have legs or are supported by posts, they may overhang posts by 12 inches. Below 27 inches, they may stick out to any depth.

Flooring

Flooring materials must be slip-resistant and level and flush with surrounding surfaces. Changes in height of ⅛ inch or less require no transition. Changes up to ½ inch require a beveled transition, and changes greater than ½ inch require a ramp.

Carpet may have a maximum pile height of ½ inch and must be fastened along all edges.

Doors and Windows

Doors and windows should be operable with a force not exceeding 5 pounds. Hardware should be lever- or push-operated type. Pulls should be U-shaped. Door hardware should be no higher than 48 inches AFF, so confirm height on predrilled doors that you specify.

CHAPTER 5

project management

Managing the project means orchestrating the timing of selections and the delivery of materials to the job site and managing the records that document the decisions, selections, and progress of the job. The tools you use to manage the process are plans, time and material schedules, and specifications. There are sample furniture plans on the CD, but the plan set for a job will also include partition, lighting, electrical, and detail plans. Schedules are succinct descriptions of materials and items for installation at the site. See Figure 5.1 for a sample portion of the health club schedule. The information on the schedule is not complete enough to place an order for materials, but it is complete enough for installers at the site to confirm that they have the correct material on hand (see Box 5.1). More complete information about selections is required for the specifications because the specifications often function as purchase documents.

Managing the records is an entire job in itself, and you may be tempted to let managing records slide into a position of secondary importance—especially if the project is small or the design fee negotiated is minimal. In such instances, it can become easy to view good record management as a luxury that the client did not purchase for the project and you should provide only the design work. You might be tempted to consider managing material records to be a favor that you will perform if you run out of other things to do. Proper

BOX 5.1 | **A Cautionary Tale**

It is important for all parties in the chain of production to understand what is to be installed on the job. Material schedules are part of the documentation that is kept at the job site, so the tradespeople have constant access to material descriptions. In the industry, *installation of materials constitutes acceptance*, so if the wrong material is accidentally delivered and installed, the transaction becomes complete. The supplier usually has no obligation to make any adjustments. If the error was theirs, they often will make adjustments (though they are not obligated to) because that is the ethical thing to do. Even though they may replace the material, they are unlikely to pay for the labor required to remove the incorrect material, repair the substrate if necessary, and install the correct material. The party responsible for covering these costs will be determined by the construction contracts.

management of materials records is part of the structure of the job, however. Even if you sign an agreement that later strikes you as a bad deal, and you don't feel that you have sufficient time (compensation) to maintain good records, remember that good management is important to the efficiency of your process and will save you time (and therefore, money) as you move through the construction phase.

	Key	Material	Description	Notes
Massage 305				
Floor				
Walls				
Ceiling				
Women's Restroom 306				
Floors				
Walls				
Walls				
Ceiling				
Partitions				
Countertop				
Men's Restroom 307				
Floors				
Walls				
Walls				
Ceiling				
Partitions				
Countertop				
Lounge 308				
Floor				
Walls				
Ceiling				
Kitchen 309				
Floor				
Walls				
Ceiling				
Countertops				

FIGURE 5.1 A portion of the material schedule for the health club project. (The complete schedule is on the CD-Rom in Chapter 5.) Use this schedule to communicate material and basic installation instructions to the contractors at the job site.

For simple construction jobs, the interior designer may be the one to perform all design tasks and prepare documentation for construction. For more involved jobs, there may also be an architect or engineer on the project. The chain of command for the project, the preparation of documents, and job observation responsibilities will vary, depending on who is responsible for coordinating the construction project.

Storing Plans

You will want to keep any plans on record that were issued to another party, even plans that were superseded during the course of the work by modifications, alterations, changes, and addendums. These plans may be electronic files maintained as CAD or PDF files. Large-format, printed plans (larger than 11 × 17 inches) are typically stored in flat files (storage cabinets with wide but shallow drawers that are deep from front to back). All plans should be marked with their date of issue. Sometimes, a detail is modified two, three, or even more times as the job progresses. One easy way to keep track of the chronology is to file a paper copy with the date of issue noted.

For extensive work, these plans may be prepared by an architect; you would keep the most recent set on hand for your reference. If an architect is supervising construction, you do not need to keep a history of plans issued, so every time you get a new plan set from the architect, put all previous plan sets into "cold storage" or throw them away if you do not have the capacity to store them. This will help you to avoid confusion. If there are no architects on the job and the plans are your own issue, *do not throw old copies away*; keep a record of *all* changes and permutations.

Keep the following types of plans in your client files:

- **Demolition and construction drawings**, referencing material to be removed, and instructions regarding the required condition of substrate and adjoining surfaces that are to remain.
- **Lighting and electrical plans**, showing the location and type of equipment that will be used.

- **Finish plans**, showing where certain materials are used; these plans will likely reference detail drawings that further describe installation techniques and dimensions.
- **Detail drawings**, including sections and elevations of construction required, the application of surfacing material, and diagrams for installation of items to be installed.
- **Furniture plans**, showing furniture locations and sizes.
- **Custom furniture plans**, including elevations and sections for built-in and freestanding furniture.

Hiring a General Contractor or Subcontractor(s)

After the procurement document set (plans, schedules, and specifications produced to solicit bids) is complete, the job will be let for bid, meaning distributed to parties interested in performing the work so they can estimate costs and submit their proposals or contracts. This is the point in the project when your client must decide with whom they would like to work. For the services rendered, general contractors typically add a percentage on top of costs as their compensation. Some jobs are small and simple enough that the clients could consider subcontracting the work themselves and saving the percentage. If this seems to be a sensible approach given the nature of the job, you, as the designer, should understand that you will probably assume responsibility for scheduling and observing the work while the client will assume responsibility for the payouts and insuring the work. When you are working with your client to decide whether or not the job warrants the help of a general contractor, consider the following:

- Complexity of the task
- How many tradespeople will be involved
- What unknowns exist (This is especially important in the case of remodeling, where service locations may not be diagrammed.)
- Specialty of the work and whether you are qualified to evaluate the quality and completeness of the finished work

- How comfortable you are with assuming these responsibilities

If the job is large in scale or complex in scope, it makes sense to have a qualified professional coordinate the work.

Finding a General Contractor

How do you find a general contractor? When recommending a general contractor to your client, shop within your network of designers and architects or cold-call another professional. Ask a subcontractor that you've worked with in the past for a good general contractor. As you gain experience in your profession, your network will grow, and you will become familiar with the quality of the work of contractors in your community. Clients often have a network of acquaintances, some of whom may recently have hired contractors.

Qualifying a Contractor

How do you qualify the contractor after you have found one? When you first contact an experienced general contractor for your project, describe the scope of the work; the location of the job and the timetable for the work, including the completion date. Ask the contractor the following questions:

- *How long have you been in business?* An established track record is an indication the contractor will stay in business long enough to finish your job.
- *May I inspect a completed job that was similar to the job about which I am inquiring?*
- *May I get references from your past clients?*
- *Which tradespeople will be your own employees and which will be subcontractors?* General contractors have more control over the scheduling of their own employees.
- *How will you supervise the job? Personal daily visits? A designated job-boss on site at all times?* Your client pays for the contractor's supervision, and the job will not run properly or stay on schedule without good supervision, so make sure you are satisfied with the contractor's supervisory style. When contractors fail to

provide good supervision, the burden of this task frequently falls on the designer.
- *Will a list of subcontractors be made available for approval by the client?* Subs earn their reputations, which precede them. A low price from a lax subcontractor is no bargain.

Ask contractors' references these questions:

- *Was the work completed to your satisfaction and on time?*
- *How often did the general contractor visit the site, and was supervision adequate?*
- *How many "extras" (work or items not in the original bid but added during the course of the work at an additional cost) were added that you felt should have been included in the bid? Were options available?*
- *Were crews of the size promised, and did the crews require excessive supervision to keep them moving?*

Contractors who are interested in bidding must have experience with the kind of work your project requires. They must have workers' compensation and liability insurance. If the work requires connecting to city services (water or power), the contractor must be bondable. Proof of all of the above qualifications must be provided to the client in the form of references and certificates.

Reviewing the Bids

How will you help your client select a general contractor? Contact contractors with whom you would like to work, and confirm that each contractor would be interested in bidding on the work.

Interview the interested contractors and conduct a "walk-through," which may be an actual site visit or simply a review of your plans if the job is for new construction. Receive their bids and compare them to one another; advise your clients, when requested, as they finalize the selection and negotiate the contract.

When bidders have been selected, you will be available for their questions as they prepare their bids to ensure that your intention has been clearly communicated. After the bids are submitted, you may be asked to review the contractor's contract and advise your client. The agreement that you may be asked to review will be between the contractor and your client. You will not be legally responsible for the completeness, validity, or terms, but your diligence in this review is vital because it will have an impact on your client's trust in your judgment. The contractor's bid should include the following:

- Identification of all parties to the contract
- Location of the job
- Detailed scope of work, describing all work requested, referencing your drawings and specifications provided for bidding and the date of the documents provided
- Description of all equipment and material to be provided under the contract
- Allowances for all equipment and material not yet specified but to be provided eventually by the contractor
- The construction schedule
- List of equipment to be provided by others and installed by the contractor. The contractor should reference specs or describe equipment to ensure that the correct installation requirements are included in the work as bid.
- Dates for change orders become required and additional charges associated with change orders are allowable.
- Procedure to be followed if hidden conditions that affect the progress of the work or require additional work to rectify are discovered later
- What insurance protects the project and who is responsible for holding the certificates
- What jurisdiction's codes will govern the project
- Who will be responsible for securing necessary permits

In addition to the preceding, the contract should also define procedural stipulations, such as the following:

- Your client must be delivered of a waiver of lien when payments are made to the general contractor. A waiver of lien is an acknowledgment by the subcontractor that he or she has been fairly paid by the general contractor for the work. Without the release granted by the waiver, the subcontractor is, in effect, still

the owner of that work. This means that a portion of the premises actually belongs to the subcontractor and the property cannot change hands (when the owner wants to sell) until the lien is cleared up.

- If some of the work required will be outside of the agreement that your client makes with the general contractor (for example, your client hires his or her own painter), the contract agreement may define the conditions that are required for the seamless cooperation among everyone's subcontractors.
- Special requests that your client has made should be listed in the contract. For example, workers may be required not to smoke on the premises. All materials and equipment needed may be required to be on hand before work commences. The contract should spell out the steps that must be taken to protect areas of the site that are not under construction. Describe the level of cleanup that is expected, and identify the party expected to provide it. What services (water? electricity?) and amenities (a toilet? drinking water?) will be available on the site during construction? The contract should provide answers to all these questions.

If the entire scope of work is not spelled out on the contractor's bid, there must be some reference that can be broadly understood to define the scope of work. For instance, the bid may read: ". . . construction work as shown on designer's plans dated . . ." The date must be supplied as part of the contract terms, and a copy of the drawings as they were at that time must be kept on file with all parties. Otherwise, subsequent revisions will be a constant source of contention.

There may be some special conditions in the contract that pertain to financial and insurance aspects:

- *Guaranteed maximum price* is often included in cost-plus contracts to insure an outside maximum cost. If the project goes over budget, the contractor bears all the additional cost.
- *Penalty and bonus clauses* are used in tandem on contracts. If the delivery date (the date the building is complete) is delayed, an agreed-

upon amount of money will be deducted from the amount paid to the contractor. If the delivery date precedes the stated completion date, the contractor will be paid additional money equal to the penalty clause amount. Penalty clauses are not usually enforceable without companion bonus clauses.

- *Shared savings* are sometimes included in lump-sum costs for construction or guaranteed maximum price arrangements. If the construction costs come in under the agreed-upon maximum, then the savings are split between the owner and contractor in accordance with the percentages listed in the contract.
- *Liquidated damages* refers to an amount of money (which must be real losses) for delayed completion of the building. These damages must be reasonable and supportable (with documentation) to be enforceable. The sum will be calculated based on the extent of the delay or the cost of work purchased to mitigate the delay and will be deducted from money paid to the contractor.

Managing Communication

As the central person in the management of an interior design project (see Chapter 2), the designer needs to understand the job responsibilities of all the other parties involved and must make sure that they each understand their roles and duties, too. Managing communication throughout the project requires maintaining a contact list of all the participants, including those whom the designer does not supervise.

Defining Each Party's Responsibilities

Managing job responsibilities in an efficient and logical manner should logically be defined at the outset. Meet with all parties on the job and define the procedural flow and timetable for the design work and clarify the role of all persons developing details and specifications for the job.

Regardless of who is responsible for developing the work as defined at this meeting, all information should be combined into a *single document* format issued through *one* entity. This

document may be the architect's plans and schedules on a job requiring an architect. It will be the interior designer's plans and schedules on jobs without an architect. When every party to the job (lighting designer, interior designer, kitchen equipment vendor for the restaurant, structure wiring consultant, and so on) has his or her own drawing submittals floating around the job site, the building tradespeople do not know what to reference, and the interface between the various systems and structures will not mesh, leading to complications and increased costs during construction. Defining the issuing party for the drawings and specs implies responsibility but does not guarantee it—the task of managing specs must be spelled out in someone's contract and he or she must be compensated.

Maintaining a Contact List

Keep a record of all parties that are involved with the project (see Figure 5.2). Include in each record the name of the party, including the company's name and the names of those with whom you will be dealing. Indicate their role or job title (general contractor, property manager, client, and so on). Include their addresses and phone numbers (cell phone and home and business phones, as pertinent) in this record and also any notes that would help you remember each contact's area of responsibility. You are likely to have information on subcontractors as well as the general contractor. Here are just a couple of examples of the usefulness of including subcontractors in your records:

- Often, the general contractor on the job supplies all but a few of the tradespeople (as when the client has a cousin in the flooring business, for instance). You would not call the general contractor with a communication for this subcontractor if the sub were outside of the contractor's management responsibility, so you would want to have that sub's information in addition to the general contractor's information.
- Even though all communications for the subcontractors are channeled through the general contractor's office, you realize that time is criti-

Client: Health Club Partners		
Contact	Address	Phone Numbers
Partners John Doe Jane Smith Carlos Sanchez	Health Club Partners 1234 Applewood Way Heartland, USA 00000	John Doe cell: 555-666-7777 Jane Smith cell: 555-777-6666 office: 555-666-6767 Carlos Sanchez cell: 555-666-7676
Architect Lead: Joan Gold Assistant: Jack Lee	Best Architects 1234 Straight Lane Heartland, USA 00000	Joan Gold: 555-222-3333 ext. 11 Jack Lee: 555-222-3333 ext. 12
Cabinetmaker Owner: Ray Milano Shop Manager: Ben	Superior Woodworking 1234 Wood Court Heartland, USA 00000	Ray cell: 555-555-1212 Ben office: 555-232-1212

FIGURE 5.2 The designer should maintain contact files with current information for all the parties involved in a project, including the client, professionals such as the architect and engineer, the general contractor and subcontractors, vendors, and installers.

cal for a particular phase of the work. You may wish to call a subcontractor directly to report that a change is being sent to the general contractor that will affect this sub's work. This way, the sub can prepare for the work to be done.

Organizing Budgets and Estimates

Keep a record of all budgets that you prepare for the client to provide a history of the job's progress as well as for your own working reference. As selections are made, you can keep track of how well you are allocating dollars. Some selections will probably be over budget, and some will be under. Your overall goal is to stay within budget parameters.

If any budget revisions are issued, keep a dated copy of each budget issued; you may want to make a note of why a revision was issued. This will help ensure that nobody forgets the reason for the change as they look back over the course of the project. For example, at the top of a revised budget, you may choose to print a note along the lines of: "Pursuant to our phone conversation [wherein you stated that the items originally selected that adhered to the budget were not to your client's liking] and at your request, I have formulated a revised budget that allows for quality levels in keeping with your expectations. The following is the revised budget, which will become our new working budget with your approval." Later in the process, when the client wonders how the budget escalated, there will be no lapses of memory as to how that was permitted to occur because you have written the history of the decision to increase the budget at the top of the new budget and reminded the client that the request originated with him or her. This does not diminish the client's disappointment, but it does help protect your relationship.

Estimates from workrooms should be kept on record, even estimates that never turned into contracts. Sometimes, a supplier that was selected to perform some phase of the work is "unselected," in which case you already have other bidders from which to choose. You also have the competitive bids in your history of the job that, for whatever reason, may be required. If you have done a lot of figuring in the process of drawing up an estimate and believe that you will want to recall how you arrived at the figure presented at a later date, you may wish to keep your notes and figures on record. For instance, a worksheet that you filled out or a plan that you marked up with your estimating process indicated will be helpful if you need to reconstruct the process for any reason.

Maintaining Schedules

Schedules used on the job include material schedules (see Figure 5.1) and timetables or construction schedules. They are both, unfortunately, called schedules and we keep them straight by contextual cues. Current copies of these schedules are kept at hand for your constant reference. Older copies, which have been revised, are kept in "cold storage" as an historical chronology of changes in case chronology and timing should ever become important.

Construction Schedules

Work schedules will be revised as the work progresses. Keep in your records any schedules dated and issued by your firm as a history of the chronology of the work. You may elect to throw away early copies of schedules issued by others that are superseded by revisions or to keep them in "cold storage" in some location other than in project records in order to avoid confusion and errors. You will reference the construction schedule. As the job moves forward, you may have to update your own records. The general contractor may not issue timetable revisions, but you still need to know when to have material that you purchased delivered to the site and when to go to the site for inspections of rough and finished work.

Material Schedules

Even on jobs on which you forward your material selections to the architect for inclusion into his or her drawing sets, you will want to keep a material schedule complete in your records as well because you will still be responsible for managing the specifications, even though they were issued by the architect. Material schedules will also change as the work progresses. For consistency's sake, the changes would, ideally, be issued through the architect's office, but the reality of this situation frequently is that you will issue the change to all parties, and the architect will be copied along with all others. If your company is issuing the schedule, then there is no question about who is responsible for maintaining and communicating information about current selections.

Ideally, all schedules and specifications will be organized into a single document for a variety of reasons:

- *Controlling for oversight.* If you believe the architect is handling something and the architect believes that you are handling it, it never shows up as a "blank" on anybody's records.
- *Controlling for duplication.* The inverse of the previous situation occurs when you both address a material selection or detail and there is conflicting information at the job site as a result.
- *Simplification of the document set.* When all material selections are presented in the same place and in the same format, it is easier for any party working on the site to find the desired information.

There are two schools of thought pertaining to the exact content of the material schedules. One approach is to use closed spec information on the material schedules, listing manufacturer and product item numbers so that the schedules on site are very complete. The other approach is to include only generic descriptions on schedules and complete information of specifications. Both have their merits.

Consider the use of closed specifications on schedules. This complete information is enough to manage the receiving and installation of materials as they are needed at the site. If the correct carpet in the wrong colorway shows up at the site, the job boss or general contractor can catch the error before the goods are installed (remember, installation constitutes acceptance in many industries). However, if a substitution was made along the way and the schedules are part of the plan set, then addendums to the schedules must be issued to and managed by the contractor.

Consider the use of open specs on the schedule and complete information on the specifications only. If the information appears in only one place, you have to make the revision in only that one place. This avoids the possibility that the specs are changed and the schedules are not and then you have job-stopping confusion on the site. On the downside, open specifications on schedules omit item numbers, which may be the only identification on the packing slip when the material shows up at the site.

Filing Contracts

Often, an estimate from a workroom becomes your contract with that firm or you issue a purchase order based on its estimate. Therefore, keep a copy of the estimate as part of your records for the contract (a purchase order is a *contract* made between you and the supplier for purchase of goods or services; a deposit request or proposal is a *contract* between you and your client for the sale of goods or services). You must keep this information on file and may elect any method that makes the most sense in light of your software and process.

Even though electronic files can now be quite complete (with scanned documents attached to a file), the preference in most studios still seems to be for maintaining paper records. The reason for this is that so many kinds of documents must attend a contract, the first being the designer's own request for a bid. This may be accompanied by a plan to help the vendor to provide a material takeoff with the bid (such as, "provide and install 3200 square feet of ceramic tile"). This bid from the vendor is submitted to the designer for review, after which a proposal to the client will be drawn up. Frequently, the client must sign a proposal; this is another document kept with the request for bid and the vendor's proposal. At this point, a purchase order to the vendor will be issued. It is common practice to file all of the above with a paper copy of the purchase order so the details, progress, and history are all together. Any orders that revise a previously issued contract should be kept with the related paperwork. So you can see that a lot of paper is generated in the natural course of the material specification and purchase. This order progression, which is kept as a series of documents, is referred to as the *paper trail* related to the order history. Even though studios all tend to keep paper records, the organization of these records is unique from one studio to another.

Managing Specifications and Purchase Orders

Specifications help you quickly find the exact information and descriptions of the work related to materials to be installed at the job site. All materials are described either in a specification for purchase by others or in the form of a purchase order. All work is described either in a memo or letter or in the form of a purchase order or contract. You will also file work orders that originate in other offices (the architect's office, for instance), so you have a record of planned, final conditions at the site.

Specifications for materials often exist in two forms in the design studio. One type is specifications issued for purchase by others. Frequently, surfacing materials fall in this category. For example, in the health club project, the contractor will very likely purchase the tile for the locker rooms. These specifications will be as complete and have attendant drawings that are as detailed as the items that your studio will purchase for the project.

The other form in which the specification could exist is a purchase order that you prepare. While the contractors like to manage the estimates and purchase of the surfacing installed, they frequently will not care to be responsible for specialty items such as decorative light fixtures. Sorting out who will purchase which materials and items for the job is part of the early planning and orchestrating sessions. Chapter 6 discusses how to prepare the specs for which you, as the designer for the project, are responsible.

Organizing Correspondence

All notes, memos, and letters sent to you by another party or sent to a third party with a copy to you should be kept on file. This category of paperwork can become quite large during the course of a project, and you may choose to subdivide it according to party into "client," "contractors," "suppliers," and so on or by topic related to a particular material specification.

Maintaining Meeting Notes

During the course of a project, there will be numerous meetings and site visits. In addition to memos distributed by you to other parties, there will be notes that you take for your own information. These will include suggestions for decisions to be made at a later date, site measures that later become part of drawings, photos of conditions that affect your work that you need as a reference, and more. Whenever there is a change or addition to a material specification or detail or to information that has already been issued, you must issue meeting minutes or an addendum to record, to summarize and clarify the change or addition. This information is often transmitted via e-mails. Your studio may file these changes electronically or print them out for attachment to physical (paper) records or both.

CHAPTER 6

specifications

As you study the materials and products for the health club project (and when you conduct research for your own real-world designs), you will encounter many kinds of specifications. Not all information contained in all of the specifications that you'll find will relate directly to your goal for the health club, which is getting the work done. It takes some focus to sift through *all* the information for the *pertinent* information required to communicate your intent. Specifications related to any given material may include the following:

- All the ingredients used to make it
- The production method employed in making it
- Its physical and performance attributes
- The best storage conditions for preserving it in good condition
- The handling and proper transportation of the material
- The installation of the material related to your specific job-site conditions
- The protection and maintenance of the material once installed
- The proper way to remove and dispose of the material

Writing Specifications for Practical Application

All of the information in a manufacturer's specification is important, but looking from the point of view of the people to whom you are communicating, consider which information matters to whom. Sift the information that you encounter so that you are delivering all necessary information to interested parties without making them slog through information that has no bearing on their work or interests.

When you are writing the specification, it is important to keep in mind who the audience is. We are all inundated with information; most people today have the problem of structuring the information so they can use it to do something.

Select Information Relevant to the Parties to the Project

Some of the specifications that you will find for materials (and that you should reference in addition to this book, just for an increased understanding of the material) attempt to cover *every* potential intensely specific circumstance. This makes them very cumbersome, and here is the danger inherent in that—tradespeople do not pick up the spec book because they need some reading material. They reference your specs because they need information. If they review your spec and think that you sure put a lot of effort into writing a spec, but it doesn't say much and that there are no instructions in it for *them,* they will get back to work based on "context clues." A tradesperson will think, "Look, here's some vinyl tile. I'll ask the general contractor where it goes and install it as I typically do." Don't deliver specs that do not do what they are supposed to do, which is to communicate clearly to suppliers and tradespeople what *they* are to do.

You might reference the standards developed by ASTM International, the organization formerly known as the American Society for Testing and Materials, in your specs. Or you might want to reference another document or other general instructions. If you refer to one of these sources, include the referent in your documents. Better yet, cull the information from the ASTM standard that pertains to your job and put that directly into your spec, just to be perfectly clear what exactly your instructions are. Specifications should be *specific.*

You will notice a number of checklists for materials and products on the CD. With so much to keep track of, it's easy to forget something, even if it's critical. Checklists can serve as "off-site" data storage for facts and procedures that might get lost in your brain.

Avoid Errors of Omission

Exercise particular diligence to avoid errors of omission in submittals of specs and drawings. When you collaborate on projects with architects, it is easy to assume that a detail under consideration is going to be handled by the architect. This is an opportunity for disappointment. Every idea that you propose should be documented by you (or your team, depending on the structure of your company). Architects are comfortable reviewing your installation detail drawings and specs and vouching for them by inserting them into their document sets. Be responsible for your own ideas and forward sufficient documentation to the appropriate parties in order to communicate your intent.

Organize Specs and Drawings

Any specification that includes instructions for assembling anything also includes or references a drawing containing an annotated diagram of the assembly. These drawings, which you will make to clarify your specifications for fabrication or installations, include the following:

- Each material, component, and accessory needed to complete the installation
- The generic name of the material, component, or accessory, even if the written spec is proprietary (that is, a particular brand). Use no proper nouns or identification numbers.
- Pertinent, exact dimensions for each to describe size and distance, as relevant
- Dimensions or items that may be allowed to vary (meaning the remaining dimensions or items are critical dimensions)
- Work or materials, shown in the specification drawing, that will be supplied or performed by others. Identify who that other is for each specified material or task, for example, "Trim collar to be provided and installed by plumber."
- If symbols are used in place of the actual appearance of an item, provide a symbol key adjacent to the drawing or in an easily located place.
- Confirm that the drawing is clear and complete in itself, but do not write extensive notes in the drawing area if they will clutter the drawing and create daunting visual chaos on the page; instead, indicate where to find the text.

As you organize your documents (specifications and drawings used in tandem to convey your design intent), keep in mind that information should ideally appear only *once* in the combination of drawings and specifications. If information is delivered in written specifications, it should not be duplicated in the drawings and vice versa. That's because as projects progress, there are inevitably numerous changes. There are various reasons for this; for example, they might be the result of new technologies, unexpected developments at the site, changes to the budget due to additional work required in another area, or any number of other developments. (Your creative contribution does not end when the drawings and specs are finalized.) If your project specs are really *tight,* you can expect up to ten percent of the project to change during construction. If information is noted in two places, you may alter documents of one type and then, believing that it has all been handled, forget to alter the other portion of the documents. So you may change the drawings and leave the written specifications unaltered and incorrect. The bottom line is that information goes into either specs or drawings but not both. Develop habits that conform with your company's system or—lacking such a system—is intuitive for you.

Follow the Rules for Spec Writing

When preparing specifications, follow these logical rules:

- Use short parcels of information and confine each sentence to one characteristic or instruction.
- Use unambiguous terms. "Provide a three-way switch at either end of the corridor" could be understood to mean at both ends or at one end. So say "both ends" or "one end."
- Avoid redundancy. The two following statements contain the redundant words "any" and "all."
  - Any lippage greater than ⅓₂" to be ground flat
  - All lippage greater than ⅓₂" to be ground flat (The gist of the instruction is *lippage greater than ⅓₂" to be ground flat.*)
- Write in the declarative or imperative mood; avoid the passive voice whenever possible because it can obscure who is responsible for some action.
  - Imperative: Install counter-height outlets every 4 feet on center.
  - Declarative: The electricians install counter-height outlets every 4 feet on center.
  - Passive: Counter-height outlets are to be installed every 4 feet on center.
- Use words that are widely understood, and avoid jargon.
- "Shall" seems to be preferred over "is to" or "must," as in "the plumber shall furnish and install . . ."
- Spell out %, +, -, , ", and '. as percent, plus, minus, degrees, inches, and feet (unless a combination of feet and inches is needed, then use the format 7'-5").
- If another standard reference spec is cited (such as an ASTM standard) or you direct the supplier to perform according to "manufacturer's specifications," you *must* read the standard that you are referencing (unless you are sure you are entirely familiar with it—and even then it doesn't

hurt) to ensure there are no contradictions or multiple options. If the reference that you are indicating is short, it will be more convenient for everyone if you just spell it out in your spec.

- Never include anything in a specification that you do not personally understand fully. Interior designers reference specifications written by other parties as they compose their specifications. These referent specs may be from the manufacturer, a standards organization, or a previous spec generated within the studio where the designer works. Designers respect and trust these sources and may feel safe just copying and pasting, but the specifications that you submit for the job become part of the construction documents, which are legal documents. It is irresponsible and professionally negligent to forward instructions that you cannot vouch for personally. Maintain the attitude that you cannot separate yourself from your work. Be responsible and mean everything personally.

Understanding the Different Kinds of Specs

The kinds of specifications that you might provide include open (descriptive), performance, and closed (proprietary).

Open or Descriptive Specification

A description of the material or product that includes material, dimensions, and qualities in sufficient detail to ensure the product will meet the program needs but does not identify a particular manufacturer's product is called an open specification. An open spec permits the supplier to fill the order with any product that matches the description of the spec. Open specs are used in the case of commodity-type products, such as dimensional wood strip flooring. They are used in cases where several manufacturers produce a product that could match the product characteristics as described. The benefit of an open spec for a widely available material (for example, 4 × 4 clay tile with matte white glaze) is that the supplier can locate material at the lowest price while working to secure the contract, saving the designer's time locating the most economical product to use while completing the project. It is a good idea to require suppliers submitting bids to submit a sample of the material with their bids to confirm that the spec was complete enough and that all expectations can be met by the proposed material. Sometimes, performance information is included with an open spec.

Performance Specification

A performance spec describes the performance of the material without necessarily identifying the material. It describes minimum standards in such areas as hardness, ease of maintenance, water resistance, stain resistance, reflectance, and all pertinent characteristics of performance, but it does not always restrict the material supplied to any particular class of materials. It is a rather rare kind of specification for product in the interior design industry and is more often included with open spec information than it is used on its own. Interior designers make more use of the performance spec when specifying the installation of materials or products using phrases like "handrail to support 250 pounds of pressure applied laterally."

Closed or Proprietary Specification

A closed spec identifies a particular manufacturer's unique or proprietary product. The closed spec must include the manufacturer's name and the manufacturer's identification of the product, such as its ID number or name. When you are adamant about the precise product that you have specified and you want to be clear that this product and no other will be acceptable, you may add the words "no substitutions" to your specification.

Manufacturers often have specifications available for their products that are written as open specifications for designers to use when they are required by their contract to use an open spec format for bids. If you use this kind of spec, it is a courtesy to bidders to add the words "such as [product ID] as manufactured by [manufacturer]" to give them a head start on what you are after. This may appear to be in conflict with the open spec requirement but, in actual practice, the bidders may submit materials that are functionally the same if materially slightly different for your consideration and approval. You always have the option of approving or rejecting the proposed substitute.

Modified Closed Specification

This specification has the appearance of a closed spec, but it can be made more open if the words "or equal" are added after the manufacturer's description or ID. This, too, allows the bidders to submit substitutes for your consideration and approval.

CHAPTER 7

Green Design and Sustainability

Green design includes sustainable site planning, pollution prevention, restoration of urban and habitat sites, access to public or alternative transportation options by building occupants, storm-water runoff management, reduction of heat island effects, maximization of open space, reduction of light pollution, water use reduction, energy conservation, recycling, conservation of materials, the use of sustainable practices and materials, attention to toxicity and general occupant health, and utilization of daylight in interior spaces. Some of these topics are of special interest as we make decisions about the material and human resources to be employed on a job, so they will be integral to most of the topics discussed in Parts Two and Three of this book.

At the level of most basic consideration, green products are:

- Renewable/sustainable
- Recycled/recyclable
- Durable
- Adaptable
- Made with low-embodied energy and locally sourced
- Sustainably installed, removed, and maintained
- Nontoxic

Renewable and Sustainable Materials

When considering a material, its renewability and sustainability can be determined by answer-ing the question: Does the material come from resources that can be easily replenished? Plants are the source for many renewable materials, but recycled material is often considered a renewable resource as well. Even renewable resources are not always sustainable (see Box 7.1). Lumber illustrates the difference between the two concepts. Trees are a renewable resource; if you chop one down, you can plant another. Using an old-growth tree, which takes hundreds of years to replace, is not as sustainable as using a fast-growing tree.

Recycled and Recyclable Materials

Basically, two sources of recyclable material are available to the manufacturer: waste from

---

BOX 7.1 | A Cautionary Tale

One of my students was researching green products and shared a hilarious example of a manufacturer "greenwashing" its product. The product claim was that it was renewable because it was made from plant- and animal-based material. Upon investigation, the product was discovered to be made from petroleum; further inquiry brought the response that oil does come from plants and animals—plankton and bacteria—so it is a renewable resource. It just takes hundreds of thousands of years to renew itself! That's why petroleum products are barely renewable and certainly not sustainable as a material source.

production of goods (trimmings, things used in the manufacturing process then discarded) and waste from products that were thrown away after use (post-consumer waste, such as soda bottles).

The carpet industry is now achieving one long-time goal of manufacturing, *cradle-to-cradle* recycling. Used carpet is delaminated (removed from its backing) and the nylon fibers are recycled into new nylon fibers and remanufactured into carpeting. Some manufacturers accept the material back at the end of its life to ensure that it will be properly recycled. Recycling is also described as down-cycling or up-cycling. A product made from recycled material that is more primitive than what it was made from, such as turning old carpeting into parking bumpers, is considered to be down-cycling. Up-cycling turns recycled content into more sophisticated or less primitive products than the original recycled content. Using fly ash from incineration as a component in Syndesis products for floor surfacing is an example of up-cycling.

Durable Materials

Determining durability is deceptively simple. Physical strength is only one part of durability. Durability cannot be evaluated by looking at the product outside of any considerations for its eventual installation; you will have to consider the end use as you evaluate the material. What kind of stress is the installed material or product subject to? An area where impact stress is likely will require a different kind of material from an area where abrasion or staining is the main stressor. Even something as simple as the right maintenance schedule can increase the longevity of a product.

Materials are frequently removed long before the end of their serviceability because they have gone out of style. Designers must resist being blown around in the whirlwind of fashion and trends. Strong aesthetic programming in the concept-development phase is vital to your design solution's congruence with its purpose and its site. This consideration is essential to specifying a project that will endure over time. Design selections driven by trends often look forced onto their surroundings. These designs become "time

capsules" that are easily identified as "yesterday's news" a decade later. Specify materials and products that are congruent with the project and site so that your solution will endure.

Speculative building exemplifies another short-shelf-life situation. Buildings are often developed speculatively, that is, the original owner intends to own the building for as short a time as possible. The new owners of the space may have needs that aren't addressed by the design solution installed for the previous owner. Because the specifier views the building as "temporary," the primary motivator in selections will be initial cost. The thing to acknowledge is that decisions related to environments that are considered temporary, for whatever reason, intensify the burden on other green characteristics. Adaptability comes immediately to mind.

Adaptability

In light of the considerations of "temporary" installations, adaptability is desirable even if your specific project programming does not indicate an emphatic need for adaptability. Can the material or item be demounted and reused if the need for it disappears in the middle of its useful life? Modular materials are often designed with this possibility in mind.

The good sense of working within modular sizes extends beyond adaptability. Most manufactured products are made in specific sizes that can be thought of as modules. When you are designing projects, find out the size of the material that will be used, then design economically within those increments to minimize waste and installation labor. For instance, drywall comes in 4 × 8, 4 × 9, 4 × 10, and 4 × 12 foot sheets. Designing to standard increments can help limit scrap and save the carpenters time. Although a carpenter's time may be considered a renewable resource, to be sure, that is no reason to be extravagant and waste it, because time is money.

Low-Embodied Energy and Use of Local Materials

"Low-embodied energy" refers to the amount of energy required by the material installed. A green material does not require lots of other resources to produce and install it. A material that is used in a condition fairly close to its natural state will often be a low-energy item relative to a material that must undergo several different processes in order to be brought to usable condition. Materials that are local and do not have to be moved in fuel-consuming transportation are low-energy compared to materials that must be transported between the various steps of their production and then delivered to the site.

Energy is required to produce and move a material or product. This would include harvesting the raw material, preparing it for production, producing it, finishing it, packaging it for transportation, and storing it until shipping (and maybe after shipping, too). The practice of material conservation should be integrated into the process, so consider the amount of waste inherent in the installation and use of the product, not just its production.

There are other costs beyond the easily measured costs of fuel and electricity consumed. If we break down the manufacturing process into a detailed series of transactions involving costs and benefits, we will discover a number of costs that are not being paid for. What if all goods and materials produced were required to have zero impact on the environment? While the granite mentioned in the Cautionary Tale (Box 7.2) is being cut, the saws are constantly cooled with water. The cost of pumping and delivering the water is very likely covered in utility bills that the supplier pays. What if the water had to be cleaned and made available for reuse? This cost is not paid under the current setup because the water is not cleaned and made available; it is simply thrown away. This is a freebie that the industry, including designers, enjoys.

For the dedicated capitalist who loves the idea of getting something for nothing, consider this benefit of taking the lead by not waiting for the government to regulate you. Look at one example summarized in the EPA Federal Register (September 11, 1998, volume 63, number 176, 48,824). The notion of regulating the emissions associated with common household products (deodorant, insecticides, glass cleaner, and simi-

BOX 7.2 | **A Cautionary Tale**

I once wanted to specify a granite with a flamed finish rather than the polished finish that was immediately available. The cost in dollars was not unreasonable, but the extension of the delivery time surprised me. That's when I learned that the granite would have to be shipped back across the ocean and the face flamed by the supplier, then shipped back to North America and trucked to Chicago. This would have significantly affected the embodied energy of the stone in question.

lar products) indicated an annualized cost of 26 million dollars. An *additional* annual cost of 990 thousand dollars for *record-keeping* would be partly *carried by industry*. Anything "carried by industry" means carried by you because the government does not pay you to provide it with any information that it decides to require. (Similarly, every time I figure my taxes to send myself a bill on the government's behalf, I wish I could deduct my usual hourly rate from the total.) So if an appeal to your ethics and social conscience doesn't move you, then let your numbers do the talking, and be personally responsible in your specifications to avoid the necessity of cumbersome government monitoring.

Sustainability in Installation, Maintenance, and Removal

The more green characteristics that a product exemplifies, the greener it is. Few products satisfy every category. When researching how green a product is, consider not just its own characteristics but the course of its entire life: its manufacturing, packing and shipping, preparation and installation, use and maintenance, and removal and disposal.

Evaluate the material under consideration in light of what is required from the time it arrives at the site. Is the installation method toxic? Does it render the material unusable for any other future purpose? Does the material have to be stripped and resealed regularly in order to be maintained in presentable condition? If so, what solvents are used to strip it? If the solvent contains *volatile organic compounds* (VOCs), it is likely that the resealing required also contains VOCs. VOCs affect people directly as well as placing a burden on the environment because systems change in response to these toxic chemicals.

Nontoxic Materials

Green design has quite naturally assumed the issue of toxicity as well. This topic centers on the presence of VOCs and chemical sensitivities of individuals. VOCs are volatile, which means they can change states from a solid or liquid to a gas. The solvents in paint thinner are an example of such compounds. You would never dream of sipping these solvents from a cup, but you are ingesting them when you breathe the fumes of these volatile compounds after they have changed from a liquid to a gas. Because these compounds are organic, they can interact with our bodies' processes and mechanisms. There is a wide range of tolerance among different people. While some people exhibit dramatic evidence of the negative effect of particular chemicals in their environment, others report no ill effects because of their bodies' current ability to achieve a healthy stasis. There is reason to suspect that with prolonged exposure to "ordinary" chemicals, our immune systems eventually diminish in their ability to bring us back to health after reaction to exposure.

According to the Environmental Protection Agency, volatile organic compounds are up to ten times more concentrated in interior environments than in the open. VOCs are emitted by many solvents, paints and varnishes, carpeting, vinyl flooring, upholstery fabrics, adhesives, caulks, and engineered wood products, as well as cleaning products.

The effects of VOCs as well as particulates and microbes—all pertinent toxicity issues—are often so subtle we accept them as normal. The next time you find yourself feeling foggy-headed, lethargic, or just plain down, take a look at your surroundings and evaluate the likelihood that there are toxins, particulates, or excessive and unfriendly microbes in your environment.

Sometimes, they are easy to identify—like that new car smell (just a noseful of VOCs)—but there is often no easily detectable culprit.

Carcinogens Common in the Products That Designers Specify

A variety of carcinogens and other toxic materials are often included in commonly specified materials:

- *Polychlorinated Biphenyls (PCBs)* are used in paint, plastic, and rubber. They are *bioaccumulative*, that is, they do not break down in the food chain. They are cancer-causing in humans.
- *Dioxin* is generated during the manufacturing of materials containing polyvinyl chloride (PVC), such as flooring, wallcoverings, paint, and plastic liners. It is also generated while bleaching and incineration during the production of materials used in interiors. They are toxic and bioaccumulative.
- *Furans* are toxic and bioaccumulative and are found in some grouting products and used in the synthesis of nylon.

Common toxic metals include the following:

- *Mercury* in electrical switches and fluorescent lamps
- *Cadmium* in plastics and pigments
- *Arsenic* in pressure-treated lumber
- *Lead* in paint

Insecticides, which are applied during the production of fibers (such as cotton) or applied during the production of materials (such as wool carpets), are designed to be toxic to insects and may be toxic to humans. You should minimize the specification of their use.

Protection against Toxins

In its most simple form, vigilance against toxins leads us down three different pathways.

1. Specify inert material.
2. Specify material that outgasses quickly or has had enough time to outgas sufficiently.
3. Encapsulate the material in a nonoffending material.

The best route is to avoid and prevent all toxins that could occur in the environment. Specify inert materials, prevent moisture (which supports the growth of microbes and molds), and filter air as it comes and goes. (In some locales, one of the biggest polluters of inside air is outside air.)

Inert materials include stone, metal, glass, and other "mineral" materials that are not organic in origin. If it is not possible to specify inert materials for your project, there are a couple of ways to deal with outgassing. *Outgassing* is the way VOCs leave a material; they turn into a gas and float out. A way to protect your chemically sensitive client is to specify material that outgasses very quickly, as many solvent-based compounds and heat-catalyzed sealants will do. They contain compounds that exit into the air but do so over a short time span, so they are not constantly leaking into the site over the course of years (see Box 7.3). The last resort is to seal offending materials completely in nonoffending materials. You could also use a salvaged or antique product that may outgas over time but, because it has been around for a long time, will emit VOC levels low enough to be tolerated.

The Costs of Green Design

Design and building decisions are always price-driven. The value of the result is always compared to the cost of acquiring it. This cost is typically evaluated in terms of dollars alone—which is shortsighted for obvious reasons, and incomplete in the long term. When comparing two bids, you should consider a number of factors beyond cost. Fortunately, the issues that seem like larger "social issues" will also have a more job-specific counterpart. For example, materials and finishes that outgas potentially harm the fabricators who handle them; they poison the environment and, closer to home for your client, they can harm the end users of the space you have designed. When calculating the full costs, consider the price, the green rating, and the social impact (are workers earning a fair wage, protected from harm, treated well, and so on?).

Green design is integral to all topics covered in this book. This is not comprehensive coverage of green design; you can find much more information through Leadership in Energy and Environmental Design or LEED (www.usgbc.org) and ASTM International (www.astm.org), but this can get you started. This chapter is devoted to the topic because the evaluation of any product follows the same guidelines. Consciously seek out green products as you are specifying for your homework assignments and as you make selections for your clients in the future.

Evaluate *each stage* of a material's production, use, and disposal by asking these questions:

- Is renewable energy used in its production? (Good luck with this one!)
- What is the packaging like? Is it made of renewable and sustainable material?
- How was it transported and how far? Was a lot of a nonrenewable fuel used because it traveled a long distance?
- Once it arrived at the job site, was it installed and finished with adhesives and coatings that are nontoxic, renewable, and sustainable?
- Does normal maintenance require the removal and reapplication of coatings?
- Are any solvent-based products required? If so, are they renewable?
- What happens when it must be disposed of? Does it go to a landfill? If so, it is not sustainable.

BOX 7.3 | **A Cautionary Tale**

I had a client whose son was very sensitive to chemicals in the environment. Her budget did not allow for expensive substrates for cabinetry and wall panels that he could tolerate easily, so we clad surfaces in plastic laminate (which out-gasses quickly) and sealed all joints after installation. The sealant also outgassed, but it did so fast enough that we were able to schedule the installation while her son was away at camp, and the environment was tolerable when he returned home. You should consider how chemicals could affect a client and the environment.

CHAPTER 8

acoustics

While all materials are acoustic materials because they interact with sound waves, thereby altering the sonic environment, the most common understanding of a material that is "acoustical" is that it will absorb sound. This is an oversimplification. A minimal understanding of sound and related issues will help you solve simple problems and communicate with acousticians.

Noise (unwanted sound) interferes with activities, reduces productivity, and causes stress. The character or quality of the spaces we create is a result of the experiences of all of our senses. The echoic quality inside an atrium space in a public building cooperates with information that we gather with our other senses and seems appropriate within the experience. In the complete absence of sound or in the presence of an unexpected quality of sound, the experience would lack congruity. This is neither good nor bad in itself, but the designer should be intentional about every aspect of the experience created. If it is your intention to create an "exotic" experience, you may decide to control the sonic environment to cause an unexpected result. If you want to create a reassuring experience, you will consider how to control sound to create an expected sonic environment as you work to achieve a good functional fit between the environment and the tasks taking place in it.

The U.S. Department of Health and Human Services has mandated that health-care providers offer confidentiality to patients who must discuss their health and other private issues with professionals in the health-care providers' offices or spaces. The health-care provider must "employ reasonable privacy safeguards to ensure that conversations about a patient are not overheard." However, "reasonable privacy safeguards" are not further defined. The designer or specifier's responsibility is not always easy to quantify when a control system of multiple parts is being assembled, so the word "reasonable" is a logical choice.

When we, as designers, are intent on controlling sound and creating a sonic environment in line with our design program, we have a small "tool kit" that we can employ. We can absorb, isolate, insulate, block, mask, and zone in our projects to diminish noise. We can bounce and aim to control, and we can focus and amplify to enhance.

Contributing to our success in managing acoustics is the location of surfaces and their potential for blocking or bouncing sound. Because the tools employed for managing sound are varied and work in combination with one another, it is not realistic to consider any isolated material or configuration—everything works together.

A minimal comprehension of the behavior of sound, plus familiarity with some measurement standards, is a good place to start as we work to address the needs identified by the Department of Health and Human Services, as well as the needs identified by our individual design programs. Our program may require that we deliver sound to locations within the project (in a presentation space or church, for instance) or introduce cancellation sound waves to obscure sound information. A primitive example of cancellation waves is white noise or music played to interfere with speech intelligibility or to obscure the presence of one sound with a competing sound.

Understanding Sound

The topic of acoustics is complex beyond the needs of our study and will not be fully addressed here. The focus within the topic of acoustics will be the materials that we employ to improve the quality of the sound or sonic environment.

Sound travels in waves, as diagrammed in Figure 8.1, but there is one other bit of information that you will find necessary as you evaluate some sources of nuisance sound. High-frequency (high-pitched) waves are short. These sound waves are easier to contain than low-frequency waves, which are sometimes long enough to "bend around" objects in their path. That thump-thump-thump of excessive base in the car next to you is not the only sound available to the driver inside it, but it is all that escapes to annoy you. The low-pitched rumble of equipment or a motor has a very long wavelength that can escape the methods used to corral the short wavelengths.

A good-quality sound environment usually requires the use of "live" and "dead" surfaces. Live surfaces bounce the sound off; they enliven and sparkle. Dead surfaces soak up and trap sound. Some bounce is desirable to create enlivened, natural-sounding sound. The periodic angles in the plan diagram (Figure 8.2) illustrate the effect of a live surface positioned to bounce the sound generated on the left into the center— rounding out the sound experience in the space.

If the space in question is deep, you will need dead surfaces, too. There is a very primitive rule of thumb called the 30-millisecond rule, which conveniently translates into a measurement that you may be able to understand more clearly as the 30-foot rule. If a sound sails past you, then bounces back to you, that is enough travel time to

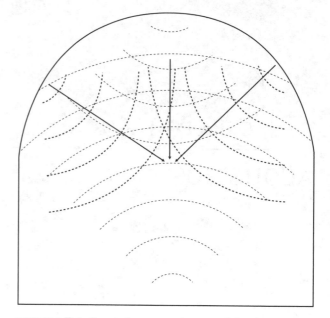

FIGURE 8.1 This diagram is presented as a reminder that sound radiates and bounces. The shape of the space works in conjunction with materials in the space to control sound. If this were a vertical section or a plan, you could predict that sound would be focused where sound waves converge. You would either actively focus or purposely absorb or baffle the sound, depending on the needs of your design program.

cause a perceptible delay in arrival. If the sound sailing past you travels beyond you, then bounces back to you over a distance of 30 feet or greater, its echo will muddle the original sound. What happens is this: You hear a spoken word and can easily comprehend it unless its own echo interferes with it. You will still hear it, but it will be harder to comprehend its meaning. So you will probably position live surfaces along the side walls and dead surface at the back wall of the space diagrammed by the plan view in Figure 8.3 to stop the echo from the back wall on the right from muddling speech generated on the left.

Rating and Measuring Sound

As you are managing the acoustics in your project with surfaces and barriers, you will encounter various ratings pertaining to materials under consideration. Even though managing acoustics in a space requires both moving and blocking sound, our industry does not tend to focus on material that promotes the movement of sound. Absorbing, diffusing, and blocking characteristics are measured, and comparisons can be drawn between materials. This is a little simplistic but

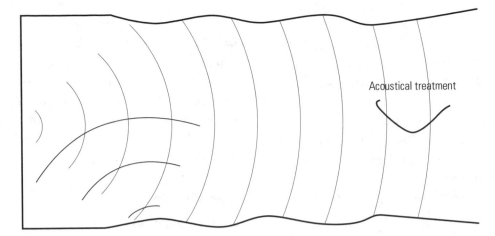

FIGURE 8.2 Sound waves in this long room could be reflected off the back wall, causing an interfering echo because of a time delay. The acoustician may suggest angling the side walls to lend dimension to the sound and adding a sound-absorbing material on the back wall to stop interfering echoes from bouncing back into the room.

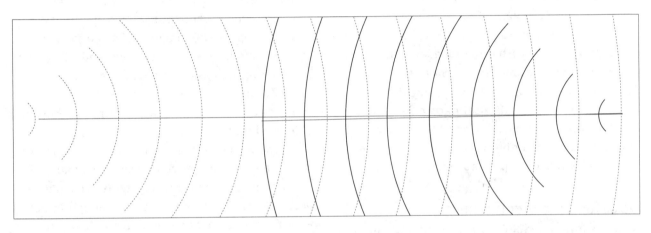

FIGURE 8.3 Without sound absorption on the back wall of a long space, the time it takes reflected sound to travel back into the center is long enough for the lag time to separate the actual sound from the reflected sound; this can occur so completely that the reflection will interfere with comprehension.

is a workable method. Measurements that are of interest to designers are privacy index, sound transmission class, impact isolation class, and noise reduction coefficient.

Privacy Index

Privacy index, or PI, measures speech intelligibility. A PI measurement of less than 60 percent offers no speech privacy and is considered poor.

A PI of 60 to 80 percent, indicating that speech is readily understandable, is considered marginal. A PI rating of 80 to 95 percent means that speech is distracting but requires effort to be understood and is considered normal or nonintrusive. A PI of 95 percent and higher indicates that confidentiality can be maintained.

Sound Transmission Class

Sound Transmission Class, or STC, measures sound moving through partitions or barriers. The number rises as efficiency increases because it measures how much sound is lost as it moves through the barrier. Sound transmission is affected by:

- The mass and stiffness of the materials used in the partition
- The thickness of the assembly
- Control of flanking and structure-borne paths ("airtight" construction)

Here are some useful numbers to clarify the value of the ratings:

- An STC of 25 to 30 means speech can be fairly readily understood.
- An STC of 35 to 45 indicates that speech is audible but not intelligible, and perceived volume falls so that, at the upper end, loud speech becomes a murmur.
- An STC of 50 renders loud speech inaudible.

Impact Isolation Class

Impact Isolation Class or Impact Insulation Class, two terms that mean the same thing, measures the amount of impact noise blocked by the barrier. A measurement of 50 is adequate, and this can almost always be achieved simply by carpeting a space. As with other measures, this is a little simplistic because it does not account for varying kinds of impact. The tapping of hard heels is a noise of a different nature from heavy footfalls on a floor assembly, so the efficiency of the assembly cannot be considered to be equal across all kinds of impact noise.

Noise Reduction Coefficient

Noise Reduction Coefficient, or NRC, measures the ability of materials to absorb sound.

- A rating of 0 means that no sound is absorbed.
- A rating of 1 means that all sound waves striking the material are absorbed.
- A standard acoustical ceiling will have a rating of about 0.55.

Speech Range Absorption

Speech Range Absorption, or SRA, measures the absorption of sounds that come specifically from speech. This will often be a different number from the NRC rating for the same product. Our ears are "tuned" to hear 1000 Hz more efficiently than 100 Hz, so materials to control speech transmission will absorb more vigorously in the range of speech; 700 Hz is considered to be the center of the critical hertz range of speech intelligibility.

Ceiling Attenuation Class

Attenuation is a weakening of sound over distance or from absorption. Ceiling Attenuation Class, or CAC, indicates the ability of a ceiling system to block sound transmission. A CAC of 40 means it reduces sound by 40 decibels. A CAC of 35 is considered a good performance rating.

Managing Sound
Decibel Reduction

A decibel, or dB, is a measure of the loudness of sound: 30 dB is a whisper; 60 dB is normal conversation; an alarm clock may be about 70 dB, which is the upper end of sound that people usually accept as a normal range. Perception of sound is dependent on personal sensitivity, content, duration, time of occurrence, and psychological factors such as emotional state and expectations. A sound level of 110 dB may be preferred at a rock concert but be entirely unreasonable in a building lobby.

General perceptional guidelines for reducing the sound level can provide a working standard for evaluation of sound control systems. A change in decibel level of 1 dB is not discernable; 3 dB seems to be the threshold of perception for change in decibel level. A change of 6 dB is clearly noticeable. A reduction of 10 dB is functionally half as loud, and 25 dB is perceived as one-fourth as loud.

Attenuation

Attenuation is an important aspect of sound transmission. Because every sound has a discrete wavelength, it makes sense to control for the length of the wave when you set out to absorb a sound. A double-stud wall construction that provides a greater distance between each side of the construction may control the migration of speech better than increasing the amount of material in the construction. For example, "A" in Figure 8.4 may be a more effective partition than "B" because the space between the two surfaces muffles the sound of a particular length better than if the cavity were packed full of insulation.

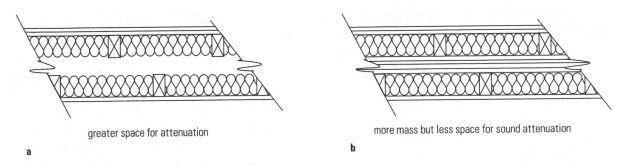

greater space for attenuation

a

more mass but less space for sound attenuation

b

FIGURE 8.4 Drawing A has more room for better sound attenuation; therefore, Drawing A will do a better job at stopping higher frequency sounds than Drawing B.

Sound Control for Different Environments

Different environments have different needs related to controlling sound. You would like to maintain quiet in libraries, contemplative spaces, museums, and in health-care facilities. In spaces such as lecture halls and classrooms, conference rooms, boardrooms, churches, and courtrooms, it is important to have good-quality speech transmission. The best balance of sound in restaurants allows for some liveliness without overwhelming the environment with sound. This holds true for most convivial atmospheres and common spaces such as malls and lobbies. In some of these same environments—places like airports and train stations—the public address system must also be audible.

Music makes different demands on a space than speech does. The hertz, or Hz, range is wider and, in the case of performance spaces where speech and music are both important, the control issues are compounded because the reverberation times for speech and music are not the same. In assembly spaces such as churches and auditoriums, some sounds should be enhanced while noise must be controlled. The doctor's office is another example of a space with overlapping demands. Reception areas and counseling areas are spaces where confidentiality and clear speech perception are both central to the function.

Sometimes, users of a space will unconsciously counter the effectiveness of sound-absorbing solutions by talking louder in an anechoic space (where materials have been added to absorb 100 percent of expected sound generated in the space), trying to "compensate" for the "dead" space. Too much of a good thing can prove to be counterproductive.

Characteristics of Sound

We are working to control the characteristics of sound when we manage the acoustics of spaces. In the acoustics portion of the design program, we identify desired behaviors of sound and sometimes quantify (state a testable range of acceptable numbers) for the following characteristics, as well as for any of the standards mentioned already (dB, speech intelligibility, etc.).

Echo

Echo is a reflected sound sufficiently delayed from the original sound that it is perceived as a separate entity. The typical culprit is the back wall. Use a material that will absorb or break up the sound.

Flutter Echo

Flutter echoes are echoes that occur in rapid succession—usually between two parallel walls. Handle flutter with sound-absorptive foam wall panels, baffles, or banners on the ceiling to absorb and diffuse sound. Use multifaceted, curved, or slotted materials.

Focused Sound

Large concave surfaces will focus sound and distort it so that sounds occurring near the focal point will be perceived as too loud relative to other sounds. Unless such areas are intended to focus sound, the sound must be managed with absorptive materials or acoustically transparent coverings that allow the sound to travel through to an area where it can be managed.

Reverberation

Reverberations are multiple sound reflections as sound bounces around in a space, creating the length of duration of the sound. The sound endures in the space, even after it is no longer being emitted by the source. Hard surfaces increase reverberation time (meaning the sound will keep bouncing around in the space instead of disappearing). Soft and uneven surfaces decrease reverberation time.

Frequency

Frequency in sound can be thought of in terms of pitch, such as a high-pitched sound or a low-pitched sound. Different materials will absorb different frequencies more effectively than others. Some cork can be very effective generally in absorbing sound, as can acoustical tiles. For specialty applications (studios, music performance spaces), materials that have been specifically engineered for the sounds that will be produced are a better choice for acoustical panels, if required. Don't forget that there will be a wider range of frequencies for music than for speech.

High-frequency waves are short and low-frequency waves can be several feet long. When the frequency corresponds exactly to one of the dimensions of the room and the new sound meets an original sound wave of matching length, a "standing wave" situation results. This produces a resonant situation, which amplifies the sound. Standing waves can reinforce each other or cancel out other wavelengths interfering with the sound.

Acoustics as a General Consideration

Assemblies change the acoustical properties of materials in the assembly. If this all sounds complicated, that is because it *is* complicated. Expert acousticians are constantly investigating and researching with physical and computer models, shaping spaces, and employing materials to create the perfect sonic environment. New materials are constantly being developed to absorb sound, and surface configurations are designed to fracture and bounce sound as necessary. Larry Kirkegaard of Kirkegaard Associates demonstrated the maniacal attention to detail that one may assume is typical of these specialists when he referred to a caulk sample board that he had on hand to test the properties of different caulks as they aged.

All components of an assembly contribute to the sound transmission and sound absorption of the assembly in some way. Construction materials that have been specifically developed for stopping, baffling, and absorbing sound can be specified in your drawings and material specs. These can be combined with surfacing materials that reflect or absorb sound as well. Construction techniques should also be specified. For example, in order to contain sound in an area, all air gaps must be sealed or closed, and this must be carefully managed with other building systems because "air gaps" are required to deliver air (and spaces are of no use without air!). Instructions to caulk all gaps with an approved caulk are noted in construction specs and instructions to the installer (Figures 8.5 and 8.6).

Manufacturers often control the testing of their own products, so the conditions under which two similar products are tested may not be identical. For instance, a material installed over a fiberglass substrate will test at a higher NRC than the very same material installed over gypsum board. The number alone is not enough to tell the whole story. When comparing two materials, review the description of the assembly that was tested to ensure that a comparison based on NRC will be valid; also, consider whether the tested assembly is close enough to your project conditions to permit you to draw conclusions about your project from the number.

You will want to work closely with HVAC engineers and tradespeople to manage duct routes, damping, and lining so sound can't travel along this hidden route to areas where it is not wanted. Ducts into areas that will generate a lot of noise (music practice rooms, theater spaces, areas with noisy equipment) may have their own duct route that does not branch to or from other areas.

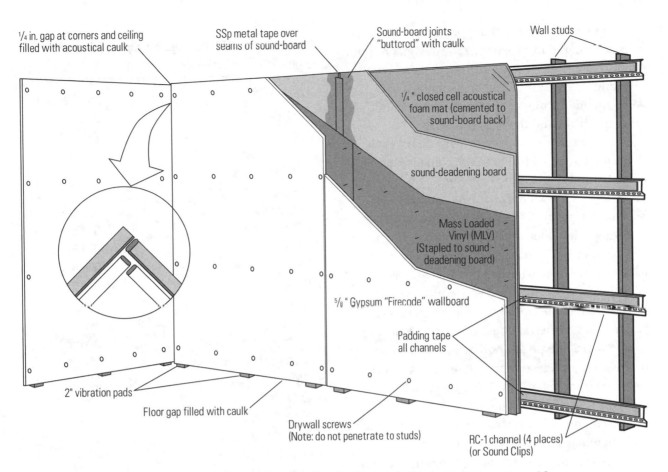

FIGURE 8.5 Design for sound containment by Super Soundproofing, San Marcos, California. *Drawing courtesy of Super Soundproofing Co.*

Labels in figure 8.5:
- ¼ in. gap at corners and ceiling filled with acoustical caulk
- SSp metal tape over seams of sound-board
- Sound-board joints "buttered" with caulk
- Wall studs
- ¼" closed cell acoustical foam mat (cemented to sound-board back)
- sound-deadening board
- Mass Loaded Vinyl (MLV) (Stapled to sound-deadening board)
- ⅝" Gypsum "Firecode" wallboard
- Padding tape all channels
- 2" vibration pads
- Floor gap filled with caulk
- Drywall screws (Note: do not penetrate to studs)
- RC-1 channel (4 places) (or Sound Clips)

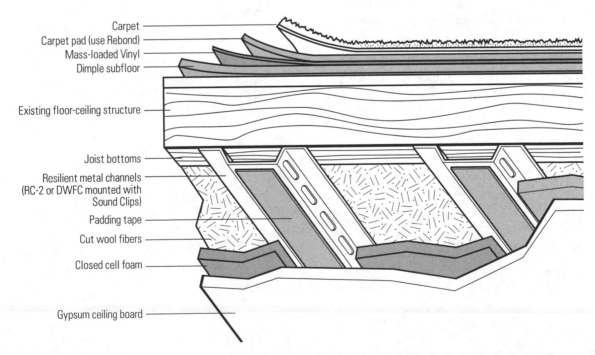

FIGURE 8.6 Design for soundproofing within floor by Super Soundproofing, San Marcos, California. *Drawings courtesy of Super Soundproofing Co.*

Labels in figure 8.6:
- Carpet
- Carpet pad (use Rebond)
- Mass-loaded Vinyl
- Dimple subfloor
- Existing floor-ceiling structure
- Joist bottoms
- Resilient metal channels (RC-2 or DWFC mounted with Sound Clips)
- Padding tape
- Cut wool fibers
- Closed cell foam
- Gypsum ceiling board

Acoustics is a topic that pertains to all materials considered in this text. Your design program should ideally address all the senses. The quality of sound in a space should be as much a part of your considerations as the quantity of sound moving within and through spaces.

As an exercise, when you learn about each material discussed in Part Two, consider the acoustical properties of the materials (along with green aspects, toxicity, and other broadly applicable characteristics). For instance, you will be studying brick later in the text. Brick has a hard surface and you would expect it to reflect sound back into the area where the sound was generated. It is also very dense, so you would expect it to have a reasonable sound transmission class rating, and most often it does. The rating will vary from one brick type to another but an STC rating in the 40-45 range and an NRC of 0-0.5 can be expected in many bricks. Table 8.1 lists NRC ratings of some common materials.

Too many live surfaces can create sonic chaos and too much dead surface area can be disconcerting—actually causing people to talk louder as they subconsciously try to normalize the environment and produce some of the expected echo that is normally present. It is very important to remember that managing the presentation of sound in spaces is not just about "mopping up all the loose sound." Managing acoustics means intentionally creating an environment where sound is useful, pleasant, and congruent with the whole experience of the space.

TABLE 8.1	**NRC Ratings for Some Common Materials**
MATERIAL	RATING
Brick painted	0–.2
Brick unpainted	0–.05
Concrete painted	0–.05
Concrete unpainted	0–.2
Marble and terrazzo	0
Linoleum on concrete	0–.05
Rubber on concrete	0–.05
Plaster	0–.05
Fabric on gypsum	0–.05
Steel	0–.1
Glass	.05–.1
Plywood	.1–.15
Concrete block painted	0–.05
Concrete block unpainted	.05–.35
Wood	.05–.13
10-oz. drapery	.05–.15
14-oz. drapery	.55
18-oz. drapery	.6
Carpet on concrete	.2–.3
Carpet on foam pad	.3–.55
Cork floor tiles ¾" thick	.1–.15
Cork wall tiles 1" thick	.3–.7
Polyurethane foam 1" thick	.3

Part TWO

Materials

CHAPTER 9

concrete

Concrete is used for both utilitarian functions and as decorative surfacing. Although available to order as standard offerings in precast units for showers and as floor tiles, concrete is often a custom (Figure 9.1a and b) and cast-in-place monolithic material. Because it is a rigid material that spans large areas, *flatwork* (floor surfaces, for instance) requires expansion joints to control cracking. These control seams should be located based on the advice of a structural engineer or architect. In order to create a vertical surface, forms must be constructed and concrete poured down into the forms. These forms can be lined with material that imparts a texture to the surface of the concrete; a moiré or wood grain is often seen, as in Figure 9.2, as are repeating bands or vertical ridges. While the horizontally placed concrete is still sufficiently plastic, a texture can be brushed onto the surface with a broom.

Custom Work

Custom work is available and easily accessible (Figure 9.3); it is a collaborative process of working with your concrete specialist to determine what is possible and sensible. Specifications should be confirmed with a sample before the actual work is performed. You may begin the process with a photo or a sample of work that the concrete fabricator has on hand. Concrete is versatile, and there are various specialties within the field, so you'll want to shop around for the right expertise and aesthetic. Drawings that you have made may be supplemented by shop drawings produced by the fabricator. A simple form may not require shop drawings, but fabricators should see the site and take their own measurements before the work begins.

Beginning with approved drawings and samples, the work will commence, but the concrete will not reach final maturity for about a month. Concrete will cure sufficiently within the span of a month to judge any custom colors and allow for the completion of any chemical reactions that could alter the appearance. The concrete must cure completely before any secondary processes (painting, acid washing, and so on) can be applied. If you are reusing your fabricator's known formula, you can probably work off of the existing shop samples with confidence. *Admixtures* (compounds added to concrete to alter its properties, such as weight or curing time) can cause unexpected visual results, so the formulation of the shop sample must be completely known in order to be reliable.

Finishes and Decorative Treatments

The finishes and decorative treatments that can be applied to concrete include dyes, paints, and acid stains.

a

b

FIGURE 9.1 Stock product of concrete tiles (a). Custom product of a fireplace surround by Flying Turtle Cast Concrete in Modesto, California (b). *Photograph of stock product by Alana Clark.*

FIGURE 9.2 When this concrete was cast into plywood forms, the water in the concrete caused the wood surface to swell; this enhanced the grain pattern that was then impressed onto the concrete.

Dyes

Dyes can be added to the mix or spread onto the surface of wet concrete. When they are mixed in, the color will be consistent throughout. When sprinkled on top of wet concrete, dyes can be distributed throughout the surface by *screeding*, one of the steps in smoothing and finishing concrete surfaces. This step is performed with a screed, a tool made of a flat plate on a handle. Sometimes, the desired effect is consistent color; sometimes, it is mottled color (Figure 9.4). The distribution of color depends on how thoroughly the surface is worked with the screed to smooth and spread the pigment.

Paint

Paint can also be used to color the surface of concrete. There are special paints formulated for concrete. As you would expect, paint sits on the surface of the concrete and is vulnerable to wearing away. Epoxy paints with extra durability are

FIGURE 9.3 The details for this custom sink would be reviewed by the installer and plumber prior to commencing fabrication.

FIGURE 9.4 This dyed concrete at River of Coffee Café was created by Tom Ralston Concrete of Santa Cruz, California.

FIGURE 9.5 This acid-stained fireplace was created by Tom Ralston Concrete of Santa Cruz, California.

used on floor surfaces; it is sometimes advisable to seal the painted concrete to provide additional protection.

Acid Stain

Acid stain (Figure 9.5) fuses chemically with the surface of concrete, but the slab must cure for 30 days prior to application. The effect is serendipitous and cannot be completely controlled. Different acids produce the different effects. Unlike a paint or stain, this coloration does not rely on pigment but on a chemical reaction.

Aggregate

The recipe for concrete is basically sand, cement, and *aggregate,* which is made up of small stones. Aggregate is naturally a part of a concrete mixture and usually sinks into the body of the mass, but it can be exposed as a decorative surface. When the design calls for exposing the aggregate (Figure 9.6), rounded or smooth material (like river rock) must be used. Producing this kind of

surface involves a lot of water; this is an insurmountable complication in most interior situations for cast-in-place (versus precast) concrete.

The aggregate can be exposed in different ways, with each producing a different visual effect. When a retardant is used, it works by inhibiting the setting up of the cement at the surface, which is in contact with the retardant. After the concrete has cured for several hours, the surface is washed with water and may be scrubbed lightly with a broom, too. This must be done by an experienced tradesperson because the right time

FIGURE 9.6 Exposed aggregate in work created by Tom Ralston Studios of Santa Cruz, California, uses a variety of stones and shark's teeth to achieve a decorative effect.

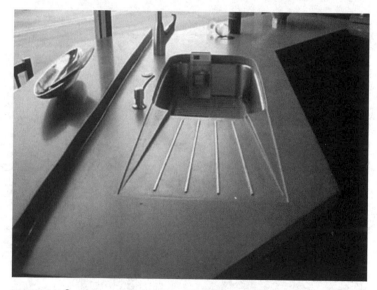

FIGURE 9.7 Custom concrete sinks can meet the style and budget requirements of a public bathroom, as in this installation by Two Stones Design in Port Byron, Illinois.

to perform this step varies; it depends more on the concrete than on the clock.

When the aggregate is exposed using an acid etch, the depth of color is somewhat retained while the surface achieves a softly weathered appearance. Because it is difficult to achieve visual consistency over a large area, it is used more successfully for small units or as a contrasting element.

When aggregate is exposed by sandblasting, the surface is covered with a haze of fine scratches upon completion. This tends to lighten the overall color, as well as create a surface that looks "drier" than the other two methods.

Exposed aggregate is an impractical selection for an existing structure because all the methods used to achieve it are too messy to perform in a finished space. It could be considered for new construction or if precast units could be produced elsewhere and simply installed as slab or tile on site.

Concrete is so versatile that you could consider almost any form (Figure 9.7) required by your project, using a combination of surface techniques to create any look that you can imagine; you are limited only by the skill and daring of your fabricator and your client's sense of adventure. Textures can be brushed or drawn on the surface with any instrument that will produce the desired effect. Tom Ralston Studios employed actual seaweed (Figure 9.8a) as a model in a multistep operation designed to reproduce the delicate texture of the leaves' veined structure in concrete. The final product (Figure 9.8b) was hand-colored to enhance the pattern precisely.

Other Materials Used with Concrete

Other materials can be used to break up an expanse of concrete that could seem monotonous in the application. Wood planks and bricks are sometimes used to form patterns in combination with areas of concrete.

Syndecrete® is a proprietary concrete (one company owns exclusive rights to produce it) that can be used in place of regular concrete (Figure 9.9) for your projects. This product is:

- A lightweight cement-based composite—lighter and denser than concrete—using natural minerals and recycled materials
- Composed of 20 percent industrial waste (milled carpet scraps, fly ash), 25 percent recycled aggregate (record albums, golf tees, video cases, wood chips, other), and 55 percent concrete
- Chemically inert, so it does not outgas VOCs
- Heat- and flame-resistant and can be coated (against food stains and water absorption) with an FDA-approved sealer
- A custom, handcrafted, precast product used for counter- and desk-tops, basins, flooring, planters
- Available in slab or tiles

The cost of Syndecrete is equal to or higher than that of granite because each job is customized based on time and materials. The surface color and texture can be controlled during fabrication.

Sealant

Concrete is subject to staining and bleaching by common substances such as foods and cleansers; it should be sealed with an approved clear sealant, or it should be coated. As with stone, sealants include penetrating and top dressing.

Film-Formers

Top dressings are also called *film-formers* when referring to concrete. Film-formers are better than penetrating sealers at resisting stains, and they are sometimes selected to enhance the concrete's color. They can also impart a gloss. Paste wax sealers are a popular film-former and can be used to increase the depth of color in concrete. Film-formers must be replenished more frequently than penetrating sealers.

Penetrating Sealants

Penetrating sealants tend to leave the appearance unaltered. Remember, if you are sealing a surface that will be used for food preparation or consumption, use a food-grade sealer. Even when protected, this is a surface that will change visually over time, and you should educate your client so that the patina is anticipated and appreciated.

Estimating Materials

Concrete as cast-in-place material is sold by the cubic yard; the setting of forms is usually calculated by the lineal foot. As a precast material, the units vary from "each" (shower pans, for instance) to "lots" of varying sizes and as square feet (as for tiles).

Qualifying Installers

Given that most concrete work is exterior, you would want to differentiate between those contractors who simply pour a lot of footings and those who understand the issues particular to

a

b

FIGURE 9.8 This highly custom concrete project (a) was created by Ralston Concrete, Santa Cruz, California. To see more images of this process, which interprets living seaweed into a beautiful concrete installation, view the shop-visit on the CD. Newly harvested seaweed was embossed to create a form to model from a custom-cast and colored final product (b).

interior work, so make sure they have experience with the kind of job you are doing.

Planning

Panels may be cast off-site and delivered in lengths of up to approximately 11 feet. A 1-½-inch-thick countertop can cantilever approximately 10 inches without being supported; beyond that, a subtop will be required. The subtop may be plywood or plate steel. A 1-½-inch-thick × 2-foot-wide concrete countertop will weigh about 18½ pounds

FIGURE 9.9 Syndecrete fireplace by Syndesis, Santa Monica, California. *Photo by Sandy Wiener.*

per square foot (just a little more than granite). If the material is sealed well (silicone, acrylic, or butcher's wax) and the sealer is renewed as required, the material should last the life of the installation. Advise clients not to cut food directly on the counter because if the sealer is cut or scraped, it must be reapplied. Hairline cracks are not a defect; your client should understand that they are a characteristic of the material. Decorate concrete countertops with dyes or material (stones, fossils, metal, other) added to wet concrete. The counter will be ground down prior to delivery.

How Green Is It?

Concrete often contains ingredients that would normally end up in landfill sites, such as fly ash (a by-product of burning coal), ground slag (a by-product of the iron and steel industries), and silica fume (a by-product of silicon production). These by-products actually improve the strength of concrete. Old concrete can be ground and reused as aggregate for new concrete installations. Concrete contributes to the thermal mass, which regulates energy use during the heating and air-conditioning seasons. The ingredients used to make concrete are usually locally available.

For horizontal, exterior applications, pervious concrete can be specified. Pervious concrete has a lower percentage of fine aggregate, which allows storm water to percolate through its mass, filtering and replenishing the groundwater at its location.

CHAPTER 10

brick

This chapter presents the brick material known as burned brick, which means it was fired in a kiln. Other types of brick include sand-lime, adobe, and cement, but they are not dealt with here.

Brick as a surfacing material for interior spaces takes a little advance planning because of its dimensions. It is thicker than most other interior surfacing that you will specify. When you are specifying for new construction, details can be devised to allow for the size, and you can easily specify *dimensional brick* (full brick). If the site will not allow for dimensional brick, you may substitute *veneer brick,* which looks like dimensional brick but is thinner and can be applied in a manner similar to a tile installation. Brick can be used for flooring and for vertical surfacing for walls. It is frequently used for accent walls and fireplaces.

Brick Production

Brick is made from clay and is formed by soft mud, stiff mud, and dry press processes. What makes these production methods interesting is that the aesthetic characteristics of the final product are affected by the amount of water in the clay. A low-water (dry press) process produces a very precisely tailored, uniform brick; when more water is present in the clay, the result is a more rusticated brick with unique characteristics.

The Soft Mud Process

In the soft mud process, water is added to 20-30 percent of the weight of the clay, which is then shaped in molds. If the manufacturer uses sand as a releasing agent in the molds, the bricks are *sand struck* (the mold that the brick is made in is lined with sand so the sticky clay will release from the mold); if water is used, the bricks are *water struck.* Soft mud brick is the least uniform type (Figure 10.1).

The Stiff Mud Process

During fabrication using the stiff mud process, clay is mixed with water to 12-15 percent of its

FIGURE 10.1 Soft mud brick. *Photograph by Alana Clark.*

FIGURE 10.2 Wire-cut extruded brick.

weight, then "de-aired" (air removed) in a vacuum chamber. It is then extruded in a column or "bat" and cut into its final size (Figure 10.2). It may then be moved through a *slurry* (watery clay mixture) to create distinctive patterns or have its surface textured. Ceramic glazes may be applied, either before the bricks are fired or after one firing, then refired for colors that are not stable at high temperatures.

The Dry Press Method

The dry press method adds water to only 10 percent of the weight of the clay. The clay is then formed in steel molds under pressure from 500 to 1,500 pounds per square inch with hydraulic or compressed air rams. The clay is then fired in a kiln, which fuses the clay.

Colors and Sizes

Because the clay used to form brick is mined out of the earth, the chemical composition varies with geographic location and with the depth from which it was gathered. The color of brick depends on its composition and the firing environment. Clay with iron oxides (common to clay) will burn to a red color in an oxidizing atmosphere and to purple in a reducing atmosphere (that is, with oxygen intake limited).

Brick comes in numerous standard sizes. Brick *pavers,* which are often used on floors, are specially designed for horizontal applications.

Pavers are thinner than the bricks used to build walls. They are normally about $3\text{-}5/8 \times 7\text{-}5/8$ inches or $3\text{-}3/4 \times 7\text{-}1/2$ inches or 4×8 inches; thickness ranges from $1\text{-}1/4$ to $2\text{-}3/4$ inches. Pavers range from $1\text{-}1/8$ to $2\text{-}1/4$ inches thick. Brick tiles range from approximately $1/2$ inch to nearly an inch in thickness.

Bricks are also available in *nominal* sizes, which means that the size is not exact. Just as with lumber, tile, and other materials, if an exact size must be known, it is best to refer to samples.

Finishes

Brick is quite impervious to water and, therefore, impervious to most staining. Bricks can be finished with any approved clear sealer to enhance their already impervious surfaces and to impart a sheen.

Salvaged Brick

Salvaged brick presents some risks when reused for structural or exterior paving applications, but these risks are not usually significant factors for consideration when specifying interior surfacing. Vertical applications requiring mortar demand good bonds, so bricks must be sufficiently cleaned to allow for good absorption and good bonds. However, because the most significant characteristics influencing brick selection for interior surfacing are aesthetic, salvaged brick can usually be safely specified.

Salvaged and reclaimed brick is commonly an option driven by material cost savings and also by a desire for a rugged appearance. The material is often salvaged from buildings that were solid masonry construction with low-fired salmon brick in the interior but better-burned bricks on the exterior.

Reclaimed brick lots often have both of these types of brick all mixed in together. In low-stress environments (interior applications would usually qualify), this randomized variation may be used to decorative effect. (Problems occur when using this material for exterior or rigorous environments.)

Because brick is so durable, salvaged brick of a character most typically available may not have the beautiful patina of age that the design program suggests, so new distressed brick (Figure 10.3) may be specified to achieve this appearance of age when required.

Brick Veneers

Brick veneers give the appearance of brick with a fraction of the depth required for brick. Brick veneer is usually the thickness of tile (½ to ⅜ inch is common). Salvaged bricks are sometimes sliced into tile. Faces will have a different appearance than interior slices.

ADVANTAGES OF THIN BRICK VENEER Thin brick veneer is most appropriate for many interior surfacing situations and it has a number of advantages:

- Interior thin brick veneer finishes can be applied by moderately skilled craftspeople.
- Thin brick veneer is very durable and longer lasting than other wallcoverings.
- Prefabrication with thin brick veneer is easily and economically done compared to brickwork.
- Better sound- and fire-resistance properties may be obtained using thin brick veneer than with some nonmasonry surfaces.
- Thin brick units are more durable than imitation brick units made from gypsum, cement, or plastics.
- Walls built with thin brick units are lighter in weight than conventional masonry veneer.
- Thin brick veneer may be used where structural support for conventional brick veneer is not available.

DISADVANTAGES OF THIN BRICK VENEER Thin brick veneer also has some disadvantages:

- The durability and overall quality of thin brick veneer systems may not be equivalent to that of brick, but for most interior surfacing applications, there should be little concern.
- Thin brick veneer cannot be used structurally.
- Sound- and fire-resistance properties are less than those of conventional brick masonry veneer.
- Thin brick veneer does not provide the thermal mass of brick, so it does not make a contribu-

FIGURE 10.3 Old Hampton distressed brick by Pine Hall, Winston-Salem, North Carolina.

tion to regulating interior temperature.
- Sound blocking from brick veneer is not as effective as from actual masonry.
- Acoustically, dimensional brick is one of the most efficient materials for reflecting all sound, even the more tenacious bass notes.

Coatings

Coatings may be considered for brick to improve some performance characteristics, such as the ability to clean away soiling or graffiti. Coatings may also be specified to enhance the gloss or color of the brick. They may be considered after sandblasting brick, which makes it more vulnerable to soiling.

Both penetrating and topical coatings are available. Film-forming or topical sealants are more frequently specified for interior surfacing materials than penetrating types because film-forming coatings solve soiling problems and enhance color.

Some coatings are designed to be "sacrificial," which means they are cleaned away with the graffiti and must be reapplied. Test for ease of removal when considering a product like this. Acrylics and urethanes work well for graffiti protection in interior spaces. Film-forming coatings can prevent the migration of moisture by sealing the surface, but they can also trap moisture trying to leave the brick and cause a cloudy appearance. They decrease the slip resistance of brick somewhat. They may need to be replenished more frequently than penetrating sealers.

The correct formulation must be used or maintenance will become a nuisance. This work should be replenished by a professional stone and masonry maintenance company as part of normal maintenance; "grocery store" products should not be applied by end users or their maintenance staffs.

Penetrating sealers work by coating rather than bridging the capillaries, so they allow the brick to breath. This prevents trapping of damaging salts within the brick. Trapped salts can deteriorate; brick and penetrating sealants are preferred for exterior walls.

Installation

For vertical surfaces, bricks are set into mortar. The mortar joints can be flush with the surface of the brick, concave (below the surface of the brick), or convex. Different formulations have different characteristics. Nonload-bearing mortar type O is sufficient for interior applications of surfacing material.

Horizontal surfaces can be set in mortar with mortar between them (so that all but the face that shows is in contact with mortar), laid loose on roofing felt with no mortar used, or set on a bed of mortar with no mortar between the bricks. Roofing felt is often asphalt-impregnated, and there are odors and toxins associated with these products.

Mortar Joints

Joints are tooled to different profiles. (Figure 10.4) Considerations related to exterior performance issues are included because interior designers frequently consult on exterior surfacing options for continuity of design.

- *Concave joint and V-shaped joint* are normally kept quite small and are formed by the use of a steel jointing tool. These joints are very effective in resisting rain penetration and are originally intended for use in areas subjected to heavy rains and high winds. As a specifier of interior surfacing material, your motivations for selecting one of these types would be visual.
- *Weathered joint* imitates erosion; the working of this joint requires care as it must be worked from below.
- *Struck joint* is a common joint in ordinary brickwork. As American masons often work from the inside of the wall, this is an easy joint to strike with a trowel. Some compaction occurs, but the small ledge does not shed water readily, resulting in a less watertight joint than other types—a consideration if you are specifying for an installation subject to water.
- *Flush joint* is the simplest joint for the mason, because it is made by holding the edge of the trowel flat against the brick and cutting in any direction. This produces an uncompacted joint with a small hairline crack where the mortar is pulled away from the brick by the cutting action. This joint is not always watertight.

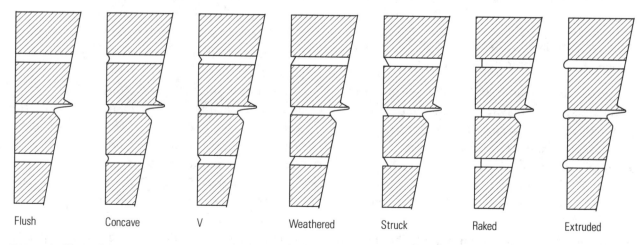

Flush   Concave   V   Weathered   Struck   Raked   Extruded

FIGURE 10.4 Mortar joints.

- *Raked joint* is produced by removing the surface of the mortar while it is still soft. While the joint may be compacted, it is difficult to make it weather-tight and it is not recommended where heavy rain, high wind, or freezing is likely to occur. This joint produces marked shadows and darkens the overall appearance of the wall.
- *Extruded joint* allows mortar to flow beyond the face of the brick as the brick is seated into position.

Horizontal Installations

Horizontal applications do not require mortar. The subfloor can be depressed (or a detail devised to safely elevate the area adjacent to the brick) and the brick can be laid on top of building felt (#15 or #30), which has been spread on top of a rigid base. A mortar bed may also be detailed if it is not advisable to loose-lay the brick (for example, if reclaimed bricks are irregular and you want to level and fill gaps). Here, the subfloor must be depressed (or the surrounding area raised) to accommodate the brick plus the setting bed thickness. A bond coat of cement and extra water (or a latex additive) may be added to the top of the mortar as the bricks are being laid and leveled (it all happens at once, not in stages) to improve the strength of the bond. This bonding coat will not factor into the calculated

depth because it is so thin (no more than 1/16-inch is recommended). When bricks are set in mortar this way, it is typical to use mortar between them. The same mortar that is used to set the brick will be used to fill the joints. Sand may also be used between bricks for exterior applications, but this is impractical for interiors where floors will be vacuumed as part of normal maintenance unless the entire installation is to be coated (for easier maintenance and to lock in sand).

An alternative to mortar between bricks would be to grout between them. The texture of the brick faces will tend to hold onto the grout that is smeared across the surface during the grouting process. This grout is impossible to remove, so unless you want this as an effect, you will want to order brick with a paraffin coating, which protects the brick face from being stained during grouting. Later, this coating is steam-cleaned away, but it's important to plan for the obvious complications related to this step.

Brick Orientations

Bricks are oriented in different directions to expose their different-sized faces to create patterns (Figure 10.5).

As the mason builds the surface, the rows are called *courses.* The patterns that display the wide

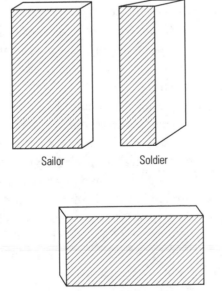

Sailor   Soldier

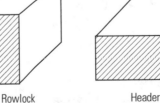

Rowlock   Header

Rowlock Strether

Stretcher

FIGURE 10.5 Brick orientations.

faces only are not used structurally and must be supported. Interior designers do not supervise structural components, but we do specify cladding for them. You may consult on the brick-work patterns to render a decision based on aesthetics, so it is a good idea to understand that some patterns are independently secure only as horizontal patterns. They can be used vertically, but they will require ties to hold them to the structural substrate.

The following are some commonly specified patterns (Figure 10.6):

- *Running bond,* the simplest of the basic pattern bonds, consists of all stretchers. Given that there are no headers in this bond, metal ties are usually used.
- *Common bond* is a variation of running bond with a course of full-length headers at regular intervals. These headers provide structural bonding, as well as pattern. Header courses usually appear at every fifth, sixth, or seventh course. A variation that has an alternating header and stretcher is also accepted as common bond, too.
- *Flemish bond* is a pattern in which each course of brick consists of alternate stretchers and headers, with the headers centered over and under the stretchers in the intervening courses above and below.
- *Monk bond* is staggered joints on courses that alternate with two stretchers centered on the headers above and below.
- *English bond* is composed of alternate courses of headers and stretchers. The headers are centered on the stretchers, and joints between stretchers in all courses are aligned vertically. Snap headers are used in courses that are not structural bonding courses.
- *Dutch bond* is a variation of English bond, which differs only in that vertical joints between the stretchers in alternate courses do not align vertically. These joints center on the faces in the courses above and below.
- *Block or stack bond* is purely a pattern bond. There is no overlapping of units because all vertical joints are aligned. Usually, this pattern is bonded to the backing with rigid steel ties. In stack bond, it is imperative that prematched or dimensionally accurate masonry units be used if the vertical alignment of the head joints is to be maintained.
- *Basket weave, herringbone,* and other patterns formed without headers or *rowlocks* (these are faces presented when bricks are used so that they reach back with their longest dimension) will be less stable in forming vertical surfaces and will have to be tied to the backing as with stack bond.

How Green Is Brick?

According to the Brick Industry Association, brick is produced in 38 of 50 states, so it is fairly local. Its high thermal mass makes it a good choice for passive solar construction. Because of its small unit dimension, waste is minimized, and brick can be used in other constructions such as roadwork. Brick is one of the most salvaged materials, thanks to its durability. Brick structures hundreds of years old are still in use today. Some bricks have recycled components, such as incinerator ash and waste glass, in their makeup. Brick is inert and is generally tolerable for people with sensitivities to toxins. Brick has a lower embodied energy cost than concrete, glass, aluminum, and even wood. The durability of brick exceeds the needs of most interior applications and, when compared to other exterior paving materials, the relatively high initial cost is paid back in about a decade. Its long life and easy maintenance make it much more economical in the long run.

Brick conserves heating and cooling energy. Based on calculations and measurements made under static conditions, brick is superior to wood and other material in providing thermal mass, which resists the transfer of heat. Because the environment is actually dynamic, not static, the performance of brick in actual use is suspected to be superior even to its own static-tested ratings because it buffers the interior against quick changes in the weather.

Variation Dutch Bond

English Bond

English Cross Bond

Stack Bond
Nonsupporting use
Horizontal or Supported Vertical

Herringbone
Nonsupporting use
Horizontal or Supported Vertical

Basket Weave
Nonsupporting use
Horizontal or Supported Vertical

Running and Stacked Bond
Nonsupporting use
Horizontal or Supported Vertical

Half Basket
Nonsupporting use
Horizontal or Supported Vertical

Running Bond

1/3 Running Bond or
Raking Stretched Bond

1/4 Running Bond or
Raking Stretched Bond

Common Bond

Variation Common Bond

Flemish Bond

Monk Bond

Dutch Bond

Basket Weave

Herringbone

Running Bond

Running and Stack Bond Mixed

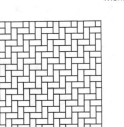

Circular and Running Bond

Stack Bond

FIGURE 10.6 Brick bonds.

Estimating

Bricks are sold by the thousand but shipped in smaller qualities. Brick tiles are sold by the square foot, just like ceramic tiles.

Estimating for quantity of brick pavers for purposes of budgeting material costs is a simple square foot takeoff, with one extra step to come up with a count. The square foot takeoff is performed just as it would be for tile or resilient material, by multiplying the length of the area by the width. To convert the square footage to paver quantity, multiply by a factor that varies with the size of the paver.

If you are using	multiply by
4 × 8 inch pavers	4.5
3-⅝ × 7-⅝ inch pavers	5.2
3-½ × 7-¾ inch pavers	5.1

For example, let's say you are performing a cost comparison of materials for your client's solarium, which is 15 × 20 feet. You are considering using 4 × 8 inch pavers. Multiply 15 × 20 for the square footage of 300 square feet and then multiply that by 4.5 to discover that you need to budget for 1350 pavers. As with any material,

there will be waste during the installation. Brick quantities should be rounded up (much like tile quantities) by 10 percent, so add 135 pavers for waste and multiply the paver price by 1485 pavers to have enough material minimally to complete the job. If you are using salvaged material or material that has a lot of variation that you may want to control for, you will add more than that to your estimate.

The same method can be used for all brick sizes. To estimate other brick sizes to quantity of bricks, use the conversion rates below to multiply the square footage by the number of bricks required per square foot.

King Size =	4.8
Builders Special =	5.33
Modular =	6.85
Colonial =	4.9
Queen Size =	5.2

A mason plus one helper can lay about 700 bricks a day. You can use this information to complete the exercise on the CD.

Brick weighs from 16 to 22 pounds per square foot.

CHAPTER 11

stone

Stone species, like tree species, share characteristics with others of the same species. Just as individual trees within each species present unique markings and coloration, individual slab lots of stone can present unexpected variations in coloration and markings. Stone material from the same quarry may vary from one area of the quarry to another. Occasionally, the new material from the quarry varies greatly from lot to lot, causing the supplier to conclude that the name originally given to the species would lead to an expectation of visual characteristics that the current material cannot fulfill. To avoid confusion when vendors order the material, a new name is used to distinguish between the two lots, which are visually dissimilar although their performance characteristics and other characteristics may be the same. This name change is still considered the "quarry name" (generic name), but it simplifies the specification process because it differentiates between two visually different stones.

It is important to view slabs with your drawings in hand, so that you can visualize how the material will look when it is installed. As an example, the variation in the slab in Figure 11.1 could appear to be two different materials if a small piece from the upper left section was used on a small section of counter and a small piece from the upper right section was used immediately across from it on an island. If you were the designer on a job that required several small pieces of stone, you might decide that limestone (Figure 11.2) had a grain pattern that would allow for more visual consistency from one area of the stone to another.

Identifying Stone Characteristics

Within categories of stones, visual characteristics such as graining or visual texture can be predicted. Granite has a pronounced speckled texture; marble has veins; limestones are visually smoother in texture, often with small fossil inclusions; and so on. General categories can also be used as a guide to porosity, abrasion resistance, resistance to etching by acids, and other physical properties.

Visual Characteristics

Both the composition and formation conditions create the stone we specify. Sedimentary stone was built up in layers, and its stratified composition shows the resulting veining. Travertine was built up as bubbling hot springs deposited materials, leaving behind the holes we still see in the material.

The ingredient that lends color to the stone may be the result of organic material—in which case, it could fade in direct sunlight. For instance, the color black results from the presence of tar or petroleum, both organic, so black marble will fade in intense sunlight. So will some peach-colored marbles because the substance that lends

FIGURE 11.1 Stone will vary considerably from one lot to the next within the same species. Luise Blue quartzite at Marble and Granite Supply International in Evanston, Illinois, is a typical example. This material not only ranges from lot to lot but also varies within the slab, so multiple pieces could display very different markings.

FIGURE 11.2 Limestone is generally a visually consistent stone with very different performance properties than quartzite, so one piece of limestone could be substituted for another. Multiple pieces cut from this slab would be visually similar to one another.

that color may also be organic in origin. Mineral colorants do not tend to fade, although some iron-based colors will "rust." Dark-colored stones with a polished surface are said to scratch easily, but, in fact, they just show scratching more clearly. A dark stone that is as hard and abrasion-resistant as a light stone may become hazy because small surface scratches show up in greater contrast on dark stone (light scratches on dark surfaces rather than light scratches on light surfaces). Unlike fading, scratched stone can be restored by polishing or touched up by *dressing*, a surface coating designed to be applied to stone.

Chemically speaking, lime- or calcite-based stones such as marble and limestone are bases, so they are susceptible to acid etching because acids dissolve bases. Hard, dense materials can be polished to a high reflectivity, but porous materials can never achieve a high shine from polishing and must be top-dressed if gloss is desired.

Tests of Physical Characteristics

The descriptions that follow are categorical properties, but there are variations among the stones in each category. It is very important to test your selection for the actual conditions that you anticipate at the site. For absorbency, put a drop of lemon juice on the stone and see how quickly it soaks in. If oil will be present, test with oil; if abrasion is expected, test with coarse emery cloth. Request sealed and unsealed samples to confirm the products' natural characteristics, as well as their characteristics after they are sealed. This is especially important for field-applied sealants meant to be reapplied as part of maintenance. You have no control over the diligence of the maintenance schedule but will be considered to be responsible for the soundness of your selection, even if it is not maintained as directed, so select a stone that is serviceable in its natural state whenever possible (see Box 11.1).

Stone Species

Stones that you may consider specifying in your interior design projects include granite, soapstone, marble, serpentine, travertine, slate, limestone, quartzite, and onyx.

Granite

A very hard, dense stone, granite has a crystalline quartz structure and is relatively uniform in visual texture, with grains that range from small to medium. Some granites are very consistent, with very little visual "movement," so it is not always imperative to hand-select the actual stone slabs, although it's always a good idea. Other granites present their granular texture in swirls and streams, the way the stars in the Milky Way seem to have movement in composition. Granite can be polished to a high gloss, as well as several degrees of "semigloss" called high hone, honed, or low hone. It is strong enough to withstand the abuse of flaming, in which the surface is alternately heated and cooled, so small chips flake off, leaving a pocked-texture surface.

Granite is often preferred over calcite-based stones (marble, limestone, travertine) that common household acids, such as orange juice or the citric acid in shaving cream, will etch. Given that granite is a natural product and not grown in a lab, some granites also contain some calcite material, so they too can be etched with acids.

A wide variety of surface textures are used on granite. The grainy visual texture (Figure 11.3) seems to be as appropriate for rustic or rough-sawn textures as for polished textures. The most impervious surface treatment is polished with a subsurface sealant.

Soapstone

Soapstone is a tough and durable stone with quartz and talc content, in addition to other minerals (Figure 11.4). You may have noticed that it is popular for small carvings. The soapstone used for carvings is selected for its higher talc content, and the soapstone used for interior and architectural work is selected for lower talc content. Even the architectural grade is softer than other stone choices and will patinate into a "used forever" appearance, which can be a good choice for a design that strives for that look overall. It does not react to heat, so there is no danger in setting hot pots directly on a soapstone surface. It is fairly impervious, but it is traditional to seal it with mineral oil.

Over time, the application of mineral oil darkens the soapstone, and eventually it is often a dark charcoal. Mineral oil is reapplied every week for a couple of months, then periodically as part of normal maintenance. When water spots start to appear, it is time to clean the surface without stripping away the previous mineral oil, then

---

BOX 11.1 | A Cautionary Tale

My client and I decided together to adhere to a strictly vintage look in her vintage condo by using Carrara marble on the countertop. It was not until modern stone fabrication tools were invented that hard materials like granite could be used for such applications, so marble was traditionally the material of choice for vintage kitchens. My client was fully informed about the potential weaknesses of the material for countertops, and said she was prepared to let the counters acquire the patina that I assured her would appear with use. Because of her comprehension of the limitations of the material, I was comfortable with the selection.

Months after completion, a potential client called who also wanted a vintage kitchen (we have many great vintage buildings in Chicago) and wanted to see a sample of my work on a vintage kitchen. My first client was pleased to have me photograph her kitchen as an example, so when I arrived at her home a little ahead of her, I just went on in with my camera and was very surprised to see that *every* part of the counter surface in her kitchen was protected with a trivet, cutting board, or place mat. When my client arrived minutes later, she was very embarrassed that I had seen how nervous she was about the countertops. Because of our very clear, up-front discussion about the material, she felt responsible and did not want to say anything to me about it.

I now tell this story to every client who expects to be comfortable with a soft or absorbent material or surface treatment on a countertop—just so the client can do some additional soul-searching before finalizing the spec. Even a fairly impervious material, such as granite, will acquire a visual inconsistency thanks to oils and moisture if the surface is honed.

FIGURE 11.3 In these samples, granite demonstrates the variety of markings within the species. Granite is a very durable stone but is often considered "too modern" for some installations. When tradition is required, a granite with more movement seems less modern in appearance.

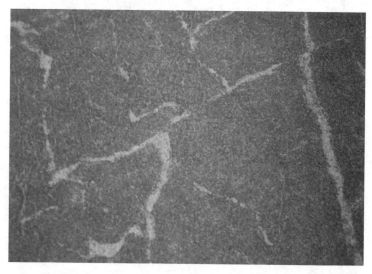

FIGURE 11.4 This soapstone is not yet sealed. As it is oiled over the life of an installation, it continues to darken; old soapstone installations look almost black.

applying fresh mineral oil. Soapstone is used for constructing big "farmhouse" sinks. People do not always elect to seal sinks because the detergents used to clean the dishes also removes the oil from the sink. The sink will darken somewhat with use but will not match any surrounding soapstone that has been sealed with oil. If a visual match between sink and counter is desired, your clients should be informed that the sink will need more frequent mineral oil applications than the counters.

Slab sizes are often smaller than for some other stones, especially now that the practice of strengthening stone with resin impregnation is becoming more common among granite and marble family options. Plan your surfacing layout for a logical rhythm of seams based on about 5-foot increments or confirm the availability of longer pieces. Soapstone can be located in large slab sizes and 9-foot sections without seams might be possible.

Marble

Marble is sometimes described as recrystallized limestone (sedimentary rock). It is softer than granite and sensitive to acid, so it's not recommended for kitchens unless your client likes the patina of an "old world" look. It will soak up oil. The most common textures are polished and honed. A honed surface is the most enduring surface because marble is somewhat soft and will scratch, but it will be more susceptible to picking up stains after having been honed rather than polished. Small scratches will occur on polished and honed surfaces but will not show up as readily on honed.

It is very important to hand-select the actual slabs to be used. You may want to mark off the exact area of stone to be used because some veining can be visually strong and placement is important. Use soap, chalk, or wax for marking instead of taping the area off. Some adhesives do not clean off without solvents, which can etch marble. If a change should occur after you have taped the surface, you may have ruined the slab for any alternative plan. If you are uncertain of the stability of your selection, ask the fabricator to inspect it prior to making a final decision. Before finalizing the selection, it is a good policy to consult the fabricator about any material that might not stand up to the abuse of fabrication. The reflection off a polished surface will highlight many veins that contain softer material and do not take polish to the same degree as the surrounding surface. Mud veins are especially soft, and an experienced fabricator can evaluate them for stability.

Like other stone species, marble has variety in visual and performance characteristics within the species (Figure 11.5). Some marbles are quite soft; you may find hard limestones, which is typically a softer species than marble, that equal the density of softer marbles. You can test the relative hardness of a marble tile by ear. Balance a tile on your fingertips and rap on it with your knuckles. Hard marbles (like pelion pink) will ring like a bell and soft marbles (thasos) will provide a soft thud.

Serpentine

Serpentine is an igneous rock largely made up of the mineral serpentine. Often referred to as green marble, it is actually a different kind of stone altogether. It is about as hard as marble. Some warping of serpentines has been reported in wet areas, so make sure you use material that is thick enough not to soak through in the presence of standing water if this will be likely in your installation. Installers often set this material with dry adhesives for this reason. The most common textures are polished and honed. It is dense and homogenous in structure, with a fine grain and no cleavage lines. Colors normally range from olive green to greenish black, but the presence of impurities in the rock may give it other colors.

Some types of serpentine are subject to deterioration due to weathering and are useful only for interior work. Black serpentine is highly resistant to chemical attack and is useful in situations where it is likely to come in contact with moisture-borne chemicals.

Travertine

Travertine is often characterized as a marble because it can take a polish. Cross-cut travertine has crevices in its face that are often filled with a

a

b

FIGURE 11.5 As is true for all stones, marble possesses a wide range of visual characteristics. In addition to the variations between different kinds of marble, each lot of marble has its own unique color and markings, as with this Negro Protoro (a) from Marble and Granite Supply International in Evanston, Illinois, and this Carrara marble (b). *Photograph of Negro Protoro by Alana Clark.*

resin for easier maintenance, especially if the stone is to be used on a floor (Figure 11.6a and b). The most common textures are polished and honed. The fill used to plug the natural voids in the material does not polish to the same high sheen as the stone does, so even when filled, it will retain the visual interest created by the holes. It has characteristics similar to marble.

Slate

Most slates will naturally have a cleft face. Occasionally, a slate will be stable enough to maintain a flat surface after the cleft face has

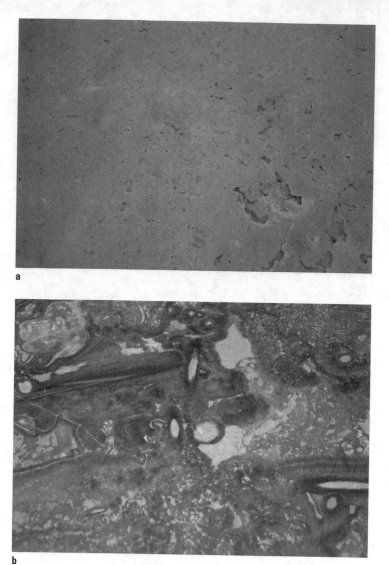

a

b

FIGURE 11.6 Holes form when Travertine slabs are percolated into existence. These holes can be left unfilled in vertical applications (a) or filled (b).

FIGURE 11.7 Classic cleft face of slate.

been abraded off. Even then, the surface may *spall* (that is, thin, waferlike chips may leave the surface) over time. It comes in a wide range of colors from yellows through pinks, reds, greens, and grays. Usually, it is found with its natural cleft face (Figure 11.7). If the material is described as gauged, that means that it has been honed to a consistent thickness. Cleft-face slate may not be consistent in thickness because material has spalled in some places.

Some slates are so stable, consistent, and flat that they are used under the felt of pool tables to provide an indisputably flat surface. Old chalkboards were once made out of similar slate. Slates from Vermont are smooth and consistent when gauged.

Slate is a relatively soft material and will soak up oil-based stains. Some of the components of the material are quite hard, but the matrix is soft. In addition to penetrating sealers, which should be used on all stones, slate is often top-dressed with wax or acrylic to enhance the color and provide a slight sheen.

Limestone

Generally, limestone is a soft stone, although some French limestones are hard enough to take a polish similar to a high hone on marble (Figure 11.8). They are a calcite-based stone, sometimes formed from the disintegration of shells. Occasionally, when the shells are still visible, the stone is referred to as shell stone. Shell stone is often more porous than limestone. Because they are calcite-based like marble and travertine, limestones are also susceptible to etching by acids. Most commonly, limestone surfaces are given a "flamed" look or honed to a high hone. Limestone surfaces are generally too soft to polish to a deep reflection.

Quartzite

Quartzite is made up of grains of quartz sand cemented together with silica and is usually distinguishable by its coarse, crystalline appearance (Figure 11.9). This natural stone should not be mistaken for man-made quartzite, which is a composite material containing quartz. Polished, natural quartzite will display more color nuance than coarse surface textures. Colors include red, brown, gray, tan, and ivory, with several colors being found in one piece. Quartzite is very hard and often comes in small slabs. For these reasons, fabricators will often charge more because their tools require more maintenance when cutting quartzite and more labor is needed to assemble a larger number of smaller pieces.

Onyx

Onyx is a term applied to translucent varieties of many different kinds of stones. It is most accurately a microcrystalline quartz, but there are calcite-based stones containing quartz that are commonly referred to as onyx. When a calcite-based stone has great translucency and depth (Figure 11.10), it is called onyx in the stone industry.

Surface Treatments

The following treatments enhance a stone's appearance or durability.

- *Polishing* produces a surface as nearly like a mirror as the stone will achieve. This treatment applies to marble, granite, serpentine, limestone, and travertine. Soft stones can't be polished to a mirrorlike surface.
- *Honing* produces a duller surface than polishing with no markings. It is often described in terms of degrees (high hone, medium hone, low hone).

FIGURE 11.8 Limestone samples at Marble and Granite Supply International in Evanston, Illinois, demonstrate a visual range.

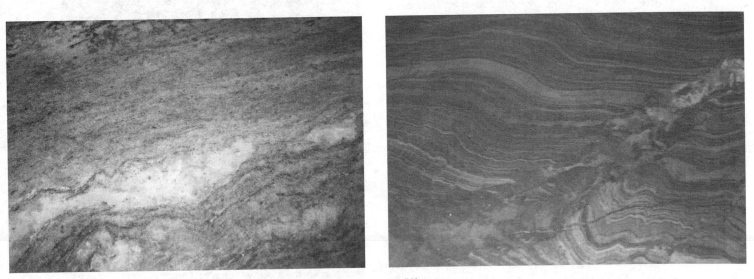

FIGURE 11.9 Quartzite is a very hard natural stone with dramatic variation among its different types.

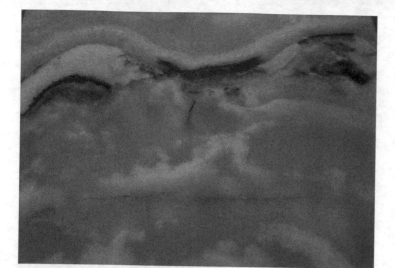

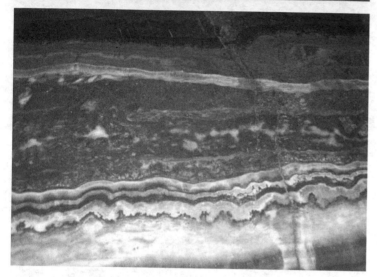

FIGURE 11.10 Onyx is prized for its translucency. Onyx tiles are sometimes used as lighting diffusers because they transmit so much light.

The degrees depend partly on the amount of polishing the surface receives and also on the hardness of the stone. A polished limestone (a relatively soft stone) can have the appearance of a honed or high-hone marble. This treatment applies to all stones except sandstone and slate.

- *Flaming*, also called thermal, uses controlled heating and cooling of the surface to produce the texture by spalling chips off. This treatment applies to granite and limestone (Figure 11.11).

- *Sandblasting* the surface with an abrasive produces fine stippling. This treatment applies to all stones.

- *Sawn-face* treatment produces a surface in which saw-marks are visible. This relatively rusticated treatment can be given to any stone.

- *Tumbling* is restricted to tiles. Marble tiles are

tumbled in a drum to simulate centuries of use and exposure to the elements. The resulting tiles have a hazy surface covered with small scratches, chipped corners, and some inconsistency in size and thickness. When installed, they may not be level, even, or consistent without extra labor on the part of the tile setter. Your client may prefer a waxed finish to keep the dark colors from looking quite so dusty, or you might specify a color-enhancing sealer to restore the color while still retaining the rustic quality of the tumbled tile.

In areas susceptible to abrasion, a honed finish will be longer-lived than a polished one. Flamed and sandblasted surfaces provide better traction but are harder to clean than polished or honed surfaces.

Slab materials that will have an exposed edge when installed (as on a countertop, for instance) also require edge treatments. They should be specified as flat polished or as receiving a profile (Figure 11.12a). The cost of the job will be increased according to the length of the exposed edge because polishing and shaping are an additional step. Individual shops will often have knives set up to produce edges that they have milled in the past. The shop may also include the

FIGURE 11.11 The appearance and slip resistance of stone surfacing partly depends on the surface texture. This granite is visually quite different in its flamed and polished forms. The color of the flamed sample could be enhanced to the color of the polished one, but the gloss would not be duplicated without a top dressing, which would then interfere with slip resistance. Slip resistance is the primary reason that granite is specified to be flamed. *Samples produced by Marble and Granite Supply International, Evanston, Illinois.*

cost of a new profile in its bid if you cannot use one of the profiles on hand. Often, the shop will charge only the cost to purchase the new "knife."

These profiles can be combined to create more complex profiles, and in cases where two layers of stone are laminated together (Figure 11.12b), they can conceal the seam. The characteristics of the stone must be considered when selecting an edge and deciding whether to build up the edge by laminating. Things to consider when building up stone edges are the resulting thickness and how that will affect the finished height of surfaces or overhang on the face of the cabinet. The mitered angle on the right in Figure 11.12b could interfere with doors and drawers opening if not "boosted" up with blocking or a subtop beneath it. Also, consider the visual characteristics of the material and its consistency. It is tricky and therefore expensive to match the markings on the piece added on to the markings on the top slab. The veining of a marble will not be easy to match up on the built-up edges, but it will be easier to achieve on the mitered design. Exposed cutouts, such as at a sink, will have to be built up, too, or they will give away the fact that the material was built up. Not all end users are equally bothered by this exposure of built-up stone. Some will be perfectly satisfied with it, but they must be informed. It will be almost impossible to match the graining at the sink cutout.

Factors Contributing to Cost

In the long run, the most economical stone is the one best matched to its purpose. The softness and absorbency of the stone are the primary limiting factors in selection. The softer the stone is, the more susceptible it will be to staining, wear, and etching. The durability and maintenance required both factor into the selection for each purpose. Marbles, limestones, and travertines are susceptible to etching by acid and alcohol and to absorption of oil, characteristics that would indicate that they are not the best selections for a kitchen. However, they are in fact used successfully in kitchens with the proper sealant, but they require maintenance.

The less maintenance a stone requires, the lower the cost over the life of the material. Color,

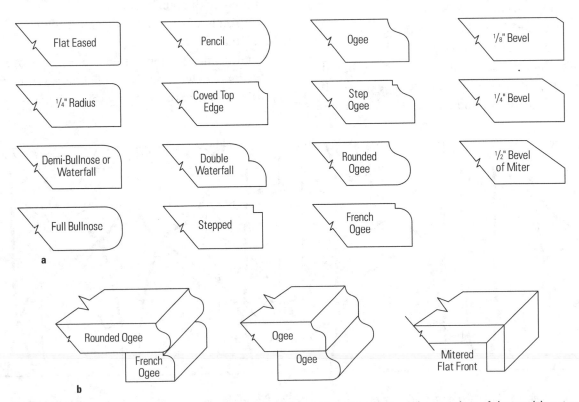

FIGURE 11.12 Edge profiles ground by knives. Knives are abrasive forms with profiles that are the negatives of the resulting stone edge (a). The exposed edges of stone slab can be detailed with profiles, which are ground by machine and finished by hand (b).

hardness, and surface treatment are the primary factors in this assessment. Many restoration alternatives are available for stones that have suffered staining or abuse, but if these problems can be avoided when selecting the stone, the total cost over the life of the installation will be reduced.

The complexity of the installation and the fabrication required also contribute to the cost. The complexity may be the result of site conditions, such as lots of prep work or a very articulated space that requires lots of cutting and fitting. There may be a pattern under consideration that will be very time-consuming; edge profiles may require a complicated fabrication effort. Laminating material to create a thicker edge also contributes to the cost of the installation.

The differences in the cost of the stones themselves contribute to the cost, often to a lesser degree than the fabrication and installation issues. However, a stone that is rare or difficult to get for some reason of terrain or local politics will be more costly. The most costly granites, currently those with blue coloration, are about eight times the cost of the cheapest granites on the market.

If slabs are polished for running match and your job requires book-matched slabs (Figure 11.13a and b), the backs of alternating slabs will have to be polished at an additional expense. If your job requires a honed surface and the materi-

al was brought in only polished, the slabs will have to be reground at additional expense. The installation of stone tile is usually about twice as costly as the installation of ceramic tile.

Working with Resources

Stone is brought into the country by various dealers who travel to all parts of the world and purchase it by the block or the slab. These dealers may also be fabricators, who buy big blocks of stone, then slice and polish it to sell it to other fabricators. Fabricators use the slabs, which are roughly rectangular in shape but are not usually neat rectangles, to fill the job orders that come in from end users and designers. They will cut it to size, then give it a specified edge profile and cutout (for a sink or cooktop or whatever the requirements) for the specific job. They will also install.

Let's follow the progression of a hypothetical installation of a marble tile for the floor and shower floor, with marble slab of the same species used for a countertop, shower seat and walls, and top of the tub deck. This progression assumes that the material will be provided and installed by the fabricator.

1. You have drawn up your plan, which calls for slab and tile.

2. Initial selections of possible stones are made by reviewing all available stone, either by visiting stone yards, looking through your library

a   b

FIGURE 11.13 Slab matches must be specified for stone in the same way that wood veneers must be matched. The two most common matches available on stone imported to the United States are polished for the running match (a) and book match (b).

samples, looking in a book or magazine that shows different stone species, then calling around to various stone suppliers to obtain actual samples of that and any similar material.

3. The stone selection is made based on the client's preferences for color and appearance and your assessment of the practical issues of maintenance. For example, a pale color will be more practical for a shower because it will show less accumulation of mineral deposits from the water. If there is iron in the water, a reddish marble may be a better selection, etc.

4. The particulars are reviewed with your pre-qualified bidders so they understand the needs of the job and the peculiarities of the site.

5. The stone is located to ensure its availability in both tile and slab. The fabricators you select and prequalify for bidding may do the searching for you or you might do it yourself. Popular stones like crema marfil are available from many sources; a less common stone may be available from only one local source, in which case, all bidders are likely to purchase from the same source. If one of your bidders for fabrication is also the local source of that stone, he or she is quite likely to figure out who the other bidders are. That fabricator is also likely to be the low bidder unless he or she represents a union shop bidding against nonunion shops. You consider cutting the 12 × 12 floor tile into 4 × 4 for the shower floor so the extra grout lines will improve slip resistance.

6. Bids are received and the fabricator selected. When you go to the warehouse, you will view the actual slabs, so you can see the variation from slab to slab. The slabs will be sequential in lots (Figure 11.14). You will typically have to purchase from the front end or the back end of the lot. Unless it is a very visually consistent lot, it is unlikely that the vendor will permit you to purchase slabs out of sequence because that would make it difficult for subsequent customers to match the slabs on their jobs. You will notice that many slabs have fiberglass mesh and resin on their back sides (Figure 11.15). Sometimes, the slabs will break when subjected to the abuse of cutting and drilling during fabrication or even while bouncing on the truck from the warehouse

to the fabricator's shop. If that does happen, all the pieces will remain in place and can be cemented back into a sound slab for the installation, thanks to the fiberglass backing. At the warehouse, all the slabs will be arranged in sequential lots of varying sizes.

7. The actual material is inspected. The tiles are compared to the slabs to make sure a good match is attainable. The slabs are inspected to make sure that the graining or patterning will be attractive when installed; they are checked for big veins that may open during fabrication. The slabs are tagged for your job and you might chalk off (or mark with a bar of white soap) the area to be used and "x" over the portions of the slab that are to be avoided. However, the supplier may forbid you from doing this until your fabricator has paid for the slabs (Figure 11.16). If there are markings that you believe indicate instability in the material, you may ask the fabricator to view the slabs before sending the truck to pick them up. The fabricator reviews the veining and rejects any material that he suspects will break during fabrication. Material that breaks can be mended, but the fabricator will avoid this cost if possible, especially if a flat fee was quoted for the installed job.

FIGURE 11.14 When you tag stone at the fabricator, you will select sequential slabs so that the material will be most visually similar and the slabs can be matched. These slabs at Marble and Granite Supply International in Evanston, Illinois, are numbered on their edges for lot and sequence.

FIGURE 11.15 Many stone slabs have mesh reinforcing on their backs to stabilize the material in case of breakage.

FIGURE 11.16 If you need to control the markings as presented on a finished piece, you may investigate that at the warehouse. When the slabs are tagged at the warehouse, you may be permitted to mark the cuts so the fabricator can see your intention most precisely. Marble and Granite Supply International in Evanston, Illinois, has permitted this designer to mark slabs with painter's tape. Some warehouses prefer wax or soap.

If there is not enough material that is acceptable, you may pick a different material or—if the size of the job warrants it—you will begin a farther-reaching search. A big commercial job may warrant a trip to the quarry in another country to select the blocks to be shipped in and sliced to the thickness required and fabricated.

Because the search is often just a matter of making phone calls to suppliers in other states, it is reasonable for your fabricator to undertake

this kind of search. There is some risk in that the fabricator will probably have to purchase the material in order to get it shipped in. In this case, the fabricator will not see it until somebody—the fabricator, the client, or you, depending on your agreements—owns it. However, that is now an unusual circumstance because the prevalence of digital cameras makes it easy to post pictures of slabs that can be viewed via the Internet.

You may also choose to reselect the material altogether or to choose a new tile or new slab that is attractive in combination with the original material selected. It is now quite common to see two compatible stones used together.

8. The material is fabricated and installed according to your instructions. If the graining or patterning of the tiles leads you to suspect that the installed tiles will have a definite direction that you want to minimize or enhance or there is so much variation that you are afraid the final installation will have an overall "blotchy" appearance that you want to avoid, you will have the installer lay the tile out so you can place and orient the tiles attractively. One hundred square feet will probably be plenty of surface to evaluate as you direct the installer. This is sometimes referred to as "dry-fitting" the tiles because they are laid out without setting material. The desired effect is then discussed to allow the tile setter to make good decisions regarding positioning and orientation of any directional material.

9. The installation is inspected before grouting because this will be your last chance to pull out any unfortunately eye-catching tiles. After tile is grouted, it is practically impossible to remove and replace without cracking adjacent tiles and making an obvious change in the surrounding grout. You will inspect one more time after grouting before the floor is covered, sealed, and protected from other tradespeople as necessary.

You may also opt to purchase the material and hire the fabrication, but of course you put yourself at risk when you then become responsible for the quality of the material. For instance, it may cause increased costs if the installer charges you for any additional work required because a fissure broke during fabrication.

CHAPTER 12

metal

The characteristics affecting the performance of metals are due to the characteristics of the metals themselves and the new characteristics that emerge when metals are combined in alloys. Unlike other composite materials, where you can assume the characteristics of the composite based on its ingredients, metals interact with each other on a molecular level and new characteristics often emerge from the union. Fortunately, you probably won't need an in-depth knowledge of metallurgy because most of the metals you will specify will be part of an assembly (metal-clad cabinetry, for instance) or a unit in a construction (metal spindles in a staircase), and you will focus on the performance specifications for the assembly.

A general understanding of the characteristics of the most commonly used metals will be sufficient for most situations. For instance, many metals will oxidize if they are exposed to air and humidity or moisture. This means that a copper-faced laminate will have characteristics of a laminate (requires adhesives to install, has a dark edge where the phenolic backing shows, and so on), as well as characteristics of the metal, which means that the face may oxidize if it is not protected by a lacquer. Iron, copper, brass, bronze, zinc, and silver will oxidize; aluminum, chrome, stainless steel, and galvanized steel will not.

Sometimes, the fact that metals oxidize is used to decorative advantage; for example, copper may be allowed to oxidize to a certain duskiness or be oxidized using an acid. Then it will be stabilized and sealed to present a brown metal finish with a copper "glow" discernable beneath it.

Kinds of Metal

Not all metals are common in interiors, so this section focuses only on the metals you will most commonly encounter as you select and specify metal surfacing and items for your projects.

Ferrous Metal

Ferrous metals contain iron. Iron works easily, oxidizes rapidly, and is susceptible to acids. It is seldom used alone for products that you will specify; it is often combined with other ingredients in alloys.

Cast iron is brittle, with very high compression strength. It is ideal for stair components and grating. Cast iron with an enamel coating is used for bathtubs and sinks.

Wrought iron is relatively soft and is corrosion- and fatigue-resistant. It is machinable and easily worked. It is often cast into bars or pipes.

The main ingredient in *steel* is iron. Steel also includes carbon; it is stronger and more resistant to corrosion than iron. Other metals can be added to the iron and carbon product to produce stainless steel. The most commonly used metal is nickel, but there are many types of stainless steel that use a number of metals in combination with iron and carbon. For example, type 304 stainless, which is used for stainless steel sinks, has 8 percent nickel and 18 percent chromium. The properties of this type of stainless steel are unique to the actual content of the alloy and include formability, weldability, and luster or sheen; it is non-magnetic. A corrosion-resistant coating forms naturally on the surface of the steel. If this coating is damaged, the material's corrosion resistance is reduced.

Nonferrous Metal

The following nonferrous metals do not contain iron.

- *Aluminum* is soft and highly resistant to corrosion. Used alone, aluminum lacks strength, but it is often used as one component in an alloy, increasing its strength.
- *Zinc* is a bright silver-colored metal; it is more corrosion-resistant than steel and is used as a plating to prevent corrosion in steel, even though it can corrode in water. It attracts minerals out of water and forms a surface scale that protects the zinc beneath it from corrosion, so it is used in some plumbing fittings. Interior designers often specify zinc sheeting for a surfacing material.
- *Copper* is resistant to corrosion but does oxidize; it resists impact and fatigue. It is used on exterior building components such as roof sheathing, gutters, and downspouts. It is also used for interior accessories and lighting and some plumbing fixtures and fittings.
- *Brass* and *bronze* are two common alloys of copper that are frequently used in interiors. Bronze can be extruded; brass cannot. Bronze is an alloy of copper and aluminum or silicon. Bronze will oxidize in the outside air to a color often referred to as verdigris. Brass is an alloy of copper and usually zinc. Some types of brass alloy are called bronze. Some nonbronze brass alloys are commercial bronze and architectural bronze.
- *Chromium* is used as an alloy to alter the characteristics of other metals (such as in steel). It is used for plating because it can achieve a high shine and because of its ability to resist corrosion. Other metals used for interiors are often chrome plated. Frequently, the metal object is first plated with nickel and then with chrome.
- *Nickel* resists corrosion and can be highly polished, so it is used for plating. It is also found in the composition of alloys. As you specify metals, you are likely to encounter two nickel-containing alloys, steel and German silver.

Forming Metals

Metal and metal alloys are formed in various ways into the surfacing materials and objects that designers specify. Not all metals are compatible with all methods, but there are numerous options available in each of these forms:

Sheets

Metal sheets are used to cover surfaces (nonstructural, not self-supporting). Metal laminates have a thin sheet of metal laminated to the same phenolic backing that plastic laminates are backed with or as solid metal sheets.

The thickness of the sheet metal is described as the gauge. Smaller numbers refer to thicker sheets of metal: 11 gauge is about ⅛-inch thick, 20 gauge is about ¹⁄₃₂-inch thick. Sheets can be formed over a substrate with corners welded to make structures like countertops and wall panels. Sheets can be fastened to other substrates with adhesives or mechanical fasteners (screws, for instance) to clad many kinds of surfaces. Metal thicker than 3 gauge (which is slightly less than ¼ inch) is usually described as plate metal, rather than sheet metal. Flat sheets and stamped sheets are examples of sheet metal products that you might specify.

- *Flat Sheets*: Whether futuristic or embossed, sheets imitating vintage tin ceilings may be pre-finished or field-finished with paint or special techniques (Figure 12.1a and b). Panels may hang in a suspended grid system or be fastened directly to the substrate with nails or glue. Depending on the system, the fasteners may remain exposed or be covered with a concealing strip held in place with mastic. Custom wall panel

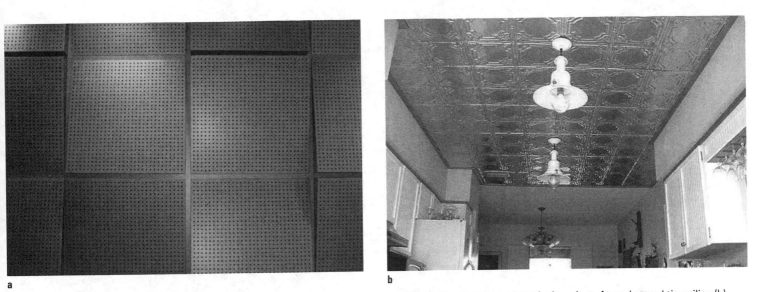

a   b

FIGURE 12.1 A perforated metal product (a) available from United States Gypsum may be combined with an acoustical product. An embossed tin ceiling (b) from Boss.

installations are formed to your specifications and installed per your drawings (Figure 12.2). Prefabricated panels come in set modular units and are purchased as a complete system.

- *Stamped Sheets:* Stamped metal is another fabrication technology. Sheet metal and bar stock (narrow strips of plate metal) are shaped against a die using heavy pressure. (A die is a sturdy form that is more durable than the material being stamped.) Embossed reproduction ceiling tiles have been stamped, as have stainless steel sinks, which are stamped in a succession of increasingly deep dies until the full depth of the bowl is achieved (Figure 12.3).

Plate

Plate is a designator used to describe very thick sheets that can be used structurally. While the thickness of a metal sheet is described by the term gauge, the thickness of a metal plate is stated in inches. For example, stainless steel plate typically ranges from 3/16 inch to 1-1/2 inches.

Cast

Casting metal means pouring molten metal into a mold. Like plate, cast metal parts can be self-supporting members of assemblies. After removal from the mold, the casting may be cleaned up by removing the metal built up at the seam between the two halves of the mold, as well as filing any

FIGURE 12.2 Custom metal wall panels by Tesko. *Photograph courtesy of Tesko Enterprises (www.teskoenterprises.com).*

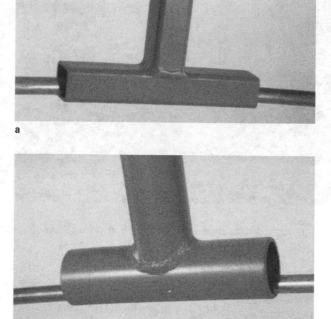

a

FIGURE 12.3 A very common stamped form. *Photograph by Alana Clark with permission of K&B Galleries, Chicago, Illinois.*

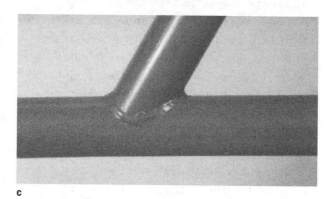

b

c

FIGURE 12.4 Cast metal.

FIGURE 12.5 Tubes are hollow metal profiles that may be square, oval, or rectangular (a). They are described in terms of their wall thickness and outside dimensions. Pipe is round hollow stock (b). Raked pipe is shown in image c. The National Ornamental and Miscellaneous Metals Association (NOMMA) uses these standard descriptors for metal pieces and constructions.

burrs smooth. The cast metal may also be forged, which means it is worked further by a metalsmith, who delivers successive blows using a machine that squeezes the metal into an altered form.

Metal can also be cast into complex forms such as grilles, screens, gates, and so on (Figure 12.4). Often, custom casting has an initial expense to produce a mold, but after that cost has been incurred, the cost of additional castings is not above average. If a piece is being duplicated from an existing item, the original may have to be destroyed to make the new mold. This process is also used to create solid metal bar stock.

Pipes and Tubes

Pipes (round profile) and tubes (square profile) of various standard sizes are used to fabricate metal components for your designs. Pipe dimensions refer to the inside clear diameter and the gauge (thickness) of the pipe wall (Figure 12.5a to c). The outside diameter depends on these two dimensions. Tube dimensions refer to the exterior size, and the thickness of the tube wall (gauge) is included in the size listed. The size may be actual (measured with calipers or other instrument) or approximate (tape measure).

Tubing and pipe can be cut and welded into complex forms such as railings. Widely available stock profiles include square, rectangular, round, and flat (Figure 12.6). Pipe is used to describe a round-profile hollow metal piece described in terms of its inside diameter with or without reference to the thickness of the pipe wall.

Quality designations for cast metal that indicate the degree of finish also have implications for cost. Foundry grade is the least costly and architectural grade is the most costly.

- *Foundry grade* will have more surface pitting and textural variations and there may be some variation from piece to piece among "identical" items. This grade is quite coarse and not appropriate for items that would be seen up close or be handled.
- *Commercial grade* items will be more uniform and smoother. The largest variations will be cleaned up, but the casting seam will still be present.
- *Architectural grade* is smoothed and sandblasted to minimize surface variations.

Extruded

The extruded metal process works something like a spritz cookie-press; metal is extruded in shapes specifically designed to perform a function. Extruded metal parts are stronger than stamped metal. Extruded metal is used to form channels, frames, and other working members of various assemblies (Figure 12.7).

Spun

Spinning metal means turning it on a lathe, similar to shaping a piece of wood (Figure 12.8). You're most likely to encounter spun metal in decorative accessory items and cabinet hardware.

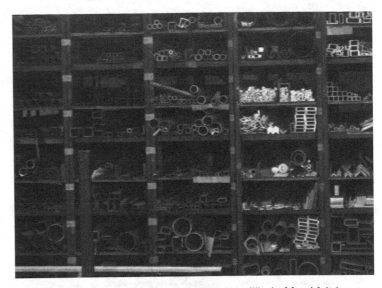

FIGURE 12.6 Stock at Tesko Enterprises, Norridge, Illinois. Metal fabricators such as Tesko Enterprises weld these parts into complex constructions for furniture and architectural details.

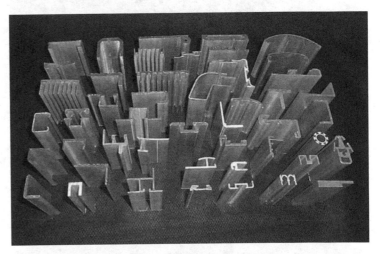

FIGURE 12.7 Extruded metal from Allied Metal Products. Production in Hong Kong fabricates extruded metal for industry.

FIGURE 12.8 These spun metal form, by Franjo in Ville Saint Laurent, Quebec, are used as stand-alone objects, such as accessories, or as components of furniture.

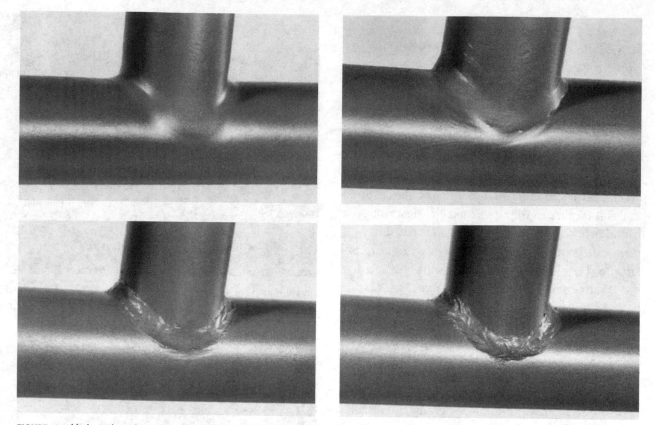

FIGURE 12.9 Various descriptors established by NOMMA as reference standards for weld quality. They range from the most cleaned up, as in the top left example, to the coarsest, as in the bottom right example, which would be used for utility and hidden parts.

Welding

Welding occurs when two pieces of metal are fused together without the aid of a metal filler. Soldering uses another metal as an adhesive to fasten two metal members together. The National Ornamental and Miscellaneous Metals Association (NOMMA) has a reference standard for the quality of metal welds (Figure 12.9).

If your job requires a lower level of finish for purposes of aesthetics or economy, you may decide to allow for a less labor-intensive weld. Standard #1 welds shown in Figure 12.9 are "cleaned up," and other standards are progressively rougher, as your particular job may require. You may also allow #4 welds if the metal is a substructure and the weld will not show.

Weaving

Metal weaving produces a nonstructural surfacing or screening material. Metal weaving uses metal wire in place of fiber, but the construction is very similar to woven textiles (Figure 12.10).

Salvaged Metal

The most frequently used salvaged material is cast metal. It is available in a surprising abundance from salvage companies, and reworking an existing piece is sometimes less costly and more interesting than purchasing or commissioning new material. This can be true even when some modifications are necessary to adapt the salvaged material to the new situation. Having a piece with some accompanying history is appealing to many people. Sometimes, the composition of old metal makes refabrication tricky, so consult the fabricator who will do the modification before making a purchase.

Finishes

Finishes refer to surface textures. The shininess of the surface of metal can vary. Bright is the highest shine, which is achieved by dipping the metal in an acid. Buffed finishes are produced by successive polishing and buffing using increasingly fine abrasives. Brushed textures are directional, with a satiny sheen produced by making tiny parallel

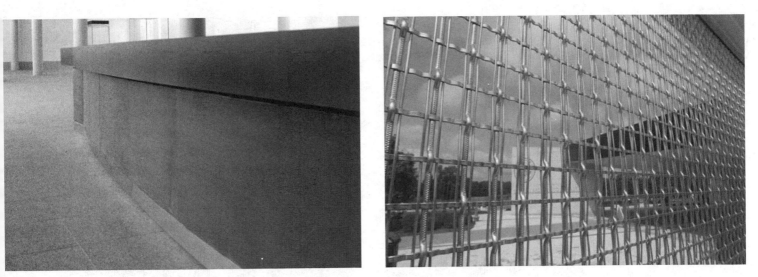

FIGURE 12.10 Woven metal from Cambridge Architectural in Cambridge, Maryland, is used for surfacing and screening.

scratches on the surface with a belt or wheel (Figure 12.11) and fine abrasives or by rubbing with steel wool. Matte is a nondirectional texture, produced by blasting the metal with sand, glass beads, or metal shot. Etched metal has a matte or frosted surface produced by treating it with acid or alkaline solutions (Figure 12.12a to c).

Plating, Coating, Patinas, and Anodizing

Plating means applying one metal to another by electrolysis, hot dipping, or electroplating. A number of materials are commonly used for plating:

- *Brass* is a long-lasting metal alloy that holds up to heavy use. Its initial expense is high because it is a costly material and requires complicated manufacturing processes. Brass may be a solid brass fitting or a brass coat applied over a base metal. Brass is a common base for other plated finishes. Titanium alloy electroplating can make brass tarnish-free in the air.
- *Chrome* is extremely hard and does not oxidize. Chrome is electrochemically deposited over nickel-plated base metal.
- *Copper* is softer than brass and is prone to corrosion and scratching. Copper may be a substrate in a multiprocess plating process. For instance, it is sometimes deposited on base metal parts that are to be chromed.
- *Gold* is used only for plating. When specifying gold-plated fixtures in a bathroom, never allow gold flash or gold wash, which can wear out in

FIGURE 12.11 Polished metal is ground to a smooth reflective surface by hand at Tesko Enterprises. Surface quality is achieved by a number of processes.

a

b

c

FIGURE 12.12 Chemetal in Easthampton, Massachusetts, produces metal-surfacing products in a wide range of varieties. This image shows three of the most common textures for metal surfaces: brushed (a), polished (b), and satin (c).

three to six months. Never expose gold plate to abrasives or acids.

- *Nickel* is frequently used for plating because of its resistance to oxidation and deep, rich luster.
- *Pewter* is an alloy of tin with brass, copper, or lead added. It is very soft and is a term that refers to the appearance of pewter, rather than the actual metal. Pewter finishes are usually chrome or nickel with a darkening overglaze of tinted lacquer.

Coatings

Coatings are applied to metal surfaces that bond to varying degrees with the metal. They are unlike alloys because they sit on the surface and are not integrated into the metal body.

Metal Coatings

Liquid copper, brass, and bronze are composed of an acrylic binder and powdered metal, creating a flexible coating over the metal substrate. These coatings will oxidize to a lesser extent than would the natural metal, and heavily oxidized effects (such as verdigris) must be encouraged with an acid or applied over the liquid coating as a faux finish where paint imitates an actual metal finish.

Patinas

True patinas are created from actual oxidation of the metal coating, which can occur over time naturally or be encouraged by acids. Formulations can be hot or cold. Hot patinas are often waxed as a last step in the process before the metal is allowed to cool down. Patinas are sometimes combined with dyes to enhance colors.

Patinas and coatings are both used to achieve similar effects, but one difference between the two is that the coating will be opaque while the patina will be a change to the actual metal surface. The patina does not obscure the surface—it is the surface.

Baked Enamel and Porcelain

A baked enamel finish is usually attracted to the metal part electrostatically (less waste in overspray), then baked on so it really clings to the surface. The final finish is roughly 0.7-1.1 millimeters thick when dry. Porcelain is also baked on. Air-dry formulas are available for touch-ups, but they are brittle and may crack if the underlying metal is deformed.

Powder-Coated Finish

A powder-coated finish is a more durable abrasion-resistant coating than paint with better weather resistance. A multistep process is used to prepare the surface, then the paint, a dry resin powder, is sprayed on. The electrostatic process prevents overspray because the particles will sail around the piece, coating all sides. The finish is then baked at 160-210°C (320-410°F). Some are thermoplastics (can be heated and softened); other formulas are thermosets (more like a "curing" process, from which the material cannot return to its original characteristics). The paint is up to 2.25-2.5 millimeters thick when finally dry.

Anodizing

Anodizing is specific to aluminum products; it is an oxide coating. Weld marks are not concealed by anodized coatings. Anodizing is not as precise in producing a consistent finish as you might expect. If you specify sheets and extruded members in the same finish, they will be difficult to match exactly.

Many colors are available, ranging from finishes that imitate other metals such as bronze, pewter, or copper to brilliant colors such as red and cobalt blue. The anodizing process actually improves the durability of the surface.

Wax

Wax is brushed onto the heated item and rubbed and buffed by hand to a smooth matte finish. It is fairly durable and easy to maintain.

Five-Stage Iron Phosphate Pretreatment

The five-stage iron phosphate pretreatment is not a final finish; it is used to prepare sheet steel for painting. It is included here so you'll understand what's involved as you are reviewing specifications for metal products you will use on your jobs. Although the five steps are listed here to satisfy the supercurious, they are unlikely to be part of your specifications for purchase:

1. Remove oil deposits and take out stains.
2. Rinse in water bath.
3. Perform an iron phosphate acid bath to etch the surface to hold the paint better.
4. Perform another water bath.
5. Seal with a water-resistant sealer.

Problems with Coating

Coatings are similar to paint. When problems occur, they can be described with the same terminology that applies to paint. These problems typically show up immediately upon curing or drying:

- Alligatoring, wrinkling, orange peeling, crazing, and cracking are terms used to distinguish between different unwanted surface textures.
- Cratering and pinholing describe pockmarking of the finish after an even application.
- Runs, sags, and drips are degrees of excess coating that began to flow before the paint could set up.

- Lap marks and framing are the result of inexpert coating labor, which layers subsequent coats unevenly.

Qualifying Custom Metal Fabricators

When you are considering fabricators for custom metalwork for your project, answer the following questions to make a good selection:

- Have they done work similar to your job?
- Have they received recognition for their work?
- Do they have the technologies required to complete the work at their disposal or can they access the required equipment?
- Will they subcontract out portions of the work to others; if so, who will be responsible for the quality of the product?
- Do they produce their own shop drawings for your review?
- What is the sampling procedure like? Will they make samples for your approval prior to commencing the work?

Judging Quality

As with all work performed to produce an item, quality differences will affect the price. We are all familiar with reproductions of modern icons, such as the popular chrome-plated Barcelona chair or Mart Stamm chair, which can be found in a mind-boggling array of prices. How do you account for the large cost difference? It comes down to the differences in quality of materials and quality of workmanship.

The decorative chrome plating used in the furniture and fixture industries involves several steps and other plating metals, in addition to chrome. (Another industrial-use plating technique, called hard-plating, involves a different process.) The base metal parts will be heavy gauge tube or solid stock that has been well machined, polished, and expertly joined with welds that are smooth and appear seamless. This well-made seam will then be ground and polished until the two members appear entirely continuous and the weld can no longer be seen or felt. Good quality chrome plating will then involve a minimum of two layers of nickel, first semi-bright nickel and then bright nickel. The actual chrome plating is very thin (measured in thousandths of an inch), and the quality of the polished surface depends entirely on the quality of the work that proceeds the actual chroming.

So, when you are confronted with a price discrepancy, such as the ones we notice with reproductions of the Barcelona or Mart Stamm chairs, evaluate the weight (heavy gauge metal). Closely inspect the welds for a smooth, seamless transition between the arms and back or at the criss-cross joints. If the piece has a polished finish, check the (hopefully) mirror quality of the reflection by holding a tape measure perpendicular to the surface and see how high up you can still read the numbers. Plating with the numbers going hazy by 3 or 4 could indicate a finish that will not be enduring, requiring regular applications of car wax just to keep it from rusting! You certainly want to be able to read clearly to the number 10 and beyond if you are looking for quality chrome. This kind of inspection will hold true for most metal items—plated or polished. If a finish is etched, brushed, satin, etc., you cannot rely on reflection, but you can still notice the quality differences between the surfaces of two different items under consideration. Look for consistency across the entire surface—is the brushing or etching or satin surface the same all over? Directional light will help while you make this determination.

CHAPTER 13

Glass

Glass is chemically a noncrystalline solid, but it is technically a liquid. However, it is such a slow-flowing liquid that it is functionally a solid. This is what gives glass (and some plastics) transparency.

Glass Production

The glass production methods that will be the most prominent in your interior specifications include float glass and cast glass. Float glass is used to produce smooth, flat sheets; cast glass is used to produce textured surfaces. Rolled glass is also used to produce flat sheets; however, this method is more commonly used in the production of decorative glass.

Float Glass Method

In the float glass method, molten glass is poured onto molten metal (tin); once hardening is complete, the glass is flat. Traditionally, flat glass sheets were made by the rolled glass method, in which molten glass was drawn on rollers, leaving marks on the face that were then ground flat. No grinding is required for the float glass method, so it is less costly to produce than plate glass, and it has become the preferred method for producing flat glass sheets. The tin side of float glass requires no further treatment; the top or "air" side is fire polished.

Cast Glass

Casting glass involves pouring glass into a mold or onto a textured surface to create a shape or surface quality. Like float glass, it can be tempered and used architecturally for doors, partitions, railings, and so on (Figure 13.1) and for furniture, light fixture diffusers, and surfacing. Unless tempered, glass produced by any method will break into sharp shards on impact.

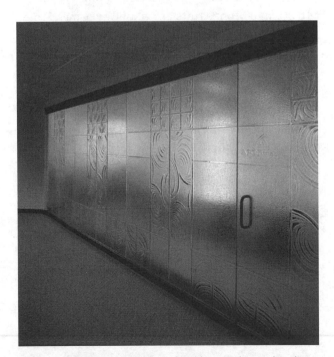

FIGURE 13.1 Custom installation of architectural cast glass by Architectural Glass Art in Louisville, Kentucky, engineered to meet aesthetic and code requirements. This entirely custom job can fulfill program requirements for pattern and signage.

Rolled Glass Method

In the rolled glass method, glass is poured from the furnace and passed between a series of rollers, producing plate or sheet glass and shaping it to the desired thickness. It is then annealed (cooled at a controlled rate) and cut to size. The two common types of rolled glass are patterned glass and wire glass.

Properties

The properties that you will consider when selecting glass for an installation include the degree of light transmittance, strength, energy efficiency, and fire resistance.

Light Transmittance

Float glass allows 75-92 percent of light to be transmitted through it, depending on the thickness of the glass. The measurement of this transparency is referred to as light transmittance. Glass may be tinted or treated to alter light transmittance. This is usually an effort to limit heat gain in buildings and protect against sun damage, but it is also used for decorative effect. Light passing through tinted glass is altered. Gray tints cause a cooling of visual effects, and bronze tints are visually warmer. From a temperature standpoint, both will reduce heat gain and limit sun damage to the interior.

As glass gets thicker, the intensity of the tint increases, so if you are requested to consult on the selection of tinted glass, be sure to review samples of the tint options in the glass thickness that will be used.

Strength

The controlled cooling process that glass undergoes as it travels away from the oven is called *annealing*. This manipulation of the cooling rate influences the strength of the glass. Glass that is cooled at a rate that's faster than the annealing ovens at the factory typically produce becomes stronger. Heat-strengthened glass is approximately twice as strong as regular annealed glass and is used where regular glass (nontempered) is permissible but increased strength is desired. Tempered glass, which is cooled even faster than heat-strengthened glass, is four times as strong as regular annealed glass. Tempered glass is considered safety glass because when it breaks it does not produce dangerous shards. Both heat-strengthened glass and tempered glass will present strain patterns, which you can see under certain lighting conditions.

Energy Efficiency

Glass used for window glazing must contribute to thermal control in the interior. Reflective glass has a thin layer of metal or metallic oxide on the outer face that reflects heat and glare while permitting light to enter. Reflective glass is sometimes also tinted.

Low-emissivity (low-E) glass is one popular reflective glass with a very specific technology. It will retain heat generated by the building's heating plant on the inside of the building while allowing the winter sun's heat to contribute to the interior. Low-E reduces glare and damage from UV rays.

Insulated glass refers more to an assembly than to a particular product. Two panes of glass are joined together while maintaining a vacuum between them created by a spacer approximately 3/16 inch thick. A moisture-absorbing material (desiccant) is used in the spacer. The entire unit is sealed.

Sometimes, two different types of glass will be used in the insulated glass assembly. Manufacturers of these assemblies refer to the characteristics of the four faces of glass used. The exterior pane facing out is surface number 1, the exterior pane facing the inside is 2, the interior pane facing the center of the assembly (facing the vacuum) is 3, and the interior pane facing the interior space is 4. The appearance of the assembly is impacted by the reflective, tinted, and patterned panes used and by the position of each in the assembly. For instance, if a reflective finish is used on surface number 1, the exterior of the building will be reflective. If it is used on the other side of the same pane—surface number 2—the glass will appear to be tinted.

Glass selected for its contribution to energy savings will be rated for its U-value (heat loss or gain through the glass) and its R-value (resistance to heat transfer). The higher the R number, the better the performance in each measurement system. The opposite is true for U-value—the lower the better.

Fire Resistance

Fire resistance is enhanced when glass is produced and then held at a high temperature until crystals begin to form in it. It is then cooled, stopping crystal formation. The resulting glass, called ceramic glass, is very heat resistant, because the crystal formation stabilizes the glass against thermal expansion. It can be fire-rated up to three hours.

Multilayer units that resemble bullet resistant glass from the edge offer fire ratings up to two hours for glass fire walls. Tested to the same standards as solid barrier walls, glass fire walls block heat, flames, and smoke. Doors with large glass panels can earn ratings up to 90 minutes.

Types of Glass

Glass is a material that is easily manipulated to produce a variety of characteristics, which depend more on the production process than on the formulation.

Tempered Glass

Tempered glass is glass held at a high temperature after its production in order to improve its strength and safety characteristics. It qualifies as safety glazing because it breaks into small cubic "beads" on impact instead of sharp shards. Tempering glass improves its tensile strength by making it slightly more flexible. (To temper means to soften; this definition makes it easier to remember that the flexibility is increased.) This improved characteristic makes it possible for tempered glass to withstand impact a little better than regular annealed glass. Tempered glass is identified by a permanent label in the corner of each piece tempered. This label, called a *bug*, cannot be removed because tempered glass cannot be cut or worked after tempering. Tempered glass that does not include this bug must be handled as a special order.

Patterned Glass

Patterned glass is passed through rollers that press a texture into one or both sides (Figure 13.2a to g). Thicknesses range from ⅛ inch to ⅜ inch, and patterns vary from one manufacturer to another, but a few standards are widely offered under various names. You would select patterned glass over clear glass if you wanted to diffuse the light or the view through the glazed panel.

Wire Glass

Wire glass has wire embedded into it. It meets fire code as long as the size of the window does not exceed the limits set by code. It is not to be mistaken for safety glass because it cannot be tempered and can break into sharp shards. The broken pieces tend to stay with the assembly because they continue to cling to the wire. Other products are as resistant to fire and are more resistant to impact than wire glass.

The wire patterns are limited to diamond or square. The classic chicken-wire pattern is available only on the resale market and should be used only decoratively. Wire glass is still preferred where vandalism is likely.

Ceramic Glass

Ceramic glass is clear glass with high impact resistance. It is sometimes used in laminated assemblies for still better impact resistance. The fire-resistive rating of this material allows for larger sheet sizes than are permissible for wire glass.

Laminated Glass

Laminated glass has a material other than glass sandwiched between two layers of glass. The inner material is usually a plastic film (PVB). The glass used can be clear, tinted, reflective, heat strengthened, or tempered. Laminated glass qualifies as safety glazing because, when it breaks, the assembly keeps the pieces from flying off. Laminated glass with a 0.3-millimeter PVB layer with two pieces of 2 millimeter glass meets the minimum requirement for safety glazing.

The inner layers are engineered for sound insulation, light control, or improved impact resistance

a

b

c

d

FIGURE 13.2 Patterned glass is available for specification on your jobs. Many patterns that you see on the market are proprietary (available only from one source) while others are classics (carried by more than one source). Samples include: antique (a); baroque (b); flute (c); krinkle (d); reeded (e); seedy (f); and water (g). Baroque, reeded, and seedy are also generic names. *Samples from Spectrum Glass, Woodinville, Washington.*

e

f

g

and security against vandalism and burglary—even bulletproof films are available. The inner layers may also be used to obscure visibility (through the use of frosted material) or to lend color.

Spandrel Glass

Spandrel glass is made from heat-strengthened or tempered glass because it is likely to absorb heat in place. The typical use of spandrel glass is to conceal mechanical areas from being seen through glass curtain walls (the spandrel is the part of the wall between the head of one window and the sill of the window above it). However, any application in which glass surface characteristics are desirable but transparency is not offers an opportunity to consider spandrel glass.

One method of making spandrel is to apply a translucent layer of material in patterns. Another method is to fuse a colored ceramic material, called a *frit*, to one surface of the glass. The glass must be either heat-strengthened or fully tempered because the frit causes the glass to absorb heat. Spandrel glass may or may not be insulated. Some codes require an open-weave glass fiber cloth or special tape to be attached to the back of the spandrel panel to ensure the panel stays in the opening if it breaks. If reflective glass is used as the spandrel application, the back surface must be obscured in some way so that the building structure does not become visible under certain light conditions.

Glass Block

Glass is available as blocks in certain standard sizes; 4 inches thick, 3-⅛ inches thick with a hollow vacuum center, or as a solid piece of glass that is

a

b

c

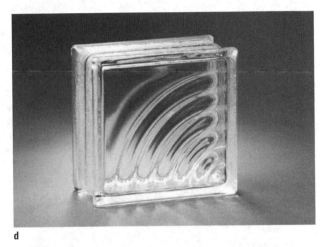

d

e

3 inches thick. It is also available in pavers 1 inch or 1-½ inches thick. Individual blocks are set in mortar or preassembled panels are installed with a mortar or silicone sealant. Accessory shapes are available for corner and end pieces. Patterned block faces provide privacy and/or decoration (Figure 13.3). Glass block walls are self-supporting but are not load-bearing walls. Specially shaped pieces are available to terminate glass block structures (Figure 13.4).

Holographic Glass

Holographic glass is a laminated product with an inner layer of holographic film. As is true with artwork that uses hologram technology, the angle of light is very important to the appearance of holographic glass. Some films are designed to give the appearance of a solid metal sheet when viewed from one angle, then become a transparent piece of glass when viewed from another. Decorative holographic glass is often very colorful and can create an illusion of great depth.

FIGURE 13.3 Glass block is a self-supporting transparent or translucent product. These patterns are by Pittsburg Corning and are all registered products. The proprietary patterns are: Argus (a), Decora (b), Essex (c), Spyra (d), and Vue (e).

One kind of holographic glass currently under development reduces the contrast between the brightness of the window area and that of the interior reaches of the space by boosting light farther into the room. This makes more natural

FIGURE 13.4 To finish the ends and edges of a glass block construction, special trims are required. These proprietary trims are also from Pittsburg Corning: Tridon (a), shown to coordinate with Decora; Encurve (b), shown to coordinate with Icescapes; End Block (c), shown to coordinate with Decora; and Hedron (d), shown to coordinate with Decora.

daylight available for use and reduces the need for added lights in the room. Balancing brightness requirements used to put extra strain on lighting systems during the day because light adaptation of workers' eyes required brighter-than-necessary light inside just to balance the brightness at the window.

Decorative Surfaces

After cooling, glass can be decorated by post-production methods that include sandblasting, silvering, painting, or carving.

Mirrors

Mirrors are made by depositing a layer of silver on one surface of the glass. The surface chosen is the air side, because the tin side does not allow silver to adhere properly. The reflective quality of the mirror depends on the thickness of the silver layer and on the thickness and color of the glass. High-quality mirrors can have copper deposited over the top of the silver layer to protect them from blackening. Mirroring can deteriorate rapidly when exposed to air, so silvered glass is usually preheated to 120–140°F and a paint-type coating is applied.

When the metal backing of a mirror deteriorates, the silver turns black. To prevent this from happening on your installation, instruct the installer to seal all edges of the mirror.

Nonglass mirrors made of Mylar are available for installation in spaces where sports or children's activities take place. Although they are clearly not glass, they fulfill the function of mirroring the environment.

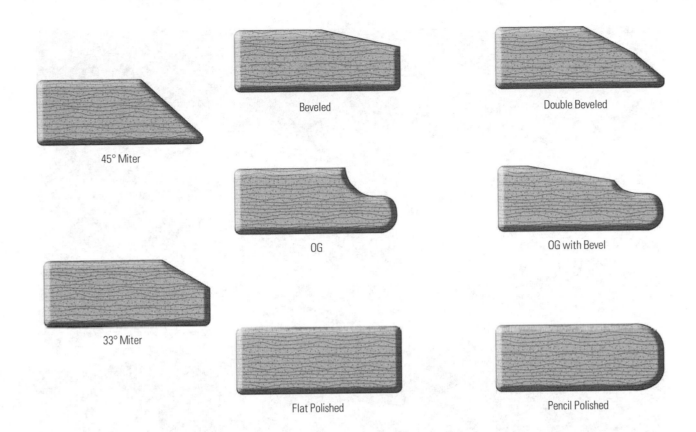

45° Miter

Beveled

Double Beveled

33° Miter

OG

OG with Bevel

Flat Polished

Pencil Polished

a

FIGURE 13.5 Glass edges (a) can be ground into shaped profiles. This process is exploited in the making of Venetian mirrors (b). *Image by Alana Clark shot with permission of Armand Lee, Chicago, Illinois.*

Edges

Almost any edge treatment that can be applied to stone can be applied to the glass portion of a mirror (Figure 13.5a), but the relative thinness of a mirror precludes complex profiles; bevels and bullnoses are the most common. Interior right angles are more difficult to grind into a special profile because the "in-corners" must be ground by hand, matching the machine-made edge along the straight section. Unless the edges of a mirror will be concealed or protected by a frame, they must be seamed, which means grinding off the sharp edge that could easily cut someone. Layers of mirror can be built up, as seen in Venetian mirrors (Figure 13.5b).

Decorative Surfaces

Mirrors, like panes of glass, can be sandblasted on either of their fronts or backs, but it's important to realize that sandblasting the back removes the reflective material from that portion of the mirror.

b

FIGURE 13.6 Back-painted glass is an art form that creates a beautiful and highly serviceable kitchen backsplash. The artist is Bruce Jackson of Gold Reverre.

They can be painted, usually on the face of the mirror, but glass panels are sometimes painted from behind (Figure 13.6). Incised lines can be carved into the glass. The surface can be decorated with carved or routed lines.

Glass Panel Installation

Glass Panels are often glued directly to the wall. This attachment may be reinforced by the use of U- or L-channel extrusions. Glass will not endure the stress of settling and a large surface must be very stable. If there is any question about movement of the surface, for example, installing a large panel, the panel can be backed with a material that's very dimensionally stable, such as plywood. The plywood backing is then glued to furring strips or hung on a cleat, rather than being glued directly to a potentially unstable wall surface. Some panels are installed on rosettes, but use of this method is less common. It involves drilling a small hole in the glass and placing a decorative rosette, like a washer, between the head of the fastener and the face of the glass.

Qualifying Installers

Review the scope of work with the installer and make sure he or she has done this kind of fabrication and installation before. Ask to see a portfolio and to speak with references who have had similar work done by the studio you are interviewing.

Inspection

You should make sure all cuts are neat and polished or edged as specified and that all seams are tight. All cover plates and escutcheon should be straight and even and conceal all cut edges. Panes of mirror or glass should be flush and aligned so that the reflection is continuous from one pane to the next. Alignments should be even.

CHAPTER 14

wood

Wood is used in many forms and locations in interiors. This chapter focuses on wood surfacing and architectural uses for millwork (wood that is given form in the woodshop and other materials that are used for trimming around rooms). The three sections of this chapter are segregated by use, but the characteristics highlighted in each apply to all the wood products discussed here and to case goods, which are the subject of Chapter 22.

Wood Flooring

When people mention wood flooring generically, they typically mean ¾-inch-thick solid wood that is 2-¼ inches wide. Wood flooring comes in many other dimensions and in laminated constructions as well. Flooring that is wider than 3 inches is considered to be plank. *Planks* up to 10 inches wide are easily available; wider ones can be available occasionally.

New Flooring

The most common woods used for flooring are oak, walnut, pine, cherry, teak, and maple. Beyond the most common woods, your client can have virtually any kind of wood available for a price. Those who are interested in environmental issues will want to specify exotic woods harvested from plantations rather than from rain forests. Ask the vendor about sustainable forestry practices employed by the supplier.

Characteristics of some of the more popular wood flooring species are outlined in Table 14.1.

PERFORMANCE ISSUES Wood shrinks and swells in response to moisture. Even climate-controlled buildings are subject to these changes, which can occur when the humidity is lowered on purpose to keep frost or condensation off of windows during a cold snap. Plain-sawn boards shrink across their width, leaving gaps between boards in dry weather; quarter-sawn boards shrink in height so the floorboards do not all align in a smooth plane. If moisture is excessive, floors swell significantly and the boards can cup or the floor can buckle. Shrinking and swelling occur as a percentage of area, so the wider the boards, the bigger will be the gaps between them. This also holds true for patterned floors laid up in parquet blocks. The blocks behave like a bigger piece of wood and all of the shrinkage within the block can be transferred to one or two gaps, making them quite large. This occasionally happens to wood plank or strip floors, too; the floors "panelize," transferring shrinkage to one large gap location. Planks are more likely to develop gaps between boards or even cracks in the board face.

Some woods are naturally harder than others. Maple, for instance, is a very hard wood. Very hard, dense wood species do not absorb stain as easily or as evenly as less dense wood. Wood will oxidize and change in color. Cherry will darken noticeably over a very short time if left natural

TABLE 14.1	Characteristics of Wood Used in Flooring
WOOD	CHARACTERISTICS
Oak	• Red oak is very common, white less so • Pronounced grain; large variety in color is possible (brown through coppery to blond) • Quite hard and durable
Maple	• Pale wood with less figuring than oak • Very hard (harder than oak) • Difficult to stain; dark colors can look blotchy
Cherry	• Fairly hard; stains reasonably well • Natural cherry oxidizes more quickly than other woods and turns copper • Stained floors change less in color over time than other popular woods • Often used as contrasting detail with other flooring material or other wood
Pine	• Soft wood • Color varies from blond to pink and light brown
Walnut	• Fairly dense wood; stains reasonably well • More expensive than other popular woods • Pronounced grain and dark brown color • Often used as contrasting detail with other flooring material or other wood
Teak	• Dense, oily wood • Water resistance makes it a good choice for locations subject to uncommon amounts of water

with a clear sealer; staining will lessen the appearance of change.

CLASSIFICATION Wood for flooring is available as dimensional or laminated. *Dimensional* wood flooring typically refers to ¾-inch-thick strip flooring that is 2-¼ inches wide. Dimensional wood strip flooring can be sanded and refinished up to five times if carefully done. Laminated wood flooring is discussed in a later section in this chapter.

You will encounter two wood classification systems describing wood qualities: One pertains to solid wood and the other to veneer. The classification system for solid wood also pertains to solid wood flooring. It ranks wood from highest to lowest quality as "Clear," "Select," "Number One Common," and "Number Two Common" (Figure 14.1a to d). Number One and Number Two are also frequently referred to as "Character Grade." Depending on your preferences from a design and application standpoint, the lowest quality may be best for your purposes. Quality is often specified as a combination; "Select and Better" is the most frequently specified quality. The other common classification system, which is often used for veneer, lists qualities as A, B, or C grade.

CUTS The direction in which the wood is sliced creates variation in the appearance and performance of the wood strips. The dense, slow winter growth varies from the fast, less dense summer growth, producing the alternating dark and light rings seen in a cross-section of the wood (Figure 14.2).

Plain-sawn wood presents more variation in the grain, with some straight-grain and some "flame-shaped" cathedraling (Figure 14.3a). *Rift-sawn* wood presents a straighter grain than plain-sawn wood (Figure 14.3b). *Quarter-sawn* wood also has a straighter grain presentation but has the cross-directional "flake" that is not present in rift-sawn. Flake is a satiny marking that runs perpendicularly to the grain of the wood (Figure 14.3c).

Both rift-sawn and quarter-sawn wood have performance characteristics that originate in the direction of the cut. The angle at which the cut is made will:

• Reduce the lateral shrinking and swelling in the boards

FIGURE 14.1 Reference standards for quality exist in several trades to which you will specify. The Wood Flooring Manufacturers Association (NOFMA) has established industry standards for quality distinctions between grades of wood flooring: clear (a), select (b), number one common (c), and number two common (d).

- Reduce the twisting, warping, and cupping
- Make the wood less prone to checking and splitting
- Produce a smoother surface because the grain is not as pronounced

Laminates

Laminated wood flooring has a thin wood face (⅛ inch is typical) bonded to a substrate (often plywood). The combined thickness of the layers is often ½ to ⅜ inch. The factory-applied finish of prefinished laminated wood floors may be unlike any that can be applied in the field. When selecting a prefinished floor, consider the ease with which tradespeople can make repairs in the field if a portion of the finish is damaged (for example, burned or scraped off of a small area). Not all

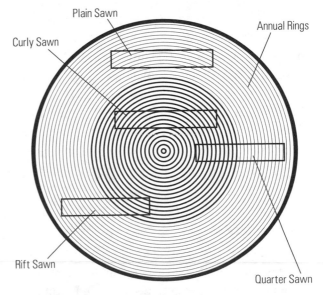

FIGURE 14.2 The grain presentation depends on how the wood was cut from the log. This visual aid will help you understand the grain patterning on boards.

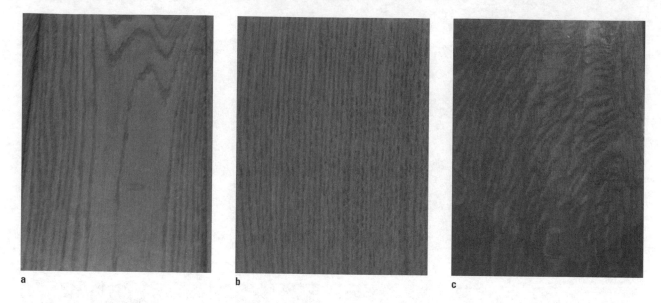

a   b   c

FIGURE 14.3 The grain patterning on individual boards derives from the cuts of wood (see Figure 14.2). For all species, the grain characteristics will be similar within the cut category. Plain sliced (a) will have more "cathedraling." Rift (b) will be the most linear and straight-grained. Quarter sawn (c) will also have a straight grain but will have flake running perpendicular to the grain.

finishes can be repaired and blended in successfully *in situ*. Some laminated product is produced with a ¼-inch-thick wood veneer top layer. These site-finished floors with a ¼-inch-thick veneer top layer can be sanded and refinished once.

Laminate floors are quite wear resistant. They consist of a high-pressure decorative laminate top surface bonded to a core that is often medium-density fiberboard. The assembly is backed by another laminate layer for stability and strength. Close inspection of some of these products may reveal a "photographic" (versus actual material) surface and the wood-grained patterns would lack the textural indication of actual wood. These floors overcome two constraints: (1) They are thin (between ¼ and ½ inch thick), allowing for a flush installation where carrying out a renovation, and (2) they are also more economical for a small area than dimensional wood. Take care to avoid placement that allows the repeat to be visible if you are using photographic laminates or multiple pieces preset in planks.

Parquet Blocks

Parquet floors consist of shorter strips of dimensional wood strip flooring arranged to form patterns. Standard pattern names include Brittany, Versailles, Bordeaux, and Herringbone (Figure 14.4a to d).

Parquet blocks may also be laminated for the sake of dimensional stability. Remember that shrinkage occurs as a percentage of the material; thus, you could find that the shrinkage for the entire block is transferred to one or two places in the pattern block.

Antique Flooring

Reclaimed or "antique" wood flooring is available, so rather than mimicking the effects and patina of aged wood, you can specify old wood that has been removed from other buildings or even railroad cars. Companies that supply this kind of product deviate from standards defining new wood in order to describe the characteristics specific to their particular products. You will need to ask pointed questions about the distress and wear, knots, and nail holes, and whether the wood has milled or square sides in order to select the appropriate grade. Some reclaimed floors are re-milled; that is to say that they are cut to standard widths and lengths, and new tongue-and-groove edging is cut. Whereas new floorboards have an undercut back to compensate for any unevenness of the subfloor, antique or reclaimed flooring that is made available to you as it was removed from its previous location may not have this undercutting. Therefore, special attention may be required for the subfloor. The flooring may not have

a

b

c

d

FIGURE 14.4 There are some generic names that you can refer to as you plan and price parquet flooring, such as Brittany (a), Versailles (b), Bordeaux (c), and Herringbone (d). *Images courtesy Birger Juell in Chicago, Illinois.*

tongue-and-groove edges and will have to be face-nailed with all fasteners counter-set and plugged or filled or will have to be delivered to a wood-shop that can mill the tongue-and-groove edges. These details will influence installation costs and methods.

Other Popular Flooring Similar to Wood

Bamboo and cork plank floors are often considered for wood flooring, particularly because of the intense interest in green building products. Bamboo is considered to be a green product because it grows very quickly; therefore, it is renewable. Cork, which is also considered to be very green, can be harvested with no damage to

the tree. Both bamboo and cork are widely available as laminate products, so consider them to share the same characteristics. They are available finished and unfinished (that is, intended to be finished at the site).

Existing Wood Flooring

Some existing wood floors that appear to be in very bad shape may be easily salvageable. When refinishing existing wood floors, it is tempting to fill gaps that have opened up. This is usually a mistake because the movement of wood will cause the filler to break, leaving what is often a jagged edge as the problem reappears. If the floor was previously waxed, it will have to be sanded a little more aggressively to remove all traces of wax; if not, the new finish will not adhere. Often, after having been waxed, a floor is unsuitable for any other finish and must continue to be waxed. If damage or staining is severe in isolated areas and cannot be removed or covered up with new colorants and sealants, you may have to piece in new floorboards. It is sometimes difficult to achieve a good match. One option is to cannibalize a hidden area, such as a closet or secondary space, for wood to use in patching a prominent place. A closely matching wood would then be installed in the hidden space. If this is not possible, various processes could be selectively applied to new boards prior to staining and finishing by an experienced floor finisher. Older floors that have shrunk a little will have a finer appearance than new wood. Therefore, even if the floor is plain-sliced, you may want to upgrade the new material to rift sawn, which has a quieter grain, so it will blend better with the older floor.

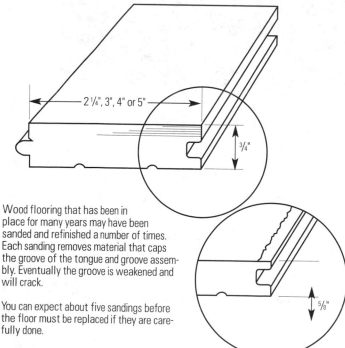

Wood flooring that has been in place for many years may have been sanded and refinished a number of times. Each sanding removes material that caps the groove of the tongue and groove assembly. Eventually the groove is weakened and will crack.

You can expect about five sandings before the floor must be replaced if they are carefully done.

FIGURE 14.5 A dimensional wood floor can be refinished three to five times with careful sanding, but eventually the groove will be worn away to the point that it will split and reveal the tongue and fasteners.

Aside from design issues and matters of personal preferences, you should consider the following:

- The soundness of the floor: Is it generally secure, tight, and nonsqueaky? Or is it splintered or damaged in too many places?
- The amount of damage: Is damage confined to the surface? If so, could it be sanded off? Could a limited number of boards be replaced if staining goes too deep? Can replacement boards needed for patching be taken from a closet or other isolated area so that a match in color and age can be made where original and replacement boards will be located side by side? Has the cause of the damage been corrected? This is especially important in cases of water damage.
- The degree of staining: Could stains be camouflaged with a darker-colored stain to avoid having to rip up the floor?
- The remaining thickness of the floor: Is thickness sufficient to permit resurfacing and finishing? Keep in mind that each sanding of the floor removes the top layer of wood, eventually weakening the strength of the top of the groove in a tongue-and-groove floor, as shown in Figure 14.5.

Floors that are in good condition but have a finish that is hazy with numerous surface scratches can be screened rather than refinished. A sanding disc that looks like window screening is used to remove only the very top layer of finish without breaking through to bare wood. The floors are then top-coated using the same formulation as the original sealant. Prefinished boards with a veneer or laminated top can also be resurfaced this way as long as the finish formula is known and can be applied in the field.

Finishing Processes

The finishing of wood includes processes applied to the bare wood. It begins with the final sanding and includes creating the surface texture, whether smooth or distressed, applying the colorants, and sealing. These processes may all occur in the field after installation or in the factory or custom shop. The most common methods for finishing wood flooring are sanding, staining, and sealing.

SPECIAL PROCESSES Special processes, which are less typical but commonly performed, include imparting textures or adjusting the wood tone before coloring. Examples of special textures are beveling edges or distressing and hand-scraping the surface (Figure 14.6). Adjusting the color before staining may involve special chemicals like bleaches. Other processes might include masking and painting or staining in controlled areas.

COLORANTS Stains are used to color wood without greatly obscuring the grain. If very dark floors are desired, the floor should be double-stained by applying the second coat while the first is still wet. The first coat opens up the pores, allowing more stain to soak in. Wetting the floor with water will also open the grain, allowing it to drink in more color.

If the finished color will vary significantly from the natural color of the wood, it is a good idea to stain the sides of the boards prior to installation. Then, when the boards shrink in dry weather, the contrast will not be so visible. If the floor color is more varied than you would like, you may request that the job be bid as stained and then sealed with one coat of a tinted sealer and two coats of clear sealer.

Some acidic formulas alter the color of wood through a chemical reaction rather than by depositing a pigment. Other chemical formulas are used to imitate the patina of aged wood when only a portion of an installation must be refinished. Where this kind of finish is desired, the job should be awarded to a shop with a lot of experience in this kind of work.

Paint can be used as a solid color or a "wash" to alter the color of the floor. Use paint specified as floor paint and seal the paint under a durable clear sealer coat.

Although bleach is more of an *uncolorant* than a colorant, it can be used to alter the color of the wood flooring. In the process of removing color, bleach weakens the wood fibers. For this reason, the process should be performed only once. With new wood flooring, samples can be made on boards assembled for the purpose of sampling, but on existing flooring, test patches should be made in inconspicuous places. Bleach

FIGURE 14.6 A hand-scraped wood floor imitates an antique floor, which would have been refinished in the days before modern sanders by hand-scraping, as in Monet's painting "Floor Scrapers." To imitate this quality, the floor will have an uneven surface. This floor also has hand-scraped beveled edges. The beveled edges serve to minimize the appearance of shrinkage between boards in dry weather.

samples will not be as easily removable as stain samples. Bleaching will lighten the inherent color of the wood, turning red oak pink, white oak green, etc. For very pale floors, it may be necessary to apply a wash to the floor after bleaching.

FINISHES AND SEALANTS Categorized by formula, sealants have different characteristics. Their inherent characteristics are often enhanced by additives that improve UV protection and provide slip resistance and other benefits in proprietary (manufacturers' secret) formulations. Sealants are available in several gloss levels.

Polyurethane finishes are oil-based and naturally very shiny. Flatting agents are available that reduce the gloss level, visually and physically softening the finish. If a satin finish is desired, specify two coats of gloss with a satin top coat to maintain the most durable finish possible. Polyurethane yellows with age.

As the term implies, water-based urethane finishes dry by water evaporation. These finishes are clear and nonyellowing. They have a milder odor than oil-modified finishes and dry in about two to three hours.

Moisture-cure urethane is a solvent-based polyurethane finish that is more durable and more moisture-resistant than other surface finishes. Moisture-cure urethane comes in non-yellowing and in ambering types and is generally available in satin or gloss. These finishes are difficult to apply and have a strong odor.

Acid-cure does not amber with age but is odorous and should be applied only by experienced floor finishers.

Penetrating sealer soaks into the wood. Because it does not enhance the durability of the wood, a surface sealer of the same basic formula or wax should be used with it.

Tung oil is a penetrating sealer that imparts an integral color or may be applied over a stained floor. It is easily repaired but requires a little more maintenance than urethane finishes.

Lacquer is easily repaired but scratches easily. It is an uncommon finish for floors but is often used for furniture.

UV-cured finishes are restricted to factory-finished flooring products because they are impractical to apply in the field. Polymer-impregnated finish, often acrylic, is also for prefinished flooring.

Wax is a liquid or paste (solvent-, not water-based) that is applied and machine-buffed to provide a protective sealant. It is unadvisable to wash a waxed floor with water because a white spot will develop where water is allowed to stand on the finish for as little as 10 minutes. If cleaning is necessary, use a combination cleaner and wax. Although seldom requested today, this sealant still has a few fans, even though it is not as easy to care for as other sealants. The visual characteristics that are admired in waxed floors (their deep color, obscured grain, obscured surface texture) can be achieved with other finishes. A floor that has been waxed cannot be sealed with urethane unless it is stripped down to clean, bare wood.

Aluminum oxide finishes are a durable coating, carrying long wear warranties; they are most popular with prefinished wood floor manufacturers.

Accessories

HVAC systems often have floor outlets and these should be addressed in your specifications. Options include wooden floor grilles to match the species and finish of the wood flooring being specified, custom metal, or prefabricated metal floor grilles. The prefab grilles come in limited colors but can be easily sprayed by the painter to blend with the color of the finished floor.

Flush wooden vents are somewhat fragile and many flooring installers prefer to provide a countersunk metal cover with a flat piece of wood that has had its face routed for air passage. These covers do not always operate as easily as they should. In addition, when floors are finished or recoated as part of regular maintenance, the contractors often do not think to remove these covers. As a result, the adjustment wheel that projects through the top is glued open or shut, as the case may be, making it impossible to adjust them without damage. Therefore, you should advise the contractor in writing to be careful about this detail every time work is done on the floors.

A more cost-efficient way of blending the floor vents with the floor is to select the standard metal floor vents and have them sprayed by a painter in a solid color that matches the general tone of the floor. Metal floor vents can also be faux-finished to imitate the graining of the floor. Floor vents can also be specified in metal and painted finishes.

Transition strips between wood and other flooring materials must be specified. Wherever two materials meet, the junction will require a detail drawing or specification. Flush sills of wood or the adjacent material are the neatest and least "fussy" way of dealing with the transition. Ideally, the two adjacent flooring surfaces will be flush when the installation is complete. Even when a flush condition can be created, the flush transition strip is still specified to lay across the ends of boards to cover the end grain there. The transition strip is not required if the adjacent material meets the side of the floor boards instead of the end. Attention to the specifics of the subfloor can allow for this if the two materials are of different thicknesses.

The greatest danger to wood flooring is gritty dirt that abrades the finish. To minimize this problem, incorporate rugs in track-off areas into your design, and specify furniture glides that do not trap dirt and grit. Felt glides that are kept clean are recommended, but if they are allowed to accumulate grit, they will scratch the floor. Therefore, if dirt will be a concern, plastic glides would be a better choice. Area rugs should be used on portions of the floor subject to water, which could otherwise seep down between boards, causing cupping or warping.

Installation

Installation of dimensional and laminate flooring requires attention to pattern, color, and finish, among other details. For laminate and parquet flooring, the underlayment is also an important concern.

DIMENSIONAL WOOD FLOORING If you are installing a simple wood strip or plank floor, you can probably convey enough information in a written specification to order the installation, although custom color will still have to be mixed on site. For a patterned floor or floor incorporating two materials, it will probably be a very good idea to draw a to-scale plan of the area showing not just the pattern but how it will be located in the space and noting the significant alignments and relationships to the architecture. A full-scale sample of the pattern with the finish specified should be provided for approval of a custom floor. Often, a custom color is mixed on site and applied directly to the floor. While the stain sample is still wet, it is a fairly good representation of the sealed color, but once it has dried, it cannot be referenced as a finish color unless wetted down with mineral spirits. All floor samples made on site will be sanded off the floor before final staining takes place.

Inspect the flooring prior to staining and sealing and again when complete but before it is covered to protect it from other tradespeople working on the site.

LAMINATE WOOD FLOORING Laminate flooring can be installed over many kinds of substrates, including an existing finished floor. Laminated flooring is usually not fastened to the floor with glue or nails. Instead, it is installed "loose" over a layer of thin foam. This installation, with the strips fastened to one another but not to the structure is referred to as a "floating floor." It leaves the assembly feeling a bit "spongy" and footfalls sound more hollow than they do against dimensional strip flooring. Laminate flooring can also be glued to the subfloor.

UNDERLAYMENTS Floating floors are installed over a sheet of material referred to as *underlayment*. The manufacturer of the flooring will recommend the correct underlayment. Flooring manufacturers sometimes produce their own proprietary material for underlayment and, unless the cost difference between it and similar products is significant, it is a good idea to consider using it. In these instances, the manufacturer will stand behind the performance of the assembly, not just the flooring product, provided your installer follows all instructions to the letter. If underlayment is required, as it is with all floating floor installations, it is a good idea to have the underlayment provided and installed by the flooring installer. The more people included in the installation chain, the greater the risk that the pieces in the process or assembly will not mesh seamlessly, and every additional tradesperson and supplier gives those involved more places to point fingers when something does not proceed or perform as expected.

The general categories of underlayment likely to be suggested are cork, standard foam, or engineered materials. Cork underlayment is used under floating and glued-down laminate floors and is sometimes used under dimensional wood flooring installations when sound abatement is needed. In the case of a floating floor, it will be dry-laid into the space. For other installation methods, it will be glued down. It is typically just under ½-inch thick. Many multiuse buildings (commercial and residential) require a sound mat of some sort under any hard-surface flooring. Because of its "generic" character, cork is often specified.

Standard foam is the most basic form of underlayment. It is about ⅛ inch thick and your installer will buy it in 100-square-foot rolls, sometimes larger. It is for above-grade applications where a sound barrier is not critical. If it is to be installed below grade, you could still use this underlayment as long as you also specified a moisture barrier.

Moisture-resistant foam or foam and film combination consists of foam underlayment, as described above, with the addition of a moisture barrier. It is about ⅛-inch thick, and your installer will purchase it in 100-square-foot or larger rolls. Install this kind of underlayment below grade or over unfinished crawl spaces.

Engineered sound-abatement products have been developed for use as underlayment. They include high-density foam, closed-cell foam, fiber pads, and rubber pads. A number of manufacturers have tweaked these premium products for special performance characteristics. Some focus on limiting transition through the assembly; others address the hollow sound of floating floor installations to create an experience more in line with a nailed-in, dimensional wood floor installation. When multiuse buildings specify sound abatement as a performance specification, you will need to carefully compare the statistics of your selected assembly to the stated requirements.

Wood Paneling

Each species of wood has its own visual and performance characteristics. Performance characteristics are very important when solid wood is to be used, but most wood used in paneling is veneer that has been laminated to an engineered substrate. Engineered substrates resist the shrinking and cracking to which solid lumber is subject. The density of the substrate influences the durability of the panel more than the thin veneer skin. Veneer is a decorative addition to the assembly.

Substrates

Common substrates for veneer are particleboard, plywood, and medium-density fiberboard (MDF) (Figure 14.7). Although your fabricator is the best person to suggest the proper substrate, you need to be aware of their general qualities so you can approve of the choices. If you do not agree with the substrate suggested by the fabricator, make sure you both have the same understanding regarding quality and characteristics.

Formaldehyde is a component of many engi-

neered wood products. It is toxic and a source of volatile organic compounds (VOCs). VOC emissions are regulated based upon parts per million of cubic volume of space. Refer to current codes for allowable emissions and work with the fabricator to determine compliance. Limits are rarely exceeded, but if compliance is in question, discuss ways of sealing the substrate.

PARTICLEBOARD Veneer is often laid up on particleboard (see Figure 14.7a), which is a solid wood composite product. It is made from wood flakes, chips, splinters, etc., formed into layers and held together by resin glues, then heated under pressure. Being layered and consisting of larger chunks, particleboard does not have uniform surface texture.

Particleboard is classified by weight per cubic foot of material. This designates the hardness of the material. Oak, as a point of comparison, has a cubic foot weight of about 40 pounds. Particleboard is available in various weights from 35 pounds to 50 pounds. The 35-pound particleboard should not be used for substrate; its main use is as a floor underlayment.

PLYWOOD Plywood (see Figure 14.7b) was once the standard substrate for cabinetry. Although most cabinetmakers will tell you that particleboard is just as good as plywood, whenever a portion of an item must be extremely stable, strong, and tightly fastened together, they will opt to use plywood as the substrate. If paneling is part of any structural assembly in the room (that is, if a wall cabinet will hang off of it), plywood may be selected for the substrate. Plywood varies in the number of plies and in the wood used. Plywood can be purchased with the face veneer already adhered as the top ply, such as warehouse-matched, birch-faced ply that is often specified for a paint finish. The substrate may be a combination of plywood and particleboard or fiberboard core. Plywood always has an odd number of plies in its construction and when the assembly (substrate and veneer) is complete, the odd number must remain. Therefore, if a veneer is applied to the exterior of the sheet, a balancing veneer will have to be applied to the interior. If an even number of plies results, the unit will warp.

a

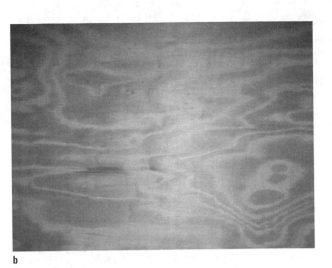

b

c

FIGURE 14.7 Substrates for flooring include: particleboard (a), which is the most common substrate; plywood (b), which is superior at holding mechanical fasteners like nails; MDF (c), which is seldom used for flooring substrate, but is a common substrate for other wood constructions.

Medium-density overlay and high-density overlay are plywood products with a resin-impregnated paper coating. They are often used for exterior painted surfaces. These are not fiber-based products. Phenolic plywood is a dimensionally stable, special-use product with a durable resin-coated finish. It is not as typical as other substrates for interior use.

MDF Medium-density fiberboard (MDF) is another common substrate (see Figure 14.7c). It is hard and very smooth, so there is no textural indication to telegraph through to the face of a smooth veneer. MDF has a weight range of 35–50 pounds per cubic foot, whereas high-density fiberboard (HDF) ranges from 50 to 80 pounds per cubic foot. MDF is avail-

able in 4 × 8 foot or 5 × 8 foot sheets in thicknesses of ½ inch, ¾ inch, and 1 inch. Thickness measurements may also be specified in metric.

Facing Material

The fabricator can counteract many of the natural characteristics of wood. For instance, the most difficult veneers to use are burls. If you look at a bundle of veneer before it is laid up, you can see that the pieces of burl are small, brittle, and lumpy. However, despite the difficulties inherent in fabrication, burl is still used in interiors because it does not pose an insurmountable complication. It is glued up in patterns defined by the designer and cured in a vacuum press (as are all veneers), resulting in a nice, big, flat board for paneling or cabinetry.

Wood Veneer

Visual characteristics of wood can often be modified to a surprising extent. By bleaching, staining, and dying with transparent dyes, white oak can become a brilliant cerulean blue or other natural or unnatural color. Similarly, an open grain can be filled or a tight-grained wood wire-brushed so the grain of the finished surface appears more open. Few characteristics cannot be changed in the shop, so what should be your criteria as you select a veneer species?

It is economical to select a wood veneer that is closest to the desired final appearance. If you want a reddish-brown wood tone, start with a species that is naturally that color, such as cherry wood, mahogany, pomelle, or anigre, and stain it the exact desired color. If you want a blond wood, start with woods that are natural blonds, such as maple, avodire, ash, or satinwood. For a brown wood, consider walnut or pecan. Pearwood is naturally pink; purple heart is naturally purple. Find the wood that most closely matches your desired color and figuring, and modify from there only as necessary. By limiting required modifications, you can more accurately predict the appearance of the final product and also control costs because every additional process costs money.

The variety of available wood species (Figure 14.8) is mind-blowing. Within the functional and aesthetic characteristics that you identify for your specific project, you will want to confirm that wood comes from sustainable sources.

Some characteristics should be considered impossible to change; for example, figuring should be selected, positioned, and oriented thoughtfully. The undertones of the natural wood color will usually linger, influencing the final color, even after bleaching, staining, and dyeing. The use of veneer over solids has some limitations, too. Veneer is best laminated to a flat, smooth surface; applying it to a complicated form with lots of separate planes is expensive. Therefore you would select, as an example, a solid

wood for ogee fillets on a panel door, even if the face of the panel were veneered. Whenever you plan to use veneers and solids together to complete your design, take care to match their visual appearances between the lot of veneer and the lot of solid wood. It is a good idea to plan for a stain finish if possible to even out inevitable differences in the color and graining between the veneers and solid wood. Veneers and solids will age differently over time; even if they match closely upon installation, they will appear different from installation and different from each other as they age. Staining will limit this change to some extent.

CUTS Veneer cuts (the way the log is sliced to produce the thin sheets of veneer) influence the visual characteristics of the veneer. Plain slicing produces areas of cathedrals and straight grain (Figure 14.9a). Quarter slicing produces a straighter grain, in which flake running perpendicular to the grain is more apparent because the flake is more reflective of light relative to the general appearance of the surrounding wood (Figure 14.9b). Rift slicing also produces a straight grain but without flake (Figure 14.9c). Rotary slicing produces the greatest amount of figuring and cathedrals (Figure 14.9d).

FIGURE 14.8 Wood selections will vary by species and are further differentiated by cut. These commonly available woods are shown as plain and rift sliced.

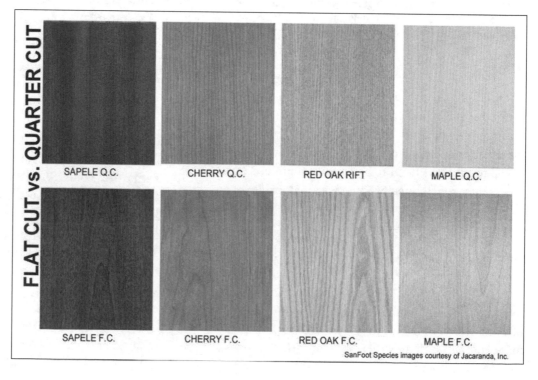

SanFoot Species images courtesy of Jacaranda, Inc.

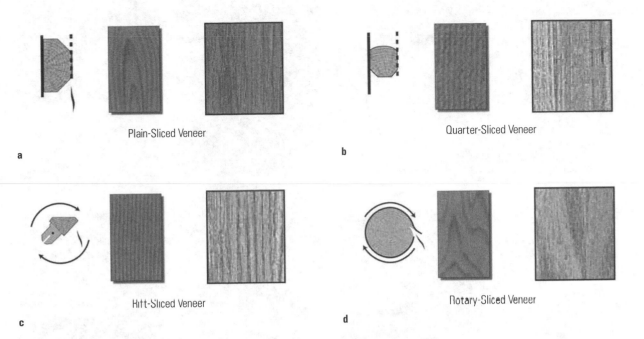

Plain-Sliced Veneer

a

Quarter-Sliced Veneer

b

Rift-Sliced Veneer

c

Rotary-Sliced Veneer

d

FIGURE 14.9 The way wood is removed from the log determines the grain pattern.

FIGURING Figuring of wood describes the markings that are the result of outside influences that disturb the growth of the tree (Figure 14.10). For example, crotch refers to wood taken from the trunk at the point where a branch has grown out; birdseyes are formed when the tree becomes diseased; pecky and spalted wood are the result of localized rot. Figuring marks occur in many species of wood in addition to those shown.

VENEER GRADES Veneer is assigned a quality grade of A, B, C, or D, similar to the quality grade assigned to dimensional wood. It is unlikely that you will ever have reason to specify grade D quality for interior work; it is a coarse grade allowing holes, knots, and worm bores. Grades A and B are the grades that you will be most likely to specify. As you specify veneer for your projects, recalling that you must always balance the two faces to end up with an odd number of layers, you might decide that the room side should be A-grade veneer, but the back, balancing side could be C-grade if it will be completely hidden after installation. You may even specify nothing for the back and leave it up to the fabricator to balance the panel with material of his or her choosing. Keep in mind that the grading is distinct from the species and the cut.

PATTERNS The way the veneer is applied to the face of the panels is called the *veneer match* and produces a variety of patterns. The kind of match specified will create the veneer pattern. These matches include diamond match, reverse diamond, end match, radial match, slip match, book match, and others.

The shop that *lays up* its own veneer (glues it to the substrate) will have the most control over the final product. Sometimes, veneer is laid up on a phenolic backing (the same backing used for plastic laminate is laid up). Be aware that a dark line under the veneer will be presented at all exposed edges. If this will be objectionable, you must note on drawings that this kind of backing is not to be used.

You may want to go to the veneer supplier (where independent cabinet workshops purchase their veneer) to inspect material to be purchased for your job. There is a lot of variation among wood veneers, even within the same species. If the exact coloration and markings must be controlled, you may want to go to the supplier and select the veneer yourself. Not every job warrants a trip to the veneer supplier, but once there, you will tag the veneer. The separate lots, called *flitches*, are groups of veneer sheets cut from the same tree and having the same or similar

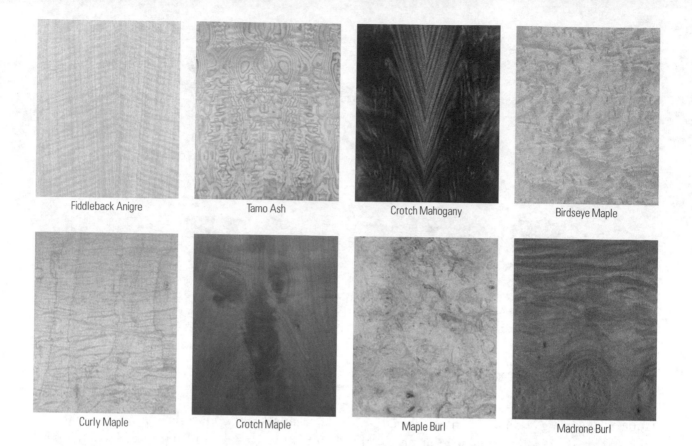

| Fiddleback Anigre | Tamo Ash | Crotch Mahogany | Birdseye Maple |
| Curly Maple | Crotch Maple | Maple Burl | Madrone Burl |

FIGURE 14.10 Some wood figuring is specific to the species, but any species may exhibit crotch, birdseye, curly grain, spalting, or burl. *SanFoot Species images courtesy of Jacarando, Inc.*

markings and grain characteristics (Figure 14.11). After you have tagged the material, your cabinet-maker will get that exact material to fill the order.

Matching

As you prepare your specifications for veneered products, whether they are panels or case goods (Chapter 22), there are essentially three kinds of relationships that you will describe. The first is the relationship of the pieces of veneer to the substrate. These include running match, center match, balance match, and end match. The second describes the arrangement on the substrate of the pieces of veneer to one another and include book slip, radial, random, diamond, reverse diamond, and box match. The third describes the panels as they relate to the surface, such as to the walls or to the cabinet faces.

The various matches (Figure 14.12a to e) describe the relationships of the pieces of veneer to the substrate. *Running match* applies the leaves (individual pieces) of veneer in sequential order, maximizing the coverage of veneer.

Balance match may contain an even or odd number of leaves of equal size. *Center match* or *center and balance match* uses an even number of veneer leaves of equal size matched with a joint in the center. In order to create a symmetrical arrangement, some of the figure may be lost. *End match* must be specified if the panels are longer than the available veneer and there is more than one horizontal row on the panel. The most commonly specified end match is a *book end match*.

The relationship between the individual pieces of veneer will also be described in your specification (Figure 14.13a to g). This relationship is often referred to as the veneer pattern or pattern match. Some of the most commonly specified matches include the following:

- *Book match* has the individual pieces laid up to create mirror images of each other; every other one is "flipped over."
- *Slip match* has individual pieces of veneer laid up sequentially, with the same side faceup for every leaf.

- *Random match* purposely mismatches the individual leaves of veneer.
- *Radial match* arranges the leaves of veneer in a starburst pattern radiating out from the center. The leaves will be cut into a triangular shape so the leaf as well as the grain radiates out.
- *Diamond match* orients the leaves of veneer at an angle in a mirror image that forms a concentric diamond pattern.
- *Reverse diamond match* orients the leaves of veneer at an angle in a mirror image moving out from the center. It is similar to the radial match, but the individual pieces of veneer are not cut into triangles, so it is only the grain figuring that radiates and not the shape of the veneer leaves.

FIGURE 14.11 At the veneer supplier, individual logs that have been sliced into veneer can be viewed by lot.

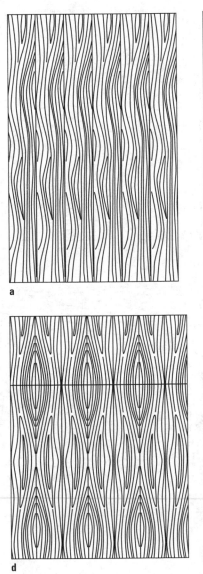

a

b

c

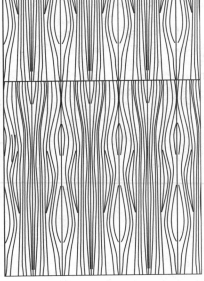

d

e

FIGURE 14.12 Running match (a) maximizes coverage with less waste. If part of a veneer sheet is left over, it is used on the adjacent panel. A small portion of grain pattern may be eliminated due to trimming. Balance match (b) utilizes leaves of equal size. Panel faces are made from equal-width veneer sheets. Grain continuity may change when a different number of veneer sheets is used on adjacent panels. Center match (c) will always use an even number of leaves of equal-width veneer sheets. This produces the most symmetrical panel. Grain continuity may change between the left and the right panels unless specified that all widths must be equal, as shown here. This is the most expensive type of matching. End matching is required when the panel is longer than the strips of veneer. Book-matched end match (d) creates a mirror image between the two rows. Continuous end match (e) carries the figuring forward to the next row.

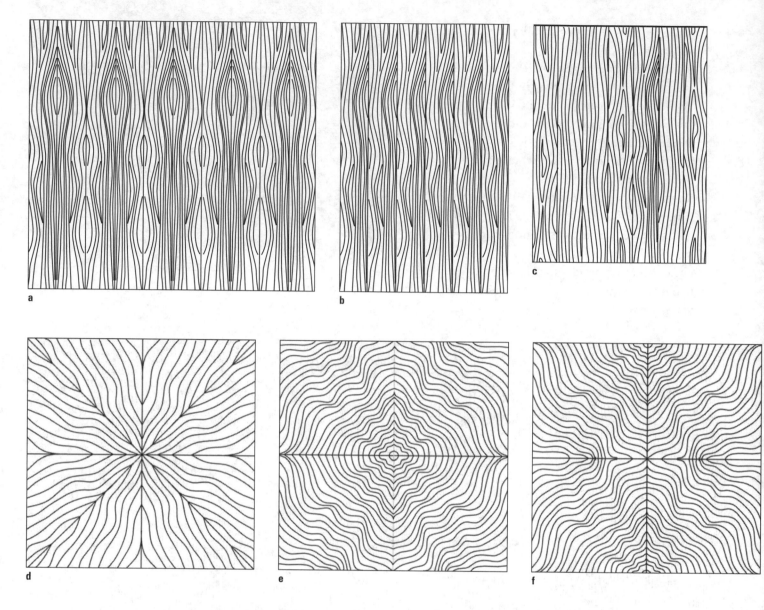

FIGURE 14.13 Patterns created when veneer is laid up on panels include the following: Book match (a) is the most common method of veneer matching. The effect is created by turning over every other piece of veneer so adjacent leaves are "opened" as if they were facing pages in a book. Veneer joints match to create a sequential pattern. Slip match (b) is most commonly used with quartered and rift cut veneers. This pattern features grain figures that repeat, but the joints do not show a grain match. Color is uniform. Random match (c) is created by selecting and randomly arranging veneer pieces from one or more flitches. A casual "boardlike" effect is achieved and veneer yield is maximized. Radial match (d) is created by matching veneer around a center point. The example here is a book-matched radial match. Diamond match (e) is like a concentric box tipped on an angle. Reverse diamond match (f) radiates out from a center point in quadrants; therefore, there are fewer pieces than radial. Box match (g) presents the grain as if they were concentric boxes. It is similar to a diamond match but squared rather than angled.

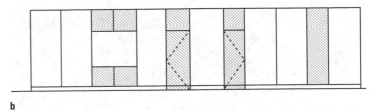

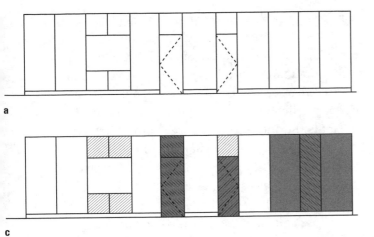

FIGURE 14.14 Panels are planned for their relationship to one another when installed. Blueprint matched panels (a) are cut to size and then veneered, so graining is continuous from one panel to the next with no ends sliced off to make the panels fit. Sequence matched panels (b) are veneered, then cut to fit; some panels do not flow seamlessly to the next but all are installed in numerical sequence for more continuity. Warehouse match (c) is also veneered, then cut to fit; this is the most economical of the matches and can be used without compromise when the lots are very similar in appearance.

- *Box match* veneers are like a diamond match, but instead of presenting the lines of the wood grain on an angle, the graining is perpendicular to the sides of the panel.

After the match of one piece of veneer to another has been specified (book match, slip match, etc.) and the relationship of the veneers to the substrate is identified (center, balance, etc.), the last piece of information needed identifies how the panels will relate to each other (Figure 14.14). There are two primary options. One is to cut the substrate to fit the wall surfaces first and then apply the veneer to the perfectly sized substrates; this option is called *blueprint matching*. The other option is to apply the veneer to the substrate and then cut the pieces to fit the room. *Sequence* and *warehouse matching* fall into this second category.

Blueprint matching (Figure 14.14a) allows for the most continuous graining. All elevations are drawn up and matching is indicated. All components are detailed and matched to adjoining members. If more than one flitch is required to fill the order, the additional flitches are carefully selected for matching. This kind of match is most easily done by the fabricator. The panels are cut for the job, then veneered.

Sequence match (Figure 14.14b) requires that the panels be laid up as sheets are drawn from the flitch. Some components will not be in sequence as the wall panels are laid up (doors, for instance, may be out of sequence because they will require a different substrate from the one

required for walls) and corners may not match because they are trimmed to fit the wall space remaining after the other panels have been installed. For this match the panels were veneered one after another, then cut to fit the job.

Warehouse match (Figure 14.14c) provides panels that are the same species in lots of 6 to 12 panels. The next lot (if more panels are required) may not be in sequence. Doors will not be in sequence and corners will not match for the same reasons as apply to sequence matching.

Other Cladding Materials

The extensive focus on wood veneer is not to suggest that it is the only option for cladding walls. Plastic laminates; wood, plastic panels, and metal laminates are often specified. The cladding materials that are available for cabinetry can also be used for panels, as well as other materials that you might consider as wallcovering so you may review those sections, too. Wood veneer is a very popular option but not the only one.

SOLID WOOD PLANKS Planks are used more often for residential than commercial installations because of fire codes (Figure 14.15). Redwood, cedar, and pine are common. Planks vary in width from 4 to 12 inches. Solid wood must be allowed to move—expand and contract—in the installation. Details between planks and at junctions between planks and other materials should conceal movement. They might have tongue-and-groove edges or be installed as a board and batten, reverse board

FIGURE 14.15 Solid wood paneling installation.

FIGURE 14.16 Reclaimed Pecky Cypress installation by Goodwins.

and batten, reveal, or spine. Remember that the battens, spines, etc. can be wood or other materials.

RECLAIMED WOOD Issues related to reclaimed paneling are consistent with those related to floors and the same inquiry should be undertaken to confirm the quality and characteristics of the available lot. A rusticated style sometimes calls for using wood reclaimed from building exteriors rather than interiors (Figure 14.16). The variety of surface characteristics and material quality cannot be predicted from lot to lot; an inspection of the lot is the only way to ensure appropriate material. If barnwood is selected, it should be reclaimed from hay barns only to avoid any possibility of persistent animal smells. If the barn is still standing, there will be fewer concerns about dampness and bugs than if the wood has been lying stacked. It is expected that the sale will include the entire barn, and the quantity may be estimated in running feet of board or square feet of coverage. This rough estimate is for your convenience and is not to be relied upon, as the seller is selling the barn and not board lengths. It is a good idea to inspect the lot and confirm availability of required lengths if your design requires long, unbroken lengths. The price may not include removing nails, bug bombing, or cleaning of any sort, so inquire about this so include that work in your budget, too.

Wood reclaimed from exteriors should be personally inspected before purchase. Wood claimed from interiors of people-serving spaces may be safely purchased via long distance after an evaluation of photos from a trustworthy seller. Wood reclaimed from industrial-use sites will fall in between the two in terms of the need for a personal inspection.

Finishes

There are two basic finishes for wood panels: penetrating and surface. Penetrating finishes include stains that add color, dyes that change the color, and bleaches, which remove the color. Surface finishes include paints (including oils, latex, low VOC, etc.), varnishes (including conversion and spar varnishes), oils, lacquers (clear and pigmented; standard and catalyzed), and waxes.

The Implementation Process

Paneling is first drawn up in plan and elevation, to scale, including any section details necessary to describe the profiles intended. All services that must be accommodated will be shown and detailed. This involves primarily electrical and HVAC. Plumbing is less crucial if it will be coming through the wall cavity into a hidden location. The drawing should contain all specifications required to explain your intent. It is standard practice to leave the selection of joints, adhesives, and fasteners up to the fabricators, aside from a general note such as "all fasteners to be concealed," unless they are to be used decoratively as well as functionally.

WORKING WITH FABRICATORS The drawing is put out to bid with one to three shops (or more if necessary). A walk-through for an existing site or a plan review for a location not yet completed will give the bidder an opportunity to ask questions regarding your intention and requirements. After reviewing bids and hiring a fabricator, the fabricator should provide you with shop drawings and finish samples prior to beginning work. If a custom profile is in question, you may request a mock-up of a rail and panel profile. These will be reviewed, changed if necessary, and then approved. You may elect to visit the shop before the panels are cut to review the veneers (laid-up or not) and make decisions regarding the selection, location, and orientation of each piece.

A second shop visit will allow you to inspect the quality of the workmanship and the correctness of the detailing before the piece goes into the finishing room. You may also view the components after they have been finished but before they are transported to the site. If there is any blending or touch-up required, it can be more easily done at the shop than on site.

It is a good idea to plan a visit to the job site at the start of the installation (after materials have been unloaded) to answer any questions the installers might have regarding your intention. Visit the site again after the installation is largely completed, but while the installers still have all of their equipment and touch-up materials on site.

QUALIFYING FABRICATORS AND INSTALLERS
Cabinet shops are the most likely fabricators and installers for this kind of work, but not all have experience with paneling. Experienced cabinet shops have very likely dealt with many of the issues involved in paneling a room, even if they have never fabricated paneling before. As with built-in cabinetry, paneling requires careful measuring and fitting of pieces that must fit tightly into spaces that are not square and plumb or even. Paneling measurements must be precise. Panels must be supported by and fastened to the walls with some kind of concealed fastener. The complexity of a paneling installation raises issues unique to paneling and any qualified fabricator must be aware of, and be prepared to address, these unique complications.

The drawings that you submit will illustrate how corners will be constructed, how details will meet openings (windows and doors), and services (switch and outlet plates, HVAC grilles, etc.). Shop drawings will further illustrate this, as well as how the fastening method suggested will affect the details.

If the paneling is to be shop-finished, the fabricator must have a clean room that is a sealed area free of airborne dust, supplied and vented separately from the rest of the shop. Often, clean rooms have a separate heating system and can function as a low-temperature oven to speed up drying time, further minimizing the risk of dust settling on a piece with tacky finish.

If the paneling is destined for an existing space, the bidders may want to have an opportunity to check conditions with a walk-through. They will be interested in how the pieces will be delivered to their location (size of access hallways and elevators). In advance of the scheduled walk-through, you will supply them with a set of drawings for their review and notes during the walk-through. Sometimes, the bidders will estimate based on drawings alone and only want to view the site if hired. After a shop has been selected and paid a deposit, they should produce shop drawings and finish samples for your approval. They will discuss how they intend to deal with surfaces that are out of plumb and complications presented by services (HVAC, electrical covers, etc.) and will show these on shop drawings.

FACTORS CONTRIBUTING TO COST The amount of labor and the difficulty of the fabrication and installation are the biggest contributors to cost.

A highly detailed design that has a lot of different profiles used in complicated combinations will be costly, as will a room with many openings and service outlets. Ironically, a very minimal design that does not allow for trim pieces that can conceal a less-than-perfect fit can also be costly, because it requires that all tolerances be exact and precise, leaving no room for error. The finish selected also contributes to the labor charge. A closed pore finish (for which the grain is filled) requires an extra step in the labor not necessary for an open pore finish. The veneer species selected (rare veneers cost more) and the pattern specified (complex pattern-matching is labor-intensive) will also affect the cost.

SURFACING SYSTEMS AND PREFINISHED SHEETS

Surfacing systems consist of panels in standard sizes and various surface veneers of wood, metal, and plastic, as well as fabric-wrapped panels, along with the hardware required to fasten them to an approved support. Some panels are specifically engineered to absorb or break up sound. Panel size will vary among manufacturers for square or rectangular panels (Figure 14.17a-c). Some panels systems are manufactured for use with freestanding office landscaping panels and include a stabilizing foot. These wall surfaces are modular and movable, so they could conceivably be taken to a new site if the owner should change locations in the future.

When working with a system, there are design restrictions beyond those that you will encounter in custom work. The panels are of a set dimension, and specific hangers are provided with the individual system. While most systems are surprisingly versatile, it would be helpful to select the system before you design the applica-

a

b

c

FIGURE 14.17 Paneling systems are designed with set increments, so the panel sizes must be designed to match the available increments. The hanging framework must be ordered from the same manufacturer. Incorporating multiple materials in your composition is easily done. The following systems are from Marlite, which creates custom and luminous panels: wood veneered (a), translucent panel (b), and tread plate (c). These examples demonstrate the range and alternative aesthetic choices available in paneling systems.

tion. You will plan for wall lengths that will fit that system and your corner details will be those that can be created with the system. For surfacing systems, unlike custom wall paneling, your fabricator (the manufacturer) and installer are likely to be different people. You may select an installer who is recommended by the manufacturer or interview installers and make your own selection. Manufacturers will sometimes offer training to installers who, after they complete the training, are certified installers of that product. If such training is made available, you will want to hire a certified installer. All information relative to the manufacture of the panels will be given to the manufacturer. This will include the description of the decorative surface, as well as the panel size, quantity, and hardware required. If a nonstandard finish is required, the manufacturer will provide a finish sample for approval.

If possible, review the site with your installer prior to ordering and check for square and plumb conditions. If the floor is very out of level, the installer can compensate by adding a small amount of height to the baseboard detail so the top of the base presents a level line for the bottom of the paneling. If the difference is so great that the difference in the height of the baseboard will be very noticeable, an additional drop in the bottom edge of the wall panels themselves may be used to trick the eye into believing that everything is square and level. In general, review with your installer the best way to correct for any defects in the site.

Prefinished sheets are available in a variety of materials and finishes. They range from wood tambour products on a flexible backing (applied with adhesives) and veneer, fabric, or vinyl-covered gypsum board product (applied with adhesives, mechanical fasteners, or clips) to vinyl sheets in thicknesses from $\frac{1}{32}$ to $\frac{1}{16}$ inch (applied with adhesives or mechanical fasteners) and baked enamel on metal.

INSPECTION You will inspect materials and installation for any paneling—system or custom—that has been installed. Material cuts should be neat with no chipping. There should be no adhesive on the surface of the material and no defect in the materials used. The finish should be as specified with no dust or drips. The installation should be as drawn, with all members appearing to be square and plumb. It is more important that everything appear to be straight than that it is to actually be straight.

Wood Trims and Other Materials Used for Similar Trims

Millwork generally conceals the junction between two materials or the transition between two planes. These are areas that could be expected to open up because of settling, or that present cut lumber edges from construction, or that have some other feature that you would like to span, hide, or ease. While these functions could be considered to be decorative, millwork trim is used unabashedly to decorate. It affects the visual proportion of space, as designers found to their dismay in the 1980s, when it was popular to install baronial-scaled moldings in modest rooms. The result was spaces that appeared mashed and squashed. Millwork carries (or adds) style. Molding articulates areas that might otherwise be too austere.

Whether made from real wood, resin, or other composition material, most millwork trims serve a largely decorative function. Picture rails, jamb stops, bar rails, corbel brackets, glazing stops, and screen beads are the trims that perform physical labor (Figure 14.18a-r).

- *Crown molding* spans the distance between the ceiling and the wall at an angle. It is not required that this trim project at an angle, but if it does, it is indisputably crown.
- Similar to crown molding is *cove molding*, but is unique because of the concave section arcing outward.
- *Baseboards* create a transition between the wall and floor; *base caps* extend the baseboards with an extra detail.
- *Bar rails* are the elbow rest at the edge of a bar.
- *Casings* trim the edges of openings like windows and doors.
- *Panel molds* are flat-backed profiles originally intended to conceal shrinkage between large panel sections.

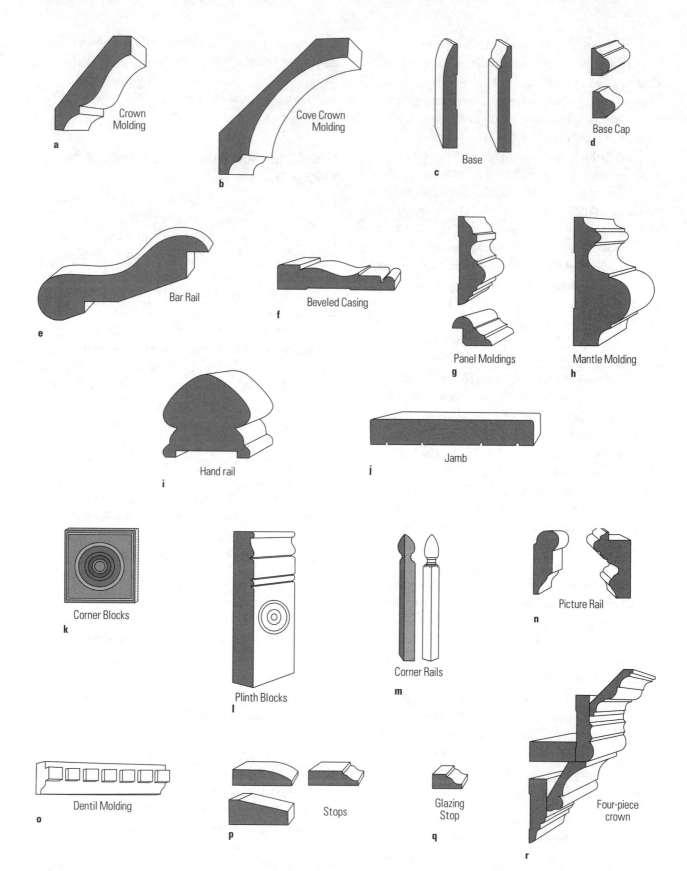

Crown Molding **a**

Cove Crown Molding **b**

Base **c**

Base Cap **d**

Bar Rail **e**

Beveled Casing **f**

Panel Moldings **g**

Mantle Molding **h**

Hand rail **i**

Jamb **j**

Corner Blocks **k**

Plinth Blocks **l**

Corner Rails **m**

Picture Rail **n**

Dentil Molding **o**

Stops **p**

Glazing Stop **q**

Four-piece crown **r**

FIGURE 14.18 The function names given to the various profiles imply where to use them, but the names do not restrict their use. You can use millwork trims in any supportable location. The four-piece crown (r) illustrates this point. It uses, from the top: a crown; then a casing, braced from behind to maintain the construction; then a cove; and finally an upside-down base. *Drawings compiled by Ferche Millwork in Rice, Minnesota.*

- *Corbel brackets* usually serve a decorative function, but when properly supported themselves, they can work to support other material units.
- *Handrails* perform the obvious function of capping the railing.
- *Jambs* cover the many structural framing members in doorways with a single piece.
- *Corner blocks* provide a casing transition from vertical to horizontal.
- *Plinth blocks* terminate the casing at the floor, creating a transition between casing and base.
- *Corner rails* protect out-corners.
- *Picture rail* is installed below the crown line (or below the ceiling if there is no crown). It was intended originally to avoid the need to poke holes in plaster walls and risk damaging the keys that hold the plaster on in order to hang artwork. Art was instead hung from wire or cord hooked into the top of the picture rail.
- A *dentil* is a shamelessly decorative piece whose only function is to jazz things up a bit.

- A *stop*, as its name implies, is a narrow strip of wood that stops the door from swinging past center.
- *Glazing stops* hold glass and window screen in place on wooden frames.

We expect molding to be made of wood because that is the material historically used. Fine carved wood moldings are frequently used (Figure 14.19a-c). Resin and composition moldings are often combined with wood trims in interiors that will have painted woodwork because, after painting, the fact that they are not wood is undetectable. Reasons for switching to a non-wood option include price and saving on labor, which also boils down to price. Primed MDF baseboard is a lower-cost option than poplar base. It also saves on priming labor, but does not come presanded, so that step in prep work must still be budgeted. Flexible molding is specified for trimming arches and circular forms. If you have such a need, you may want to select the flexible trim

a

b

c

FIGURE 14.19 Trim products may be materials other than wood or combinations. This crown molding is both solid wood and a composition material, or *compo* as trades sometimes call it. Well-made carving of such an elaborate design would be expensive. An alternative that you see is an embossed detail which does not have the high relief of this compo section. Once this trim is painted it will appear to be a very expensive hand-carved relief when it is a combination of solid wood and compo. *Trim by White River, Fayetteville, Arkansas.*

a

c

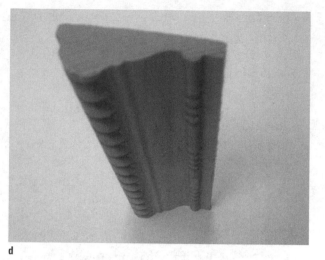

d

b

FIGURE 14.20 The millwork trim industry provides materials for detailing architecture that are produced from a number of materials. Plaster medallion and resin corbel bracket imitate wood but are made of other materials that are intended for a painted finish. Mantelpieces are available in standard sizes that are likely to fit prefab fireplaces but could be customized or modified to accommodate custom-build masonry units. Solid wood casing for paint or stain (d). *Products for detailing by White River, Fayetteville, Arkansas.*

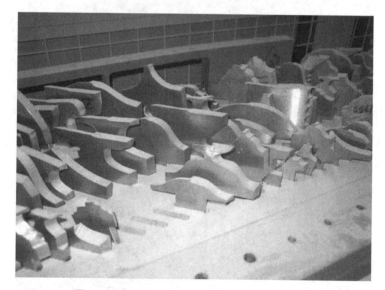

FIGURE 14.21 These custom knives were cut to provide specific profiles for wood edges. The knives are fitted into a sleeve that rotates them at high speed. They slice a solid wood block into the negative of their shape.

profile first because the selection is more limited, then proceed with other selections that will be compatible with the flexible molding. Special items like domes, niche shells, mantles, and others are widely available. Companies that handle millwork trim may also carry plaster ceiling medallions and fireplace mantles (Figure 14.20a-d).

Custom profiles can be milled in wood for small orders because the cost of cutting a knife is small (Figure 14.21). When a custom profile is needed, you will need to add about $300 to the budget for the knife, which is a small enough percentage of the whole job. It pays for itself when matching existing profiles that are to remain by avoiding the need to remove and destroy existing molding throughout to achieve a match.

You may forward your selections to the architect for inclusion in his or her material schedules or forward them in your own material schedules. The exact sizes and profiles will be shown on your elevations, but if you have any compound moldings (such as the four-piece molding in Figure 14.18r), a dimensioned drawing should be included with your drawing set.

CHAPTER 15

carpets and rugs

This chapter covers carpets and area rugs. The distinction between the two topics lies in their predominant methods of manufacture. There is also the assumption that carpet is fastened from wall to wall as a surfacing material and that area rugs lie loosely. There is a little crossover between the two, but these distinctions should help you organize the information generally in your mind.

Fibers

Carpet provides sound absorbency and thermal insulation properties superior to other floor surfacing materials. It is considered a textile and is made from the same fibers from which other textiles are made.

Wool

Wool is generally considered the most expensive fiber choice for carpets. (Although silk is more costly, it is not typically used.) In terms of quality, wool is the standard by which other fibers are measured. It is soft and resilient and can be bleached and dyed to any color. It is naturally stain-resistant (not stain-proof) and is naturally flame-resistant. It ages gracefully. Although nylon is often more abrasion-resistant and more durable, in terms of appearance, it will "ugly out" before it wears out. In contrast, wool attains a patina of age that many people find acceptable. Wool is subject to static electricity; in some installations, it may require special treatment to combat this.

People with chemical sensitivities will be interested in the kind of pest-repellant treatment that has been applied to the carpet to deter moths. Some people are sensitive to wool itself. If crushing of fibers is the most likely kind of abuse that the carpet will suffer (flattening from footfalls, relocation of furniture within the room, etc.) and price is not a restriction, then wool would be a good choice for the area.

Nylon

Nylon is considered the most durable fiber in terms of abrasion resistance. It also resists mildew, moths, and mold. It is hydrophobic, that is, it does not easily absorb water and waterborne stains. Nylon has been around since the 1940s and has been developed and improved over time. You may hear fibers described as first-, second-, third-, fourth-, fifth-, and sixth-generation nylon—with each generation improving upon the preceding generations:

- Second-generation fiber hides soiling.
- Third generation improves soil-hiding ability, delusters the yarns (so they aren't as glittery), and reduces the static buildup problem.
- Fourth generation makes yarn soil-resistant and introduces antimicrobial treatments, for use in hospital and sports facilities.

- Fifth generation yarn allows easier cleaning once it becomes soiled.
- Sixth generation makes the carpet more resilient and stronger.

Nylon is naturally subject to the accumulation of static electricity. Fiber engineering has produced carpets especially constructed to reduce static buildup. Nylon is unlikely to cause an allergic reaction; after it has had a chance to outgas, it is safe for use by most people with chemical sensitivities. Unless it is solution-dyed, it can fade in sunlight.

Olefin

Olefin has good resistance to waterborne stains because it is hydrophobic, but it has an affinity for oil-borne stains because it is oleophillic. It offers good fade resistance because it is solution-dyed, which means the color is introduced into the "soup" from which the yarn filaments are spun. Olefin is durable against abrasion, but it crushes easily and relies on construction to overcome this problem (low dense loop construction is typical). Olefin is a relatively cheap choice compared to other fibers.

Acrylics

Acrylic fiber is soft and resilient and compares well to wool in many characteristics. It has low abrasion resistance and can sometimes pill. It can be solution-dyed, making it resistant to fading. It is mostly used as a component in blends.

Polyester

Polyester is soft, dyes well, and resists fading and wear, but it has poor resilience and relies on high density to overcome this weakness. Because it has a "high bulk," some manufacturers skimp on the density. Low-density carpets show crushing as the yarns "fall over," showing their sides. It can be made from recycled plastic bottles.

Cotton

Cotton is soft and dyeable, but it's subject to wear and it stains easily. It is uncommon in carpet because of its wear and staining weaknesses, but it is irresistibly soft under bare feet. Any carpet will suffer if cleaned improperly, and cotton must be cleaned carefully. When cleaned with water and air-dried, cotton fibers clump together, so it can be difficult to restore the carpet's appearance—get cleaning instructions from the manufacturer and pass them along to your client.

Linen

Linen is another less typical fiber for carpet, but you will encounter it, often in combination with wool. Linen is strong and dyes well. Make sure you get specific cleaning instructions from the manufacturer. Linen, like cotton, must be carefully cleaned because it is especially fussy and can easily mat or flatten after being cleaned with water.

Silk

Silk, as found in broadloom, is typically part of the patterning in a wool carpet. While silk is a strong fiber, it is not resilient. The luster and fine denier is used decoratively as a contrast to the carpet's field.

Jute

Jute fiber also has an affinity for dyes, so many bright colors are available. As with sisal (see below), natural jute varies in color from light tans to browns. When exposed to sunlight, jute can change color. It can be cleaned by shampooing or dry-cleaning.

Seagrass

Seagrass (Figure 15.1a) is a popular natural fiber that is also woven into area rugs. Seagrass can be recognized by its grassy, haylike scent and coloring, which dissipate with time. Colors range from sage-green hues to olive. It has a naturally smooth texture and sheen.

Sisal

Sisal (Figure 15.1c) is often used wall to wall. As a natural fiber, it is subject to pests and to crushing, and it can he degraded and stained by water-borne solutions. Natural sisal has a wide range of color variations, which depend not only on the origin of the fiber but also on the time of year it was harvested, with spring harvests being a little greener than later harvests. The color changes over time; the greenness fades to a "straw" color, but spring harvests may stay a little greener than fall harvests. These fibers can be dyed and stenciled to color and decorate them, but they are frequently left natural. Sisal is a little scratchy under bare feet.

Fabrication Characteristics

The two most prominent considerations in the construction of carpet are the yarn and the construction method.

Yarn

Synthetic fibers are processed before being spun into carpet yarn. The acronym BCF stands for *bulked continuous filament* and refers to synthetic fibers in a continuous form for perhaps miles long. These long fibers are gathered into yarn bundles and texturized to increase bulk and cover. Texturizing changes the straight filaments into kinked or curled configurations. BCF fibers are twisted and bulked before being heat-set.

BULKING *Bulking* is processing yarn to fluff it up and give more coverage with the same weight. Bulking also adds to fiber resiliency. Crimping creates bulk in individual filaments by creating a saw-tooth, zigzag, or random curl relative to the fiber.

Staple fibers are chopped-up BCFs, rather than a continuous filament. They arrive at the carpet mill in bales, very large cubical bundles like cotton bales. The bales are opened up and blended with other bales of staple to ensure uniformity. The fibers are "carded," spun, and twisted with other strands of yarn to make the final yarn.

PLY Ply refers to the number of individual strands twisted together. Single and multi-ply yarns are heat-set to make the new texture permanent. The number of plies and the amount of twist that is set into the yarn contributes to its

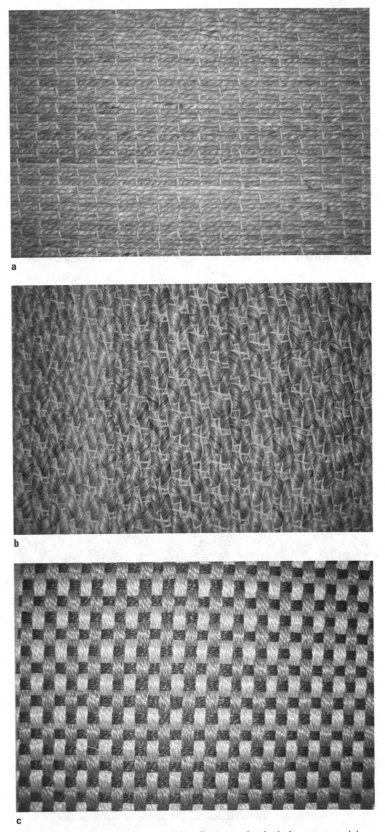

FIGURE 15.1 Plant-based fibers used as floorcovering include: seagrass (a), abaca (b), and sisal (c). Seagrass is sometimes called water hyacinth—a pest plant that clogs waterways in the Far East but is now being put to good use when harvested for floorcovering. Abaca, which comes from banana leaves, presents a lot of natural variation in its fiber. Sisal is a scratchy fiber but a tight, flat weave like this one will minimize that quality.

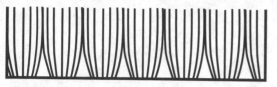

FIGURE 15.2 A low-twist yarn is used to produce a carpet quality referred to as velvet, which shows traffic patterns readily.

FIGURE 15.4 High-twist yarns are the most obscuring when it comes to showing footfall in traffic areas. They maintain an acceptable appearance more naturally than lower-twist yarns.

FIGURE 15.3 Velvet plush construction has a smooth, formal appearance in which individual tufts are less distinct. A medium twist is generally referred to as Saxony plush (as shown above), in which individual yarn tufts are more distinguishable.

appearance and performance. Velvet plush uses a low-twist yarn (Figure 15.2). A high-twist yarn shows less evidence of traffic than low-twist, so foot traffic leaves lots of shoeprints on velvet. The Saxony plush (Figure 15.3) will show fewer footprints than the velvet plush (Figure 15.4) and the frieze will show the least of all due to the increased twist.

In addition to fiber characteristics, yarn gets some of its characteristics from the denier (thickness of the yarn) and the number of plies (number of yarns that are twisted together) (Figure 15.5a-c). Increasing the number of plies produces a thicker yarn with greater resilience or memory. This has a big impact on the appearance of the carpet. Dense construction of small-denier yarns, such as the single-ply yarns used in velvet plush, will produce carpet with an elegant, formal aesthetic. It will show every footprint. Thicker denier, multi-ply yarns will produce a carpet that's grainier in appearance, less formal, and better at camouflaging footprints. These types of yarns also add to the resilience of the goods.

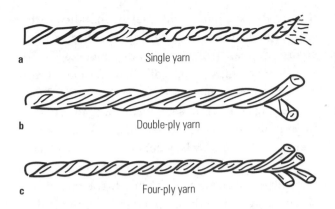

a   Single yarn

b   Double-ply yarn

c   Four-ply yarn

FIGURE 15.5 The number of yarns twisted together is referred to as ply—single-ply yarn (a), double-ply yarn (b), and four-ply yarn (c).

Construction Methods

Carpet is manufactured by a variety of processes, each of which yields a product with different characteristics.

TUFTING Most of the broad loom carpet manufactured in the United States is tufted. The face yarns are looped through the backing and then sealed in place with latex or some similar secondary backing. A tufting machine is usually 12 feet wide with hundreds of needles that punch loops of yarn into the primary backing. The tufting machine produces a level loop, multilevel loop, cut pile, and cut-and-loop pile.

A looper forms the pile and determines the pile height. Loopers with a cutting knife attached are used to produce cut-pile or plush carpet. A loop-pile machine does not have knives, so it leaves the loops uncut. Structures are sheered after tufting is complete (Figure 15.6a-c).

WEAVING Woven carpets use the most expensive method of construction. The backing and the face are produced simultaneously. Complex patterns are possible with woven carpets. The three most important weaving methods for carpet are Axminster, velvet, and Wilton.

An Axminster loom has control over each tuft of yarn making up the carpet. Axminster carpets are usually complicated designs and are always cut-pile. Spools of yarn that feed the loom can hold different colors and even different kinds of yarn.

a

b

c

FIGURE 15.6 The way carpet is sheered or not sheered is defined by general terms. Looped face (a) means that the loops are not sheered at all. Uncut loops create the surface. Random sheered (b) means just what the name implies: Loops are randomly cut. Various qualities of sheering (c) refer to the examples where the upper left is loop-face, the upper right is random sheered, the lower left is loop-and-cut pile, and the lower right is a cut-pile velvet. *Sample pad courtesy of Watson Smith Carpets.*

In the velvet loom, the pile yarn loops are formed over "wires," one wire for each row of tufts. The wires are then pulled out, leaving a row of tufts. A knife blade, similar to a razor blade, may be attached to the end of the wire. As the wire is extracted, the tuft is cut to form a cut-pile carpet. If no blade is attached, the carpet remains a loop pile.

The Wilton loom regulates the delivery of pile yarns into the loom to form a pattern. Sculptured carpets are made by controlling pile height and by cutting or not cutting, leaving loops.

FLOCKING Short fiber called flock is adhered, usually by electrostatic processes, to a base fabric, creating a very short pile material with a velour texture. A secondary backing adds body and dimensional stability. A few flocked carpets are made for bedrooms and bathrooms, but most are used in vehicles: cars, planes, and buses. The short fiber and construction resist the appearance of crushing.

FUSION BONDING Fusion-bonded carpet has yarns that are inserted into liquid vinyl, which hardens, locking the yarn in place. It is especially applicable to the production of carpet tiles.

KNITTING The knitting process loops yarn in a manner similar to hand knitting, then a coat of latex and secondary backing material is applied to the fabric back to provide dimensional stability. Variations in color, pattern, and texture are possible in knit carpet.

NEEDLE-PUNCHED Needle-punched carpet is made by barbed felting needles punching batting into a base fabric. This forms a flat felted-looking carpet mainly used for indoor-outdoor carpeting and some carpet tiles. A coating of weather-resistant latex or similar material is applied to the back.

Modular Tiles

Usually available in 18–36-inch tiles with PVC backings, modular units are convenient over raised access flooring because individual tiles can be removed to allow access to cabling and electrical connections under the raised flooring. Tiles also allow for easy replacement in heavy-traffic locations without the disruption that would come with having to remove all the furniture in an area

to replace broadloom. They may be installed with regular adhesives or peel-and-stick adhesive strips; they can also be simply dry laid.

Tile backing systems can also offer moisture barriers from the base of the pile yarn to the floor, preventing spills from seeping down to the subfloor. In modular tiles, as well as with broadloom, a moisture barrier may be valuable in humid areas or health-care environments, where spills are inevitable and cleaning is frequent. The moisture barrier provided by the carpet itself and the sealing technique used for the seams may lessen the potential for bacterial growth and provide lower long-term maintenance costs.

Construction Measurements

The three main descriptive measurements for carpet are gauge (width), stitch rate (length), and pile height (height).

Gauge

Gauge is the distance between the needles. For example, $\frac{1}{8}$ gauge simply means there is $\frac{1}{8}$ inch between each needle or there are eight needles per inch of width.

Stitch Rate

Stitch rate (or stitches per inch or SPI) defines the number of times per inch a stitch occurs, just as gauge expresses the frequency of tufts across the width. Stitch rate is the number of times an individual needle inserts a tuft into the primary backing as the primary backing moves one inch through the tufting machine. Therefore, eight stitches per inch means that, as the primary backing moves through the tufting machine, a single needle forms eight tufts or stitches per inch.

Pile Height

Pile height is the length (expressed in decimal parts of one inch) of the tuft from the primary backing to the tip. All other factors being equal, a carpet with a higher pile height will possess more yarn on the wearing surface and may possibly be more durable.

Other Measurements

A number of other measurements are related to carpet construction:

- *Denier or yarn denier:* Unit of weight for the size of a single filament or yarn bundle. The higher the denier, the heavier (thicker) the yarn and the more resilience it will offer, but also the coarser it will be.
- *Density or pile density:* The weight of a pile yarn (including portions in the backing) in a unit volume of carpet is expressed in ounces per cubic yard. Also called "average pile yarn weight." The closer the tufts are to one another, the denser the pile. All other things being equal, the greater the pile density, the greater the wearability of the carpet and the longer it will last.
- *Face (or pile) weight:* The total weight of the face yarns in the carpet. The more ounces per square yard, the denser the pile and, potentially, the greater the wearability of the carpet.
- *Twist:* Twist is the process whereby two or more spun yarns are twisted together. Twist is counted by the number of turns per inch (TPI) of the yarn. The performance of cut-pile carpet is dependent on the rate of twist and twist retention. Heat-setting helps stabilize yarn twist by subjecting the yarn to high-temperature steam under pressure. A high twist will result in a frieze, a medium twist will produce a Saxony, and low twist will result in a velour or Saxony plush style. Loop pile styles have closed loops, so twist is not a major factor.
- *Tuft bind:* Tuft bind is the relative strength of the attachment of the yarn loops to the backing of the carpet.

Colors and Patterns

Fibers are dyed by a few different methods. They can be categorized as pre-dyed and post-dyed. Pre-dyed methods include the following:

- *Solution-dyeing:* The "soup" that synthetic fibers are made from is colored before the material is made into fibers.
- *Stock-dyeing:* The fibers are dumped into a vat and dyed before they are made into yarn and sold to the carpet manufacturer.

- *Skein-dyeing:* The yarns are dyed. This is a more expensive way of coloring carpets but is typical of custom carpets.
- *Space-dyeing:* This produces random color distribution as yarn is wound and printed with three colors in stripes: The overlap of colors gives the effect of more colors. Warp yarns can also be space-dyed, but colors are less random. Space-dyed yarns are often found in loop-style contract carpets.

Post-dyed carpet is dyed after the goods are made into carpeting. The following are post-dyed methods:

- *Beck-dyeing:* This is primarily for solid colors. This method is performed after tufting but before other finishing processes (such as attaching the secondary backing). Large rolls in rope form of uncolored carpet (greige goods) are placed in a large vat of dye solution (dye beck), heated to high temperatures, agitated continually while it is soaking up the dye, making the color come out very even from end to end and side to side. It is then removed, washed, and dried. This is most commonly used for cut-pile carpet.
- *Piece-dyeing:* Carpet is dyed after it is made up. This is common for residential carpet, which is not as dense as commercial carpet and for which smaller quantities can be dyed as needed.
- *Continuous-dyeing:* Greige goods (undyed carpet) are rinsed, and then passed under a dye applicator, which spreads or sprays dyes evenly across the entire width of the carpet. The carpet then enters a steam chamber, where the dyes are "set" into the fibers. This method is for longer runs of both solid and multicolor applications.
- *Printing:* Much as from an ink-jet printer, colors are sprayed from closely spaced jets. Pattern changes are made on the computer, so no screens are required. Removing screens from the process eliminates the possibility of crushing, which was a problem with screened patterns.
- *Differential-dyeing:* Tufted carpet with yarns chemically treated so that when placed in a dye bath, each yarn type will react differently

to the dye, resulting in different shades of the same color.

Backing

The primary backing into which the tufts are inserted may be made of jute, kraftcord (yarn made from twisted craft paper), cotton, and woven or nonwoven synthetics. The most common primary backing material is polypropylene.

Latex is applied to the back of the carpet. As the carpet passes under the puddle of latex, a blade forces the latex down and around all the yarn on the back of the carpet, which locks the yarn into the primary backing. A second coat of latex is applied to hold the secondary backing onto the tufted material, which gives the carpet its dimensional stability. The new carpet smell is from a by-product of the latex.

Dimensional stability, primarily imparted by the secondary backing, is the ability of carpet to retain its size and shape after installation.

Traditionally, secondary backing was made of jute. Jute backing has several major problems, such as the potential for browning and rotting. Most secondary backing today is woven polypropylene.

Durability

Durability is often categorized in terms of residential and commercial and traffic. Residential-grade carpet is for lower-traffic situations, while it is generally understood that a commercial grade will be more durable. Within these two broad differentiations, there are traffic categories. Light, medium, and heavy categories will depend on assessments that you will have to make regarding the kind of use and abuse that an area will receive. For instance, a light-use residential application may include stairs. Stairs suffer more abuse in normal usage, so you may upgrade a light-use classification to medium or heavy to accommodate the stairs. You may take other precautions to protect the life cycle of the installation, perhaps ordering extra carpet for the stairs, folding one tread depth under the first riser, and then shifting the risers to the treads at some point in the future.

Custom carpeting can be specified when your need is very specific. Minimum dollar or minimum quantity restrictions will often come into play. Often, suppliers will have samples of different qualities that can be done up in wool in custom colors and the variety available is impressive. Commercial goods can often be ordered through custom programs in combinations of stock colors. Often, custom goods can be wider than 12 feet.

Carpet Life Cycle

Carpet is degraded by grit and dirt, which is a special problem because carpet traps the grit that will eventually abrade the fibers and wear them out. Regular vacuuming is required for durability as much as for general cleanliness. In addition to vacuuming, carpet maintenance should include the following:

- Keep outdoor areas clean so less soil is tracked into the carpeted area. Shovel to clear snow and ice rather than relying on chemicals or sand.
- Use mats, grates, or removable rugs in track-off areas. The rug should be big enough to require two or three steps to cross.
- Place chair pads under desks to prevent dirt from being ground into carpet. Restrict food and beverage consumption (and spills) to specific areas.
- Maintain the HVAC system, changing filters frequently. That will help remove particles from the air and prevent them from ending up in the carpet.

The life cycle of carpeting depends upon the kind of traffic an area is subjected to, on the carpet itself, and on the regular maintenance it receives. The cost of selecting carpet versus another floor surfacing encompasses more than just the cost of new carpet (materials and installation). Also figure in the cost of maintenance and replacement costs. The cost of regular maintenance (rigorous regular vacuuming and spot cleaning) has been proven to be lower than the cost of periodic chemical cleaning without the benefit of regular maintenance. The International Sanitary Supply Association estimates that it costs approximately $500.00 to remove one pound of dirt from carpet in a commercial environment. Because carpet can be maintained by unskilled labor using simple equipment, the cost of maintaining carpet is actually lower than the cost of maintaining most other floorcoverings. Maintenance cost can be reduced further by installing midtoned or multicolored carpets, which show less soil and lint than pale or dark colors. Pale colors tend to show soiling, while dark colors tend to show lint and debris.

Allergens and Carpet

People with allergies are sometimes unable to tolerate carpeting for the simple reason that it traps a lot of dirt and becomes a veritable jungle of dust mites and microbes, which thrive on shed skin cells and the other foods available to them, even in the cleanest of environments. Generally, the denser the carpet is, the more soil-resistant it will be because dirt cannot fall down into the pile as easily. Some people are allergic to wool. Synthetic fibers will be more hypoallergenic and resistant to consumption by moths or other pests.

People with chemical sensitivities must contend with the outgassing of VOCs from the fibers of the carpet and the padding, as well as the adhesives in glue-down installations. Additional chemicals are purposely applied to carpets for stain, microbe, and static resistance. Because the manufacturers want the properties instilled to be lasting, they are chemically formulated to endure (unlike the VOCs, which may outgas relatively quickly, leaving the carpet tolerable). Carpet can function as a "sink," accumulating VOCs that have been released from other sources. It also traps small particulates that might otherwise be airborne and find their way into people's lungs.

Appearance Retention

For appearance retention, dense carpet with a low pile height is best. This information is provided by the manufacturer for close comparisons, but this is also something that you can discern to some extent by sticking the ends of your fingers down into the pile during initial selection because you can feel the difference.

Too much carpeting ends up in landfills every year. Responsible manufacturers have devised ways of minimizing this through carpet lease programs, recycling programs, and the restoration and resale of used carpet, as well as through recycling.

Kinds of Pads

The correct pad extends the life of the carpet and improves maintenence. When selecting a pad, it is a good idea to put a piece of the padding under the carpet on a hard surface and test the two together. When a cheap pad is used, not only is the installation hard underfoot, but the tape used to seam the carpet can telegraph every seam location through highlighting. Always specify good padding or ask for a sample of the padding that the installer intends to use.

Generally speaking, the firmer the pad, the less strain the carpet backing will have to endure; the softer the pad, the less crushing will occur on the face of the carpet. So, a happy medium is your goal in selecting the perfect pad for the carpet and for client preferences relative to the way it feels underfoot.

In selecting and specifying pads, it is advisable to consult with the manufacturer and installer. Do not allow the installation of a pad that you believe is inappropriate or of poor quality, but remember that you want the manufacturer to warranty the goods and the installer to guarantee the installation, and this includes the performance of the padding selected. If two pads are equal in quality and the installer is partial to one of them, you would likely be wise to concede to the installer's preferences rather than make yourself responsible for the life of the padding.

Waffle Rubber

The waffle part of the padding gives it a thickness that is mostly air (Figure 15.7), and as a result, any of this type of padding rated less than 90 ounces is still too soft for today's plastic-backed carpets. Also, the rubber used to make these pads may contain clay-type binders that break down with use. Rub your thumb over the surface of a rubber pad and make sure that it

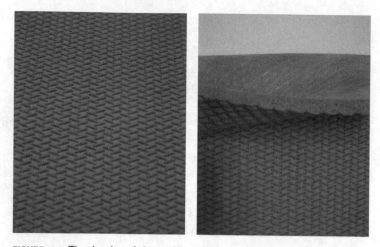

FIGURE 15.7 The density of the waffle pad is variable with more air in some portions. The fibrous topping allows the carpet to slide over the surface as it is stretched into place. *Sample pad courtesy of Watson Smith Carpets.*

FIGURE 15.8 The foam pad is an economy selection for light traffic areas. *Sample pad courtesy of Watson Smith Carpets.*

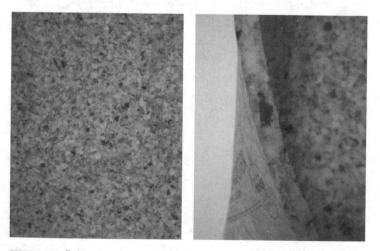

FIGURE 15.9 Rebond can be made from production waste foam and various densities are possible. It is often the standard offering if no pad is specified. *Sample pad courtesy of Watson Smith Carpets.*

doesn't break down easily. A better pad will not crumble.

Slab Rubber

Unlike the waffle rubber padding, slab rubber does not contain big ripples of air. This pad feels much like 7-pound rebond, but will resist furniture indentation and crushing for a much longer period of time.

Foam Padding

This type of padding is made from urethane foam and is available in different densities and thicknesses. Generally, this type of pad is recommended for light traffic only. Urethane foam may be a homogenous foam or a composite of shredded foams bonded to a "skin," (see Rebond below) which can be a fiber or a plastic that allows the carpet to slide as it is stretched over the padding (Figure 15.8).

Rebond

Rebond padding (Figure 15.9) is used most often by the floor-covering industry. It is made from scraps of the high-density foams used in furniture making that are bonded together. Rebond padding comes in various thicknesses and densities. The density is rated at so many pounds per cubic foot. For example, a 5-pound rebond pad would weigh 5 pounds per cubic foot. The Carpet and Rug Institute (CRI) recommends at least a 5-pound pad that's ⅜ inch thick for light residential traffic, and a 6-pound pad that's ⅜ inch thick for heavy residential traffic.

Fiber

Fiber pads are used when one wants to limit the movement in a piece of carpet. This pad can be made from jute, or hair mixed with jute, or synthetic fiber, or recycled textile fiber. It should be between ⅜ and ⁷⁄₁₆ inch thick. Fiber is felted, which produces a firm-feeling pad. Originally made out of animal hair, they are often synthetic fibers although they are sometimes referred to as "hair" or rubberized hair. This is a relatively expensive kind of pad.

Frothed Foam

Superdense urethane (Figure 15.10) is approximately 5/16-inch thick and extremely durable. This pad (Figure 15.11) has virtually no VOC offgassing; can be used under all carpets; and will reduce furniture indentations and prolong the life of your carpet better than any rebond, fiber, waffle rubber, or prime foam. It costs about the same as a good slab rubber padding and should last as long.

Installation of Carpet

The following installation methods apply to broadloom. The glue-in methods also pertain to tiles.

Tackless Method

In the tackless method, thin strips of wood (usually plywood) with rows of small "teeth" are nailed or glued around the perimeter of the area to be carpeted. Padding is laid down within the area defined by the tack strips and the carpet is stretched into place by means of a power stretcher or knee kickers. The excess carpet is cut off and the cut edge is poked down in between the strip and the wall. Sometimes, a baseboard or other molding is installed afterwards, but before specifying this kind of installation, consider the difficulties in replacing the carpet if the trim must be removed to accomplish the replacement.

Glue-Down Method

Carpet with or without any integral padding is glued directly to the floor. This is a good installation for gyms or areas where carts or equipment will be moved frequently. Double glue-down installations have the pad glued to the floor and the carpet glued to the pad. If this kind of installation is required, let the installer know prior to the specification of the pad. When installing glue-down, confirm the offgassing adhesive will not cause a problem for anyone (people with chemical sensitivities) or anything (the bouquet of wine can be ruined by the offgassing glues) in the environment.

FIGURE 15.10 Dense urethane foam padding is considered an upgraded, premium pad. *Sample pad courtesy of Watson Smith Carpets.*

FIGURE 15.11 This very firm, low-VOC pad addresses the increasing awareness of the damage done to living systems like human bodies by volatile organic compounds. The elderly and young children are the most vulnerable, so this is a pad that you may specify in spaces where children will spend time on the floor.

Installation on Stairs

Installation methods for stairs include waterfall (Figure 15.12), where the carpet is effectively one continuous run from top to bottom, and tacked at the back of each tread at the bottom of each riser.

Installation on curved stairs might require that each riser-tread unit be cut independently of other riser-tread units or that risers and treads are each cut independently and secured under the nosing, at the bottom of each riser at the back of each tread. This method of installing carpet on stairs is called cap and band.

An installation of a single continuous piece that has the tailored appearance of cap and band

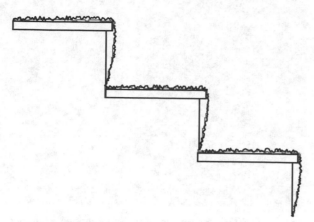

FIGURE 15.12 Waterfall installation on stairs shows the profile of the carpet installation tacked at the crook between the riser and the tread.

FIGURE 15.13 Hollywood or cap and band will have the same appearance in profile because both are tacked under the nosing and in the crook between the riser and the tread.

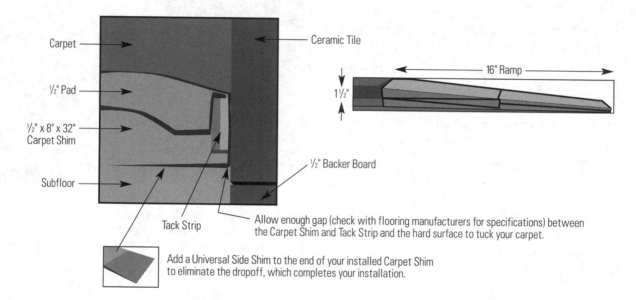

Carpet

Ceramic Tile

½" Pad

½" x 8" x 32" Carpet Shim

16" Ramp

1½"

½" Backer Board

Subfloor

Tack Strip

Allow enough gap (check with flooring manufacturers for specifications) between the Carpet Shim and Tack Strip and the hard surface to tuck your carpet.

Add a Universal Side Shim to the end of your installed Carpet Shim to eliminate the dropoff, which completes your installation.

FIGURE 15.14 Carpet shims by Carpet Shims Ltd. can ramp from a thin carpet to a thicker floor surfacing in a retrofit situation when the substrate cannot economically be altered. *Image by Carpet Shims Ltd.*

is called Hollywood (Figure 15.13). For a Hollywood installation, carpet is tacked under the nosing and in the crook between the riser and the tread. The way cap and band and Hollywood are tacked creates a similar appearance.

One common complication when remodeling an interior is that subfloors are already established, which makes adjoining materials of varying thicknesses a little more complicated. When a thin carpet must abut a thicker material surface, there are ways to "boost" the carpet up to have a better relationship with the companion floor. One way to handle the difference is to "float the floor up" with a cement-type product. Ideally, the area under a thinner carpet will be floated so that it is still level throughout the space but "lifted" to bring the carpet level with the adjoining surface. A cement product could also be ramped up to the thicker material, spanning a distance that would minimize perception of the change. Carpet shims may be purchased to ramp up to the thicker flooring adjacent to the carpet (Figure 15.14).

Installation of Carpet Tiles

Carpet tiles may be loose-laid or glued down. Whether or not they are glued in, you will want to specify the positioning and arrangement of the tiles.

Plan the positioning and orientation of the carpet tiles on a to-scale plan (Figure 15.15). The product that you select will be available in set sizes that will, ideally, allow for full tiles throughout. This is rarely possible so, just as with other tile products (stone, ceramic, resilient), plan the location of cut tiles as you position the product in your plan. It is common practice to begin the tile installation in the center of the space and work outward toward the perimeter, but this is not a hard and fast rule and the conditions at the site may indicate a different starting point. The manufacturer may recommend a specific match based on the pattern. Very simple photo-management software makes it easy to duplicate a digital image of the tile and repeat it to confirm that a particular orientation will yield the effect you want (Figure 15.16a and b).

Carpet Services Available

During the course of ordering carpet, you will probably engage the services of a measurer who will determine the quantity to be ordered, a supplier who will sell the carpet, and an installer who will receive the carpet, seam it, and install it over a pad, which the installer will most often supply. These services can all be supplied by the same shop.

Generally the process goes something like this:

The carpet is selected and to-scale plans are sent to the suppliers from whom you are requesting a bid. The suppliers use these

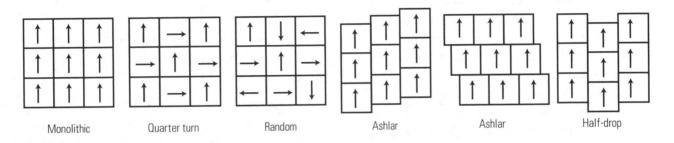

Monolithic Quarter turn Random Ashlar Ashlar Half-drop

FIGURE 15.15 Carpet tiles offer not only the benefits of modularity for replacement and reconfiguration but also additional design flexibility because individual units can be arranged with differing relationships between the tiles. In order from appearance: Monolithic, Quarter Turn, Random, Ashlar, Ashlar, and Half-Drop.

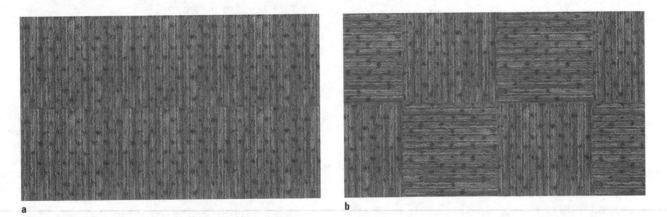

a b

FIGURE 15.16 The same carpet tile can achieve a variety of looks. These two patterns were easily investigated by shooting a digital image and using simple photo-management software to try out these two options for arrangement. Pattern a is monolithic; pattern b is a quarter turn, creating a checkerboard effect.

plans for estimating yardage and labor charges if they will also install the goods. They will need to know what the goods are (including width, repeat, and match) and about any special conditions at the site, such as the following:

- If they must be prepared to move furniture.
- If the access to the space will make it difficult to move large rolls of carpet into the space, etc.
- If the floor contains a radiant heat system that must not be disrupted by fasteners.
- If adjacent flooring is thicker, which would necessitate ramping or carpet shims (see Figure 15.14).
- If the floor must be patched, leveled, or sealed.
- If stair installation is wall-to-wall or runner with bound edges, and if treads and spindles must be wrapped.

Do not omit any special requirements from your bid requests to installers working up estimates. You will be billed for all additional work required and of course it is better to know all charges up front. Installers will sometimes bid just the installation, with additional work performed on a time and materials basis. The time-and-materials approach always has the potential risk of escalating the price significantly. It is a good idea to explore all likely total costs up front to make sure that the installation as described in the bid request is in line with your budget. Even if installers are reluctant to quote the additional work on the bid, they should be able to give you a good ballpark notion of the probable cost of all the work requested.

Reviewing the Bids

Bids should include not only quantities and descriptions of the materials and labor but also a seaming diagram that shows the location of the seams and the direction of the carpet. Carpet has a grain that sometimes produces a definite light and dark side, so all goods must run in the same direction. Confirm quantities and evaluate the appropriateness of padding, installation methods, and fasteners. Are special services noted and priced (furniture moving, disposal of old carpet,

storage instructions for large leftover pieces to be kept for patching, etc.) and is the seaming diagram correct?

Checking the Seaming Diagram

You will want the fewest seams that are practical, given the space and the carpet dimensions. Seams should be in inconspicuous places, such as in closets, under areas planned for large pieces of furniture, and away from bright light and windows. You want the seams placed in low-stress locations, away from doorways and other major traffic areas; if seams must fall within traffic areas, they will be less vulnerable if they run parallel to traffic rather than perpendicular to it. The goods should run parallel to traffic on stairs. You want to avoid seams in any location where traffic will change direction because this will stress the carpet, making the seam more obvious.

Estimating

Estimating is most easily done on a to-scale plan. The following illustrates a method for estimating broadloom accurately:

1. Draw the goods onto the plan in scale, showing the correct width and the seam locations to derive the running feet of carpeting needed (as it comes off the roll). Remember, you have to buy the full carpet width even if you don't need it, so the required length of goods will be multiplied by the width of the goods, not by the width of the room.
2. Lay out the width of the stairs and see how many stair widths you can fit on one width of carpet. If the stairs curve (so they are wider at one side than the other), use the deepest part of the tread in your calculation. Running all goods in the same direction on curved stairs means carpet on each tread has the same relationship to the tread, with the grain parallel to the traffic direction. You may want to draw each pie-shape tread on a to-scale pattern repeat as illustrated in Figure 15.17 to be sure of quantity.
3. Measure the height and width of the treads and risers and multiply that number by the

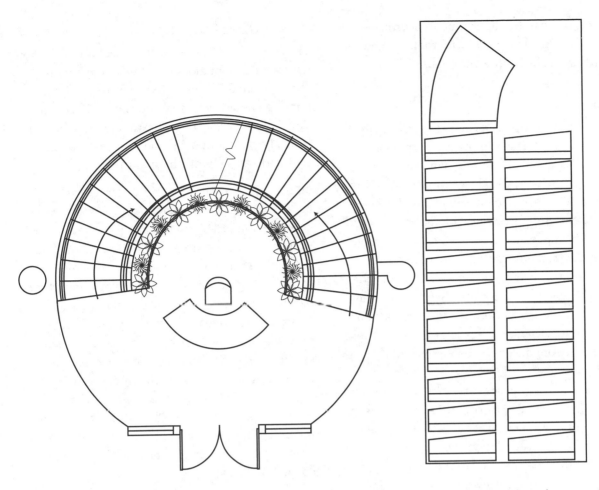

FIGURE 15.17 These diagrams illustrate an estimation of carpet on stairs. Carpet must run continuously on the grain even as the stairs curve for aesthetic and durability reasons. This installation would be cap and band.

number of steps to get the lineal feet of carpeting required for the stairs.

4. Divide that number (from item 3, above) by the number of stair widths you can get out of a single width of carpet (from item 2). This will give you the running feet of goods required for the stairs.

5. Add the stair running feet of goods to the rest of the running feet of goods (add 4 and 1). Remember to round up to full pattern repeats.

6. Multiply the running feet by the width of the goods to get square feet and divide that number by 9 to get square yards.

Area Rugs

Construction and options vary greatly among rugs in this category—including everything from pile rugs to tapestries; canvas that is painted or stained; animal skins dyed, stenciled, or natural;

rag rugs in all kinds of "scrap" cloth or leather or suede; felted rugs; and many others.

The major classifier in this area distinguishes between handmade and machine-made products. As a general rule, handmade product is considered the higher-quality option, even though it usually lacks the "perfection" of machine-made product. Handmade product generally starts out at a higher price point and retains more value over time.

Many custom options exist among handmade rugs. Artists working in the different techniques are often willing to work on commissions to create your designs, as well as to create or modify some standards among their own designs in alignment with the needs of your client's space. This process is more easily controlled when the designer works and communicates directly with the rug-maker, but custom rug specifications can be communicated with success through your local vendors, who then communicate with weavers in other locales.

Finding a Rug

The best way to shop for a rug is to visit rug dealers that you trust. Have your floor plan, fabric, and finish samples in hand. Depending on the job, your client, and your usual working relationship, you may make arrangements to bring likely possibilities to the site for review. You may collect photos of the best possibilities to send to your client. Take any fabric samples with you and shoot a photo with the fabric lying on the rug so the client can see the color relationships. Bring a tape measure to confirm the accuracy of the sizes listed on tags. Photos and sizes are required 1) as a comparison of rugs from different resources and 2) for an initial review by the client.

If you exhaust the resources in your area and still do not have the right rug, this item is easy to buy from a more distant resource. Usually, new rugs are more universal, and the new rugs in New York are going to be similar to the new rugs you will find in Chicago. However, for semi-antique and antique rugs, it might even pay to extend your search to other cities while you are shopping locally. Call dealers in other cities that carry the kind of rug you are looking for; describe as precisely as you can what it is you need, even talking about the rugs that you found locally that were *almost* right and listing the things that made them not work, as well as the things that made them near-misses. The dealer will send pictures or rugs for your review. Likely candidates should be shipped in. You will make whatever arrangements both you and the dealer find comfortable. If you have an ongoing relationship with the dealer, he or she may just box up the rugs and send them. If your relationship is new, the dealer may ask for a check or credit card information for security. Dealers may or may not pay for shipping; often, they'll pay for shipping to you and you'll pay the return shipping if you do not keep the rug. Confirm all arrangements and get your client's approval for all charges.

What to Look For

The rug that you select will, first of all, work well with your design and appeal to you and your client; second, it will be in a condition that is durable enough to withstand the environment. This factor will be variable from job to job. Third, it will be of the highest quality available consistent with your client's budget range.

SIZE Size is the first limiting characteristic because rugs are often close approximations of several standard sizes, but many of the examples that you will view are one-of-a-kind items. When planning a room, it is a good idea to plan it around a "standard" size, but as you shop, be prepared to resketch your plan lightly (take a pencil) in alternative sizes that you may see, to determine whether they work. A little larger or smaller selection is to be expected because even handmade rugs produced with the intention of adhering to a standard size can be a little off after final processes are complete. This is a good thing to remember if ordering a rug from a handmade rug program—the size cannot be strictly controlled down to the inch.

Table 15.1 shows standard sizes.

TABLE 15.1	Rug Sizes	
2' × 3'	6' × 9'	10' × 14'
2' × 4'	7' × 10'	12' × 15'
3' × 5'	8' × 10'	12' × 18'
4' × 6'	9' × 12'	13' × 20'
5' × 8'	10' × 13'	14' × 21'

YARN QUALITY Yarn quality depends on the species, environment, and health of the animal used as the source of the fiber, if the fiber is animal hair. Wool should be in good condition, not dried out. You should be able to feel the lanolin on your fingertips. The yarn should feel springy, not "crunchy," when you squeeze it. If an old rug sheds, don't buy it. New rugs may have sheared ends still in the pile, but after a rug is completed, it often goes through a series of washings, and most new rugs will have very little loose fiber in them. A visual inspection of the wool is not going to be enough because there are many post-production treatments called washes that alter the luster. The fact that a rug has been treated or washed is not an indication of overall quality, as rugs of all quality ranges are treated or washed.

If you are not certain that what looks like silk is really silk, remove and burn a small piece of yarn (with the dealer's permission, of course). Mercerized cotton has sometimes been used to create a silk look because it is soft and lustrous, as is silk, but it does not wash up the same. This substitution is acceptable if identified, but rugs change hands a few times en route to their destination and the information may be deleted from the description along the way. Your reputable dealer will have already confirmed the fiber prior to putting the rug on the selling floor. Your reputable dealer will also not object to this test and, if you have doubts, will probably happily perform it for you if your interest is strong and your doubts are genuine. If cotton has been used, confirm cleaning instructions with the dealer because cotton does not always wash up well.

AGE The age of a rug is an important classifier; age adds value to a rug in the same way that it adds value to collectible furniture. The following list provides age classifications for area rugs.

Classification by age:

- 15 years or less = new
- 15–50 years = semi-antique
- 50–75 years = antique
- More than 75 years = classical antique

WEAR If the rug is not new, look at the back to inspect for poor mends. Evaluate whether it is in a condition that will hold up at the site. Check to see how much pile is left. Look at the back for evidence of water damage. Check places where one color transitions to another to see if any of the color has migrated to surrounding areas. Reds are especially prone to color migration (Figure 15.18).

FORMAL ASPECTS OF DESIGN Preferences for the nature of the design are highly personal, but the quality of the design can be evaluated outside of these personal design preferences.

If there is a medallion, it should be centered. Lines that are intended to be straight should be so. If the design uses a repeated motif, it should be fairly uniform, but it need not be slavishly so; small, charming variations that are revealed upon close inspection indicate the handmade process. The design should be well balanced. Lustrous colors are valued among connoisseurs, but fashionably faded colors are generally acceptable. Nomadic rugs often have color changes along the weft. This is called *abrash* and it should be subtle and gradual. Abrash and small asymmetries are common, but they must be attractive and not damaging to the design. If it isn't charming, it's a defect.

CONSTRUCTION ISSUES Look for warp yarns; you should see very little of them and none at all in some weaves. The sides or selvages should be evenly wound. Extra wefts may be inserted into the selvage to stiffen and protect it. Leather strips may be sewn along the edges to keep them flat. The rug should lie flat with fairly straight sides, especially if new. Run your hand over the pile and feel for undulations, which can indicate improper shearing or excessive, harsh washing. The rug's edges should be perpendicular.

KNOT COUNT Knot count is no longer considered the be-all indicator of good quality. Different desired looks are achieved by varying the knot count, but it should support the fineness of the pattern. A fine curve will disappear into "speckles" if the knot count is too low to hold the yarns in the correct location to support the pattern.

COST There is not always a direct relationship between quality and cost. Other factors that may affect cost are design, rarity, and accessibility.

COLOR Compare individual colors in different parts of the rug. Abrash is usually the result of natural dyes, although it is sometimes imitated in rugs with chemical dyes, where color can be more strictly controlled. Some new rugs rely almost entirely on abrash for all their patterning (Figure 15.19).

REPAIRS Look at the back for repairs. It is sometimes impossible to find a well-done repair from

FIGURE 15.18 When reviewing a vintage or antique rug for purchase you are likely to find some small areas where color has migrated. This is an undesirable characteristic and is most likely to show up around patches of red as noted by the arrow.

FIGURE 15.19 Abrash may be incidental or integral to the design. This modern rug relies on the abrash as a significant contribution to the design of the rug. *Copyright 1995, Michaelian & Kohlberg, Inc.*

the face side. Repairs are common and acceptable in older rugs (Figure 15.20a-d), especially if the alternative is a worn area in disrepair! Poorly made repairs can be removed and re-repaired, so a good-quality rug with a poor repair is not an unfixable problem.

Kinds of Area Rugs to Choose From

The kinds of area rugs that you could consider for your project are numerous; only a few of the most popular options are mentioned here. The most popular of all falls into the category of "oriental."

The sheer variety of options is worthy of a lifetime of study, but as a practical matter, you will learn here only how to select, specify, and acquire them for your jobs. Other handmade and machine-made options are also covered here, including constructions of staple fiber, yarn, fabric, leather, and other textiles that have been felted, woven, knotted, hooked, braided, sewn, and so on.

ORIENTALS There are many different kinds, styles, and weaves that are classified by age, origin, and sometimes also by style, although the region of origin is often considered to define the style, too. Age classifications follow the standards listed on page 133. Because different regions have their own characteristic pattern organization and kind of knot, the region name is usually synonymous with the style name. For example, there are more than 70 regions in Iran (or Persia, as it is known in the rug world) that are referenced to denote rug styles.

Years of study are required to become knowledgeable in this area and, until you develop the specialty, you must find the best dealers and rely on them to evaluate the quality of the product that they resell. You must work with someone that you can trust to be your guide and to educate you over time. The appraisal of oriental rugs is a field unto itself, and many factors play into the value of a rug, some tangible and some intangible. Like the art market, the rug market is often influenced by factors that have nothing to do with the physical attributes of a rug. The uniqueness of the design of a rug, political situations that make rugs from a certain area difficult to get, and other factors complicate the valuation of a piece for purposes of investment. Making an appropriate selection for your design is a little easier.

- *Patterns:* Many kinds of oriental rugs are meant to be symmetrical, although few are precisely and perfectly symmetrical. There is an old adage that imperfections and flaws were purposely woven in because of the belief that only God could create perfection. If the flaws are not unattractive, they are not defects, but when in doubt, reject the goods with imperfections that do not "charm" you. This is an area where an accurate assessment will, to some

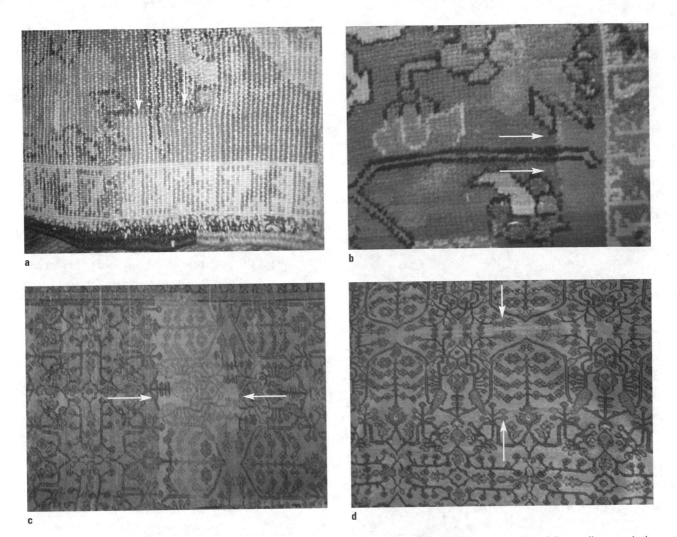

a

b

c

d

FIGURE 15.20 Repairs are very common among the vintage and antique carpets that you will find, so a good repair is usually not a deal breaker. Poor repairs can be redone if the rug is worthy of the effort. The dealer will usually include the repair in the negotiated price of the rug, but you should confirm this as you come to agreement. The first example (a) shows a well-made repair on the left side of the image, seen here from the back, stabilizing the rug without distortion. The second example (b) shows the same repair from the front, now on the right side of the image: a color shift is slightly visible and the knot count is slightly higher in the repair than in the surrounding area to compensate for the finer yarn used by the person making the repair. The third example (c) shows that this important antique rug must have had extensive wear or damage because such a large area was repaired. It is generally easier to see repairs from the back than from the front. The fourth example (d) shows the same area of the same rug from the front and the junction between the repair and the original portion is barely discernable. *Photographed at Minasian Carpets, Evanston, Illinois.*

extent, take a trained eye, but knowledge of elements and principles of design is a good basis from which to start.

- *Yarn Count:* Some people still consider yarn count in an appraisal of value, but quality is a more accurate word than value. A rug with 50-100 knots per inch will have a more primitive quality than a rug with 100-300 knots per inch. If you are viewing two rugs of the same style in two densities, the rug with the higher yarn count is likely to cost more, but the appearance also changes. Very intricate and small patterns demand a high knot count to

control the presentation (Figures 15.21 and 15.22a-c). The borders between two colors will be sharper with a high knot count and curves will be smoother if the knot count is high. Large areas of color may be well presented with a lower knot count, which furthermore has a pleasing texture for a more casual interior (Figure 15.23). Therefore, a direct comparison of knot count does not tell the whole story about quality. Individual rugs must be evaluated on all their characteristics.

- *Styles:* Historically, any style names were actually the location of fabrication or initial sale,

FIGURE 15.21 A high knot count is a necessity for an intricately detailed rug with fine tracery in the design like this silk rug. Silk is not inclined to "stand up" on its own so yarns need their neighboring yarns to hold them upright; thus, the dense yarn count actually helps to maintain good presentation of the pattern. *Photographed at Minasian Rugs, Evanston, Illinois.*

referring to an actual town or village. As rugs have been traded for many years, design motifs from one area have had time to infiltrate or influence others, making identification of the rugs a more complicated matter. Just the same, there are enough consistencies to allow you to become familiar with stylistic generalities. This location name is a communication tool when discussing rugs with your dealers.

• *The Production Process:* Consider the Turkish rugs that you find on the market as an example of the production process. Nomadic tribes herd sheep into high mountain meadows in the summer. The low temperatures there produce a lanolin-rich (oily) wool. The fleece is combed repeatedly during the winter, and then sheared in early spring. The wool is washed and sorted for length, and then teased to separate and fluff the fibers. Then the wool is spun by hand into yarn. The wool is then dyed with vegetable dyes, such as madder root for red, walnut hulls for dark brown, indigo for blue, pomegranate skins and acorn shells for camel, etc. In most of the rug-producing cultures, the weaving is done by women, who work on vertically oriented looms with cotton warps (or sometimes wool, camel hair, or silk if rugs are to be woven with silk). The patterns are produced from memory and are rarely drawn. Motifs are learned through repetition. When complete, the rug is cut from the loom, stretched out on the ground, and sheared by hand.

There is a vociferous effort being made around the world to end child labor. Child labor has been a fact of life in the rug industry for centuries, but it is no longer acceptable. An organization called Rugmark inspects production facilities to ensure that no child labor is being used. When you are meeting with a new dealer, ask whether the rugs you are being shown meet Rugmark's standards.

You can also ask about another organization called Arzurug. This program has helped carpet weavers in northern and central Afghanistan by providing technical and financial assistance to women weavers, social assistance to their families, access to health care for mothers, and education

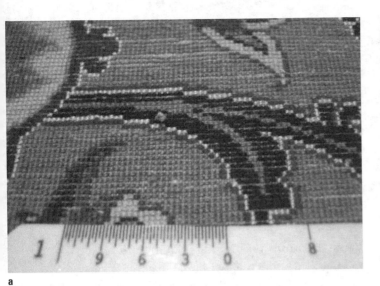
a

b

and literacy programs. In addition to creating sustainable employment for the women, the program aims to establish additional roles for women in the carpet production chain, such as spinning and carding wool, and graph-making.

SEMICUSTOM PILE RUGS Some manufacturers offer rugs that can be made up in their patterns in certain sizes with certain limited colors selected from their standard color offerings. These rugs are available with a pile construction, flat weaves, as well as chain stitch, needlepoint, and other construction methods.

PIECED RUGS A pieced rug is another type of custom area rug. Broadloom is cut and pasted with heat tape to form a custom pattern, and the edges are bound to create an area rug. Often, local installers can provide this kind of custom fabrication. They often "sub" it out as well, so ask if they do the work in-house—if not, you may be able to get a lower price by finding your own direct source and avoiding their markup. This legwork will take time, however, so if your client is purchasing your service on an hourly basis, you will not spend three hours visiting shops and inspecting work just to save your client $200 in production costs.

You will make a drawing and indicate either the broadloom from their program or give them a closed spec for the goods to be used. If they have a program of standard offerings, it will probably save you money because you do not have to

c

FIGURE 15.22 A fine wool rug with an intricate pattern also benefits from a high-knot count (a). The fine tracery (b) is crisp and quite consistent, but if this rug were produced with a lower knot count the pattern would suffer for it. The overall design (c) is also very intricate. *Images shot at Minasian Rugs, Evanston, Illinois.*

FIGURE 15.23 These rugs have a low knot count but the pattern is appropriate to the count and the design is well rendered at 100 knots per square inch. The rugs shown in Figures 15.21 and 15.22 would have been poorly rendered in 100 knots per inch. *Photographed at Minasian Rugs, Evanston, Illinois.*

purchase a lot of waste carpet that will not become part of your rug. Quite often, with this approach, you do not receive a rendering from them, so you will have to create all of the tools required for checking the design composition and color relationships.

This option would be considered if cost was a factor, if there was some other benefit in having a synthetic yarn (allergies or cleaning properties), or if the best solution per your program called for the visual consistency of a machine-made product. The edges of the broadloom will be bound. Popular options for binding include cotton tape to blend with the pile, twill tape to contrast or blend with the pile, leather (be careful with this one because it complicates the cleaning of the rug), or leather-look vinyl, which will be an attractive visual accent whether it blends with or contrasts with the color of the rug.

FLOOR CLOTHS Floor cloths are painted onto a textile backing and are very washable. Highly customized, one-of-a-kind designs are available because floor cloths are often "one-off" items, which means each one is unique. Vintage floor cloths may be dry and a little stiff, but new floor cloths are pliable and can be rolled like a painting for transport because that is essentially what they are.

RAG RUGS Manufacturers may have semi-custom offerings of various colors and certain patterns. Workshops can produce totally custom rag rugs, dyeing rags to match a color sample and laying them into the loom to create the pattern as directed. Unless the rug is pieced (two strips woven separately, then sewn together), the width of the rugs is limited by the size of the loom, with the largest possible size being twice the width of the loom when a double weave technique is used (see Box 15.1). Often, a person or company will represent many weavers who have different abilities (including skills and loom sizes) and specialties (Figure 15.24).

Standard rug patterns are offered by many weavers and ready-made rag rugs are also available. This technique can use a number of different woven patterns that are common to woven fabric, so a variety of patterns and textures can be

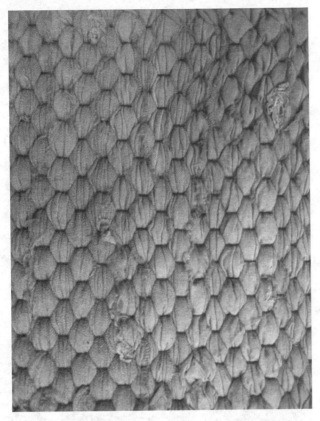

FIGURE 15.24 Rag rugs are still a craft tradition in the United States, and small independent weavers still fill some of the demand for rag rugs.

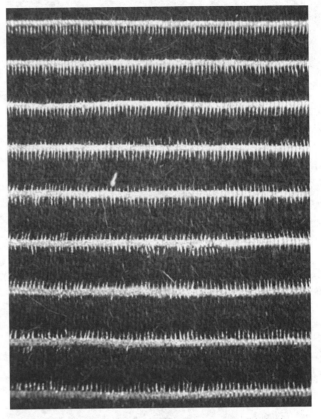

FIGURE 15.25 Daring combinations of fiber are possible in the custom rug market, like this wool-and-steel example.

achieved. The rag strips may also be knotted in (like a pile rug) to create a "fluffy" vs. flat surface; rags may be braided. These rugs are typically cotton rag on a cotton warp, but that will not prevent a creative designer working with an experienced weaver from doing other fabrics and warps.

CUSTOM RUGS OF UNUSUAL MATERIALS Woven leather rugs are constructed in a manner similar to rag rugs, but leather strips are used in place of cotton rags. Figure 15.25 shows a combination of wool and steel.

HOOKED RUGS Hooked rugs are handmade by hooking the yarn through a canvas backing. Rug hooking has long been a hand-craft tradition in the United States and many vintage selections are available. The craft is still alive and well, with artisans working in reproduction and modern designs.

FELT RUGS Felt rugs are made of wool fiber that has not been processed into yarn. Instead, it is

matted with heat, hot water, pressure, and controlled friction to lock the fibers together (Figure 15.26a and b). This is a very hands-on process (or feet-on, depending on the methods of the individual fabricator) as the fibers and felt strips or felt sheets cut to shape are dyed and distributed according to the design, which is laid out on a mat or canvas. The assembled tufts are sprinkled with hot water and rolled up inside the mat or canvas. The matting takes place as the rug is rolled back and forth inside the mat or canvas. The finished rugs are rinsed and air-dried.

BRAIDED RUGS Braided rugs are made of rag or yarn; the pattern is defined by the construction to a large degree.

TAPESTRY RUGS These are flat woven rugs (with no pile) with intricate patterns and multiple colors. The pattern is woven into the body of the rug. Sometimes, the name tapestry is applied to needlepoint rugs (there is some confusion about French and English interpretations of the word

a

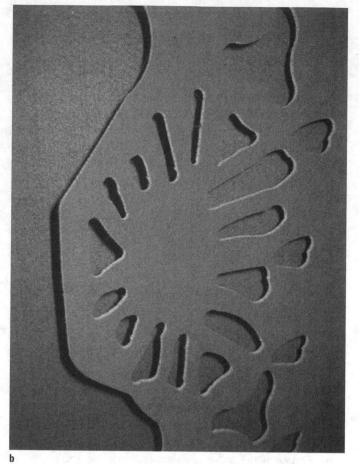

b

FIGURE 15.26 Felting rugs is an ancient craft. Modern rug-makers work in traditional and machine-assisted methods. Manipulation of color and the felting process itself lends variety to this craft. A rug by Festive Fibers (a) is made by traditional methods with lots of hands-on physical labor bringing the rug into being. Laser-cut borders (b) also appear on felted rugs—an unfathomable notion for the original rug-felters eight thousand years ago.

FIGURE 15.27 Needlepoint rugs have their "tails" remaining on the back. *Courtesy of S & H Rugs Danbury, Connecticut.*

tapestry), but generally the distinction seems to be that tapestries are woven and needlepoint falls in the embroidery family.

NEEDLEPOINT RUGS Needlepoint rugs are flat rugs with patterns that have been stitched onto a canvas back. When you flip them over, the "tails" of yarn where the artist changed color are left hanging, so additional yarn is sometimes available for making small repairs to the face (Figure 15.27).

Care and Maintenance

The basic care and cleaning of the various rugs varies among the different types of rugs. Most rugs are washed with water, but leather or leather-bound rugs are not.

RESTORATION Rug dealers will usually restore vintage and antique rugs that they sell, and this is typically included in the price. They are also a resource for restoring your client's own rug. Restorers are capable of mending a rug so meticulously that it is difficult to locate a mend from the back and impossible from the front side. Keep this fact in mind as you inspect examples of their mending capabilities before hiring them.

CLEANING Cleaning services for oriental rugs will wash rugs. The rugs must then be spread in an area with a lot of air circulating within it so that the rugs dry as quickly as possible before they become musty-smelling. For the other types of rugs mentioned here, it is a good idea to get instructions from the individual fabricator on caring for the rug. Processes and materials differ, even within the same technique, and the care that the rug will require will vary with the materials and construction techniques used.

Custom Rugs

The transaction process is similar from one type of rug to another. Let's consider this example of the process for the purchase of a custom pile rug.

Most fabricators of custom pile rugs will work only in wool yarn, although nylon-yarn custom rugs are available from a few resources. They are no less costly than wool rugs, but they offer an alternative to those who are allergic to wool fiber. The same wide variety of colors is available for both nylon and wool rugs.

The rug can be priced out when it is in the form of a line drawing and the number of colors required is known. Make a to-scale drawing of the rug you would like to have made up and submit it for pricing along with other specifications about yarn, such as denier or general thickness; describe the pile height and density. It is very easy to introduce a specialty yarn. You may want to request samples for quality if you are unfamiliar with the work of a particular fabricator who is bidding. Discuss any nonnegotiables with the fabricator to make sure the process will yield a satisfactory result.

After a fabricator has been selected and pricing has been approved, you will send a copy of your to-scale drawing with your purchase order, along with color samples keyed to match the col-

ors that you will require. The vendors representing custom rug-makers often have some color samples on hand from which to choose. It is not always possible to find exact color matches in the sales rep's shop, in which case you will indicate the exact color with a paint chip, a piece of fabric, or some other reference to define the color that you are matching. The side of a yarn *pom* (a small sample of bundled yarns) has a paler appearance than the cut end. Therefore, in your documentation, it's important to indicate whether the pom that they dye to match your sample pom should be a side-to-side match, a side-to-end match, or an end-to-side match.

Some length of time after you place your order and pay a deposit, you will receive a pom set for color approval from the company. These poms are often poms that the fabricator has on hand and believes to be a match, or they are yarns that have been dyed to match in a "beaker" (small quantity). With the first pom set or some time after that, you will receive a large-scale line drawing of the entire rug, perhaps with a portion colored in. There may be some back-and-forth at this stage, but it is important that your requirements be met exactly at each juncture.

After the fabricator receives your approval on a complete pom set, he or she will likely make up a large (2 feet by 2 feet or thereabouts) sample called a strike-off, which is an example of the construction technique, showing a portion of your actual pattern in the colors that you have selected. In your order, specify that the sample produced should present all of the colors as they will be juxtaposed on the finished rug, creating all the possible color combinations and, as nearly as possible, the proportions, so you can see how the colors affect and influence one another. The effects of simultaneous contrast come powerfully into play with heathered effects and outlining. In order to fulfill this request, the strike-off may not adhere strictly to the final design.

There may be more reworking at this stage. If this is the case, another sample will probably be required. Sometimes, only one sample is included in the price, so do not be frivolous, but do be thorough and buy a second sample if you need it. The pain will be huge if you are disappointed in the final product. It is sometimes the habit of the fabricator to dye all the yarn needed for the rug when the yarn for the sample is dyed, but just as frequently, the dyeing is done after the sample is approved. It's a good idea to inquire about the process when finalizing the price because if the yarn is dyed before the sample is made, there may be an additional cost if you change a color after review of the sample.

After the approval of the sample and any adjustments to the rendering, you may receive one last pom set for approval. These poms will be from the large quantity of yarn that the fabricator will use to make the rug. This is your last chance to disapprove of a color. It will cost you money to withhold approval at this stage unless the fabricator has failed to make a match. If the match is accurate, but your client has changed his or her mind for some reason about a color or a key fabric in your fabric scheme, you (or your client, depending on your contract with your client) will pay for new goods to be dyed again and a new sample to be made. However, you will not have doubled up any production costs, just sampling costs.

After your approval of these poms, the rug will go into production, possibly in another country; lead times are often long. The rug will probably be received by your supplier, and the supplier is likely to offer delivery and spreading services, usually for an additional charge. The rug spreaders do not usually expect to move furniture, so if that will be required, check to make sure they will do that. If not, have the rug sent to a local delivery service and pay the service to deliver and spread it. When the rug arrives in town, take the

| BOX 15.1 | **A Cautionary Tale** |

Here's an example that illustrates the variations likely in the handmade rug process: Twenty years ago, it was fashionable to slipcover the furniture in the summer and a client needed a summer rug to go with the summer slipcover scheme. When a large area rug is lifted up, the floor beneath it is lighter; this is especially obvious at the perimeter of the rug, so it was very important for the summer rug to be exactly the same size as the winter rug. The size of the loomed rag rug selected could not be so precisely controlled; the process did not allow for it. I worked with the weaver to refine the border detail so we would have some leeway after the run was complete to add to it if it was short. Fortunately, it was short by such a small amount that the weaver was able to block (steam and stretch) it to the correct size. Understanding the possible limitations of the process affected the design a little, but it also made it possible to control the product. It is not always the case that an area rug must be so precisely the specified size, but if size is a nonnegotiable characteristic, that should be discussed when you are collecting bids.

drawing and sample poms and check it over before delivery if possible. Some warehouses are not spotlessly clean with great lighting, so the inspection must often take place when you receive the rug at the client's site.

Other kinds of custom area rugs will follow a similar process. Although the sampling process may vary a little, all custom rugs—with the exception of pieced broadloom—require a sample.

CHAPTER 16

ResiLient FLooring

Resilient flooring is functional flooring for schools, laboratories, clean rooms, computer rooms, supermarkets, stores, lobbies, storage areas, spas, dormitories, libraries, health-care facilities, and other areas where easy maintenance, low cost, and durability are required. It is preferred in health-care facilities because it is impervious to water, resists stains, and can be disinfected easily. Many styles have a high-tech or industrial appeal that allows resilient flooring to make an aesthetic statement that cannot be duplicated with any other material.

When specified for residences, resilient flooring is used in kitchens, laundry areas, and service areas. People with chemical and dust sensitivities can live with these floors because they can be cleaned easily and do not tend to trap dust.

Most resilient floors have a linoleum and decorative surface protected by a wear layer. Solid materials like vinyl or rubber are exceptions to this.

Resilient floors can become scratched, stained, or gouged, and they may develop bumps, bubbles, or curled edges, if not installed properly. Heavy foot traffic or the constant movement of furniture can cause wear patterns. They fade in direct sunlight, so sun exposure must be considered when specifying.

Types of Resilient Flooring

The most commonly used materials are linoleum and vinyl. Other options include rubber, cork, leather, and composite materials.

Linoleum

Linoleum is composed of natural materials and it is biodegradable. Therefore, it is subject to damage from excessive or standing water. It is manufactured by oxidizing linseed oil to form a thick mixture called linoleum cement. The cement is cooled and mixed with pine resin and wood flour to form sheets on a jute backing. Linoleum comes in tiles and sheets. Its colors go all the way through the depth of the material.

Linoleum is a green product because its components are:

- Manufactured from readily renewable natural raw materials.
- Highly recyclable and all production waste is currently recycled.
- Durable. Linoleum will retain its attractive appearance for decades when properly maintained.

It is also hygienic; its natural inherent properties actually halt the growth of many microorganisms. Its naturally antistatic properties repel dust and dirt, making it easy to maintain a clean and healthy environment.

Sheets are often available approximately 6-feet wide. It is also available in tiles sized 12 × 12 inches and 18 × 18 inches. Sheets can be cut and configured to produce many patterns.

Vinyl

Pure vinyl, vinyl, and vinyl composition products contain varying degrees of fillers. Pure vinyl flooring contains only vinyl. "Solid" vinyl contains mineral aggregate, pigments, plasticizers, and stabilizers, which are introduced into the body of the tile. Numerous styles apply to a variety of installations (Figure 16.1a and b). Vinyl is available as sheets or tiles. Commercial sheets are available in 6- and 12-foot widths approximately 70–100 feet long. Tiles are usually available in 12 × 12 inches, 18 × 18 inches, up to 36 × 36 inches and in two thicknesses—¹⁄₁₆ and ⅛ inch. They may have a clear vinyl or urethane finish. Precision-ground edges produce a floor that can have the appearance of a one-piece sheet vinyl installation. Some specialty products are available to help disperse static electricity. These materials are installed as a system of specialty tiles, grounding strips, and conductive adhesive. Other products are designed to provide greater slip resistance.

A variety of sheet vinyl goods are available:

- *Inlaid sheet flooring* combines inlaid vinyl chips in a matrix that is usually attached to a felt (or vinyl or fiberglass) backing, frequently with a protective topcoat. With inlaid sheet flooring, the color or pattern is an integral part of the wear layer.

- *Cushioned sheet flooring* has an overlay of a printed foam layer that creates a textured surface that can replicate other materials. Cushioned products are soft and may not wear as well as other products. It is important to confirm that individual products in this category meet fire code requirements for your specific job.

- *Homogeneous sheet flooring* is solid, which means the material is consistent in color and pattern throughout its full thickness; in other words, the whole thickness is the wear layer. Homogeneous flooring must be at least 50 percent vinyl.

- *Heterogeneous sheet flooring* is a laminated product having, at minimum, a cushioned or felted bottom layer, and a decorative, printed, or patterned layer topped by a clear wear layer. It may be smooth or embossed and may be

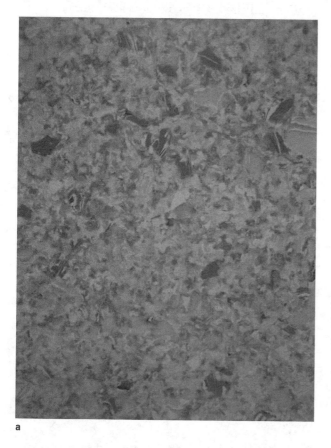

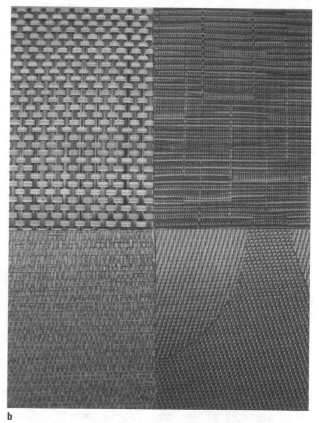

FIGURE 16.1 Solid vinyl tile can imitate a terrazzo (a). Woven vinyl product for floors (b) has good slip resistance, easy maintenance, and moisture-resistance characteristics like a solid vinyl.

cushioned to enhance sound absorption or underfoot comfort.

- *Performance-backed sheet flooring*, another laminated product, can be either homogeneous or heterogeneous with a backing of closed-cell PVC foam for use in applications where increased shock absorption or sound control are critical to the design program.
- *Slip-retardant sheet flooring*, either heat-welded or flash-coved, offers a seamlessness not available with tile. It also, typically, has a higher resistance to staining than tile. Some manufacturers offer a still higher degree of stain resistance. These products are usually urethane-enhanced.
- *Static-control sheet flooring* dissipates electricity. Common applications are hospital operating rooms and clean rooms.

The sheet vinyl that is popular for residential use is a slightly different product. Residential grades have a surface that has been built up out of tiny granules fused together by heat and pressure, often over a cushioning layer of foam. It is usually available in 12-foot widths and continuous lengths up to 90 or even 100 feet. This sheet vinyl flooring derives its durability from its upper layer, called the *wear layer*, which is a clear vinyl resin available in different thicknesses. The thicker the wear layer, the more expensive and longer lasting the product will be. The thickness of wear layers can range from 0.005 inch to 0.025 inch.

Many sheet vinyl floors have a very high gloss, achieved by adding a urethane on top of the clear, vinyl wear layer. These urethanes are as durable as the urethanes that are used on hardwood flooring.

Sheet vinyls can be installed to be very impervious to water, especially when "welded" with accessory items such as coved bases. This makes them ideal for spaces with rigorous standards of sanitation (like health-care facilities). They emit very low volatile organic compounds (VOCs) after installation. They offer some cushioning without the maintenance complications of carpet. Patterns tend to have better appearance retention than solids and organic patterns stay clean looking longer than geometric patterns. Even if you

are more of an advocate of clean than of "clean looking," you still must concede that there are high-traffic installations where it is unsafe or inconvenient to be continuously mopping the floor (24-hour environments like emergency rooms come to mind), so soil-hiding is an important characteristic under some circumstances.

Special glues have been developed to join pieces together. This glue, or "seam sealer," actually welds the two pieces of flooring together into one solid piece.

Rubber

Rubber flooring is also available as tiles or rolls. Rubber and synthetic rubber (composed of styrene butadiene, very fine mineral aggregate, stabilizers, pigments, and wax) are both degraded by oil but are otherwise durable flooring. They require regular buffing to maintain their appearance because they tend to show scuffs. Rubber flooring is naturally slip-resistant. Most rubber flooring offers a coefficient of friction of 0.8 or higher. Some products have a granular nonslip feature or strip to provide even more traction. Sheeting is sold in rolls that are typically 3-6 feet wide and approximately 40 feet long, with heavier-gauge material shipped in shorter lengths (Figure 16.2a-f). Rubber tiles are available in various sizes ranging from approximately 18 inches square to 36 inches square.

Cork

Cork flooring is available in tiles ranging from ⅛ to 2 inches thick in varying sizes. Cork "planks" are also available. They typically have an engineered product backing them and sometimes have an additional cushion layer. They typically have tongue-and-groove edges. Cork planks straddle the line between resilient and solid flooring and their characteristics relate more to solid than to resilient flooring. Cork is also a component in tiles that have vinyl backing, a cork core, a separate cork veneer face, and a vinyl top surface.

Cork shares some characteristics with wood (comes from trees; expands and contracts because it is susceptible to water absorption). It is available unfinished or prefinished with wax or

a

b

c

d

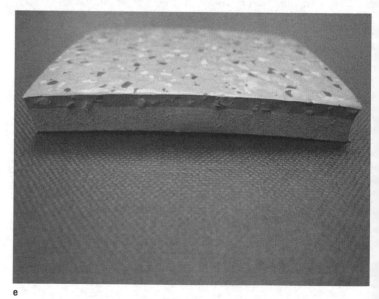

e

FIGURE 16.2 Standard rubber tile surface textures (a). Recycled rubber flooring by Ecosurfaces Burke Mercer (b). Ecostone by Ecosurfaces Burke Mercer (c). Interlocking modular tiles by Ecosurfaces Burke Mercer (d) allow for moving or replacing individual tiles. Rubber tile (e) with integral cushioning for sports locations and other areas where slip resistance and a softer surface are required. The custom capabilities (f) of rubber flooring is appealing for large-area spaces where a meaningful pattern, such as this map in a schoolroom, could contribute to the design program with a very serviceable surface.

f

polyurethane (Figure 16.3a and b). In its natural (unfinished) state, cork is susceptible to staining, so it must be sealed. Unfinished cork floors can be stained (like wood flooring) using a water-based stain. After the stain has dried completely, three coats of water-based urethane are applied according to the manufacturer's instructions.

Cork flooring is antistatic, sound absorbing, and insulating (both heat and cold); it can be tolerated by people with allergies. It can withstand heavy traffic and weight and has a "memory," so it recovers well from compression. It is considered especially comfortable to stand on. Cork flooring products are available with a range of visual characteristics (Figure 16.4).

Leather

Leather tiles are cut from the back area of very heavyweight skins (Figure 16.5a). They are full thickness from unsplit hides because thicker skins are more stable and consistent. Tiles are available in different shapes and sizes in both natural and dyed colors. Color and texture variations are present in both natural and dyed leather tiles.

Leather tiles must be sealed to protect them from staining. In addition to any sealant applied at the factory, leather tiles should be waxed two or three times on site (Figure 16.5b). They will develop a patina over time when exposed to natural light. Explain to your client that these changes in the appearance of the material are normal and desirable characteristics as the material mellows with age. Leather tiles are considered comfortable underfoot and, if properly cared for, acquire a patina with age.

Composite

As new technologies and needs surface, research leads to new products. As with any material that is a combination of two other materials, composite flooring products will retain characteristics of both component materials. The push for green products has led to the development of materials with recycled content and to products that combine two or more sustainable materials to take

a | b

FIGURE 16.3 Cork flooring (a) shown unfinished for finishing on site and pre-finished with a urethane top coat. The softer sheen of wax compared to urethane (b). Wax satisfies a desire for naturalness, but urethane is easier to maintain over time.

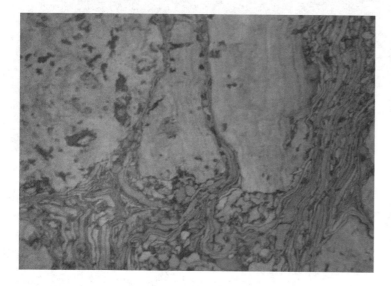

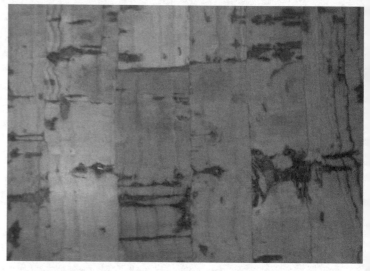

FIGURE 16.4 Cork is a natural product. Strict control of visual characteristics is not possible; however, variations within a range can be selected. It is a good idea to get current samples whenever possible.

a

b

FIGURE 16.5 Leather tiles are a luxury product for light-traffic situations (a). Leather floors are waxed at installation (b). Other than waxing, there is no recommended way to clean leather floors; they are similar to antique-wood flooring in this respect. The wax acts as a top dressing and should be periodically cleaned and replenished to maintain the floor.

advantage of the strengths of all the component materials. Refer to manufacturers' literature to confirm the characteristics, installation, and care information for all materials specified, especially for composite materials because combinations may call for new installation procedures or maintenance products.

Installation

Although you will be relying on a professional installer, you need to know enough about the installation of the flooring material you have specified to be able to evaluate the installer's work.

Qualifying Installers

The installer selected should have experience with the product selected. Furthermore, there are certification qualifications available through the Floor Covering Installation Board (FCIB) and Certified Floorcovering Installers (CFI).

Installation Instructions

A written specification to the installer is adequate for simply installing tiles. As with any flooring material, a special pattern or particular instructions regarding alignments or relationships to the architecture should be shown on a drawing that is reviewed with the installer on site prior to the installation.

Moisture Control

Rooms with floors at or below grade level sometimes have moisture problems that can cause the flooring to come loose, especially around the edges of the room. In these cases, the moisture problem must be solved before installing or repairing an earlier installation. If there is a risk of moisture migration from below-grade concrete slab floors, a moisture barrier (often a 6-millimeter film of polyethylene) is required. On top of this barrier, a plywood subfloor is installed and the tiles are glued to the subfloor.

Subflooring

Resilient flooring is a thin, flexible material, so any unevenness in the subfloor will telegraph through to the surface in a very short amount of time. Although 35-pound particleboard with square edges is often used as a subfloor, particleboard will absorb water; this is a limiting factor in the total assembly. Many resilient flooring materials can stand up to water, but if water should leak down to the subfloor, the installation will be ruined. Sometimes, particleboard is covered over with MDF board to produce a really hard, smooth surface. Plywood subfloor is often specified as A-C, with the higher-quality surface (A) facing up so the resilient flooring material is adhered to the smooth, better-quality surface. If heavy water spills are anticipated, the perimeter of the room should be caulked prior to installing molding or baseboards.

Transitions

Resilient flooring products are often thinner than adjoining materials and you must specify how the edges and transitions will be handled. A variety of metal transition strips are manufactured for this precise purpose; they range from a very minimal "terrazzo" type edging to broader strips that bridge more pronounced differences in material thickness (Figure 16.6). Another transition area to be specified is the transition between the floor and the wall. In addition to more traditional products, resilient products such as vinyl base strips are available in a number of solid colors to accompany the resilient flooring that you specify (Figure 16.7).

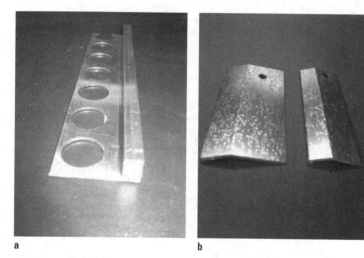

a   b

FIGURE 16.6 Transitions between usually thinner resilient products and adjoining surfaces must be detailed carefully to meet code in commercial installation and provide an attractive transition in any installation. A variety of products are available. Generally a minimal transition is preferred, and if flooring substrates can be specified to make the finished installation flush with adjoining flooring, then a very minimal terrazzo edging can be specified (a). If a minimal transition is not possible, you may have to specify a transition strip, which provides more of a "bridge" from one material to the next (b).

FIGURE 16.7 In commercial installations, it is quite common to specify a vinyl base for resilient material and for carpeted areas. Manufacturers tend to color-coordinate across the industry, so coordinating base and stair accessories can be companionable when paired with resilient flooring material.

CHAPTER 17

TiLe

When considering a tile surface for your project, you will address all the components of the installation, including the material the tile is made of, how it is formed, the surface quality, the finish on the body of the tile, the size of the tile, the installation method, the grout, and sealants.

Composition

Tiles are made from a variety of materials. The most common tile body is clay, including porcelain. Other materials made into tiles include glass, stone, concrete, metal, brick, and composite.

Clay

Clay is mined from the earth, not born in a vat, so the characteristics of natural clay vary. White clay bodies are suitable for wall tile; porcelain clay, gray, tan, and terra-cotta clay bodies can be used on walls or floors. Tile color and coarseness are inherent properties of the clay.

Clay tiles that are handmade have slightly irregular shapes and surfaces. The term "handmade" may mean that they have been formed by hand or that they have been machine-made (with an intentional variation in surfaces, edges, and size) and only glazed by hand. Tiles identified as "machine-made" are more consistent in surface and size.

Clay tiles are fired in kilns at high temperature, which causes a molecular change in the material. Before the tiles are fired, they can be broken, mixed with water, and reconstituted as plastic (moldable) clay. After firing, they are forever modified and can no longer return to a plastic condition. Tiles that are fired once are referred to as *monocoturra*; those that are fired twice are more impervious and are referred to as *bicoturra*.

Clay tiles are generally ¼ to ⅜ inch thick. Terra-cotta tiles (Figure 17.1) are thicker—sometimes 1 inch or more. If an exact dimension is required (for example, as when tiles are being used side by side in a pattern), the thickness of a sample should be measured rather than relying on manufacturer's literature. If tiles are glazed past the edge of their faces so no unfinished clay is visible on the edge after grouting, the change in dimension may make an interesting design detail.

Porcelain

Porcelain tiles (Figure 17.2a) have a porcelain clay body that is consistent all the way through, with pigment mixed into the clay (rather than sitting on top as a glaze), so wear will not be obvious in high-traffic situations. Porcelain tiles are usually formed by pressing very dry clay into a mold. The use of fine-grained porcelain clay and a mold with very little water creates a very uniform product.

FIGURE 17.1 Terra-cotta tiles may be unglazed to show their natural clay faces for aesthetic reasons. These distressed or reclaimed tiles are unglazed.

Porcelain tiles typically have no additional finish. They do not need to be glazed in order to be impervious to staining. Porcelain tiles are available with a variety of surface qualities.

- *Polished* surfaces are not the result of a glaze or applied surface treatment. Instead, they are mechanically produced (ground like polished stone) to a hard, smooth, shiny surface.
- *Matte surfaces* provide good slip resistance. They have a flat, even, "fine-stipple-like" texture.
- *Textured surfaces* create excellent slip resistance. The texture may be random and "natural," similar to the cleft of a stone (Figure 17.2b) or consistent, such as the raised pattern of a geometric relief or a grainy additive that rises up above the surface of the tile.

Very large tiles can be produced from durable porcelain clays. When the installer installs very large tiles (or very uneven tiles), the backs should be *buttered* (spread with pliable mastic) to eliminate any voids that may otherwise be present in the setting material. Voids left under the material are apt to allow the tile to crack under pressure.

a

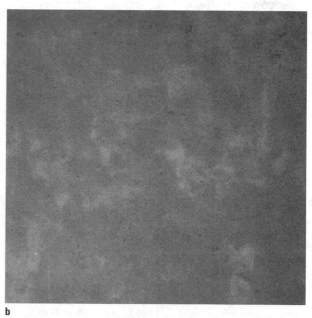

b

FIGURE 17.2 Natural stone tile is often imitated with more durable porcelain for the most abusive environments where natural stone would be difficult to maintain. Durable porcelain tile (a) would be a good substitute for the natural stone (b) if you were specifying for a space with a lot of foot traffic. *Photographed by permission of The Tile Gallery in Chicago, Illinois.*

Glass

Glass tiles are formed by casting glass into molds. Glass tiles might have integral color or baked-on color enamel. The enamel creates opacity as well as adding color in the tile. Tiles can be clear glass (Figure 17.3) or translucent glass with polished or matte surfaces. If you are specifying clear glass tiles, request that the installer make up a sample board with a few pieces set up and grouted for approval. This sample will show whether the mastic can be evenly applied so the surface visible underneath is smooth. Trowels used to spread mastic have serrated edges and can leave a striped grout bed, which may remain even after the tile is pressed into position. You may want to include "knock the notches down" (smooth out these ridges) in your installer's instructions.

FIGURE 17.3 This clear glass mosaic must be expertly installed because the mastic will not be hidden as it would if this tile were opaque. The installer must knock down the notches left in the mastic by the serrated trowel so there is no striped mastic showing through the installation when it is complete.
Photographed by permission of The Tile Gallery in Chicago, Illinois, courtesy of Boyce and Bean Natural Glass and Clay Co.

Glass tiles are impervious to many chemicals and can withstand cleaning by cleaning agents in common use.

Recycled glass tiles are readily available. Some have an iridescent surface, which is not a glaze but is integral to the material.

Glass mosaic (Figure 17.4) tiles are small (as small as ¼-inch square) and are available with flat or irregular surfaces. Irregular surfaces can be ground flat after installation if desired but are usually left as-is because of the charming variation of the textured surface that results (Figure 17.5). As with most tiles smaller than 6 × 6 inches, mosaic tiles are sold mounted in 12 × 12 inch squares. They may be mesh-backed (mounted face up to fiber mesh) or paper-faced (mounted face down on paper). It is important for the installer to maintain the spacing predetermined by the mounted tiles for a seamless installation that does not highlight the 12 × 12 inch squares. This is trickier with paper-faced tiles because the installer cannot see the relationship until after the setting material has cured and the paper can be washed off the face of the tile.

Stone

Stone tiles will have the characteristics per species described in Chapter 11. Stone tiles are distinguished from stone slab by length, width, and thickness; stone tiles will typically be ¼ to ⅜ inch thick. Stones with uneven surfaces, like cleft-face slate (Figure 17.6), will present the same installation requirements as uneven tiles, such as terra-cotta.

Concrete

Concrete tiles for interior use (Figure 17.7) are available in many sizes and colors. They have characteristics of concrete (see Chapter 9, Concrete) and can be finished with polyurethane or acrylic to prevent some kinds of staining. They can also be used for exterior surfaces and, if thick enough, resist damage from freezing. When used outdoors, they are sealed but not top-dressed with polyurethane or acrylic. Concrete tiles cure to set up (that is, undergo a chemical reaction as opposed to a process) and are not fired in tile kilns at high temperatures, so a variety of materials can

FIGURE 17.4 This clear glass tile demonstrates one of the decorative possibilities of glass tile as each is individually decorated with a colored glass composition. Because it too is clear, the same installation cautions apply as in Figure 17.3. *Photographed by permission of The Tile Gallery in Chicago, Illinois, courtesy of Dolce Glass Tile.*

FIGURE 17.5 Glass is a versatile product and need not always be sleek and modern. This rusticated glass tile has a natural irregularity but still displays the translucency of glass as light penetrates the material. *Photographed by permission of The Tile Gallery in Chicago, Illinois, courtesy of Oceanside Glass Tile.*

FIGURE 17.6 Many varieties of stone are available as tile. Stone tile is cut thinner than stone slab. *Photographed by permission of The Tile Gallery in Chicago, Illinois.*

FIGURE 17.7 Concrete tile may be tinted to imitate other material that imitates terra-cotta tile. *Photographed by Alana Clark.*

be embedded in the tile body. Examples of unusual materials that can be embedded include golf tees or chips of semiprecious stones. Composite tiles that contain recycled or reclaimed material can increase the "green" quotient of an installation.

Metal

Solid metal tiles (Figures 17.8 and 17.9) have characteristics inherent to the metal selected (Chapter 12, Metals). Clay-body tiles with metallic glazes are sometimes used instead of metal tiles. Metallic glazes abrade more easily than other glazes and are not suitable for floors.

Brick

Face bricks (thin bricks and pavers) are truly brick. They are included here as a reminder of products that you could specify in place of tiles because this material resembles tile in applications and installation. Bricks are resistant to staining but should still be sealed (see Chapter 10, Brick).

Composite

Composite tiles are a combination of two or more materials, often including natural stone and resin or cement (for more information about composite materials, see Chapter 18, Terrazzo). The size and material combination varies. Tiles can be composed of small chips or larger pieces of stone. The color often derives from a pigmented matrix and the color of the companion material.

Surface Characteristics

Surface characteristics are derived from the body of the tile and the glaze. The body of the tile may be exposed (unglazed) and can also be textured with a relief of some kind. Both glazed and unglazed tiles can have surface texture from relief patterning (Figure 17.10) or granules added to the face of the tile for slip resistance.

Unglazed Tiles

Unglazed tiles rely on the quality of the tile body for their color and other characteristics. Terra-

FIGURE 17.8 Stainless steel tiles by Crossville.

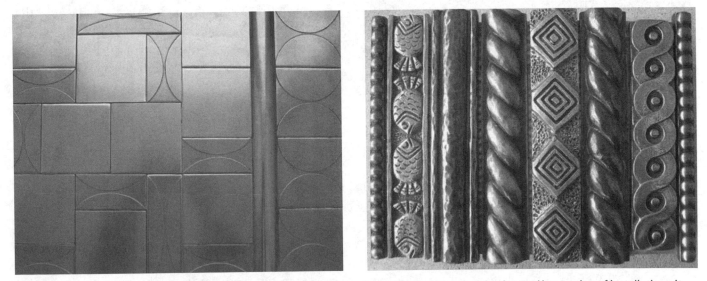

FIGURE 17.9 The versatility of metal tile for different aesthetic programs allows this durable material to be used in a number of installations. It can be very crisp and modern and also very rustic or visually soft. *Photographed by permission of The Tile Gallery in Chicago, Illinois, courtesy of Flux Studios.*

FIGURE 17.10 Because tile made from clay starts life as a very plastic medium, a limitless variety of surface relief patterns and textures is possible. *Photographed by permission of The Tile Gallery in Chicago, Illinois, courtesy of Quemere International.*

FIGURE 17.11 This porcelain series by Crossville is available in three surface qualities. Not produced by a glaze, the gloss version is a very impervious polished surface.

cotta tiles (see Figure 17.1) are porous with a natural matte texture that is difficult to clean. This difficulty extends to the cleaning of grout from the face. When creating a spec for your installer, add to your instructions, "Window pane-ing of grout on face of tile is unacceptable; use grout release, all grout to be cleaned from face of tiles," or words to that effect.

Unglazed quarry tiles and porcelain tiles (also made of clay) are generally considered to be stain-resistant. Quarry tiles may be factory-sealed against staining. Tiles may be a smooth,

consistent color across their faces or have a variegated pattern (often resembling wood grain) that goes all the way through the tile. Tiles with a flashed surface have one side that is darker than the other, gradually fading into the pale edge. This type of surface is seen in quarry tiles and in brick; it is created when a fire in the kiln creates an oxygen deficit.

Porcelain tiles are not sealed; the surface is very durable and serviceable (Figure 17.11). They are often designed to imitate more vulnerable stone tiles for areas where a stone look is desired but more durability is required.

Glazed Tiles

Glazed tiles have surface characteristics similar to glass; they are usually impervious to water and staining but have some of the same vulnerabilities (chipping, scratching). Glazes show wear over time, especially glossy finishes. Glossy finishes are generally considered to be unsuitable for floors because they show scratches and are slippery, but they can be installed in light-use areas as an accent.

Crackle glazes are more susceptible to staining. The intentional cracks in the glaze are decorative and are sometimes used to imitate old tile for vintage looks. The cracks are sometimes inked to enhance them (Figure 17.12). Because the glazed surface has been compromised, the tiles are vulnerable to infiltration of moisture. They are not advisable for high-moisture environments like steam showers or saunas but are acceptable for regular showers.

Layout

Given that structures are not usually square and plumb, it is sensible to design details that allow for imperfections. Do not design an installation with a lot of critical dimensions that require adhering to strict horizontals and verticals.

A drawing will help ensure that the correct number of tiles is ordered. This is especially important if the tile has a long lead time or is costly. While most tiles are sold by the square foot, some of the more expensive new tiles, trim tiles, antique tiles, and some salvaged tiles are sold by the tile.

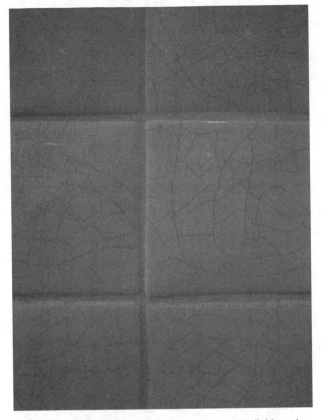

FIGURE 17.12 Hundreds of glaze formulations are available and many are proprietary secrets. Crackle glaze is purposely distressed to imitate aged tiles. *Photographed by permission of The Tile Gallery in Chicago, Illinois.*

Their cost warrants the added precaution of a drawing because they usually are not returnable, unlike many stock tile overages, which are returnable with a restocking fee (you pay shipping, too).

A drawing will clarify instructions regarding acceptable placement of cut tiles versus full tiles, as well as alignments. For example, should wall grout lines align with floor grout lines or be purposely offset? A drawing of the tile layout tells the installer the location of the tile. It describes the pattern (if there is one) and the relationship of the pattern, tiles, or joints to any features in the architecture; it addresses how to deal with services (switches, junction boxes, or electrical outlets, vents for HVAC). It also identifies the trims that are required and where to use them (Figure 17.13).

Installation

The three main components in a tile installation are (1) the selection and installation of the substrate, (2) the setting of the tile, and (3) the grouting of the tile.

Substrate

The substrate for flooring must be appropriate to the tile selection and the use. The floor must be entirely rigid. Any "give" or "springiness" will lead to cracked or loose tiles. The sheets that make up the substrate should be flush with one another. The greatest allowable change in surface according to most standards is $\frac{1}{32}$ inch up or down. Any point that rises above the surrounding substrate could cause a stress crack in the tile or grout. Tile is bonded directly to the substrate, so any movement in the substrate will cause cracking of the tile installation.

Several substrate products are available:

- *Water-resistant "green board"* or blue board should be specified as the substrate if any water will be used during the installation such as tile installed with mortar. Green board has a gypsum core laminated with a paperlike covering that is water-resistant. In contrast, the face of regular gypsum board is paper; therefore, regular gypsum board should be used as a tile substrate only if the area will remain dry during use and tile is to be installed with adhesive and grouted with an epoxy or other waterless grout. "Blue board" is designed as a substrate for plaster, so it also resists moisture while providing a good bond. The gypsum core will disintegrate if water reaches it.

Trims:

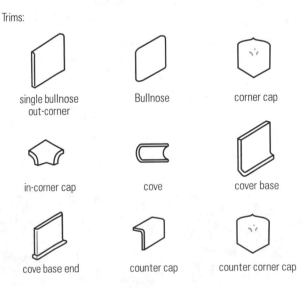

single bullnose out-corner   Bullnose   corner cap

in-corner cap   cove   cover base

cove base end   counter cap   counter corner cap

FIGURE 17.13 The various trims desired to finish off the edges of your installation must be ordered separately. Most trim pieces are sold by the tile.

- *Cementitious backerboard* (cement board) is available in fiber-reinforced or glass-mesh-faced sheets. These substrates contain no gypsum and are water-impervious sheets, so they're able to withstand excessive exposure to water; in fact, you could soak them in a swimming pool without damage.
- *Plywood* of exterior grade is designed to resist delaminating in the presence of moisture and can be used as a backing for tile, although this is a less common choice.

Mortar is applied to the substrate to prepare it to receive a tiled surface. Mortar consists of cement mixed with sand, water, and sometimes hydrated lime.

Setting

The more uneven the tile (handmade or slate tile, for example), the thicker the setting material must be in order to keep faces as level and flush as possible.

Tiles should be evenly spaced and laid according to plan with all trims used as required. The layout should be dry-fitted if necessary to ensure that there are no tiny "slivers" of tile along the perimeter and yet the installation is "balanced" on any important feature. A rule of thumb is that the layout should present no tile that is half of the full width. A slight change in the width of the grout line can sometimes make the difference between a logical, beautiful installation and one that calls attention to itself for all the wrong reasons,

If the selected tile will have a lot of variation (Figure 17.14) in it (a handmade tile with a mottled glaze or flashed surface, for instance), a "dry fit" is advisable. At the very least, you will want to open a few boxes and look at the actual material, especially if it comes set up on a mesh back-

ing. The contractor will most likely lay the tile as it is set up on the mesh. If one box is different from another, you will want the contractor to remove the mesh, mix the batches up, and set the tiles individually for even dispersal of the varieties within your order. At the very least, the tile setter should open several boxes and mix them up as they are laid to avoid a patchy installation.

Several setting methods are used:

- *Wetset* is used on a substrate or mortar bed that has not hardened or is at least still not cured. The adhesive is mixed using cement, water, and sometimes sand.
- *Thinset* refers to an adhesive made of cement, sand, and methylcellulose, which holds water, allowing the installer to set dry tile. This layer would be ¼ to ⅜ inch thick (plan for this thickness in your details). Various formulations are available from different manufacturers, with each offering a different set of characteristics, such as higher bonding properties, faster drying times, higher water resistance, and reduced shrinkage factors. White is usually used for walls and counters; gray thinset is used for floors. The installer might also use white thinset on the floor if a pale grout has been specified.
- *Thickset* material consists of 1-¼-inch-thick cement; in some cases, reinforcing wire or galvanized lath is incorporated. Thickset should be considered if you want to level out unevenness in the substrate, incorporate slope in the tile layer if needed (for example, slope to a drain), reinforce the substrate for complete rigidity (for wood framing), or create sufficient thickness for burying radiant heating or other tubing.
- *Organic adhesive* or mastic is used like thinset to bond tile directly to a backing or substrate. It can be used on floors and walls. Organic adhesives

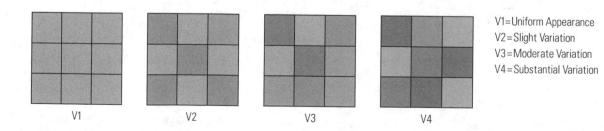

V1 = Uniform Appearance
V2 = Slight Variation
V3 = Moderate Variation
V4 = Substantial Variation

V1   V2   V3   V4

FIGURE 17.14 Standards for describing variation in tile designed for random effects are required for specification purposes.

come premixed in watertight containers. Type 1 mastic is used for walls and floors; type 2 is used for walls.

If you intend to use two tiles of different thicknesses next to each other, and the differences in thickness are minor, a thinset installation could make up the difference. If differences are greater, you may have to instruct the installer to "back butter" (slather more mastic on the back before positioning) the thinner tiles to boost their surfaces into flush alignment with the thicker tiles.

Grouts

After the tile has been adhered to the substrate and the setting has cured, the installation is grouted. You will need to specify the type and color of grout.

TYPES OF GROUT Four basic types of grout are available:

- *Portland cement-based grouts* are the most common. They are naturally gray or white, depending on the color of the cement used. They are available pigmented in many colors and they may be sanded or unsanded. Sanded grout is used for most installations. It cleans up easily, making it good for porous surfaces. The sand in sanded grout limits the amount of shrinkage, so sanded grout is less likely to crack. Care must be taken on polished tiles as the sand may scratch polished surfaces. Unsanded grout is used for close-butt joints and should not be used on joints wider than ⅛ inch because shrinkage will cause cracks in the grout joint.
- *Epoxy grouts* are available as two- or three-part systems. This type of grout must be used immediately after it's mixed up. It is nonporous, chemically resistant, and easy to clean. Epoxy grouts are more expensive to buy and install, but in some circumstances (for example, restaurants and other places where sterility is important), the extra cost is considered to be worth it for the ease of maintenance. They may be "sanded" for wider grout joints, but the sand will probably be a specially selected mineral

filler. Modified epoxy grout is composed of epoxy and Portland cement. Its characteristics are similar to those of Portland cement grout, but it is harder and forms better bonds.
- *Silicone rubber* grout cures rapidly and is resistant to hot oil, steam, humidity, and prolonged temperature extremes. It should not be used on food preparation surfaces.
- *Furan resin grout* is highly resistant to certain chemicals, especially acids. It cures within minutes because furan is a very volatile chemical. The installer should follow the manufacturer's directions, and tiles should be prewaxed to prevent grout from adhering to tile faces. Grout residue is removed from the tile faces by steam cleaning. This type of grout is most typically available in black. Furan is toxic and the toxins are bioaccumulative, which means that they build up in organisms.

LATEX ADDITIVES Latex additives are incorporated into the grout for better adhesion and application of the grout; they reduce absorbency and shrinkage.

COLOR Grout is available in a range of colors (Figure 17.15). The tile setter should be instructed to make up a test sample on a board with the tile from the lot ordered and the grout mixed up from the grout ordered for the job. Keep in mind that each time grout is mixed, even if from the same bag, the color will vary slightly. There is no way to control this precisely, so be very practical about accepting or rejecting a color sample.

An associated issue regarding the variation of grout color is that the contractor will be working quickly to grout an entire surface with a single batch of grout before the grout begins to set up (cure) because the next batch mixed from the same bag, using the same source of water, will vary slightly. If the grout specified is a contrasting color to that of the tile, a test sample should be made before applying grout to make sure there is no absorption by the tile of the colored grout. Beware of black grout as a contrast; it is difficult to completely clean off of the face of the tile. As a "matching" grout, expect it to fade to "charcoal" in a short period of time. Also, be aware that grout changes color over time. This includes

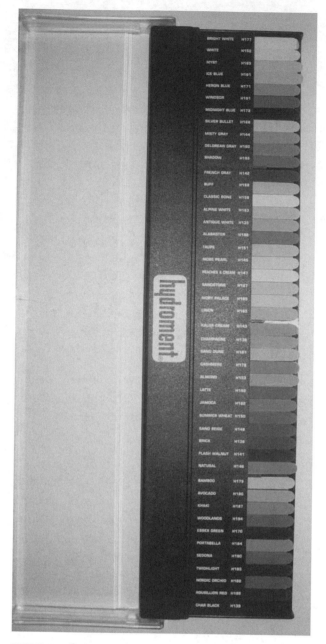

FIGURE 17.15 Grout manufacturers assemble sample sets for designers to keep on hand for selection of color. The colors in the set will be available in a variety of formulations by each manufacturer.

grout samples; when your samples are three or four years old, it is time to request new samples, even if the colors are still current.

GROUT SEALANTS All grout should be sealed as soon after installation as the manufacturer will allow (28+ days). The best possible situation is one in which all traffic will stay off of the floor until the sealant has been applied and has dried. However,

grout has to cure for such a long time that this is not always possible. If an area must be used during the curing process, the grout must be cleaned and allowed to dry thoroughly prior to sealing.

Factors Contributing to Cost

Materials can vary dramatically in cost and can be the biggest cost variable in the job. Installation costs can rise with the complexity of the job. Any preparation required prior to installation will, of course, contribute to the cost. For example, if the existing substrate is inadequate, it must be improved before installing tile, so the cost will be higher.

If the tile setter is simply laying down pre-grouted sheets on a large flat area, the square foot cost will be lower than if there are many different trim pieces to accommodate, complicated architecture, or a complex design or pattern. The per-hour charge for a highly skilled installer will be higher than for someone whose expertise does not stretch beyond the simplest installations.

The method of setting also factors into the price. The care required to install uneven tiles or tiles with variegated coloration is time-consuming. Uneven tiles must be pressed into place in a thick bed to create the most even surface. This not only requires careful judgment (and possibly a more skilled and, therefore, more costly installer) but also time. Variegated color also requires skill in placing and orienting tiles to achieve a nicely uniform mottled appearance versus a blotchy installation. Your expectation with respect to these two items in particular must be communicated to the installer. If you suspect that your intention for the installation is not fully understood, you may have to be available to assist in the decision making during the installation (this means you must be on site).

Qualifying Installers

Qualifying installers becomes more involved as the demands of the job become more complex. The best way to determine the capability of the installers is to question them about their experience with the kind of installation that you have in mind and to see some of their work.

CHAPTER 18

Terrazzo and other composite materials containing stone

Terrazzo has been used as a flooring material for hundreds of years. Modern engineering has created composite stone products that are similar to traditional terrazzo but have different performance characteristics.

Types of Composite Flooring

Three types of composite flooring are used today: terrazzo, engineered stone, and terrazzo tile.

Terrazzo

Terrazzo is a composite material that consists of aggregate (stone or glass chips) (Figure 18.1a and b) bound together by a matrix of cement or resin. It can be poured in place or purchased precast in custom or standard units. The color varies, depending on the aggregate in it and the color of the binder matrix. If poured in place, terrazzo must cure and then be ground flat, polished, and sealed. If installed as tiles, it will come pre-ground.

Portland cement matrix and epoxy matrix are the two binders used. Durability is affected by the binder, with epoxy resins being the most durable. Poured-in-place terrazzo (monolithic) with a Portland cement binder will be 2-½ inches thick with a mortar bed and requires metal divider strips at control joints. Terrazzo with an epoxy binder may be ⅜-inch thick and may not require a mortar bed; it does not require metal strips at joints, but they are often incorporated anyway for decorative effect.

Terrazzo has some inherently "green" characteristics. It is a nonporous surface that does not support microbial growth, mold, or mildew. Portland cement matrix is an inert material, so it contains no VOCs. It is low maintenance and, when poured in place, locally produced. Terrazzo is a durable material.

Engineered Stone

Engineered stone products are often a combination of natural stone chips in a polymer binder. They may resemble natural granite in appearance. Some of these materials are available in "slab" sizes (for example, 4 × 4 feet or 4 × 8 feet). The same considerations that apply to stone and to terrazzo apply to most of these composite materials. They will stain, scratch, and chip just like natural stone. They require rigid substrates, as does natural stone. Sometimes, the binder used allows for characteristics that would not be found in natural stone; composite materials are often more flexible, which prevents cracking to some degree. Some products can actually be heated and bent around curves.

Terrazzo Tile

Terrazzo tile comes in various sizes and thicknesses that are common to tile (⅜-inch, ⅝-inch, and others per individual product). Tiles are ordered by

a

b

FIGURE 18.1 Stone chips (a) are graded by size. Glass aggregate (b) allows for more intense color. Recycled glass is readily available for use as terrazzo aggregate. Aggregate specified may be as fine as sand (bagged lower right section of sample sets).

FIGURE 18.2 This exotic combination by Caretti Terrazzo in Morton Grove, Illinois, uses mirrored glass aggregate and metal shavings in the aggregate mix. The mirrored glass does not adhere well to the Portland cement matrix, so most likely an epoxy will be suggested by the installer.

FIGURE 18.3 Rustic terrazzo shares some similarities with exposed aggregate concrete in that the aggregate selected must be rounded, not chipped, and sharp. Rustic terrazzo is not ground flat. *Sample produced by Caretti Terrazzo, Morton Grove, Illinois.*

the manufacturer's ID number. If they are not factory sealed, a sealer or grout release is applied at the site. Refer to Chapter 17 for more information about tile specifications and installation.

Components

Composite stone flooring has three basic components (1) aggregate (chips) (Figures 18.2 and 18.3), (2) the binder matrix, and (3) divider strips. Among these components, however, many different options may be specified.

Aggregate

Aggregate is traditionally marble chips. Marble is soft enough to grind flat, yet still is a durable, serviceable material for flooring surfaces.

Marble chips used in terrazzo are graded according to size from #0 (with chips from 1/16- to 1/8-inch) through #8 (with chips from 1 to 1-1/8 inch). Customary sizes for toppings are standard #1 and #2 (spanning 1/8- to 3/8-inch); intermediate #1, #2, #3, and #4 (spanning 1/8- to 5/8-inch), and Venetian #3-4 mixed, #7-8 mixed, or #4-7 mixed (Figure 18.4a-e). Table 18.1 explains the abbreviations used to denote commonly encountered aggregate compilations.

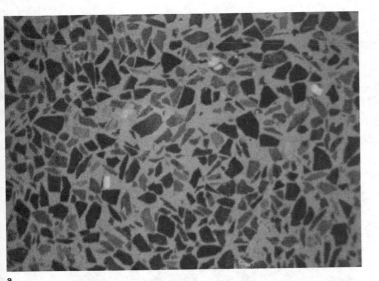

a

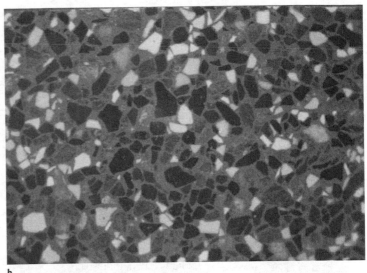

b

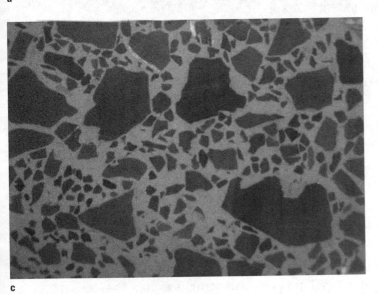

c

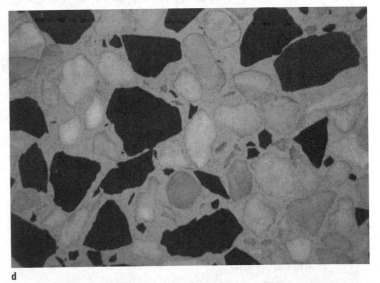

d

Matrix Binder

Three basic types of matrices are common: cementitious, modified cementitious, and resinous epoxy. The binder matrix can be pigmented to produce various colors.

- *Cementitious* Portland cement is naturally gray, but it can be produced as white if the color is controlled during manufacturing. It can be tinted with pigments similar to grout.
- *Modified Cementitious* Polyacrylate is a composition resinous material that has proven to be an excellent binder in thinset terrazzo.
- *Resinous* Epoxy or polyester is a two-component, thermal-setting resinous material that is also excellent for thinset terrazzo.

e

FIGURE 18.4 These samples, produced by Caretti Terrazzo in Morton Grove, Illinois, demonstrate the possible range in the selection of aggregate size alone. The largest aggregate, which is called Palladiana terrazzo (e), is the most labor-intensive terrazzo to cast because the slabs are often broken and hand-fitted onsite.

TABLE 18.1	Commonly Used Terrazzo Compilations	
ABBREVIATION TERM	DESCRIPTION	
S	**Standard terrazzo** · Marble chip sizes #1 ($\frac{1}{4}$-inch) and #2 ($\frac{3}{8}$-inch) in equal parts in combination with Portland cement, gray or white, with or without color pigments	
TS	**Thinset terrazzo** · Marble chip sizes #1 ($\frac{1}{4}$-inch) and smaller in combination with resin or cement binders, with or without color pigments	
V	**Venetian terrazzo** · Marble chip sizes #1 ($\frac{1}{4}$-inch) through #8 (1–$\frac{1}{8}$ inch) in combination with Portland cement, gray or white, with or without color pigments	
R	**Rustic terrazzo** · Uniformly textured terrazzo that uses marble chips, granite, riverbed stone, or other aggregates in combination with Portland cement, gray or white, with or without color pigments Note: This system requires that the matrix be depressed to expose more of the aggregate. It is not ground flat during finishing.	
C	**Conductive-type terrazzo** · Density of 60 percent or less of marble chips (size #1 or smaller) in combination with carbon black matrix Note: This system is specially designed to conduct electricity, eliminating buildup of static electricity.	
P	**Palladiana** · Thin, random, fractured slabs of marble with joints of standard-type terrazzo between each piece of marble	

Divider Strips

Divider strips are often made of an alloy of zinc, brass, or plastic (Figure 18.5a-c). Brass and plastic may have a reaction with some resinous materials and should be specified only if proven safe with the binder specified.

Installation

Depending on whether terrazzo is poured on site or precast, installation will involve some or all of the following steps: (1) selection of the aggregate and matrix (for poured-on-site terrazzo) (Figure 18.6) or the precast material, (2) preparation of the substrate and underbed, (3) pouring of the aggregate compilation or placement of the preformed composite, and (4) curing and finishing (grouting, polishing, and sealing) (Figure 18.7).

Substrate

The thickness of the terrazzo is not the whole story. You can see from the preceding descriptions that some systems can be installed directly on the structure, but some systems require additional material in the underbed and can increase the thickness significantly. A precast material with small chips in a polyester resin matrix will be about $\frac{1}{4}$ inch thick, monolithic (poured in place) material will be about $\frac{1}{2}$ inch thick, and Venetian will be about 2-$\frac{3}{4}$ inches thick. These systems require a 3-inch slab depression with an additional dead load capacity of 30–35 pounds per square foot.

Sand-cushioned systems have much better resistance to substrate movement because of their isolation from the structural slab; they are ideal for renovations where thickset granite or marble is being removed. This is normally the most expensive and time-consuming terrazzo installation.

Installation Systems

Installation systems are identified by the three types of matrix: cementitious, modified cementitious, and resinous.

CEMENTITIOUS MATRIX In *bonded* installations, a cement matrix is adhered to underbed the system for interior and exterior areas where conditions require 1-$\frac{1}{4}$ to 1-$\frac{3}{4}$ inches of recessed depth to be filled in addition to the $\frac{1}{2}$-inch terrazzo topping. The thickness is 1-$\frac{3}{4}$ to 2-$\frac{1}{4}$ inches, including a $\frac{1}{2}$-inch terrazzo topping; the weight is 18–22 pounds per square foot.

a

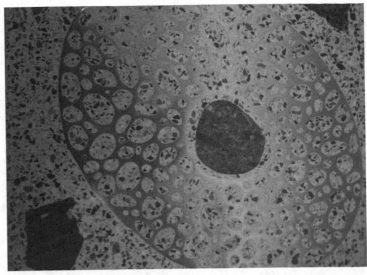

b

In sand-cushioned installations, an isolation sheet and sand layer separate the terrazzo from the underbed. This is considered to be the best system. Thickness is 2-½ to 3 inches, including a ½-inch terrazzo topping, and it weighs about 25-30 pounds per square foot.

In monolithic installations, a cement matrix veneer is poured on the concrete slab. It depends on the concrete quality for flatness and crack prevention. It is for on-grade or below-grade installations only. The thickness is a ½-inch terrazzo topping, and it weighs about 5-7 pounds per square foot.

MODIFIED CEMENTITIOUS MATRIX In modified cementitious polyacrylate installations, a polymer-modified Portland cement veneer is poured on a level concrete slab. The polymer provides strength to allow for thinner applications of cementitious systems. Thickness is a nominal ³/₈-inch polyacrylate with terrazzo topping. Chip sizes used are #0, #1, and #2, and it weighs about 4.5 pounds per square foot.

RESINOUS MATRIX In resinous epoxy installations, veneer is placed on a level concrete slab. It can be specified with marble, glass, synthetic, or granite aggregates. This system is considered to be the best thinset system. Thickness is nominally a ¼- or ³/₈-inch epoxy terrazzo topping; #0-#1 chips are most common, but #2 chips may be used for ³/₈-inch installations, and it will weigh about 3-4 pounds per square foot.

c

FIGURE 18.5 Metal inserts are traditional in terrazzo installations. They are usually metal divider strips but occasionally decorative metal inserts. Divider strips (a) were traditionally employed to control cracking. They contribute to the decorative quality of the terrazzo whether they are functional, as shown here, or purely decorative. Decorative metal (b) is used as part of the design in this terrazzo. When metal is used for decoration it will be laser-cut plate of durable thickness matching the thickness of the terrazzo (c). *Samples produced by Caretti Terrazzo, Morton Grove, Illinois.*

Curing and Finishing

Other tradespeople must be kept off the flooring until the terrazzo has been ground, polished, and protected with Masonite. Terrazzo containing Portland cement or natural stone must be sealed.

FIGURES 18.6 Begin the selection process by reviewing samples at the installer's location, where countless options and existing samples can help you narrow your search, as here at the Caretti Terrazzo showroom in Morton Grove, Illinois. Caretti Terrazzo is a member of the Krez Group.

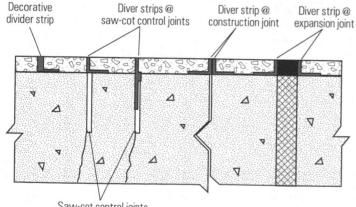

Decorative divider strip   Diver strips @ saw-cot control joints   Diver strip @ construction joint   Diver strip @ expansion joint

Saw-cot control joints

FIGURE 18.7 The various profiles available for terrazzo installation are functionally different. Work with your installer to select the correct options and finishes.

Factors Contributing to Cost

Brass divider strips are more expensive than white metals, as are divider strips wider than ⅛ inch. Designs with small areas and lots of color changes, curved shapes, or diagonal patterns, chip sizes larger than #2 (⅜-inch), and exotic aggregates are also more costly than other choices. Portland matrix is more labor-intensive and, therefore, more expensive than other matrices (as shown in Figure 18.2).

CHAPTER 19

waLLcoverings

Types Of Wallcovering

Any material that can adhere to walls and later be removed without damage to the wall can be used as "wallpaper." The following discussion reviews materials commonly sold specifically for that purpose. However, with proper sizing and preparation, followed by careful and durable installation, your creativity can expand beyond these materials.

Paper

Printed paper is exactly what its name implies. A number of colors are printed via a small variety of methods to produce the image on the surface. Each additional color requires an additional screen, cylinder, or block. Labor must be increasingly meticulous as the registration (the alignment of each successive screen, block, or cylinder pass) must be precise and accurate. The more colors and the more complex a pattern is, the higher the cost will be (Figure 19.1a and b).

a

b

FIGURE 19.1 Hand-blocked wallcovering will display some off-register markings because the human hand is not as precise as a machine. In this precise pattern (a) the misalignment is easy to find in the white border next to color areas. This pattern utilizes a moderately large number of screens. Eleven different color layers create this pattern. In this less-precise pattern (b) the off-register marks are not as noticeable. If you are hoping to find the imperfection in the product as evidence of its hand-produced nature, you may want to consider how the pattern displays or does not display the evidence.

There are two basic methods of decorating the paper: machine printing or hand printing. In machine printing, cylinders are engraved to trap ink in the voids on the roller. The surface of the roller is carved away and ink is applied to the raised surface, which transfers ink to the paper. Alternately, in rotary screening, ink is forced through unobstructed portions of mesh, much like in a silk-screening process.

Hand-printed paper may be screen or block printed. In screen printing, mesh is sealed to obstruct the transfer of ink through to the paper. In block printing, the faces of the blocks are carved away to delete the background and ink is applied to the raised surface for transfer to the paper. Small defects and irregularities are to be expected from hand-printed papers (see Figure 19.1). These are considered to be the charming quirkiness of a handmade product, but a gross defect, such as a large, noticeable, unattractive, off-register lot, is cause for rejection of goods. You should retain all samples and strike-offs to support your point in case of defective goods or a quality dispute.

Coated paper consists of a paper substrate and decorative face, as in wallpaper as described already, but with a thin layer of acrylic. This layer of acrylic provides protection and light washability (Figure 19.2a and b).

Other kinds of wallpaper include torn craft or rice paper, which arrives in pieces approximately 15 × 25 inches, and any other paper product that can be glued to the wall, whether backed or unbacked. If you are deviating from the products that are commercially offered as wallpaper, you probably need to do some product evaluation. For example, you will want to weigh the potential for fading and long-term stability because acidic paper will deteriorate and turn brown. Also, consider the level of preparation required; aside from the usual sizing of the wall surface, you may have to prepare the material itself in some way. And don't forget any finishing that may be needed to seal the material after installation.

Materials Other than Paper

Any materials, backed or unbacked, that can be glued to the wall can be used as wallcoverings. The many choices include grass- and string-faced papers, veneers, foils, cloth, and vinyl.

GRASS CLOTH Grass cloth is paper faced with long woven grasses that are left natural or dyed (Figure 19.3). Paperhangers can avoid an uneven appearance by rotating every other panel as they install. The seams always show. Special clear paste is required to avoid staining the face of the goods. Some grass cloths will shrink as the glue

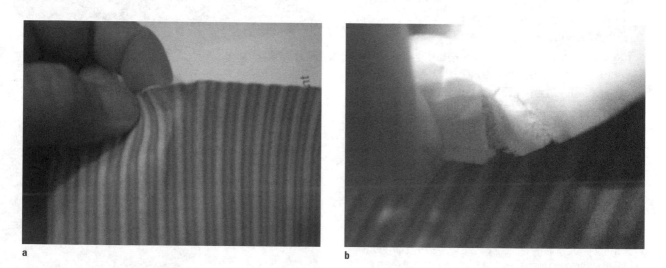

a   b

FIGURE 19.2 A light acrylic coat does not provide the protection that a heavy vinyl layer can afford. You can check the thickness of the top layer by pulling the sample to find out if it will hold up to rigorous environments. A vinyl face of a wallcovering that stretches (a) indicates that it has a durable surface. A paper backing that tears before the vinyl breaks (b) confirms that it is suitable for areas that must be occasionally scrubbed.

cures, so the hanger may not trim the top and bottom of the sheets until the glue is dry.

STRING String papers have continuous rows of strings laid side by side on a paper backing (Figure 19.4). The strings run parallel to the vertical seams, so the seams can be well hidden. These coverings are especially porous and vulnerable to soiling, and cats cannot resist clawing them.

WOOD AND CORK VENEER Wood and cork veneer wallcoverings are real wood veneers that are backed with paper or mesh for flexibility (Figure 19.5). They are available in different unit dimensions, so check with the manufacturer before estimating. Products that are three feet wide are fairly common, but narrower and wider widths are also available. Some manufacturers sell this material by the panel (8 or 9 feet long), others by the roll. The veneer surface is ready for finishing on site or may come prefinished.

FOIL AND MYLAR Foil and Mylar wallcoverings, which are backed with paper, are reflective and can show every imperfection in the wall surface, so prep work may be more intensive than merely sizing the walls. Foils are actual metals and can oxidize under the wrong conditions. Mylar films are reflective plastics that imitate foils.

CLOTH Cloth can be backed with paper, a knit fabric backing, a foam backing, acrylic backing, or left unbacked (Figure 19.6). The backing process may stretch some sections more than others. Paper-backed fabrics do not always arrive strictly on grain and the backing does not allow for any movement if the hanger should have to "fudge" the alignment of a pattern, for instance. A woven-fabric scrim backing will allow for some movement if necessary.

Textile wallcoverings (cloth and string) should be treated with a stain-repellent finish to make it easier to remove any adhesives from the face of the product after installation.

Cloth wallcoverings can also have vinyl-laminated faces, which will improve washability and protect the fabric from damage.

VINYL Vinyl is the most cleanable kind of applied wallpaper because it is hydrophobic and won't be

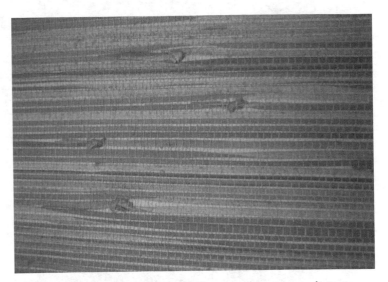

FIGURE 19.3 Grass cloth has vegetable fibers glued to a paper substrate. The seams on this paper will always show so it is important to consider the seaming plan with the hanger so the rhythm of panels is acceptable.

FIGURE 19.4 String paper has string glued to the paper substrate. This paper will not show its seams as readily as grass cloth.

damaged by a little water. Many vinyl wallpapers are considered scrubbable and can withstand cleaning products, so they are good choices for areas subject to moisture and dirt. However, vinyl doesn't breathe, so the proper adhesives must be used to prevent the growth of mildew. Vinyl wallpapers are available in a variety of forms:

- *Paper-backed vinyl* is a paper substrate with a 2-5-millimeter vinyl layer applied to the substrate in liquid form. The decorative layer is printed on the vinyl.
- *Fabric-backed vinyl* has a woven or nonwoven substrate to which up to 10 millimeters of vinyl

FIGURE 19.5 The voids in the sample on an angle allow contrasting paper to show through to decorative effect similar to the fills in travertine.

FIGURE 19.6 Fabric can be purchased paper-backed or can be laminated to paper. When you select fabric that's already adhered to the paper substrate, you are more assured of consistency in the application than when you have fabric laminated per order by a third party.

have been applied in liquid form. The vinyl may be printed or embossed.

- *Solid vinyl* consists of film vinyl that is laminated to a paper or fabric substrate. It is more durable than paper-backed or fabric-backed vinyl wallcoverings, which have only a vinyl coating.

Borders

Borders are narrower wallcoverings designed to be hung horizontally. A unit of border paper is referred to as a spool instead of a roll.

Custom Wallcovering

Some manufacturers will custom-color any of their designs on any of their grounds (the paper or vinyl that serves as the base material for the patterned wallpaper). Minimum quantities usually apply and there is often a setup charge in addition to the usual costs. Custom colors and patterns can be hand-blocked onto any suitable ground.

The custom process will increase the delivery time of the order. You will need time to investigate the possible design impact of color combinations in relation to the pattern selected. You may need more than one strike-off (sample) as color combinations may have unexpected results (simultaneous contrast and other color theory effects). Include the time for production of the strike-off, as well as for transportation of the strike-off between the fabricator, your office, and your client. It is advisable to have the unit cost per strike-off stated up front if there is a limit on the number of strike-offs that will be produced as part of the order cost.

Backings

Products offered for sale as wallcoverings are typically backed with a material that is compatible with the covering. If you are selecting a backing for a product that is not sold as wallcovering, but you intend to use it that way, the different characteristics of various backings should be considered.

- *Woven* (light = scrim, heavy - drill or cotton twill) backings allow for flexibility so the paperhanger can make minor adjustments, if necessary, while hanging. The various weights should correspond to the material being backed. The backing should be lighter in weight than the face.
- *Nonwoven* backings will be dimensionally stable because of the randomized orientation of the fiber and fiber content of the backing. This backing will also be flexible, allowing for adjustment.
- *Knit* backing is a fine open knit and allows for adjustment at the site because it is so flexible.
- *Paper* backing fixes the dimensions of the covering and is not flexible, so the paperhanger cannot make adjustments onsite. This selection should be reserved for coverings that are also very stable, such as tightly woven chintz or materials that do not require any pattern match.
- *Acrylic or latex* backing maintains flexibility and, because it is applied in liquid form, it bonds fibers together. This backing would be selected for a fabric likely to unravel at the cut edges or where you expected that adjustments would be needed at the site.
- *Lining paper* is an undecorated paper wallcovering. It may be installed on the wall prior to the installation of the decorative wallcovering over it. Special *bridging lining* would be selected to mask texture on the wall if necessary.

Durability Ratings

You will encounter two systems of rating the durability of wallcoverings. One relates to all wallcoverings and the other describes commercial wallcoverings specifically.

Ratings Applicable to All Wallcoverings

- Class I: Decorative
- Class II: Decorative and serviceable (more washable and colorfast)
- Class III: Decorative with good serviceability. Medium use for abrasion and stain resistance. Meets strength and crocking-resistant standards
- Class IV: Decorative with full serviceability, heavy consumer and light commercial use; meets strength, crocking, and tear-resistance criteria
- Class V: Medium commercial serviceability; high abrasion and crocking resistance, color-fast and tear resistant
- Class VI: Full commercial serviceability; in addition to above criteria resists cold cracking, heat aging, and shrinkage.

Ratings Applicable to Commercial Wallcoverings

- Type I: Light duty for offices, hotel rooms
- Type II: Medium duty for reception areas, corridors, classrooms
- Type III: Heavy duty for hospital corridors and other heavy-use with moving equipment

Instructions on the handling and installation of wallcoverings are usually included with the shipment and may be given in the form of symbols (Figure 19.7).

Sizes

Wallcoverings are manufactured in several standard sizes. American rolls are 27 inches wide, European rolls are 22 inches wide, grass cloths are 36 inches wide, and vinyl is 54 inches wide (Table 19.1). Most papers are priced by the single roll but sold in double or triple rolls to reduce waste (Figure 19.8). Unless a cutting charge is offered, allowing you to purchase an off-number of rolls, you will have to round up to the nearest multiple. Vinyls are often sold by the yard or the bolt. Bolts commonly contain 30, 50, or 60 yards. The only way to know for sure how much wallcovering comes in a single unit (bolt, roll, double roll) is to ask the supplier. The number will probably be stated in terms of yards per roll or bolt and feet or square feet for rolls.

Installation
Prep Work

In addition to the prep work required for painting (including priming with the recommended primer, usually alkyd), other work may be required. Old wallpaper may have to be removed,

TABLE 19.1	**Rolls of Wallcovering**		
TYPE OF ROLL	WIDTH	LENGTH OF GOODS	COVERAGE SOLD
American Rolls	27"	4.5 to 5 yards per single 30 to 33 sf/roll	Double to triple
European Rolls	20.5"	5.5 yards per single 27.5 sf/roll	Single or double
English Rolls	20.5"	11 yards per single 55 per roll	Single
Borders	No Standard	5 yards spools, 5 lineal yards	Spool
Vinyl	54"	Sold per yard 30 to 35 yard bolts	13.5 sf/yard per yard

→|○ No match	↑↓ Reverse alternate lengths	☼ Good light fastness
→|← Straight match	∼ Spongeable	↗ Strippable
→|← Half drop match	≈ Washable	↗ Peelable
$\frac{50}{25}$ **cm** Distance between repeat Distance offset	≋ Super-Washable	Pre-pasted
↑ Direction of hanging	▥ Scrubbable	Paste the wall (Unpasted paper)
	☼ Sufficient light fastness	Past the paper

FIGURE 19.7 International symbols for characteristics and performance of wallcoverings are a necessity in today's world market.

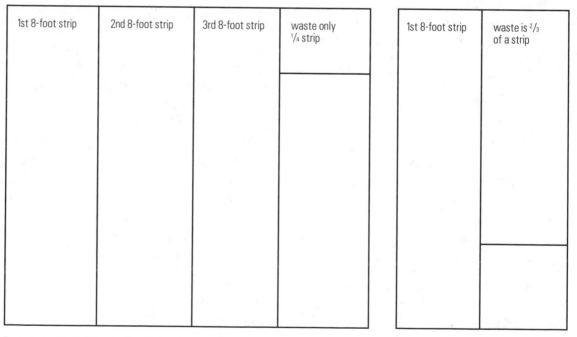

For typical ceiling heights, double rolls have less waste.

Ceiling rolls leave more unused, wasted goods.

FIGURE 19.8 Single-versus-double-roll yields demonstrate the material savings for two rolls of wallcovering left contiguous as opposed to that which has been cut into separate rolls. It is priced by the single roll but shipped in doubles.

walls may need to be sized, or glossy surfaces may need to be sanded so that the adhesive will stick. All holes and cracks must be repaired. If the walls are not smooth enough, a liner paper may be installed. If walls have a textured finish, sanding them may be sufficient preparation or they may have to be skim coated (coat of plaster applied). If the walls are primed with a color similar to the color of the wallcovering, any small opening that develops from paper shrinkage as the glue dries will be less noticeable. The trim must be painted before the paper is hung.

Qualifying Installers

You will interview the installer about similar work that he or she has done in the past and ask how the work was done, what issues came up in the hanging, and how they were handled. If possible, you should review photos of similar installations. If the job is especially tricky and the material is costly (if you are using a hand-blocked fabric with some inconsistency in the match, for instance), you may ask to see a completed installation of a similar material, even if it is not recent. While inspecting the installation you should evaluate (1) how neatly the matching was done and, if an exact match was not possible, whether the seams are inconspicuous, (2) whether the seams are clean (with no glue, wrinkles, etc.), and (3) whether the overall job appears to run on grain and the pattern is well-placed relative to architectural details. You should also interview previous clients of the hanger and ask about the quality of the installation, the accuracy of the estimates for material and time, and the professionalism of the workers (that is, their general tidiness and courtesy).

Inspection

You will need to check the seams for a tight, accurate match and make sure there is no adhesive on the face of the paper. Make sure that natural material (cork, grass cloth, etc.) was installed in a manner that minimizes the effect of variations in the panels and that fabric orientation is consistent (fabric may reflect light differently depending on which way it is hung). There should be no bubbles or dents. All cuts should be straight and neat and, if covering switch plates, concealed behind them. If HVAC grilles are covered, be sure the slices between veins are straight and neat, the covering is adhering tightly to the entire surface, and the corners of covered plates and grilles are neatly folded and tightly adhered. On fabric or string wallcoverings, any cuts should not show fraying or loose edges.

For restorations of historic places, follow the installation techniques that were originally used with the addition of one more step—installing acid-free liner paper. Historically, the plaster was sized with diluted glue and a lining paper was installed using cooked wheat paste. Then a layer of 100 percent cotton muslin was installed on top of the blank lining paper and the decorative wallpaper was installed on top of that. Today, we add a second layer of acid-free lining paper beneath the decorative paper to ensure the longevity of the installation.

Factors Contributing to Cost

The difficulty in hanging the wallcovering will be the single largest labor factor. Most wallpapers are so consistent that paperhangers will figure their installation costs on a flat fee per roll of paper hung. If a hand-blocked fabric is being used, the hanger may charge on a time and material basis to allow for degrees of possible variation. If this is the case, try to obtain a not-to-exceed price. Keep in mind that the maximum agreed-on price that will be charged often becomes the final fee. Materials are likely to represent the greatest price variation.

Estimating

General rules of thumb can be used if the roughest of takeoffs is sufficient. For example, every American roll will cover about 30 square feet of wall surface. Subtract a half roll for every door or window of similar size. If the wallcovering is metric, add an extra roll for every four American rolls. Patterned wallcovering will result in some waste. For a repeat of up to 6 inches, reduce the 30 square feet coverage rule to 25; for 7-12 inch repeats, the coverage will be closer to 22 square feet; for 13–18 inch repeats, it drops to 20 square feet; and for 19–23 inch repeats, it will be about 18 square feet.

Calculating Quantities for Cost Comparisons

If a more precise estimate is required for cost comparisons, you may want to use an estimating method called the strip method, which accounts for every panel of wallcovering required. On a to-scale plan, determine the best starting point for the installation (for example, a corner where the mismatched pattern will not be obvious) and make a tick-mark indicating every panel edge. This will indicate the number of panels required. Calculate the length required by rounding up each panel length until it contains a number of full repeats. For example, if the wall height indicates that 10.3 repeats will be required, round up to 11 repeats for the new length, and multiply that by the number of panels needed.

The strip method is the most precise way to estimate wallcovering and it is the method that professional paperhangers use.

1. Measure the perimeter of the room and divide by the width of the paper to determine the number of panels or, alternately, tick off the panel widths on a drawing (Figure 19.9).
2. Calculate the total running length of paper required by multiplying the number of panels by the length of the panels. There is a rule of thumb that directs you to deduct a roll for every two openings, but Figure 19.10 illustrates a configuration that disallows any subtraction of material for an opening, so this rule of thumb is for the quick takeoff for producing a ballpark estimate only.
3. Repeats are important in determining the quantity of wallcovering required. The kind of match—drop match, side match (Figure 19.11a and b)—does not have as much impact on quantity as the size of the repeat does, but the kind of match should also be relayed to the paperhanger before finalizing quantity. Divide the size of the vertical repeat into the height of the wall and round up to the next full repeat. Multiply that number by the vertical length of the repeat.

4. Divide the running length required by the length available in a single unit (single roll if sold by the roll, bolt if sold by the bolt, in a single yard if sold by the yard, etc.) to arrive at the number of units required. Add one full repeat per roll to your order so you can start the first cut where you want it.

Obtaining an Estimate

When it is time to draft the proposal to your client, you will obtain written estimates from one or more paperhangers. The installer will tell you how much paper to deliver to the job site or to their receiving room. Along with your request for bid, you should forward:

- A description of the job: location, room name, condition
- Scope of work: washing, sizing, other work required in addition to hanging. Include any special instruction from the manufacturer in the scope of work list.
- Description of the material: type of wallcovering (paper-faced vinyl, paper, etc.), unit of measure (yard, American roll, etc.), width, and repeat

Include a to-scale plan and information on how to gain access if the hanger wants to inspect the job site before bidding. If you need the bid by a certain date or if there is a deadline for completing the work, you should also include that information with your request for bid.

Custom-Upholstered Panels

Like custom wood wall panels, upholstered panels will be drawn up in elevation and put out to bid. You will probably prefer to have the fabricator handle installation as well. Drapery workrooms often supply this kind of service. Some upholstery shops also do this kind of work. Panels will require some kind of stable substrate. Homasote fiber board is often used; it can be backed with MDF or other material to strengthen it, if necessary. Panels can be padded with a layer of foam or polyester batting. They can be hung on the wall with cleats or Velcro hook-and-loop fasteners or some other concealed method that is de-mountable. The panels should probably not be

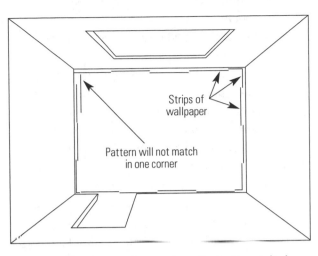

FIGURE 19.9 The most precise way to estimate the required quantity of wallcovering is the strip method. It will also help you to visualize how the pattern of seams may lay out if you have a wallcovering in which the seams cannot be well hidden.

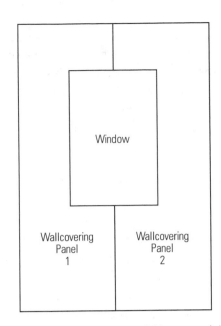

FIGURE 19.10 Formulas do not always yield accurate information. A formula may tell you that you can deduct so much wallcoverings for openings, but if the opening and the wallcovering meet in an undesirable manner, you may not have enough paper to correct the problem.

a   b

FIGURE 19.11 A match may be described as a straight/side match (a), a half-drop match (b), or another match. This information should be given to the estimator when you are ready to place the order. More paper than estimated may not be required, but it is better to have overage on hand than to come up short.

glued because this would make it impossible to change the fabric without damaging the panel substrate and the wall. Walls may be padded out and fabric panels tacked top and bottom and a millwork trim or fabric welt added to cover all tack locations.

Upholstered panels demand more consideration for service outlets than wood panels do. The same issues apply but are compounded by maintenance considerations. Areas such as HVAC vents (returns as well as supplies) and switch plates will be subject to soiling. HVAC grilles are problematic because wherever a lot of air is moving past a textile, there will be extra soiling. Switch plates will accumulate dirt from hands. Areas adjacent to open windows are vulnerable to soiling as well. Cleats for hanging artwork will have to be modified so the artwork does not "dimple" the upholstery.

The fabric width should exceed the panel width to avoid having a seam on the face of the panel. Repeats will have to be figured into the planning and placement and all of this information must be clearly communicated to the fabricator in drawings and notes. You may want to inspect the panels at the shop prior to their delivery to the site to make sure that the panels are covered as instructed, that the panels are on grain and free of unwanted tucks and puckers, and that the padding is smooth and of the proper puffiness. Correcting or adjusting panels will be easier at the shop than onsite.

CHAPTER 20

waLL surfaces and paint

The quality of your paint job depends on the surface, paint selection, and the skill of the painters. You will find a broad range of quality among the surfacing, selection, and labor, and the precise circumstances of the job and budget will indicate the most appropriate quality level. As with most items and work that you will specify, you get what you pay for. It is an unspoken expectation that a college student painting houses over the summer break will not provide the same quality work as a full-time, skilled craftperson. Price differences can be startling when work is released for bids if there are differences among the skill levels of the bidders and the scope of work is loosely defined.

Because painting work comes toward the end of the project, there is a temptation to skimp on the quality of the painting labor (resulting from budgeting at the outset or cost overruns during construction), and compared to other kinds of work that you will specify, painting is fairly easily redone at a later date. In the hierarchy of the task, the most important work is the preparation of the substrate. The substrate should allow for no compromise.

Substrates

Paint is one material surface that is secondary to its substrate—the ceiling, trim, and walls. The biggest factor differentiating a good paint job from a terrible one is the surface on which the paint is applied, so this discussion begins with material substrates.

Plaster

Traditionally, walls and ceilings have been plastered. Wooden lath was fastened crosswise to studs and joists, leaving spaces through which the plaster oozed. The part that oozed through the lath holding the plaster to the walls and ceilings was referred to as the "keys." Over time, wooden lath expands and contracts, and eventually the keys break off because of movement of the structure, so the plaster is no longer firmly affixed to the substrate. Plaster in rooms with smaller areas tends to survive longer than that in large continuous areas in equally sound structures and similar conditions. Today, diamond expanded metal mesh is used in place of traditional wooden lath.

Plasterwork is becoming very scarce but may be required for jobs if old plaster is damaged or missing in limited areas or if the structure is historically significant. It usually takes years of training and experience to get a feel for plastering, and good plasterers are not easy to locate. The plasterer must work the plaster sufficiently but not overwork it until it starts to brown out (cure to sufficient stability), at which time it must be worked again to a smooth surface. Most tradespeople don't have the opportunity to acquire the necessary experience because plasterwork is rarely specified. So, it is more likely that you will specify plasterwork repairs than actual plastering.

In order for the installation to be successful, the plasterer must start with a proper mix of ingredients; proportion is very important for all layers, as is timing. The coats must be timed so the previous coat is set but not too dry. The surface must be properly worked as the plasterer wields the trowel during the application. If new work is being installed on top of old work, the original formula must be used or the layers may not bond properly. The temperature of the environment has to be controlled and cannot be too hot or too cold. Although you may want to seal up the house while the work is in progress, you don't want it to get too damp either! Even a skim coating puts a lot of moisture in the air, and plaster releases even more water. Although the look of a hand-troweled surface and the solid feel of plaster walls are appealing, it is easy to understand why the building industry has switched to drywall, given the complications of plaster.

FORMULATIONS The plasterer doing your repair work may suggest one of two general formulations: lime plaster (limestone) or gypsum plaster (gypsum rock). Older plaster was a lime formulation, made from powdered limestone. The first two coats contain fibers (traditionally animal hair, but now vegetable fibers are typically used) and sand and are about ⅜ inch thick. The top coat has no fiber and very little sand, and is very thin, about ⅛ inch thick. Lime plaster is harder than gypsum plaster, but it takes months to dry out. If the repair work requires that the plaster be applied directly to a masonry substrate (no lath on the back of a chimney, for instance), the plasterer will probably use lime plaster (and there will probably be vegetable fiber rather than animal hair in the first two coats).

Gypsum plaster sets up quickly and dries in weeks instead of months. It does not use animal hair. You may find metal lath under gypsum plaster. Plaster on metal lath will be thinner—around ½ inch thick instead of nearly an inch thick. Plaster is also applied to *blue board* (a specially treated gypsum board with a paper face that makes a good bond with plaster) and skim coated.

The top plaster coat may be tinted, eliminating the need for painting work.

LATH You will encounter three common types of laths: wood, metal, and gypsum. Wooden lath consists of thin wood strips fastened horizontally across studs or joists and is usually found in structures built before the 1930s. Metal lath may be painted or galvanized and is typically diamond expanded metal mesh. Gypsum lath, usually referred to as blue board, has a paper face specifically designed to absorb water, so it forms a good bond with plaster skim coats. An obsolete product called rock lath came in smaller sizes than blue board, but you may hear blue board called rock lath.

Wallboard

Different wallboard varieties address different site and surfacing needs. Green board is water-resistive and is specified when humidity is likely or when the surface is being prepared for tile that will be thinset. The thinset mixture contains water and the water resistance of green board makes it a better choice. Some installers request blue board as a substrate in bathrooms because the surface soaks up water and supposedly forms a better bond with water-containing mastics. For areas that will be wet (such as shower surrounds), cement board is totally impervious to water. You can soak it in water without damage. For painted surfaces, regular gray-faced gypsum board is sufficient. Specify ⅝-inch-thick board for walls receiving a single layer of drywall. Code dictates that commercial spaces have walls with fire-resistive capabilities. The wall construction will be dictated by occupancy, use, and building construction type (frame, heavy timber, masonry, etc.). Fire-resistive partitions will use varying combinations of different thicknesses (Figure 20.1a-g).

Primers

Primer is used to even out the surface of the substrate so the paint application will have an even appearance. It also creates a good bond between the substrate and the paint. Primers hold the binders in the finish to the surface, preventing them from soaking into the surface and causing inconsistencies in the gloss level. It may be specified in your documents or you may enter a performance specification and allow the painter to select the primer to suit the needs of the job.

Two categories of primer are enamel underbodies and sealers. Enamel underbodies are selected to conceal minor imperfections. These primers have more pigment than sealer and can be easily

a

b

c

d

e

f

g

FIGURE 20.1 The following sample constructions use various wallboard products that demonstrate various fire-resistive characteristics. One layer of ⅝-inch sheetrock on each side of 2 × 4-inch wooden studs, 16 or 24 inches in the center (apart), with joints finished for a 1-hour fire rating (a). One layer of Durock cement board on one side and ⅝-inch sheetrock on the other side of 3⅝-inch 20-gauge steel studs with joints finished with 3-inch Thermafiber insulation in the cavity for a 1-hour fire rating (b). Two layers of ⅝-inch sheetrock on each side of 2 × 4 wooden studs, 16 inches in the center (apart), with face layer joints finished for a 2-hour fire rating (c). Three layers of ½-inch sheetrock on each side of 1⅝-inch 25-gauge steel studs, 24 inches in the center (apart), with face layer joints finished for a 3-hour fire rating (d). One layer of ¾-inch sheetrock with 3 ½-inch 25-gauge steel studs, 24 inches in the center, with 3-inch Thermafiber insulation in the cavity for a 2-hour fire rating (e). Two layers of ½-inch sheetrock over 1⅝-inch 25-gauge steel studs, with the face layer joints finished for a 2-hour fire rating (f). Four layers of ½-inch sheetrock on each side of 1⅝-inch 25-gauge steel studs for a 4-hour fire rating (g). *Images photographed by permission of United States Gypsum Corporation.*

sanded. Sealers hold back anything on the surface that might bleed through the finish coats and prevent damage from alkaline "hot spots" in plaster. Sealers may be especially formulated for particular situations like sealing knots in wood, suppressing stains, or creating a surface compatible with latex paint if the original finish was oil-based.

Primers may be alkyd or water-based (latex) primers. Latex is more flexible, but it will raise the grain of bare woodwork because water makes the grain swell. Oil will not raise the grain in the same way. Woodwork can be shellacked to seal knots and sap. Stain-killing primers can be used if there are stains that would continue to bleed through coats of paint (for example, painted graffiti or ballpoint pen) or if anything on the substrate might react with the paint. The substrate, site conditions, and planned use will indicate the proper primer (and paint). Different materials (metals, brick, wood plaster, concrete, etc.) require primers with different characteristics. The job's location (above or below grade) also influences the selection of primer as can the planned use (heavy-traffic floor paint, spaces with temperature fluctuations, other conditions).

Paint

Paint is specified by formula, color, and gloss level.

Formulations

Latex and oil paint are the two broad formula categories commonly referenced. Oil-based paints can still be understood by the traditional meaning—that the solvent is oil-based. The term "latex" derives from the original water-based paint formulation, which used synthetic latex rubber. Although this formula is no longer available, the term is still used to indicate various types of water-based paint.

Oils traditionally used in paint include linseed oil, tung oil, and soya oil, but now the designation "oil paint" also includes alkyds (modified oils). Alkyds dry harder and faster than traditional oils. The extra durability for which oil paint is known is due to the fact that it does not simply dry but oxidizes in a way that produces extra hardness, which is referred to as hard surface tack. This characteristic is preferred for window sashes, which must slide without sticking.

The oxidation process continues over the life of the paint job, and the paint eventually becomes vulnerable to cracking and chipping. The oxidation also causes yellowing in areas not exposed to sunlight. Oil paints dry more slowly, so they have time to "level out," leaving fewer brush marks.

Oil-based paints are being replaced (in some jurisdictions by mandate of law) by water-based paint. Water-based systems include acrylic, vinyl acrylic, acrylics and styrene acrylics, polyvinyl acetate, and waterborne epoxies.

Acrylics offer good adhesion; they are thermoplastic, flexible, and resistant to damage from moisture. Vinyl acrylics, which form a breathable film, are thermoplastic, nonyellowing, and alkali-resistant. Styrene acrylics have good film strength and resist moisture. Polyvinyl acetate forms a breathable film, is nearly odorless, and has good alkali resistance. Waterborne epoxies are nonyellowing and have low VOCs.

Water-based paint is easy to use because painters don't have to keep stirring it and it cleans up with water. It does not give off solvent fumes, although it does have an odor and many latex formulas outgas VOCs. VOC levels are identified as parts per volume using the metric measurement of grams per liter (g/l), although paint is still sold by the gallon in the United States. Some latex paint formulations claim zero VOCs and are virtually odor-free. There may still be some toxicity related to colorants and additives, but getting the solvent down to zero is a big step toward healthier environments. Good-quality paint will have a higher percentage of solids per volume of solvent. The solvents are the part that releases VOCs. Quality has an indirect relationship to organic compounds, but more pigment and less solvent per volume does contribute to the reduction of outgassed organic compounds.

Water-based formulas cannot yet achieve the hard "tack" of oil-based paint. They do not perform as well on moving parts such as doors and window sashes because they are always a little stickier. Oil paints level themselves out over their long drying times, a fact that is responsible for the oil-paint adage, "less paint, more painting." That is good advice for oil but bad advice for latex. Water-based paint dries faster than oil;

therefore, it must be applied very quickly with as little reworking of the surface as possible to prevent brush and roller marks. When latex paint is to be used on woodwork, many painting companies now mask off the entire room, leaving only the millwork exposed and then spray the paint on. No brushing means no brush marks; however, you still must watch for drips and sags.

Gloss Level

In addition to formula and color, paint cannot be adequately described without a gloss level designation. Standard gloss level designations include the following: gloss, semigloss, satin, eggshell, and flat. Manufacturers have proprietary formulas for specific gloss levels and may also designate their own descriptive names for some sheen levels (for example, Benjamin Moore's soft satin, called Pearl).

Gloss paint produces a reflective surface and is defined as having 75-85 percent sheen, meaning that 75-85 percent of the light striking the surface bounces off. Oil-based gloss paint is the most durable and most stain-resistant type of paint. It is also the most cleanable, so it is a good choice for areas with heavy traffic. Because it is so reflective, every surface imperfection will be visible; gloss paint should only be applied after expert preparation of the surface. In utility spaces where washability is more important than appearance, it is usually acceptable to use gloss paint on less-than-perfect surfaces.

Semigloss paint is a step down from gloss paint in sheen. Its performance is similar, just a bit less so: a little less shiny, a little less washable, a little less demanding of a perfect surface. It is still easy to clean and still fairly shiny. Semigloss paint is specified more often than gloss paint and is frequently used on millwork trim and as accent areas. Semigloss is defined as having 40-55 percent sheen.

Satin is the next step down on the gloss continuum. It has a soft sheen, but is less able to endure rigorous cleaning than higher-gloss paints. However, it still allows cleaning with a soft cloth and mild soap to remove fingerprints. Satin is defined as having 25-40 percent sheen.

Eggshell is very close to the sheen of satin, and a side-by-side comparison of samples may be needed to discern the difference. This similarity in appearance can be used to good advantage, by applying eggshell to the walls and satin to the trim, for instance. Eggshell is washable and has a sheen of 10-25 percent.

Flat paint is defined as having a sheen of 0-10 percent. It is the most forgiving of imperfections in walls; although it does not make bad prep work invisible, it is the best choice for situations in which the budget allows only minimal prep work. The velvet appearance of flat paint on ceilings could not be duplicated on walls until new formulations for washable flat appeared on the market. Ceramic technologies have replaced the fillers that once gave paint its opacity, making the surface slightly more durable than regular flat paint, which cannot be rubbed without damaging the surface (so that washing demanded repainting). A washable flat formula appears a little more reflective than flat formulations.

Paint for Use on Special Materials and Surfaces

Other paint formulas are designed for special uses. For example, high-performance epoxy coatings are used for high-traffic floors, and additives are introduced to paints to provide antifungal or antimicrobial properties. Some companies will produce custom coatings in large quantities, working with you to define the characteristics desired, then develop a formula to meet your needs. The many differing surfaces specified for paint finishes demand a variety of paint formulations. Your painter should be permitted to select the formulation to be used because he or she will be expected to stand behind the performance of the completed work. Understand that if you specify the formulation, you will be the liable party if the installation should fail for any reason. Many designers restrict their specs to manufacturer, color, and gloss level. Formulations recommended for various surfaces include:

- Cement ceilings, walls, columns: Cementitious paint (like a thin mortar) with a flat finish
- Cement floors: Urethanes or epoxy polyamide
- Concrete block (above grade): Cementitious latex specially formulated for use on concrete

blocks with a filler finish, epoxy polyester, or below grade cementitious only

- Particleboard or flake board: Alkyd undercoat with a latex top coat or alkyd undercoat and top coat
- Metals: Alkyd base paint

Additives may be used to impart additional desirable qualities. These additives are chemical compounds such as driers, defoamers, antiskinning agents, coalescing agents, thickeners, biocides, dispersants, and antisetting agents.

Other Surfacing Materials and Finishes

Plaster or stuccolike surfacing mixtures create an actual (rather than visual only) texture on a surface. Stucco is a traditional cement-based product that is still in use, along with new acrylic products that are troweled or sprayed onto the surface being texturized. Dryvit is one widely known product that allows for a range of textures. Earlier generations of the material were susceptible to damage when bumped, but newer formulations are sturdier.

Fresco is essentially a thin-coat plaster with an integral color that can be worked or troweled to a hard, textured surface. Because fresco is not a film, dings will only chip the surface. The integral color is present throughout the depth of the material, so the appearance of a small chip can be minimized, if necessary, with a light sanding. Venetian plaster products (Figure 20.2) are examples of such a finish.

Paint techniques are very popular now and can be achieved using a variety of methods. Some techniques that you will specify may require a textured undercoat. This undercoat may be as delicate as tissue paper (Figure 20.3) or as bold as a buildup of a composite (Figure 20.4). Many techniques require multiple steps to achieve (Figure 20.5a-c). They range from random spatters to a tightly controlled trompe l'oeil. Textural effects are possible when paint layers of differing formulations react to each other in controlled ways, such as alligator technique (Figure 20.6). Commonly used techniques include striaé (Figure 20.7a), linen-look (Figure 20.7b), sponge or ragging, faux finishes such as a simulated wood

FIGURE 20.2 Venetian plaster products are produced in a manner similar to classic tinted plaster techniques, but new formulations are even more durable, flexible, and water-resistant. *Courtesy of Hester Painting and Decorating, Skokie, Illinois.*

grain called faux bois (Figure 20.8a and b), or other simulated materials. Many of these finishes, certainly the multi-layer techniques, employ a *glaze*, a thinned-down paint that is applied by some method over a solid base color. The glaze can be any formulation that allows the painter to work the medium as necessary to achieve the finish desired. For instance, the faux tortoise technique depends on the incompatibility of two or more glazes that repel each other rather than combine with each other.

The use of stencils (Figure 20.9) allows for a repetition that resembles printed patterns on wallpaper. Metal leaf (Figure 20.10) is not paint, but is included here because it is a surfacing material employed for the same function. These thin foils on small pieces of paper (less than 6 inches square) are so fine that painters cannot handle them with their bare hands—the heat from their skin is enough to attach the leaf to their fingers. The material and labor are expensive for metal-leaf surfaces. Metallic paints contain actual metal powder and may be substituted for actual leaf to meet budget restrictions. Recall that metal will retain its characteristics, regardless of the application, so the properties of these finishes include those of the paint vehicle, as well as the properties of the metal in them (see Box 20.1).

Installation

New substrates will usually be in more predictable condition than substrates that have been

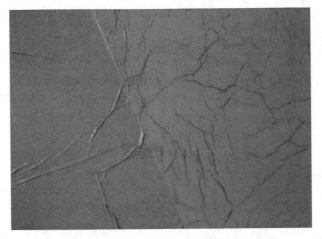

FIGURE 20.3 Regular paper forms the underlayer of the sample on the left, and tissue paper forms the underlayer of the sample on the right. *Courtesy of Hester Painting and Decorating, Skokie, Illinois.*

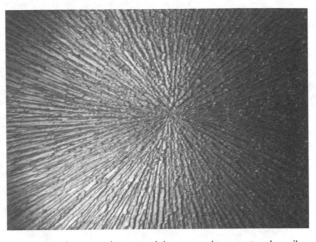

FIGURE 20.4 A composite material was used to create a heavily textured surface for a metallic paint coat. *Courtesy of Hester Painting and Decorating, Skokie, Illinois.*

a

b

c

FIGURE 20.5 Many techniques require more than one coat. A base coat of flat color was given an actual texture with two layers of tinted texture (a). A base coat was skim-coated with a tinted texture (b). A lightly textured base coat was ragged with two successive layers of glaze (c). These samples display successive layers building the finish up toward the center. *Courtesy of Hester Painting and Decorating, Skokie, Illinois.*

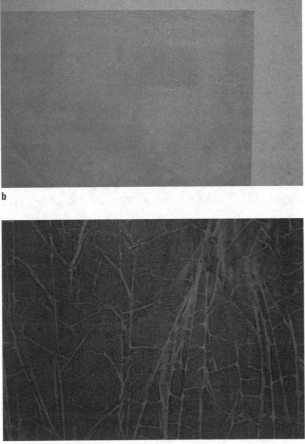

FIGURE 20.6 This alligator skin technique requires careful management of two paint formulations to create this visual texture. *Courtesy of Hester Painting and Decorating, Skokie, Illinois.*

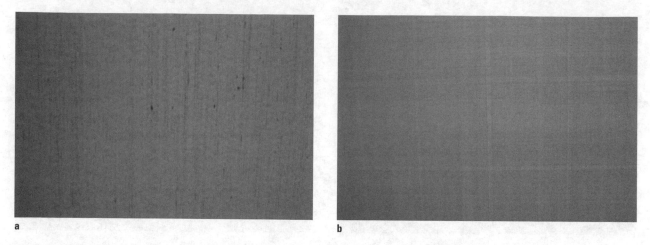

a

b

FIGURE 20.7 Two classic techniques utilize similar methods and materials. Striaé (a), pronounced *stree-ay*, drags the overglaze in one direction. The linen technique (b) drags the glaze in two directions. *Courtesy of Hester Painting and Decorating, Skokie, Illinois.*

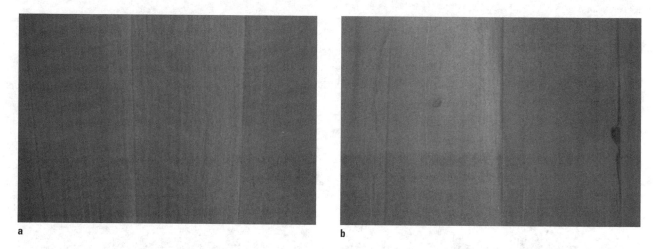
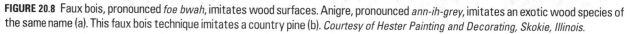

a

b

FIGURE 20.8 Faux bois, pronounced *foe bwah*, imitates wood surfaces. Anigre, pronounced *ann-ih-grey*, imitates an exotic wood species of the same name (a). This faux bois technique imitates a country pine (b). *Courtesy of Hester Painting and Decorating, Skokie, Illinois.*

in use for years. The older the surface material, the more likely the surface will require repair. While you are in the early planning stages and preparing budgets for your client, you should have a rough idea of the work involved in bringing surfaces to acceptable condition so that you can formulate sensible plans for the quality and timing of the completed work.

Plaster Prep Work

You may encounter many different conditions in existing spaces. You should work with an experienced painter to judge these conditions and devise the best course of action. Different degrees of damage will indicate different approaches to the prep work. While collecting bids, you will probably enlist the opinions of bidders on the best repair options during the walk-

throughs. The following scenarios are presented in order from minor to major repair options:

- If the plaster top coat is crazed with fine cracks going in every direction rather than oriented along a single direction, the painter may recommend washing and skim coating or, if the surface has more noticeable crazing, canvassing the walls (installing panels of canvas fabric to smooth them out).
- If walls have minor cracking here and there, the painter may suggest scoring the crack with a V-shaped tool like a can opener. The crack will then be filled with patching compound. If it looks like the crack has been repaired previously or you have reason to suspect it is from seasonal movement, the crack should be patched with fiberglass tape, spackling, and painting.

A metal paint that I specified for a client's ceiling contained silver powder in its formulation. The painter did a beautiful job of painting the surface to resemble individual sheets of metal leaf. About a week after installation, the client called the painter and me to the house to look at the ceiling, which was marked at regular intervals by a dusky stripe that spanned the entire width of the ceiling. Upon investigation, we discovered that the chemicals in each spackled joint had oxidized the paint and that we should have used a special sealing primer.

FIGURE 20.9 Stencils may be cut to create crisp patterns with a heavy application or a delicate pattern, as shown here with a glaze. *Courtesy of Hester Painting and Decorating, Skokie, Illinois*

- If areas of plaster are loose but the installation is sound for the most part, the painter may recommend tightening the loose areas back down by putting plaster washers (Figure 20.11) on drywall screws and screwing through the plaster into the lath, and then skimming the surface.
- If the area is larger and looser, then bad areas should be broken out and replastered. It is sometimes a good idea to apply metal lath on top of wooden lath in the areas to be patched to make the patch more secure. If the area is large and the structure is not historically significant, it may be acceptable to patch the area with a piece of drywall. A carpenter will cut away the loose plaster and cut drywall to conform to the area removed. More than one layer of drywall may be needed to build the patch up to the thickness of the plaster.
- If large areas of the installation have deteriorated, breaking out the bad areas and entirely replastering or drywalling may be advisable.

FIGURE 20.10 Metal leaf is extremely thin and must be removed from its tissue paper backing and applied to the surface by burnishing. Actual metal is used, so characteristics of the metal will remain constant. This means that oxidizing metals must be sealed.

Other techniques are employed for demanding restoration work and are not common practice. If you are working on a registered historical building, you may work with a specialist who recommends some of these techniques in order to save plasterwork that, under normal-use conditions, would simply be replaced.

In either drywall or plaster installations, you may encounter water damage or settling cracks. There is no point in repairing the surface and painting if the cause of the problem has not been corrected; thus, the repair should be done first and then the resulting damage corrected. It is especially tricky to locate the source of leaks, and clients should be prepared for a couple of wrong

guesses as to the source of the water. Be sure to allow time in the schedule to complete this sleuthing before the work proceeds.

Prep Work for New Construction

After the drywallers have installed the drywall sheets and the corner beads and have taped and spackled the seams and out-corners, the spackle is feathered out and sanded smooth. The walls may also be fully skim-coated with a special spackle coat. This is, of course, more costly because spackling work is usually restricted to screw and seam locations, but skim coating covers the entire wall. The material list is slightly

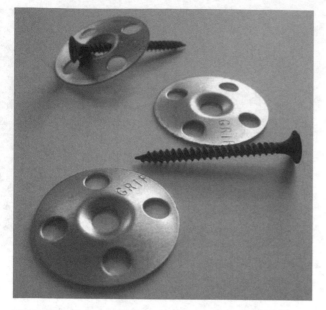

FIGURE 20.11 Rodenhouse plaster washers are used to tighten plaster to the lath if some of the fingers or keys have broken off.

different, too. The seams may be taped and spackled, but a special spackle that cures like plaster (called hot mud) may be used. The surface is worked and troweled like a plaster wall finish coat. Both the material and labor costs are increased for skim coating, but if the budget allows for it, it is a much superior installation. It is more durable and more solid-sounding. We experience spaces with all our senses and can hear quality construction in the way sound moves, or doesn't move, through spaces. This kind of finishing is referred to as a Level 5 finish.

Level 5 finishes are understood to mean that the flat joints will have tape embedded into joint compound and will receive two separate coats of joint compound to cover the tape. The in-corners will have the tape embedded in joint compound and receive one covering coat of joint compound. The fasteners will receive three separate layers of joint compound. After the tape and fasteners have been covered with the requisite number of coats, the entire wall will be skim-coated. There will be no tool marks or ridges and the entire surface will be smooth and consistent.

Finished spaces can also be given a Level 4 finish if a textured paint will be used or if a medium-weight wallcovering is specified. A Level 4 finish is similar to a Level 5 finish but omits the skim coat.

You may occasionally specify a Level 3 finish if you will be using a very heavy, textured, com-

mercial wallcovering or a heavily textured paint finish. Level 3 finishes will have the tape embedded in joint compound and covered with joint compound. Fastener heads will receive two coats of joint compound in two separate operations. All joint compound will be smooth and free of ridges and tool marks.

Level 2 and Level 1 finishes are used for unseen areas, such as wall surfaces extending into the plenum for sound barriers and fire-stopping. Level 0 is for temporary partitions put up during construction to protect areas from construction dirt and noise.

If the painter will not be taping and spackling, it is a good idea to include instructions in your specs mandating that the painter will be responsible for approving the tapers' work. Again, because the painter must be responsible for the quality of the finished job, if he or she is not contracted to do the taping and spackling and separate tapers will be hired, the painter must be given some say about the conditions under which he or she is expected to do the painting work. If that is not allowed, then you lose control over the quality of the finished job.

The walls are first primed. Ideally, the primer color should be similar to the finished wall color, but painters frequently use white. White is usually fine, but if you intend to use a very dark or bright color, you may request that the primer be tinted. This gives you one more chance to confirm the color selection and makes it easier for the painter to achieve complete coverage.

Once the primer coat has been applied, it is easier to see any surface imperfections before the final coats of paint are applied. Many good painters will graze the wall surface with a bright light to check the quality of the prep work before proceeding with painting. You can do the same kind of check with a flashlight if your painter is disinclined to check his or her own work.

You must be aware of the kinds of problems that can and cannot be corrected at this stage. The painter cannot correct a large shallow bow in the wall. If there is a gross deformation, the problem will have to be corrected by the contractor who installed the studs because the problem is most likely a warped stud or sole plate that is causing the studs to be out of alignment with one another. Because this problem can only be corrected by removing the drywall sheet(s) and affected studs and replacing them with good material, everyone is happier when this is noticed sooner rather than later. Problems that are correctable by the painter are drips and globs in the paint, dents or roughness under the paint where the paper face of the drywall was scuffed or torn or the spackle is not smooth, and areas where the paint has not covered completely. It is unlikely that drywall has been nailed to the studs in new construction, but in buildings that are 30 or more years old, nails were used and you will need to look for nail pops, which should be pulled, screwed, and spackled.

Special preparation may be needed for the particular finish selected. A stain-killing primer must be used as a base for metallic paints (paints that use metal powder as part of their formulation) because the drywall compound may oxidize the metal, creating a stripe wherever there is a seam in the drywall. This happens very quickly, within a week or so. If woodwork has been stripped down to bare wood, there could be areas that need to be sealed to prevent sap from rising through the paint.

Millwork trims may have many layers of old paint on them. Sometimes, this paint is loose—stretched across an "in-corner," for instance, or flaked off. If the woodwork's finish is in bad condition, it should be stripped or replaced. Stripping paint is costly, but it makes sense if the damaged paint is confined to a small area of a large job with trim that is otherwise fine and consistent throughout. If the paint is in poor condition throughout the entire job, it is, unfortunately, cheaper to remove all trim and replace it with new trim. Another alternative is to "cut into" the detailing to remove all loose paint. Specially shaped tools are used to drag the loose paint off the woodwork profiles. This work must be carefully done by experienced tradespeople because these tools are sharp enough to cut into the wood. The woodwork is then hand-sanded to try to minimize the differences at the junction between the painted and scraped portions, although it is rarely entirely undetectable. The successive layers of new paint will further minimize the difference between areas with many layers of old paint and those with bare wood where all paint has been removed. This is a compromise to control price; the best solution is always to strip the woodwork or replace it. If only a few sections of the trim will be replaced on a job with old original woodwork, the existing woodwork is likely to have several layers of old paint. The new work will look "crisper and flatter" than the existing areas unless you specify extra layers of paint for the new work.

Qualifying Painters

A wide range of skill levels are available for hire. Depending on your needs, you will be choosing someone between Michelangelo and a bio-extension of a paint gun. If you are managing rental property and need a lot of area sprayed white, do not hire a highly skilled painter because the quality expectations do not justify that level of expertise (or expense). Painting is one area where it is possible to cut costs if necessary. Unlike structural work, it can always be done again properly when funds become available. However, if you plan to paint twice to achieve appropriate quality, consider the cost of the initial job *plus* the final job as the real cost when opting to cut this corner. New construction settles and a few of my clients over the years have elected to delay the "real" paint job for two or three years in cases when I suggested using the paint techniques described above.

Review the work and the level of perfection required with your painters. Go and see similar techniques at other sites where the painters have worked, review their portfolios, and interview their references.

The following hypothetical scenario outlines the steps in working with a painter: Imagine that you want to hire a painter. You define the scope of work with the client and select all the finishes and colors, then:

1. Meet your prequalified painting contractor(s) on the site for a walk-through. (Even if the job was bid from a set of plans, there will eventually be a walk-through to confirm all the assumptions made during bidding.) For new construction, the painter will want to inspect the condition of the surfaces to be painted to make sure they are in the condition expected (and thus in the condition upon which the bid was based). Conditions will be reviewed with

the painter and suggestions will be made regarding proper preparation of the surfaces for the painting work described in the scope of work. If the scope of the job has changed because conditions are not as expected, the bid will also change.

2. After all is understood and agreed upon, the contractor will be hired and paid a deposit. Often, the payouts are one third, one third, and one third, but sometimes they are half down and half on completion if the job will not take long.

3. The color is selected or custom-mixed with the painter. It is a good idea to check the color on the site with the painter, who will have universal pigments on hand to adjust the color as needed. To custom-mix with the painter, give him or her a color that is close to the color you want (a paint manufacturer's product number, for instance). Meet the painter on the site with all of your material samples needed for comparison. The painter should paint a big (18+ inches square) sample using the pint or quart that he or she purchased and allow it to dry on the wall. You will review and, if necessary, adjust the color with the painter, who will add pigments as needed, drying the samples with a blow dryer or heat gun so you can see the final, dried color.

4. When you believe you have mixed the correct color, the painter should paint it on several surfaces throughout the area so you can check it in bright light, diffuse and indirect light, and in shadow, as well as in natural and artificial light and all lighting conditions that you can effect. If it still looks right, and your client approves, the painter will purchase all the paint needed for the job, custom-mixed by his or her supplier to match the color that you just created.

Unless there is a need for a stain-killing or other special primer, the primer could be custom-mixed to your selected color. This not only helps the painter with coverage, it allows your client to experience the color more nearly as it will be in the final coat. If there should be a change of heart, adjustments can be made before the final coats go on. For the cost of a few gallons of paint, you can still make a change at this point if necessary. You may want to check the color of the batch mixed by the supplier; sometimes, they are slightly off, which may or may not be a material difference. If it is not a dead-on match but is still a good color, you may choose to accept the batch.

If you want a glaze technique (a faux linen or sponge, for example) the proceedings are just slightly different. You would still prequalify the painters, describe the scope of work, and do a walk-through, as well as select the colors (plural) to be used. However, you will need to select a base color, as well as one or more glaze colors. It helps to have an understanding of how colors mix and affect one another. If you lack experience with this, you could take a painting course (fine arts), train yourself by experimenting with paints, or work with your painter to mix and adjust each color individually. Working with the painter is probably the most efficient way to proceed because you can mock up the color interactions, if not the actual technique, right then and there. After the colors have been selected, the painter should make a large sample (18 × 18 inches) on a board. Check this sample at the site by carrying it into several different lighting conditions available there. Request any adjustments necessary and have the painter make a new sample if the change is significant.

Accessories that are to be painted (switch plate covers, outlet covers, floor or wall vents) must be metal in order to hold paint. Occasionally, clients will request that the painter faux-grain the floor vents to blend with a wood floor. This can get expensive; sometimes, simply spraying the vents in a mid-range tone from the general flooring helps to blend them in.

Inspection

You may find it beneficial to evaluate the paint work in process. Aside from confirming that everything is still on schedule, you are looking at the same things that you would check at the end of the job: that the prep work is adequate, the color is correct, the level of gloss is as specified, the work is being neatly done, and all areas to be painted are being painted. After the job is complete, recheck all of these features, as well as the cleanup on windows and hardware (especially hinges) and other finished surfaces. Make sure there are no runs or drips or "globs" in the painted surfaces. Arrange to have all artwork, window coverings, and anything else that was removed for the paint work reinstalled if necessary.

CHAPTER 21

Plastic Laminates

This chapter covers laminates that are typically used as surfacing material; it does not include specialty laminates for structural use or those for use in explosive environments, laminates for carving, laminates for industrial uses, or building sheathing. The laminates covered are the products typically specified by interior designers who are assembling working and living spaces; they include high-pressure laminate and low-pressure laminate.

High-Pressure and Low-Pressure Laminate

There are two basic types of high-pressure laminate: *Nonforming* laminates are rigid and will tend to remain as straight sheets in your application, and *forming* laminates have been adjusted in the curing process to allow more flexibility so they can be bent under heat. This post-production adjustment is called *post-forming.*

Construction

The construction of laminate involves essentially bonding layers of paper together with resins to produce a surfacing veneer with properties that vary only slightly among product categories. Melamine is a resin-saturated overlay for decorative surfaces. Low-pressure laminate is a melamine resin-saturated paper with color or a gravure print. High-pressure laminate is Kraft paper saturated with phenolic resin. These layers are compressed at between 1000 and 1200 pounds per square inch for one hour at more than 280 degrees Fahrenheit to produce a more durable surface than low-pressure melamine.

Thickness

The thickness of laminates varies and has a direct relationship to serviceability for vertical and horizontal grades. Horizontal grade has a more durable wear layer to handle the extra abrasion that one would expect on horizontal surfaces. There is variation among different manufacturers' products, but the approximate thickness for vertical grade is .03 inch, and horizontal grade is .05 inch thick. The thickness of post-forming grade is generally somewhere in between.

Surfaces

The components of plastic laminate pertain mostly to the color and pattern of the decorative layer and to the gloss level. Several manufacturers offer a variety of papers for use as decorative layers, so pursuing custom color options is often unnecessary. Available surfaces are typically gloss or textured. The manufacturers have their own matte surface textures; not all product offerings will be available in all texture options, so you'll need to confirm the available textures once you have made the initial color or pattern selection.

Specialty backings and surfacing formulations that address special-use situations are available from manufacturers. There are specialty laminates and adhesives to address user requirements for fire resistance, abrasion resistance, chemical resistance, use as a dry-marker surface, and rigorous indoor-air-quality restrictions. Nondecorative sheets for use as liners or backers for other materials or as finishes or balancing layers for multiple-ply constructions are also available.

Sheet Size

Sheet sizes vary slightly among manufacturers. Generally, sheets can be found in widths from 30 to 60 inches and in lengths from 8 to 12 feet.

Seams

It is a good idea to avoid seams in your design wherever possible because the nature of the material makes it hard to minimize their appearance. It is important to include the seam locations in your drawings. One reason to do so is that simply drawing the seams on your plans or elevations will force you to consider their impact on your plans and designs. The other reason is to communicate your intent to the bidders and fabricators. Balance seams left and right of a prominent elevation or feature in your design, and try to keep them away from cutouts or the location of any feature in the design or any equipment that stands there. Avoid small pieces and irregular rhythms whenever possible. Just as with carpet and other materials that you will plan for projects, you may have to create a hierarchy of importance as you review these guidelines for seaming related to your designs because it is not always possible to address all of these suggestions in your seam plan.

Custom Laminates

Manufacturers can use your custom artwork on the decorative layer of a laminate product that you can special order (Figure 21.1). Contact the manufacturer for instructions on e-file size (for artwork) and file type (tiff, jpeg, and bmp are common) and for the recommended laminate for your application.

FIGURE 21.1 Custom laminate work executed by Wilsonart.

Color-through laminates are similar to high-pressure laminates, except that colored sheets are used for all layers so there will be no brown backer layers showing at cut edges.

Laminates should be bonded to particleboard, medium-density fiberboard (MDF), or plywood with one A face (to which the laminate will be applied). The characteristics of the substrate are important because this material is never used alone; it is always adhered to the substrate and, furthermore, is part of an assembly. For example, laminate is a popular material for countertops. Countertops in kitchens contain sinks. Water is not a problem for laminate—it is water-resistant. However, it *is* a problem for many wood-based substrates, so the substrate must be protected from water penetration. If water reaches most substrates, they will swell up, breaking the adhesive bonds between the laminate and substrate. It is common practice to use only overmounted sinks in laminate and seal the cut edge of the substrate against water drawn in by capillary action (Figure 21.2). Recall the other characteristics of engineered substrates (Chapter 14) as you consider the selection of substrates, which must have accessories fastened to them and field-assembled joints.

Your quality fabricator will follow all the manufacturers' recommendations for proper adhesives and techniques, including handling, cutting, and drilling of their material. Many laminate manufacturers recommend their own proprietary adhesives and, unless there is a good reason to use something else, you should have your fabricator use the proprietary adhesives to further ensure a trouble-free installation.

Laminates are one of the most economical surfacing materials available and if a laminate meets your program needs in functional and aesthetic areas, it will be easy on the budget. Just to illustrate, a marble countertop costs 15 times more than the current price of laminate countertops from a building center (material-only price).

Solid Surfacing

Manufacturers of plastic laminate typically offer solid surface materials, too. This material is often used to make accessories that a designer may want to integrate into designs such as sinks, soap holders, and other molded objects, which can be "seamlessly" adhered to the material (Figure 21.3a-c).

Physical Properties

These materials range from ⅛ to 1 inch thick. Sheet sizes are similar to laminate sheet sizes. Formulations are proprietary (that is, unique to the specific manufacturer's products), and performance varies from one product to another. The most popular materials are acrylic and polyester. Polyester is less expensive than acrylic, but the seams are mechanically bonded rather than chemically bonded, as acrylic seams are.

Bonding

Chemical bonds are more durable than mechanical bonds, so if you need to join two sheets for use in a rigorous environment, you may want to explore acrylic options first. If acrylic materials are to be used in the environment, such as in dental labs where acrylic bonding is part of assembling forms and models, the acrylic being used can bond with the acrylic solid surfacing material. For these cases, you may want to consider polyester because it resists some chemicals better than acrylic can. Some fabricators prefer the ease of fabrication that acrylic offers over polyester material characteristics.

Thermoplastic and Thermoset Formulas

Thermoplastic and thermoset formulas have different capabilities and performance characteristics, so you will want to match your program to the material. Thermoplastic means that it softens when heated, and thermoset means that heat cures and hardens it into permanent form. Hot water can "etch" and dull the surface of thermoplastic formulations, but they can usually be buffed back to their original condition. Generally, thermoset materials are difficult to heat bend, and stress marks may become visible on the surface.

Color-Through

All products in this category are color-through, which means the color of the material is consis-

FIGURE 21.2 Plexicor Karran sinks are undermounted in laminate tops by a special process that protects the substrate from moisture damage (see shop visit on the CD-Rom).

a

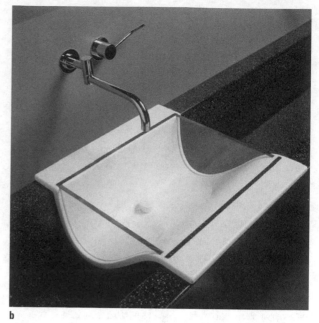

b

c

FIGURE 21.3 Corian can be worked like wood and heat-formed. A countertop (a) was worked with the same tools and methods used to shape wood. Solid surfacing (b) is water-resistant and dimensionally stable. Unique custom designs have been created out of Corian when designers compete for recognition in contests and contribute to fund-raising efforts, as in an installation for a Design Industries Fighting AIDS benefit (c). *Images courtesy of DuPont Corian.*

tent throughout its entire thickness. Because of this, stains and burns can be removed with light sanding and buffing.

Many installation instructions from manufacturers suggest that this material should not be bonded to other material substrates, but the details should employ "floating" constructions (such as a counter that sits on top of cabinetry) or mechanical fasteners. These requirements will affect the details of your custom constructions, so refer to product literature as you finalize the construction documents so you design buildable details.

Acrylic

Acrylic is another solid surfacing material and is also used in interior products in a solid, clear form. It is a chemically clear, colorless resin, but it can have color introduced into the material before forming. It is thermoplastic and can be heat-formed at about 350 degrees Fahrenheit.

Acrylic is a soft material and can be scratched by abrasives; shallow scratches can be buffed out. It will deform under pressure or weight; thicker material is stronger. Like glass, it is good at resisting impact when it is thick. It is vulnerable to some chemicals and to ammonia, which is present in many cleaning products and will make the surface cloudy, so your client must be informed to ensure the material will be properly cleaned.

As component parts, acrylic is available as sheets and rods (round and square) for forms that are built or constructed using chemical bonding agents. It can also be cast into molds and heat-formed. Thicknesses range from $\frac{1}{8}$ inch to 1 inch. Special formulations offer UV protection. You might consider acrylic for locations where glass would be too heavy.

Lucite and Lexan are two major proprietary materials of this type. Lucite is like a super-strong acrylic, and Lexan is a proprietary material owned by GE.

part
Three

Constructions, Products, and Systems

CHAPTER 22

case Goods and cabinets

The term "case goods" is used to describe "hard" furniture as opposed to upholstered furniture or soft goods (bedding, draperies etc.). Case goods, which are freestanding, are differentiated from cabinetry, which is usually built in. Woodworking shops build custom cabinetry, custom furniture, manufactured cabinetry, and manufactured furniture. Although the materials, production, and quality issues are similar, there are some logistical differences between custom and stock and between built-in and freestanding items, which will be covered in this chapter.

In the past, both cabinetry and case goods were constructed of solid wood. Today, these items are often constructed from an engineered substrate covered with a facing material (veneer), with some portions of solid wood. You may want to review the wood information in Chapter 14, especially the discussion of paneling, to refresh your memory about the characteristics of different species of wood.

Substrates

Substrates common to the construction of case goods and cabinets are MDF particleboard and plywood. The substrate also may be a combination of plywood and particleboard, possibly with a fiberboard core such as medium-density fiberboard (MDF) (Figure 22.1a-e).

Although you can find furniture in building centers made out of it, 35-pound particleboard should not be used for furniture; its main use is as a floor underlayment. Particleboard does not generally hold on to screws as well as plywood does, and it is not the best substrate for load-bearing joints. Developments such as the biscuit joiner, which makes secure joints in particle board possible, and special fasteners called confirmats, have allowed for mechanical fastening of particle substrates, expanding the uses of particleboards.

Plywood can be purchased with the face veneer already adhered as the top ply; this product is called warehouse match and is used for cabinetry. It is described as "ash-face plywood," "mahogany-face plywood," etc. You will usually specify A-grade plywood for surfaces that show in normal use and on the exterior, and may allow the use of B-grade plywood on a concealed interior if you are trimming costs.

As with substrates for paneling, your fabricator is the best person to suggest the proper substrate for case goods and cabinets. However, you should be knowledgeable about the general qualities of the options available so you can understand and approve the fabricator's choices. As with paneling choices, if you do not agree with the substrate suggested by the fabricator, make sure you both have the same understanding regarding its quality and characteristics.

If the finish surface is not attached to the substrate, the shop will apply the facing veneer. This is called "laying up" the material. Facing

a

b

c

d

e

FIGURE 22.1 Plywood is a good substrate for other surfacing material such as veneer and laminate. It would not be used for a lacquered finish because the grain on the face (a) is very textural. Plywood layers (b) are always an odd number so that material will not warp. When a surfacing material is adhered to one side of a plywood construction, a balancing layer must be applied to the other face for that reason. Cabinet trades sometimes refer to plywood as veneer core. Particleboard (c) is formed from coarse chops of wood; it is not suitable for lacquered finishes, but it is acceptable as a substrate for other surfacing materials. It is suitable for use in case goods at a density of 40 pounds per cubic foot and greater. It must be sealed against infiltration of moisture because it will swell and quickly and dramatically deform. The edges are especially vulnerable. When particleboard is used for some of the layering in plywood, it is called particle core. MDF (d) has a finer grain than particleboard. Cabinet trades sometimes refer to this as hardboard. The smooth face of MDF (e) is a good surface for lacquered finishes, thin surfacing materials, and laminates.

materials typically include laminate, wood veneer (for stain or paint finish), metal, or MDF with laminate or for paint or lacquer finish. Solid wood lumber or millwork (solid wood pieces cut with knives into shaped profiles) may also be used.

Joinery

Solid wood members can be joined together using various methods (Figure 22.2). One method is to shape the edges of the two pieces to be joined to form "positive" and "negative" ends that fit together like pieces of a puzzle. Examples include mortise and tenon, rabbet, dovetail, dado, shoulder, and half lap joints. Another method of joining pieces involves inserting a dowel, metal fastener, biscuit, or spline into the two pieces, as seen in the miter, biscuit, and butt joints. These joints would

most likely be glued as well. Portions of the case-work may be glued and screwed together.

The fabricator will suggest the type of joint to be used. Sometimes, the joint is part of the detailing, as in Shaker or Mission-style furniture, in which the finger joints or mortise and tenon joinery is an exposed design feature. If there is an aesthetic motive and the joint will show, you may request a particular joint based on its visual appeal for the fabricator's approval (because the fabricator is the one who must stand behind the stability and longevity of the work). The shop drawings–drawings prepared by the fabricator as confirmation of details and a guide to production–will show the suggested joints. As a responsible member of the design team, you will review and approve of the joints, along with the shop drawings, before the piece is produced.

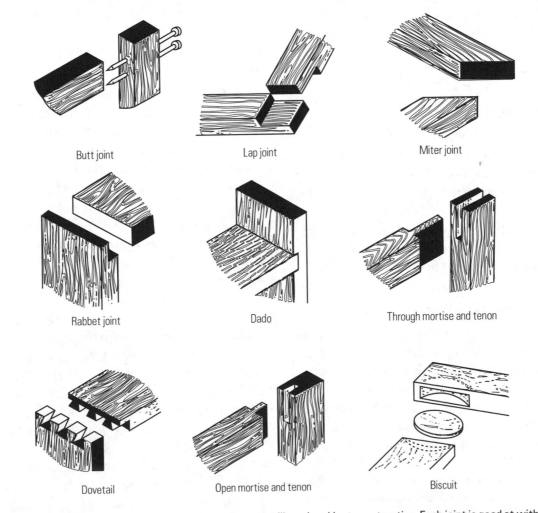

Butt joint Lap joint Miter joint

Rabbet joint Dado Through mortise and tenon

Dovetail Open mortise and tenon Biscuit

FIGURE 22.2 These are the most common wood joinery that you will see in cabinet construction. Each joint is good at withstanding a particular kind of stress.

Several factors will determine the type of joint used. The first of these is the substrate. Characteristics of some materials will not permit milling of the positive- and negative-style joints described previously. The function of the piece, the stresses that the joint is likely to endure, and the location of the joint within the cabinet will also suggest the kind of joint to be used. Consider the kinds of stresses each of the joints shown in Figure 22.2 would bear. The dado would be good at withstanding a vertical load but would not handle the horizontal stress to which a drawer is subjected well. Cost is another factor that may influence these decisions, and dadoed drawer boxes are sometimes found in low-end furniture drawers.

Another determining factor in selecting the kind of joint is the necessity of having the piece *knocked down* (disassembled so that it can fit through doorways as it is being delivered to its location). Some joints are easier to *field assemble* (put together on site) than others, and if the piece knocks down, there will be some joints that are field assembled.

Case Construction

There are many opinions regarding the specs for top-quality cabinetry. The choices of solid versus veneer and framed versus frameless construction are topics of disagreement related to quality. The information in this section is provided to help you consider the implications and characteristics of various options and thus choose the one that best fits the design program for a particular project.

Framed versus Frameless

Traditionally, cabinets were constructed as frame units and many fabricators fiercely support this construction. Other fabricators are nonchalant about frame style and still others say that frame units are inconvenient and wasteful. If your design allows for one and not the other, you may actually be limiting the number of shops that will be willing to bid. The choice of framed or frameless does not restrict style; either option can be styled to fit any aesthetic. Although framed is a traditional construction, frameless cabinets can be given the appearance of framed construction

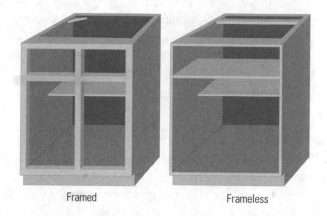

Framed   Frameless

FIGURE 22.3 Framed cabinets are more traditional than frameless ones and are believed by some to be of stronger construction. Frameless construction, however, eliminates restriction of the opening.

with the application of a false face frame. Access to the interior is unobstructed with frameless construction (Figure 22.3).

Door Styles

The relationship of the door to the case can be arranged in three basic ways (Figure 22.4): inset doors are set into the frame, fully exposing the frame all around the door; full overlay doors cover the entire frame, except for the small gap required to keep the doors from binding; and partial overlay doors are set onto the face frame, exposing some of the case, but not all. This relationship may influence the decision to use framed or frameless construction. Inset doors work better on frame cases and full-overlay doors will look the same on framed and frameless units.

The doors in Figure 22.4a-c show a traditional five-piece construction, which includes four framing rails and a center panel. The profiles in Figure 22.5 illustrate the construction. Notice how the center panel is "loose," dadoed into the rail. This allows for expansion and contraction of the wood center panel inside the drawer frame. This kind of detail is also used for decorative effect when the center panel is an engineered wood product faced with veneer. Because the engineered substrate is dimensionally stable, the expansion that five-piece construction allows for is not needed.

a   b   c

FIGURE 22.4 These images illustrate the relationship between doors and cases. The example on the left is a full inset door (a). The hinge on the left side shows the limits of the door leaf and the start of the face frame. The example in the center (b) is a full overlay door. The gaps between doors and drawers would be fairly tight—within ⅛ inch. The cabinet case is effectively concealed with full overlay. The example on the right (c) shows a partial overlay, a construction very similar to the full overlay but exposing more of the cabinet case with wider gaps between door and drawer faces.

Surfaces

The surfacing materials used for case goods and cabinets include wood, laminates, thermofoils, and veneers.

WOOD Some wood species have more visual consistency than others. Cabinets constructed of solid wood sometimes display this fact in their color and grain. For example, the door shown in (Figure 22.6a) is clearly solid wood: you can see the distinction between the two planks that were joined to build the door. This variation is something to call to your client's attention. If this natural variation in wood from one plank to another is not acceptable, a veneer product should be considered, because that is the only way to ensure uniformity (Figure 22.6b).

In slab-style doors, the wood grain is responsible for the entire aesthetic. If solid wood is desired and variation between planks is not to the client's liking, you could consider a more elaborate five-piece door construction. In such construction, the visual action helps distract attention from the variations across the surface of the door. The variations are still there, but the added visual complexity seems to soften their impact. Be aware that, even if showroom displays do not exhibit these natural variations, the cabinetry delivered to the job site may still contain it. This is often a nonnegotiable situation, so prepare your client for the likelihood that there will be a visible distinction between individual wood members of solid wood cabinetry.

PLASTIC LAMINATE Most plastic laminate products consist of three layers: a backing layer, a decorative layer, and a protective layer of plastic. There are small differences in formulations, as well as in the decorative layers. Solid material eliminates the dark line that many people find objectionable in plastic laminate furniture. If the brown edge is not a design feature that you want to employ intentionally, you can design to minimize or eliminate it. Further information about plastic laminates is provided in Chapter 21.

METAL LAMINATE Metal laminates can be a solid metal product or a product similar to plastic laminate with a backing layer (often phenolic) faced with a top layer of metal. Metal laminates can be adhered to the same substrates as plastic lami-

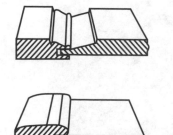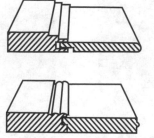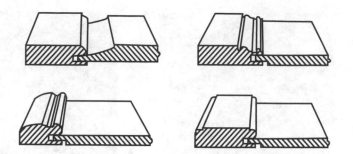

FIGURE 22.5 Five-piece panel construction means that side, top, and bottom rails surround a center panel. It is the most popular door assembly for solid wood because it allows some movement of the center panel: As wood responds to changes in moisture, the "loose" panel in the center moves within the rails without cracking.

a   b

FIGURE 22.6 Solid wood (a) is not as easily matched as veneers, so variations between individual wood members are likely. Stained finishes can minimize the variation of solid wood members to ensure that differences are less visually pronounced. Veneer cabinetry (b) allows for a more visually consistent surface. *Photograph of solid wood door variation by Alana Clark*

nate and wood veneer. Their faces present the characteristics of the metals used. A review of the information on metals in Chapter 12 will help you understand the relevant durability and performance issues. Metal laminates are usually used for vertical surfaces and light-duty horizontal surfaces. They are available in a variety of styles to address many design programs (Figure 22.7a-c). They will patinate, acquiring surface scratches, so keep in mind the likely wear and tear when you are considering metal laminate.

THERMOFOILS These products are reserved for economy grades of cabinetry. They consist of a very thin vinyl layer, usually in a solid color or a photo-transfer wood grain, on an engineered substrate. Thermofoil shares some characteristics with plastic laminate but, unlike plastic laminate, can conform to intricate profiles cut into the substrate, imitating a raised panel cabinet door. Thermofoil is a new technology and does not have a long track record. There is some indication that the material yellows with exposure to heat, indicating that thermofoils are more suitable for low-heat environments such as baths, entertainment, and living spaces. Thermofoil products are a budget-driven option.

VENEERS Wood veneer is a layered component that consists of a thin layer of wood possibly laminated to a backing material. Wood veneer is available in different thicknesses up to ⅛ inch. Refer to Chapter 14 for more information about wood veneer. The choice of wood species, cut, and figuring will impart visual characteristics, as will special processes such as bleaching, staining, and dyeing with transparent dyes. It is economical to select a wood that comes the closest to the desired appearance for color and figuring and then modify it as little as necessary. Making the fewest modifications helps hold down the cost and allows you to predict the appearance of the final product more closely.

Veneer is sometimes laid up on a phenolic backing (the same material onto which plastic laminate is laid up). The dark line to which people object under laminate will be present at all edges. If this will be unacceptable, you must note on drawings that this kind of backing is not to be used. For a review of veneer cuts and matching, see the discussion in Chapter 14.

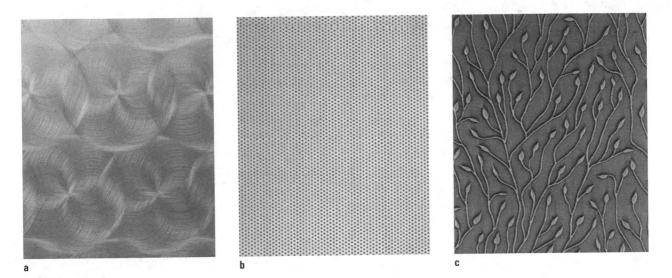

a   b   c

FIGURE 22.7 Metal laminate products are one example from the available variety. Production techniques and materials vary from one product to the next, and all the specs must be understood during the selection process. Solid aluminum (a) is polished with a special router to create the controlled surface scratches that give this laminate its texture. Solid aluminum (b) is perforated to create this product. The pewter vine pattern (c) is a high-pressure relief with a thin layer of metal foil pressed onto phenolic backer. The material is then polished to brighten up the raised leaf pattern. *All images courtesy of Chemetal.*

Hardware

Most cabinetry requires hinges, drawer slides, and pulls. Many cabinetmakers have their own preference for functional hardware and you will only have to define the function. Rarely, a new function will require a search for the requisite hardware or custom fabrication; when this occurs, the fabricator will do the initial research to find suitable hardware.

Hardware manufacturers offer components with differing qualities. You should review an open specification ("full extension glides to support 'x' number of pounds") or a closed specification ("Accuride number ––") to determine if the quality of the hardware is suitable to your specific purpose. Function usually dictates the selection of hardware, but because the construction and design details will vary according to the kind of hardware used, function is not the only determining factor. For instance, whereas a concealed, self-closing hinge is often preferred for cabinet doors, such hinges are large and unattractive. Thus, for a glazed door (that is, a door with a glass panel) you might opt for a smaller hinge at the sacrifice of the self-closing property.

Finishes

Some surfaces require protective sealants. Depending on the material and intent, the finish may be transparent like a stain and sealant or opaque like a lacquer or paint. Transparent finishes for cabinetry are similar to those for wood floors and paneling. There are two basic finishes: penetrating finishes (such as stains, which add color; dyes, which change the color; bleaches, which remove the color; and oils) and sealants, which provide a protective coating.

The best finish is dictated by the use and desired appearance of the piece. It is a good idea to involve your fabricator in the final specification of the finish and sealant if you want the benefit of performance guarantees. As with other decisions involving fabrication, your fabricator can be expected to stand behind the durability and appearance retention of a finish that he or she recommends. The following description of general categories will help you communicate with your fabricator:

VARNISHES Numerous proprietary formulations are available and the general characteristics of a specific product within any product category will vary from one manufacturer to another. The general characteristics of different finishes can best be understood by grouping finishes into two broad categories based on how they set up. The first group are finishes that set up through evaporation of a solvent, which includes lacquers, shellacs, and water-cured products (in which the water is not the solvent but rather a carrier for the emulsion). The term "nonconversion" varnish is applied to this group. This term makes intuitive sense because the formula is still intact and the material has not been converted into another substance. In contrast, the second group of finishes, which can be thought of as reactive, set up due to a chemical change rather than through evaporation. These finishes make up the conversion group of varnishes. The evaporative group (nonconversion varnish) can be more easily repaired in the field because they can be redissolved in their solvents, which makes it easier for new material of the same formula to adhere to the existing finish. However, because solvent-based finishes soak into the wood, they will deepen the color slightly more than finishes that sit on top of the wood.

Gloss level is measured in sheen (just as length is measured in feet and inches) and is usually discussed in terms of flat, satin, semigloss, and gloss. Most finish formulas yield a gloss finish. If a lower sheen is desired, flatting agents are added to the formula. Sheen is described in terms of percentages of reflectance. A difference in sheen of less than 20 percent is difficult to detect from one sample to the next. Flat finish yields a range of 15 to 30 percent sheen; satin is 31 to 45 percent; semigloss is 46 to 60 percent; and gloss is 60 percent or greater.

Many professional cabinetmakers prefer lacquer finishes. The most commonly used lacquers are nitrocellulose, which ambers over time (this is most evident on pale woods); acrylic-modified lacquer, which is similar in performance to nitrocellulose but does not yellow; and catalyzed lacquers, which are easy to apply but have very good durability. Formaldehyde, which is a known irritant for people with chemical sensitivities, is an ingredient in catalyzed lacquer. This can pose a problem for sensitive people before the material

sets up, but once the solvent has migrated and the finish has dried, the remaining formaldehydes are encapsulated enough to be tolerated by most people.

OTHER SEALANTS Other finishes include waxes, oils, and shellac. These are not the preferred finishing systems for most jobs but may be appropriate in some special circumstances.

- *Wax* is not normally used alone as a finish for furniture but may be used over other sealants, such as lacquers or shellac. It is an easily repaired protective coat but will develop a white ring if water is allowed to remain on the surface for several minutes.
- *Oils* do not form a durable film. They are penetrating and soak into the wood where they cure, forming a solid, but the solid is relatively soft. Boiled linseed oil and tung oil are occasionally used to seal furniture.
- *Shellac* is a soft finish that is naturally ambering, although some premixed products can be bleached and left clear or tinted. It can be dissolved by alcohol.

Installation of Custom Cabinetry

Custom cabinetry, as a product, has a lot in common with manufactured case goods, but the process of completing a job using custom cabinetry requires more planning, communication, and documentation.

Qualifying Fabricators for Custom Work

Referrals are the best way to locate a cabinetmaker. After finding a fabricator, you will need to assess the quality of his or her work. You can get an idea of the complexity of the work produced from a portfolio, but a quality assessment often takes an actual field inspection. You can interview previous clients, but you are limited by their knowledge and level of expectation, so seeing actual work is the best way to understand the capabilities of a particular shop.

When interviewing cabinetmakers, ask how long they've been in business, how many employees they have, and whether they use subcontractors. Do they work in the material that you have in mind? Some shops will do beautiful work in laminate but will not work in wood veneer. If you are specifying a wood finish, do they have a clean room (a room with a separate air system from the rest of the shop so no dust particles from sanding will be blown onto your piece while the finish is wet)? If they send the piece out to a finisher, you will have to check the quality and credentials of that shop as well. Even though unacceptable work is contractually the shop's problem, you want to make sure before you start that the shop is capable of doing the kind and quality of work that you expect. If the shop cannot make the work right, you will certainly lose time and most probably some money in the process. Therefore, don't assume that the low bidder is automatically compelled to deliver the quality of the high bidder; they often cannot do so.

Working with Fabricators

If more than one tradesperson is required to complete a piece, there will be combined meetings to keep all parties coordinated. If specific equipment must be accommodated, there will be meetings with the supplier of that equipment, the fabricator, and possibly the client as well.

Typical Procedure for Custom Work

Custom cabinetry is produced from a very detailed drawing. The design process is complicated and many variables influence decisions. The following steps outline this process.

Step 1. The requirements of the piece are defined and the function is accommodated with all the design details selected. The finish selection is based on aesthetic as well as functional considerations. The piece is drafted up with all notes required to communicate the details as well as your overall intent. The drawings that you produce are approved by the client, then submitted to fabricators (typically one to three) for their bids.

Step 2. The bids and suggestions by fabricators are reviewed and one of the bidders is selected for hire and paid a deposit.

Step 3. The fabricator produces shop drawings from which the piece will be built, as well as finish samples for your client's or your own

approval. You review the shop drawings to make sure you agree with the visual and functional aspects as drawn. You assess the finish sample for color and finish. Sometimes, two samples are submitted: one for finish, the other for color.

As you review the shop drawings, you may mark them with additional notes, including any changes required, using a noticeably contrasting marker. This is called "red-lining" because red is the usual color chosen (Figure 22.8). You then sign the drawings "approved with changes noted." You may copy the drawings or transfer all notes made onto a duplicate set of shop drawings, which are your records of the changes and additions. Unless changes are enormous, no further drawings will be produced; your red-lined set goes into the shop for fabrication. If many details must be reworked, the fabricator may opt to produce another set of drawings. The finish sample will be assessed to make sure that the correct material has been used, that the color is correct, and that the finish is as specified.

For wood veneer cabinets, you may actually go to the veneer supplier (where independent cabinet workshops purchase their veneer). There is a lot of variation among wood veneers even within the same species. At the veneer supplier, you will tag the flitches, (which are groups of veneer "sheets" cut from the same tree and having the same or similar markings and grain characteristics). This ensures that you will get exactly the material you want. When your shop sends in the order, the flitches that you traced will ship out. It would also be at this stage that you would select any other actual materials to be used (a stone slab for a countertop, for instance).

Step 4. You will most likely review the piece at least once in the shop to inspect the details and quality. The first shop visit should take place when the piece is "assembled." Prior to the application of the finish, the piece is put together as much as is practical in order to check the fit of the components. This is a good time to inspect to make sure all detailing is as drawn, as well as to inspect the quality of the workmanship. Check the tightness of permanent joints (remembering that some joints will be field assembled and will not be permanently adhered at this time), the

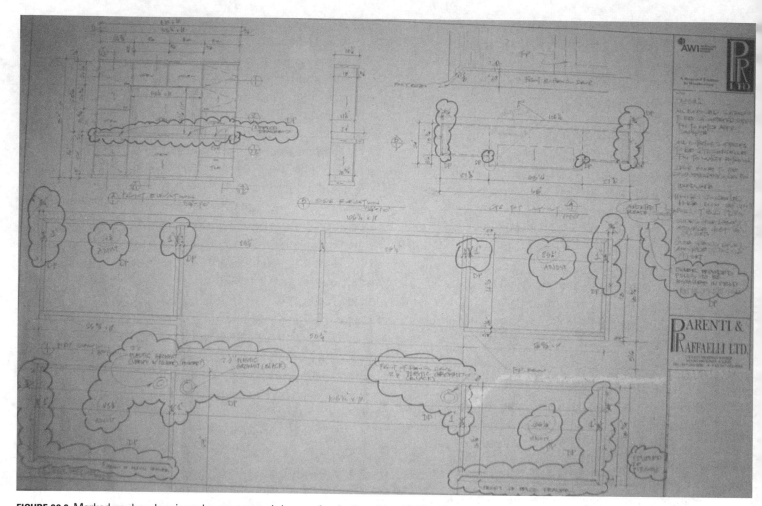

FIGURE 22.8 Marked-up shop drawings show requested changes for the Parenti and Raffaelli cabinet shop. The drawings were signed by the designer with the note "with changes as noted," so these drawings can go into the workshop to be used as a guide for production. If the changes were extensive, another set of drawings would have been produced to confirm that all details could be built.

smoothness of the cuts, and the matching of wood grain. A second inspection is advisable after the pieces are finished. They might not be reassembled again before they are delivered to the site, but you can check the finish quality (drips, dust, cloudiness) and correctness (closed or open grain, color, gloss level).

Step 5. The piece is then delivered to the site for installation. You will need to arrange a time to inspect the piece after the assembly is complete but before the installers leave. You will inspect for, among other things, the fit of all pieces, damage, and the function and alignment of doors and drawers.

Specifications for custom cabinetry always include detail drawings along with written specifications. Frequently, a wood sample for color,

finish, or both will be submitted for exact matching or as a close example of your expectations. Hardware specifications will be part of the material specs, as well as open or closed specs for other materials to be incorporated (stone tops, glass doors, metal inserts, contrasting inlays, and so on). All materials listed will be located and shown on the drawings submitted. Performance requirements will sometimes be submitted, especially if open specifications are used for any material or equipment. Confirm all assemblies to be used. If panels are to be veneered on one surface, the opposite surface must also be veneered with the same number of layers to prevent warping. This is true even if the substrate is an engineered product (particleboard or MDF). These materials are warp-resistant but not warp-proof.

Estimating

Many fabricators operate within general rules of thumb when it comes to gross estimates. You will need to budget anywhere from $500 to $1,200 per running foot for custom work. The actual dollar figure will depend on quality, the specific shop, materials used, and the complexity of the piece. Some cabinetmakers who rely on referrals from designers give designers a break in pricing (similar to a designer discount); others will actually raise this initial rough estimate because designers are sometimes more demanding of quality than end users. There is no standard, so ask if you can have a discount when you begin working with a new shop if your business model depends on a markup.

Special Issues for Built-Ins

Built-in cabinetry will often be designed to accommodate building services (HVAC, electrical, plumbing). Sometimes, service locations can be changed or rerouted. At other times, the service must stay where it is, especially if it is part of the function of the cabinet (plumbing for a sink, for instance). Often, air vents are routed out through the base of a built-in or through the crown molding detail. If an electrical outlet falls within an area that will be covered with cabinetry, the box must be omitted or made accessible through the cabinetry. Not all locations are plumb and square. Often, filler strips must be incorporated into the design and scribed (cut to follow the slant or waviness of the wall or ceiling surface) to fit.

Installation of SemiCustom and Stock Cabinets

Kitchen cabinetry is a topic unto itself. Manufacturers offer many stock cabinet styles with varying customization options. Kitchen specialists also offer completely custom-designed kitchens—in which case, the conditions and considerations for custom work apply in their entirety.

Working with Specialists

The goal of presenting the following information is to describe the workings of this part of the industry and define the relationship between the generalist and the kitchen specialist. There are numerous possible structures for your working relationship with any specialist. Clarity regarding authority and responsibility is central to a successful relationship whenever a generalist shares a client with a specialist. Lack of clarity here creates confusion and inefficiency, driving up production costs (what it costs the designers to complete the sale) and sometimes job costs as the client bears the cost of last-minute changes and delays.

The two scenarios that follow demonstrate the range of possible working relationships between the generalist and the kitchen specialist, along with the corresponding shift of authority and responsibility. By viewing this interaction as a continuum, you will be better prepared to define how your particular working relationship with the kitchen specialist will be organized.

In the first scenario, the generalist assumes full responsibility for the overall design and selection of stock cabinets and materials and competitively bids the job. When this scenario is in place between you and your client, you have full control of the design direction, including all functional and aesthetic details and selections. You may submit your fully detailed plans for bid to one to three contractors, who will supply and handle the buildout. If you have noted on your drawings that the bidders are to take their own measurements and ensure that the work constructed will fit as shown on the drawings, you can expect that responsibility to fall on the fabricator. If you omit this stipulation, the bidders may build to your plans and it is then your responsibility to ensure that the cabinetry will fit and that all conveniences desired by your client are included. You may sell the work to your client or you may have the supplier contract directly with your client. Your responsibility is undiminished in the latter; you will still be expected to stand behind the entire job.

At the other end of the continuum, the generalist may produce plan views that he or she has drafted to typical kitchen cabinet standards, but his or her role is that of managing the interface between the kitchen and the adjacent spaces and assisting the client in the selection of stock cabinets and materials to be used.

The generalist may also participate in kitchen planning with the kitchen specialist and the client, but the responsibility for the design in this scenario is shifted to the kitchen designer.

Here, the generalist participates in the selection of the cabinet style and finishes, and evaluates the kitchen specialist's plans for congruency with the remainder of the work and the rest of the structure.

This continuum of involvement from fully responsible to merely decorating demonstrates the range of possible relationships. When you are negotiating the job, you should make clear your expected level of involvement and the attendant responsibility that you intend to assume. All manner of relationships are feasible, and the only thing that will never work is for you to have responsibility without compensation adequate to permit your involvement to the level required to fulfill all stated expectations.

Standards for Stock Cabinetry

As you participate in the design of the kitchen layout, some standards in the industry are helpful to remember:

- Cabinetry is designed as individual boxes with consistency in component elements (doors, drawers, details) so that when the kitchen is assembled, visual continuity is ensured. This is unlike custom cabinetry, wherein a single case will hold many different units.
- Cabinetry box widths are sized on 3-inch increments (12 inches wide, 15 inches wide, 18 inches wide, etc.) for base cabinets, wall cabinets, and "talls," which are sometimes called pantry cabinets. Cabinetry box heights have more limited size options.
- Base units are sized to accommodate appliances, so they are standardized to be consistently 34-½ inches tall and 24 inches deep. Different manufacturers will offer other depths, such as 13-inch-deep cabinets to align with upper cabinet depths, so check individual offerings to ensure the size you need will be available in the line under consideration.

- Upper cabinets are typically 13 inches deep in varying heights in 3-inch increments, starting as short as 12 inches and going up to 48 inches.

Judging the Quality of Stock Cabinets

You should never make a recommendation based on written specs alone. Always inspect cabinetry samples in person before making suggestions to your client. You can save yourself some running around if you review written specs to reduce the number of cabinets that you will see in person. In the case of kitchen cabinets, as with most products, you get what you pay for. If your client has extreme budget restrictions, you will accept lower quality standards, but you should never agree to participate in a kitchen project of which you cannot be proud. Clients never agree to post a disclaimer on a completed job absolving the designer of responsibility for poor quality.

Inspect Samples

In addition to the written specs (which you reviewed as a preliminary check), you will want to see actual cabinet samples at the vendor's showroom. The cabinet companies that made the first cut as the result of acceptable material and method descriptions in their written specs usually will have kitchen vignettes available for review at their dealer's locations.

Visual Consistency

Look for visual consistency among and between parts. Remember to account for the inherent differences between wood species for wood finishes. Your expectations for cabinetry made of a species that typically has a lot of visual variation, such as cherry, will be less rigorous than for a species that is visually consistent, such as maple. After taking such differences into account, notice how well-matched the parts of the cabinet display are from box to box, from box to doors or drawers. Especially in five-piece construction, check the quality of the match between all parts of the door and the drawer face.

Quality of the Finish

Stains and tinted lacquers are sometimes used to even out inconsistencies between wood members. Look closely at the wood grain: Is it obscured by heavy pigment? This is usually not what clients hope for when they purchase wood cabinetry. Clear sealers that allow the natural markings of well-matched pieces are desired here.

The modern spray technologies most shops possess ensure that the quality of the sprayed finish is rarely defective. All the same, you should inspect for the quality of the finish coat and for work that precedes sealing. The finish should be clean, with no small debris caught under the finish. It should be consistent; if a touch-up was required, you may notice a variation in the way the light glances off the surface. It should be free of drips and sags. Inspect for the quality of the prep work, too. Feel the smoothness of the sanded finishes under the finish, especially in areas that would be difficult to sand, such as in-corners and shaped edges. Good quality will have eased out-corners, with the sharp out-corners sanded slightly to remove the sharp crease.

Special Techniques

If the piece is distressed, notice the realism of the distressing. Is it theatrically exaggerated or does it imitate the timeworn look of cabinetry that was carefully used for a century? Subtlety is essential to good-quality distressing. When you see good distressing, it will have some of the following characteristics:

- Pattern of distressing: The distressing should occur in areas where use and handling would be expected. For example, out-corners and raised edges would have dings and even small chips. These marks should not be crushed or crisp but should have been eased with hand-sanding prior to finishing. Natural-looking distressing should also occur around the hardware and latches. There may be additional, random slight dents in other areas as well. Again, these areas should be sanded for smooth wear and not be severely deep or sharp. The concentration of wear will occur in the vulnerable areas, with only occasional and subtle distressing marks elsewhere.

- Worm holes: These should be small, neat, and clustered, not sprinkled all over. They are made with a slender tool about the size of a pin and may be darkened on their interior if the overall cabinet color is dark.

- Overglazing: Any glazing should provide moderate contrast to the overall color, and its location should conform tightly to the grooves and corners where it is left on. The implication of glazing is that a piece was conscientiously cleaned over the course of its long life and some slight grime accumulated in expected places over many years. The effect of poorly wiped glazes is that the piece was left moldering in mud and then cleaned with a broom. Leave the latter for stage sets, not fine interiors.

- Ink spatters: Opinion is surprisingly contentious about such tiny marks. Some designers contend they are a dead giveaway to a fake. In a heavy-use space such as a kitchen, however, they provide a visual "break" in the surface, which is very practical. Use your own eye to evaluate the careful selection of ink for the cabinet color and the artistry exhibited in the amount and location of spatter.

Dealing with Defective Items

When a defective item is delivered to the site, the part is usually quickly replaced. When this is required, allow for the extra time needed to ship the defective piece back for purposes of matching (unless that is the basis of your complaint). While the manufacturer has all the parts on hand, it is a much simpler matter to compare the visual characteristics of one part to another and provide for visual consistency. After the kitchen has shipped, it is much harder to provide a matching part. It is fair, correct, and actually a favor to the fabricator when you make clear your expectations for a satisfactory match *as judged by you*. It is expensive to ship parts back and forth, but the costs are compounded when unsatisfactory replacements are shipped back and forth.

Installation of Case Goods

By now, you probably realize that the divisions between custom, semicustom, and stock are quite blurred. This holds true for case goods, as well as cabinetry. Some shops participate in the design of items they build, but others do not alter any feature or detail of the case goods they sell. A seamless spectrum spans the distance between these extremes.

Manufactured pieces use the same construction methods, facing materials, and finishes listed for cabinetry. These pieces are standard components or standard pieces that may have some optional or custom details or finish options. The main difference between custom and manufactured pieces is that manufactured pieces are selected rather than designed. There are obviously restrictions when standard pieces or components are used, but the process is much simplified. You may have to design the configuration, but much of the design detailing is already done for you.

The same shop may make both custom pieces for designers and standard furniture, sometimes for more than one "manufacturer." It is fairly common for a manufacturer to subcontract production in more than one geographic region to save on freight charges and reduce lead times. I was very surprised the first time I had a meeting with my local cabinetmaker about a custom piece and saw a bench that I had ordered from a California-based company in production in his Chicago shop. It was also reassuring to see it in such good hands.

Many levels of quality are available. Because you get what you pay for, one quality level will be more appropriate than another, depending on the application. Higher-quality pieces will have thicker "parts" (for example, tops will be 1-½ inch or thicker) and veneer will run consistently across all faces (running vertically on drawer faces, as well as doors). Design details may include more difficult constructions (like flush, inset doors versus full overlay). No substrate or backing material will be visible. Wood and veneer will have been carefully selected for consistency in color and graining, and grain may be filled. Medium-quality pieces will have thinner members (1-½ inch might be the maximum for tops), and detailing will be simplified. Grain will run horizontally on drawers and vertically on doors. Wood members and wood veneer may not have been selected as carefully for consistency. You may notice backing material at edges of veneered members, but no substrate will show. Low-quality or economy-grade pieces will have thinner material; tops will probably only be ¾ inch thick. Photographic wood or plastic laminate may be substituted for actual veneer or combined with actual wood for shaped pieces.

Assessing Quality

Wood used should be well chosen for consistent grain characteristics and color, not only within the single piece of wood itself but also for consistency from one piece of wood to another used for the item. Check the match of veneers used. The veneer used for table leaves should have grain that flows consistently from the table to the leaves.

Drawers should have dovetail or French dovetail joints and have little play when wiggled side to side. Exposed interiors should be smooth and finished to match the exterior. Press on the bottom of the drawer to make sure the material is thick and sturdy.

Doors and drawers and table leaves should line up. Slides should operate smoothly, catches work properly, and pulls be of good quality.

Carving and details should be well formed and sanded smooth. Wood finishes should not obscure the grain; they should be even and rich-looking. The top coat should be smooth with no dust trapped in the finish and no drips or thin spots.

Factors Contributing to Cost

Factors that add to the cost of the piece are both tangible and intangible. Tangible factors derive from materials and labor expenses incurred by the fabricator. If a piece is especially difficult to construct due to its own details or complications presented by the installation, it will be more costly. If the piece uses costly materials, the price will go up. The bulk of the cost is typically in the labor part of the equation related to complexity. Intangible factors in the price include such "components" as the reputation of the designer or fabricator. A famous designer's work is more costly than work by an unknown. Certain fabricators, designers, and vendors have prestige and, therefore, can command a higher price for a product that may be identical in every way to a piece from a less prestigious shop. A much-desired style can command higher prices. Pieces that satisfy the aesthetic criteria of analytical people could be more costly. Items that are manufactured in foreign markets where the dollar happens to be weak will be more costly. As a designer, you will have to make the determination as to the value of the benefit derived from the particular characteristic that is adding to the cost. Intangible factors are not less "real" than tangible ones; they are simply prioritized along with tangible factors and the return for dollars paid is accounted for.

You will assess a variety of tangible factors:

- Cost of the materials used
- Complexity of the construction
- Complexity of the installation
- Quality of workmanship

You will also assess a variety of intangible factors:

- Proportions
- Materials selected
- Timeliness
- Design techniques

These items may be considered "matters of opinion" but will give you a beginning basis for assessment.

In assessing the proportions, evaluate whether the members work harmoniously with one another, either supporting a consistent scale or contrasting in a surprising way that can be supported not only intellectually (hierarchy of importance) but visually (do elements create a sense of tension that is resolved within the piece or do they create an "unsettling" quality and is the effect appropriate for the installation?). This assessment will include an analysis of the arrangement and selection or hierarchy of elements and principles of design. Hierarchy (which elements and principles are employed) is to strategy as emphasis is to tactics: What is the intention of the design and what furthers that intention?

Evaluate the material selection. Does the piece exhibit restraint in its vocabulary? Is there a logic to the use of materials from both a functional standpoint and a visual standpoint? Do the materials create a sense of interest within a generally unified presentation or do they "pull" against each other, vying for attention in a way that visually pulls the piece apart in conflict? Have quality materials been worked with meticulous craftsmanship? Are the materials an obvious choice, and is that appropriate to the installation or would something less conventional be more appropriate?

Assess the timeliness of the piece. Does it embody a relation between itself as an object and life at this point in time or life as presented in the context of the decor you are creating?

Evaluating the design technique can be more difficult. There are cheap tricks (obvious and forceful), expensive tricks (complicated and rare), and elegant tricks (readily available materials and components used succinctly in novel ways). All methods are valid, but you must assess whether the method used by the selection under consideration is appropriate to the context. A cheap trick in the pool house is perfect but not in the front room (unless it is so witty that it escapes censure through the sublime).

This kind of assessment will be based on individual criteria that you will develop over time. The ability to assess selections objectively is one factor that differentiates a professional designer from a layperson. Everyone has preferences and visceral reactions to pieces and concepts, but your ability to logically assess these intangible characteristics is one of the primary reasons that your clients hire you. Clients will have their own gut reactions but have a right to demand that you be more than simply reactionary. In fairness, you should be prepared to deliver objective evaluation with forethought and some expertise.

When considering an antique's intangible and tangible factors, you employ the same quality assessments that you use to judge the quality of a manufactured piece of furniture. You should consider at a minimum:

- Age
- Condition of the structural members
- Wear and patina of the surfaces
- Charm. A piece that had a very specific and obsolete function often is considered to have more interest or charm than a more functional piece.

- Importance in terms of history of ownership, called *provenance.* A famous previous owner adds to the cost of a piece.
- Attribution. A piece produced by a known craftsman or workshop will have higher value than one whose maker is unknown.
- Color. Often, some quirk in oxidation or other factor makes the color unusual in some way.
- Amount of restoration required.

Hundreds of other factors also come into play.

Try to purchase from a reputable dealer with whom you have an ongoing relationship. You can train your eye over time to recognize the subtle differences between old wood and new. Review the history of manufacture; if a table is said to be 400 years old and the planks that make up the top have edges that are very even and straight, you should be very suspicious because the technology of the time was too limited to produce such a crisp edge. Perform your own initial appraisal but, unless you know a lot about antiques, do not attempt to authenticate the date of a piece. Hire an appraiser who specializes in the kind of piece you are considering.

Old pieces often require restoration. This work should be done by a shop that specializes in restoration of antiques. Determining the amount and type of restoration work is both an art and a science. A piece can be devalued by improper restoration or too much restoration. This is a nebulous assessment that is partly based on the character of the piece; sometimes, a worn finish is preferable (as in the chipped, alligatored, painted folk furniture that came into vogue in the early 1990s, for instance).

Sometimes, the restoration is not confined to the structure of the piece. Companies that work to restore belongings after a fire will often have ozone chambers, which can eliminate musty or smoky-smelling odors but are not as effective in reducing "barn" smells. Baking soda placed in a dish inside a drawer absorbs musty smells.

Reworking Pieces for New Function

Often, large pieces must be disassembled and then field assembled in order to get them through narrow passageways or up in elevators to their new location. It is currently a popular idea to house electronic components in a cabinet and occasionally the cabinet selected is an antique that must have its interior reworked to accommodate the equipment. Sometimes, doors must be modified to "pocket" next to a TV compartment. This work is done by a special cabinet shop that has experience working on projects like this or by a cabinet shop with an overseer who can understand the issues involved and work with you on devising the method that will change the exterior appearance of the piece as little as possible. New interior parts would be finished to match the interior as closely as possible.

Sometimes, the interior of an antique piece is upholstered to hide the rough surfaces of the cabinet that were not originally intended to be visible during use. This would be the case for a cabinet being modified to house a TV.

Working with Out-of-Town Resources

Contact with out-of-town dealers usually involves a review of photos initially. You may contact resources with a description of what is needed; they will then send photos, dimensions, and prices for you to consider. Any pieces that interest you should be seen in person prior to purchase. Compare the cost of bringing the piece into town (and returning it if it is not suitable) with the cost of flying out to see the piece. If there are a few pieces that are likely candidates in close proximity to one another and the budget warrants the trip, you or your client may opt to visit pieces at distant dealers.

Ordering

Your order should include information about the physical characteristics of the piece (condition, size, material, age, unique details, and any other information that describes the unique piece), as well as detailed descriptions of all work to be performed by the dealer (restoration, fitting out the interior for new function, etc.). You may even produce drawings if necessary to explain your expectations relative to size and modification of any details.

CHAPTER 23

upholstery

Upholstery encompasses items that have padding and fabric fastened to a framework. Generally, this includes seating and bed frames, but there are some items in other categories of interior goods (padded upholstered coffee table bases and padded window cornices, for instance) that can also be considered to be upholstered.

Custom Upholstery

Because seating comfort is such a person-centered judgment, it is quite common to build upholstered lounge seating to spec. The upholstery business resembles the case goods and cabinet industry in that there is a nearly seamless flow from stock items to custom items with lots of optional variation between the ends of the spectrum.

Construction

Quality upholstery work conforms to particular specifications and workroom practices. It is important to work with a shop accustomed to producing quality work because once the piece is complete, you will not be able to see many of the details that indicate good practices. Discerning the quality of upholstered furniture is a matter of reviewing specs and inspecting samples. When interviewing an upholstery workroom, ask to see samples of work for quality evaluation. Between your questions and inspection, you should confirm the following specs and practices for components of upholstered furniture:

FRAMES Frames should be made of kiln-dried hardwood (ash, maple, oak, walnut). Construction should be double-doweled with corner blocks glued and screwed. Some contemporary furniture may have a metal frame. If so, the frame should be welded, not mechanically fastened together.

SPRINGS Springs should be eight-way, hand-tied in the deck and back. A metal clip is sometimes used in place of jute twine to fasten springs together in the frame, and many upholsterers are of the opinion that this is more durable and contributes to higher quality. You will have to decide this one for yourself. I believe the hand-tied springs are a superior construction detail, allowing the upholsterer to create the proper shape. Not all frames have springs. Slender contemporary designs do not allow for springs and use webbing (jute or rubber) instead. Sinuous springs are acceptable for tight backs. Small, individually pocketed (in muslin) springs (Marshall units) are also used on sofa backs.

CUSHIONS Cushions may have foam, down, spring-down (springs wrapped with a down blanket), a Marshall unit, or even cotton padding at their core. Cushions with a foam or spring core will likely be wrapped in a layer of polyester batting (poly-batt) or down. Cushions may be 20 percent down and 80 percent feather (designated as 20/80).

PADDING Padding should be even and of consistent thickness. Check proportions on sectionals, because there are often inconsistencies in padding between pieces. Padding on the frame may be foam wrapped with polyester and covered in muslin prior to upholstering or horsehair and cotton padding covered with burlap, then cotton, and finally muslin. Foam of the appropriate firmness should be used; a good upholsterer keeps several densities on hand. Foam for button-tufting of vertical surfaces may be soft to allow for deep tufting. If horizontal surfaces are tufted (the top of an ottoman, for instance), the foam padding should have a triple-layer laminated construction that is firm on the bottom, medium in the middle, and soft at the top to pad the piece properly and allow for good tufting details. Padding on the frame should be firmer than that used for seat cushion cores.

FABRIC Fabric application should be taut, smooth, and consistent. The tucks and seams should be neat, the location of seams consistent (especially relative to their location on the frame), and the seams should be precisely positioned at the corners, not shifted around to the front side of one corner and the back of another. The pattern must match consistently from top to bottom and side to side. The motifs should be well-positioned and balanced. Welting should be straight, even in dimension, and smooth on cushions and frames. If the fabric cannot be *railroaded* (applied to the piece horizontally so there are no seams on a wide sofa back (Figure 23.1), the seams that will occur along the back, as well as on any continuous seat cushions or on the tight back, should be aligned with cushions or relate to the design, rather than being driven by the fabric width alone.

QUALITY The criteria for quality will vary with the type of construction presented. In all cases, the frame should be sturdy and you should not be able to feel its crisp, sharp edges easily through the padding. All exposed surfaces—whether they are wood, metal, or other material—should have a quality finish that is smooth and free of defects to the surface or finish. If wood, the finish should be free of burrs, blobs, dust, etc. If metal, it should have a smooth finish with three coats of plating, if applicable. The piece should have comfortable proportions and relationships (this

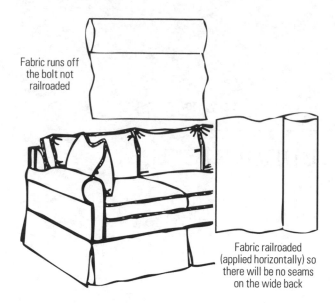

Fabric runs off the bolt not railroaded

Fabric railroaded (applied horizontally) so there will be no seams on the wide back

FIGURE 23.1 Some fabrics can be applied as railroaded to eliminate seams in long items such as sofas. Examples of fabric that cannot be railroaded include pile, some prints, and fabrics that are used elsewhere, such as drapes. Various configurations for custom upholstered lounge seating are possible by assembling combinations of the images throughout this chapter. *Drawing courtesy of Avery Boardman Furniture, New York.*

includes dimensions such as seat depth, as well as relationships such as the slope of the back, tilt of the deck, etc.). The fabric should be neatly applied with all seams straight and consistent.

COMFORT When building a piece of custom upholstered furniture, it is a good idea to sit in several pieces of upholstery to evaluate comfort. Note the height of the arm and back that is preferred, the slope of the back, the tilt of the seat deck, the fill of cushions, and all other components that make up the piece. You will need to be as specific and thorough as possible in your instructions to the upholsterer. Some modifications can be easily made after testing (softness of cushions or firmness of padding, for example), but others are more involved (such as changing the slope of the back or the depth of the seat). When test-sitting a piece, check all of the components (padding and cushion fill, slope height, depth of parts, etc).

Styles

Figures 23.2 through 23.7 provide a sampling of the many style options available from one manufacturer, Avery Boardman, at the time of this book's printing. Many other custom details are illustrated on the company's website. Familiarize yourself with common styles for each category listed below:

- Loose backs
- Tight backs
- Arms
- Seats
- Bases
- Skirts

Banquettes and Other Upholstered Items

Banquettes and other built-in seating may be delivered complete or built on site. As with any custom item, a complete and precise drawing should be produced to show all construction details. If the piece is to be delivered to the site and installed complete, make sure that it can knock down as necessary to be delivered to its location. If it is to be built on site, make sure that the details will allow for upholstery without the benefit of shop tools (air guns, sewing machines, etc.), as it will have to be upholstered by tacking and trimming by hand. Banquettes may be partially assembled in the shop and have portions covered on site. The more work that can be done in the shop, the more expert the installation can be.

Lambrequins, upholstered headboards, and upholstered box springs are less complicated constructions than sofas and chairs. Usually, these items are simply padded with foam or polyester batting and covered with fabric. They may be trimmed with decorative braid or cording, or button-tufted, but generally they are quite simple. Nonetheless they will require a drawing showing all dimensions and details.

Beyond issues of quality and style, there will be special requirements indicated by the design program. If a large piece must be delivered through a tight access space, provisions must be made to "break down" the item. This can often be easily accomplished if known in advance. A sectional is sometimes planned for such a circumstance because it naturally arrives in several smaller pieces.

Loose Back Square

Loose Back Round

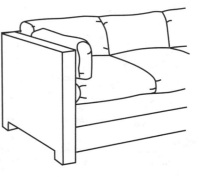
Loose Back Bullnose

Loose Back "Scatter Back"

Loose Back "T" Cushion

Loose Back Knife Edge

FIGURE 23.2 Loose back cushion styles. *Drawing courtesy of Avery Boardman Furniture, New York.*

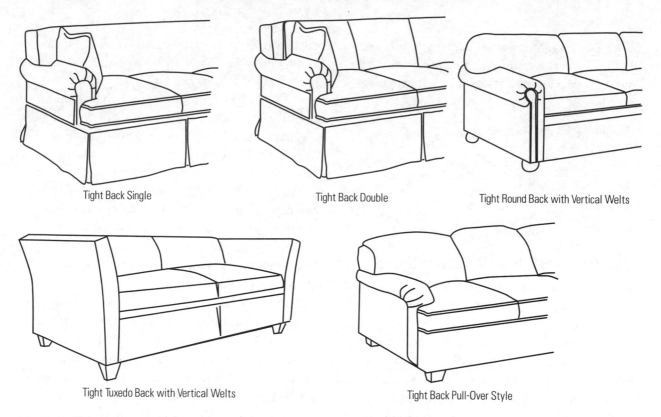

Tight Back Single

Tight Back Double

Tight Round Back with Vertical Welts

Tight Tuxedo Back with Vertical Welts

Tight Back Pull-Over Style

FIGURE 23.3 Tight back cushion styles. *Drawing courtesy of Avery Boardman Furniture, New York.*

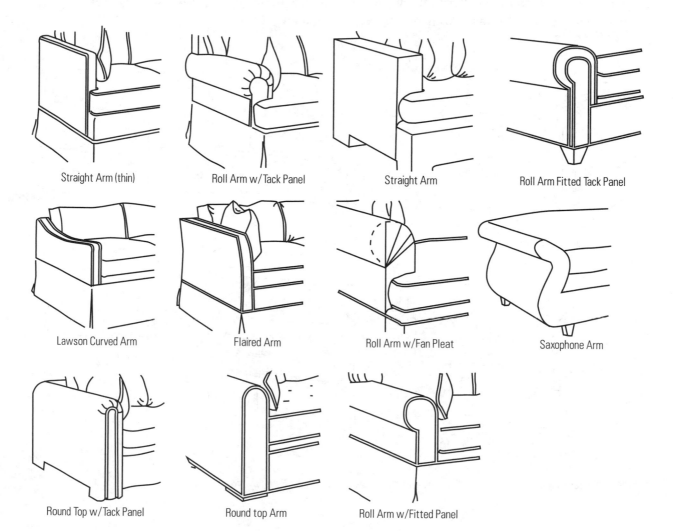

Straight Arm (thin)

Roll Arm w/Tack Panel

Straight Arm

Roll Arm Fitted Tack Panel

Lawson Curved Arm

Flaired Arm

Roll Arm w/Fan Pleat

Saxophone Arm

Round Top w/Tack Panel

Round top Arm

Roll Arm w/Fitted Panel

FIGURE 23.4 Arm styles. *Drawing courtesy of Avery Boardman Furniture, New York.*

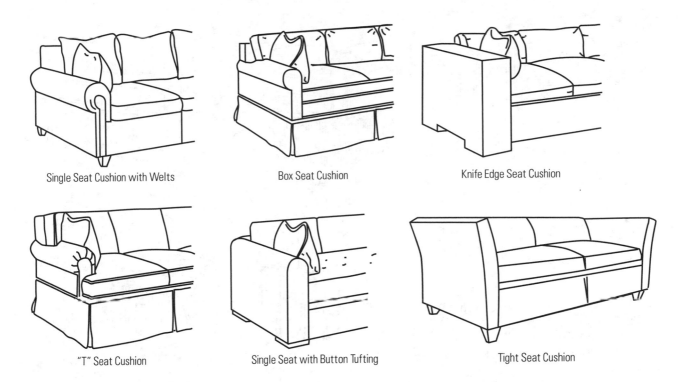

Single Seat Cushion with Welts

Box Seat Cushion

Knife Edge Seat Cushion

"T" Seat Cushion

Single Seat with Button Tufting

Tight Seat Cushion

FIGURE 23.5 Seat cushion styles. *Drawing courtesy of Avery Boardman Furniture, New York.*

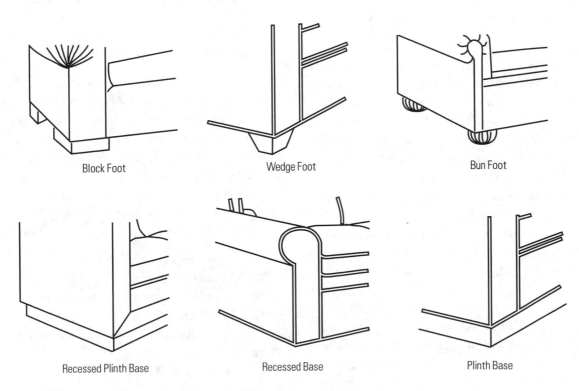

Block Foot

Wedge Foot

Bun Foot

Recessed Plinth Base

Recessed Base

Plinth Base

FIGURE 23.6 Base styles. *Drawing courtesy of Avery Boardman Furniture, New York.*

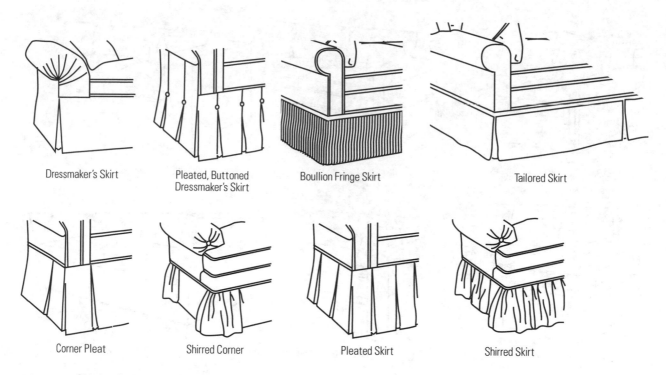

FIGURE 23.7 Skirt styles. *Drawing courtesy of Avery Boardman Furniture, New York.*

| Dressmaker's Skirt | Pleated, Buttoned Dressmaker's Skirt | Boullion Fringe Skirt | Tailored Skirt |

| Corner Pleat | Shirred Corner | Pleated Skirt | Shirred Skirt |

Design Process

The design process typically involves the following steps:

1. The piece is designed according to the needs of the clients for size, comfort, details, etc. It is drawn to scale and a fabric is selected. The specifications will include all details and materials, including padding, fills, frame, etc.

2. The drawings are submitted for bid. The information submitted includes a description of the fabric so the upholsterers who are bidding can estimate yardage.

3. Bids are reviewed; a fabricator is selected and paid a deposit; and the fabric is ordered.

4. The piece is tested by the client after it has been assembled and padded and at least one seat and one back cushion have been stuffed. The client will check for the comfort of the cushion fill and the appropriateness of the dimensions (seat depth and height, arm height, back height, and so forth), as well as the back slope and the padding of the frame. Padding is especially important over the arms, keeping in mind that the finish fabric will most likely lend some additional stiffness.

5. After approval of the muslin-covered piece, the finish fabric can be cut and applied.

Selecting upholstery for the elderly often requires a more rigorous assessment of comfort, as elderly people experience more discomfort when sitting for extended periods. Before the selection is finalized, the client should sit in the chair for 30 minutes if possible. The following checklist should be strictly adhered to as insurance against an uncomfortable chair.

While the client is seated, confirm that:

- The client's feet are flat on the floor.
- The client is comfortable.
- The client can make use of the backrest.
- The client's thighs are fully supported.
- There is a small space behind the client's knees.
- The client can shift his or her position with ease.
- The chair is wide enough for comfort.
- The seat tilt is comfortable (6 degrees is average).

- The seat is well-padded.
- The back slope is comfortable for the kind of sitting that will take place (dining, lounging, card-playing, knitting, etc. are all different from one another).
- The backrest supports the full length of the back, but does not push the head forward if it extends behind the head.
- The backrest is padded and comfortable all along its height.
- The armrests are padded at the area of the elbow.
- The armrests are low enough so as to not interfere with needlework, reading, or other activities that require motion or cause the client to hunch his or her shoulders.
- The armrests are the correct height and length.
- The handgrips that assist in rising are comfortable to hold (a rounded wooden end is often preferred).

A number of other issues must also be taken into consideration:

- Does the chair comply with fire and safety recommendations?
- Is the chair sturdy and stable?
- Do the legs splay out in a manner that might pose a tripping hazard?
- Would a freestanding footrest be desired or does it also pose a tripping hazard?

Factors Contributing to Cost

Both materials and labor factor into the price of an upholstered piece. If a piece is complex (or in the case of reupholstery, the modifications are extensive) the price will go up. The kind of padding and fills will affect the price (down is significantly more costly than synthetic fills). The process can also contribute to the cost. For example, if the client would like to have the entire piece covered with muslin for a test-sit and review of the entire construction, the cost will rise due to the labor involved in the application of muslin, which is not typically factored in. The covering can contribute a large percentage of the cost; for instance, the cost for leather alone can be as much as that for the entire construction of the piece covered in fabric.

Manufactured Upholstery

Manufactured upholstery is no different from custom. It is, in fact, so similar that often the cost of shipping an upholstered piece from the manufacturer's factory in another state may make a standard piece higher in cost than the same item made to order by a local shop. The disadvantage of not being able to test-sit a piece of furniture during production can be offset if a local sample can be reviewed and tested in a showroom. Remember that the fabric contributes to the comfort of a piece—a stiff fabric (or leather) on a showroom sample will give the cushions more body than a softer fabric and vice versa. Many manufacturers offer numerous alternatives to the arm style, back height, skirt detail, etc. Some pieces can be partially disassembled to move through small openings and assembled on site (as with many reclining chairs).

Sectional sofas are delivered in smaller components and "assembled" in the room. Consider the base or foot detail prior to ordering. Sometimes, a foot on a sectional is a little busy-looking if it has been designed as a decorative detail. Occasionally, a plinth base will be recessed on the sides as well as in front, leaving a dust-catch in a gap between the pieces at the base.

If you are ordering a single piece, a cut sheet or copy of a catalog page showing the piece and written description listing unique details are sufficient. For a sectional, you may also elect to include a plan view showing the components assembled to reinforce the information regarding left-facing and right-facing arms, as well as other details. When inspecting the piece at the warehouse prior to delivery to the site, you will review all points listed earlier in the discussion of assessment of quality for custom-upholstered furniture, as well as confirm that the correct pieces have been shipped.

Reupholstery

Reupholstery should be reserved for good-quality pieces that are comfortable and in good condition structurally. It is often a good idea to assess the condition of the padding on the frame and to replace cushion fills at the time of reupholstery.

Minor changes can be made to pieces economically while they are stripped down to the frame for reupholstery. The assessment should be made with the advice of your upholsterer. The seaming detailing, the thickness of the padding, the skirt or foot, the thickness of the cushion, and other minor changes can often be easily made. The height of the back, the width of the arms, and other changes to the frame will be more complicated and should be reviewed with the upholsterer prior to finalizing the specifications; not all frame changes can be economically accomplished. Exposed wooden portions can be upholstered more easily than upholstered portions can be left exposed (numerous nail holes will show, even if the kind of wood used is suitable for finishing). When considering stylistic changes, it helps to have "X-ray eyes." If you can discern the construction of the frame, it will be easier to imagine what changes will be easy and which will require modifications to the frame, thereby increasing the cost of the work substantially.

CHAPTER 24

Doors

Doors are pretty familiar items and I am tempted to dispense with the obvious and just get down to what (in addition to the obvious) you'll want to know on the job. A short list of door styles should serve to remind you how much you already know about doors. The styles that you might use in your designs include:

- Swinging doors—single or double leaves
- Pivot doors
- Bifold doors
- Dutch doors
- Sliding doors
- Surface sliding doors
- Pocket doors
- Coiling partitions and accordion doors for very large openings

Standard Doors

Doors come in numerous standard sizes and combinations of height, width, and thickness to give you a lot of flexibility to obtain a door of the desired size without the need to have it custom built. If a door must be custom built, that can be easily done, but always try to use a standard size whenever possible. The decision about which kind of door to use is a logical one, as the following examples will illustrate. If a door must be hung in an existing opening and must match other doors that are simultaneously visible or you are replicating a door that could not be found as standard for

any reason, it would be tempting to build a custom door. If you were specifying multiple doors, fire-rated doors, or doors for new construction where the openings can be sized to fit standard sizes, you would want to specify standard doors.

Sizes

There is a wide range of standard door sizes:

- Width: 2 feet, 2 feet 4 inches, 2 feet 6 inches, 2 feet 8 inches, 3 feet, 3 feet 4 inches, 3 feet 6 inches, 3 feet 8 inches, and 4 feet
- Height: 6 feet 8 inches, 7 feet, 7 feet 2 inches, 7 feet 10 inches, and 8 feet
- Thickness: 1-3/8 inch (typical for residential), 1-3/4 inch (typical for commercial), and 2 inches

Prehung versus Loose Leaf-Doors

Both standard and custom doors can be installed prehung or loose leaf. The prehung door arrives in its jamb and will be set into the door bucks that the rough carpenter has built to size. It may even have trim attached to one side. More frequently, however, the doors are trimmed and cased on site.

Loose-leaf doors arrive as the door only. They can be ordered with hinges attached so the carpenter does not have to mortise the hinges into the door and frame on site. When ordering special hinges for loose-leaf doors, order the following number of hinges per door:

- Three hinges for a standard interior door of less than 7 feet
- Four hinges for 7- to 12-foot doors
- Five hinges for 12- to 15-foot doors
- Six hinges for taller doors

The rule of thumb for positioning hinges is to place the top of the top hinge 5 inches below the top of the door and the bottom of the bottom hinge 10 inches above the floor, with equal spacing in between. The weight of the door will also influence the number of hinges required. For instance, a standard interior oak door could weigh about 7 pounds per square foot, but a hollow core door is only 2 pounds per square foot. If a mirror will be affixed to the door, add 3.28 pounds per square foot and calculate the additional thickness when selecting hardware.

Right- versus Left-Handed Doors

Doors that swing on hinges are described as right-hand, left-hand, regular bevel, or reverse bevel. The hand of the door is determined by the hinge location as judged from the "outside"—that is, the most public side—of the door, often the hallway. If the hinges are on the right, it is a right-hand door; if on the left, it is a left-hand door. If the door opens by standing on the public side and pushing the door open away from you, it is a *regular bevel*. If it opens by pulling the door toward you into the public space, it is a *reverse bevel*. This information is critical for the purchase of hardware.

Sliding and Prehung Doors

In addition to doors that swing on hinges, you may design for a door that slides. Examples include pocket doors, which slide on an overhead track (Figure 24.1a and b), and sliding doors, which have rails mounted to the floor and another track in the door header. Sliding doors must be designed with flush floor details to avoid having a surface-mounted track that bumps up above the floor surface. This is a nuisance, even in closets. Door openings that have neither the necessary clearance for a swinging door nor the wall space or opening width for a pocket or slider can be

a   b

FIGURE 24.1 Johnson Hardware produces a kit that contains the hardware required for a typical pocket door installation (a). You can see the rollers for the top assembly that would hang in the top track with their plates fastened to the top of the door leaf. The guides for the bottom of the door would be mounted to the floor. Johnson Hardware also produces the "pocket" portion of a pocket door, called the door buck (b), which will be entirely concealed in the wall space (the portion on the right of the image) and in the head jamb above the opening. The door will slide from the opening into this hidden pocket clearance.

designed for bifold doors or a surface sliding door on wall-mounted tracks.

Hardware

A review of hardware mechanisms for the different functions illuminates the need for detailing when planning for doors. For example, shoji sliders may be detailed with a track in the floor and head rail or they may require a head rail and a floor guide, depending on surface materials (that is, whether it is possible to install a track flush into the floor) and number of panels (a pair can use floor guides, but multiples must have tracks). Wall-mounted sliding hardware can be visually awkward and look like a retro-fit if not detailed to integrate well into both the design and the construction. Figures 24.2 through 24.4 illustrate hardware used for multi-panel sliding doors, bifold doors, and shutters.

Acoustics

Acoustic separation of spaces will vary with the door style, as well as with construction. Doors that come to rest against stops block sound better than sliding doors, which usually have small gaps between panels and walls to prevent the parts from dragging against each other and damaging surfaces (unless gaskets can be applied to the construction). These little gaps will permit sound to move easily between spaces. The acoustic qualities of various door types are discussed in more detail later.

Door Construction

The door leaf, which is the part of the construction that moves to expose the opening, may be constructed in various ways from a variety of materials, with any number of surface "skins."

Hollow Core

There are limited reasons for specifying hollow-core doors. The most frequent reason is cost: They are cheaper than other door constructions. If you are concerned that children in the family might suffer mashed fingers (something that is not common in door use, but circumstances might present a worry like this in specific instances), a

FIGURE 24.2 Multipanel sliding door hardware from Johnson Hardware allows a large span to be covered or opened. Confirm the weight of your door to make sure you are ordering the correct hardware because such hardware is available in a variety of weight classes.

FIGURE 24.3 This image of bifold (meaning two leaves) hardware from Johnson Hardware shows the portion of the track concealed from view after most installations are complete. It also shows the solid wood hinge rail and top rail in this veneer skin door that may be hollow core but still requires solid wood for fastening the hardware.

FIGURE 24.4 You need not stop at bifold, as this image from Johnson Hardware illustrates.

hollow-core door may be the best spec for the program. Generally, however, they are not preferred. Hollow-core doors (for interior use only) are not entirely hollow; they contain a honeycombed core interior panel. Their characteristics are:

- Laminated construction
- Framework of metal or wood

- Core of expanded foam, honeycomb, grid, or tube matrix. (Expanded-foam cores offer good insulating properties.)
- Plywood and veneer face (wood, laminate, hardboard, or metal)

Hollow-core doors have solid wood at the sides for mounting latches, locks, and hinges. They usually have solid wood at the top and bottom so they can be shaved down if necessary to adjust the fit if the framework is wood. (This is more difficult if the face is metal.) Sound travels easily through these doors, and they can be damaged by rough handling.

Solid Core

As noted, solid-core doors are preferred over hollow-core ones. In addition to providing a better sound barrier, they feel noticeably more substantial and, therefore, suggest better quality. Doors with expanded-foam cores have good insulating properties; those with particleboard and wood-block cores are dimensionally stable and more inherently rigid. The characteristics of solid-core doors are:

- Laminated construction
- Framework of wood or metal. (Staved cores or particleboard cores may also have an intermediate sheet of metal.)
- Plywood and veneer face, or veneer face only

Veneer-faced doors have a number of plies installed over the core. The number of plies and the quality of the top or face veneer are variable. In addition to the species of wood used, you will select the cut of the veneer and describe the kind of matching that will be acceptable. To ensure that the graining is consistent and continuous with the wall panels in a paneled room, you may hire the fabricator to make the door as well as the panels, rather than specifying a manufactured door. A door with a high-pressure laminate face will be constructed in a manner similar to veneer-faced flush doors. Solid-core doors are good insulators and sound-blockers, but these characteristics can be further improved if weather-stripping is used. They can be shaved down to adjust the fit if the framework is wood, but again, this is more difficult if the face is metal.

Flat Panel Solid Wood

Solid planks jointed together will have the vulnerability to checking and cracking for which solid wood is known. This specification would be limited to situations where a design could not be easily or economically produced with an engineered base material, which would otherwise always be the more sensible way to make a door. Even if the aesthetics called for a plank door, you might want to try to design the look of a plank door onto a stable substrate. A door with heavy all-over carving may have to be solid wood planks. These doors have a variety of characteristics:

- Better-quality doors with curved pieces (oval or round windows in the door, for instance) have raised molding ringing the curved cutout.
- The molding will often be in several pieces. This is an indication of better quality because the wood is oriented in the direction of greatest strength to prevent cracking.
- Solid wood doors are fairly good insulators and sound-blockers. Both of these inherent characteristics of wood are affected by the fit of the door and the condition of any weather-stripping. Solid doors can be trimmed or shaved to fit if necessary.
- They are constructed of solid wood; therefore, they are vulnerable to shrinkage and swelling with changes in humidity.

Raised Panel Solid Wood

Solid wood doors with the framework exposed consist of a top rail, lock rail, and bottom rail, with possible intermediate rails. Mortise and tenon joint or doweled construction is typical for the rails. Occasionally, the rails will be glued in addition to the joint. The center panels are loose to allow for expansion and contraction. High-quality exterior doors may have a split panel, which allows the interior and exterior faces to expand and contract independently of each other. For interior doors, the center panel may be louvers. If the center panel is solid (not louvers), the door will block sound well. Acoustic isolation can be improved further if the door is fitted with weather-stripping.

Doors constructed of solid planks are less common than those with panel construction. They are heavy and likely to crack. They will be good insulators and sound blockers if the fit and weather-stripping are appropriate. These doors have a number of characteristics:

- They are constructed of solid wood; therefore, they are vulnerable to shrinkage and swelling.
- In some doors, the center panel is constructed of planks as described previously. Because the panel is loose at the edges, any shrinkage is transferred there and should not crack the center panel (Figure 24.5).
- If the door is painted, seasonal shrinking and swelling is likely to crack the paint at the perimeter of the panel.

Hardboard

High-density fiberboard (HDF) doors can have the appearance of a panel door because they are molded into a raised-panel style over a core. Made from wood fiber, hardboard is neither moisture- nor flame-resistant unless treated.

Depending on its core, a hardboard door may be a good insulator. It can be shaved down to adjust the fit. Doors may be constructed with recycled content, thus contributing to green design efforts.

Fiberglass

Fiberglass doors have molded surfaces over a polystyrene core. Depending on the type of core, this door may be a good insulator.

Metal Doors

Metal doors are most often used for commercial installations. A variety of doors may be selected, including all-steel doors, sometime in combination with glass; storm doors with glass; all-steel doors; and all-glass doors that use aluminum and steel frames. Steel doors are selected for security doors. The interior and exterior skins are steel with an insulating core. It is common for a portion of a metal door to be glazed (that is, to have a window installed). Steel doors are often molded to imitate a panel door. They are used in both residential and commercial settings and are categorized as either one or the other, although residential-quality doors can be used in settings that require only light commercial use.

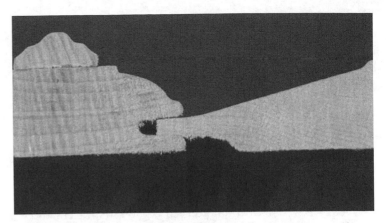

FIGURE 24.5 This section of rail and panel shows how the center panel is captured by the side rails of the door with a dado joint; it is not fastened into place so the wood can expand and contract without binding or breaking bonds because there are no bonds to break. *Photograph by Alana Clark.*

Steel-clad doors may have hollow cores or have particleboard, wood block, urethane, or expanded polystyrene-foam cores. They typically have solid wood blocks at the stiles and rails, and in the area surrounding the lock and knob. They usually receive a painted finish and might be galvanized, primed, or have a baked enamel finish. They are often available in several different configurations of single or double doors with side lights and transoms. Depending on their core material, they could be well-insulated and good sound-blockers. Although they may have wood bottom and top rails, typically they cannot be shaved to accommodate a change in floor finish.

Metal doors that must provide a thermal break may use wood as part of the door to minimize the transfer of heat and cold through the door. Wooden mounting areas for hardware will be concealed by metal skins. Glazed areas should be tempered or laminated glass.

All-glass doors are used for interior doors and shower doors. They often have top and bottom rails of metal. Per code, they should contain tempered or laminated glass for safety.

Institutional Doors

An institutional designation usually indicates a more durable version of whatever is being specified, and that is also true with respect to doors. The difference in specs between a solid-core door and an institutional-grade door will be the thickness of the facing material, the kind of core, and possibly the incorporation of metal protection, either concealed or surface-mounted. Institutional doors have a number of characteristics:

- They are thicker and heavier than standard doors.
- They feature laminated construction.
- The framework is constructed of wood or metal.
- They have a grid core, and ladder-type or vertical stiffeners with or without foam insulation.
- The face is made of plywood and veneer.

Institutional doors are good insulators and sound-blockers if their fit and weather-stripping are appropriate. They can be shaved down to adjust the fit if the framework is wood, but this is more difficult if the face is metal.

Door Systems

Commercial buildings frequently have multiple units of standard metal and glass doors set in a companion framing system that also includes stationary panels (windows). These systems are sometimes referred to as *store-front doors*. They should be selected early in the design process so that any standard sizes and components can be integrated into the design as it develops.

Fire and Safety Considerations

The main safety concern in specifying doors is the fire rating, but even if a door does not have to be fire-rated, the safety features of any glass should be considered.

Fire Doors

The fire code requires that doors in defined locations in a commercial project and between a residence and an attached garage be fire-rated. This means that the door and frame can withstand exposure to smoke and flames for a specified period of one to four hours. Fire-rated doors bear a label identifying them as such on the hinge end (which is held against the frame when closed). In addition to resisting flame, the door, depending on its location, may also be required to resist the transfer of heat through the door or to block the passage of gasses. In addition to instructions that define the characteristics of the door, fire-rated doors must have acceptable hardware and closers.

Detailed definitions of door locations and type are found in the code book. Generally speaking, you will seek this information in the code book under any of a number of circumstances:

- The door has an exit sign next to or above it.
- It leads to stairwells or horizontal exit routes.
- It divides a large area into smaller "fire areas" per code square-foot maximums.
- It leads from a distinctly separate room into a hallway or into another distinctly separate room.

A compliant fire-rated door will have a number of characteristics:

- Have the required label attached, describing its tested rating
- Have steel ball-bearing hinges
- Be self-closing and self-latching

Glazing

Fire codes require the use of fire-resistive glass of limited dimensions, depending on the rating. For example, in an A-rated 3-hour door, no glass is likely to be permitted. In a B-rated 1.5-hour door in vertical shafts, 100 square inches is the maximum allowable. In a C-rated 1.5-hour exterior door, no glass is allowed.

Safety codes require tempered or laminated glass for some circumstances. You will need to confirm the required rating according to local codes before selecting windows in doors that must be fire-rated. Glass used in fire-rated doors is usually wire glass or ceramic glass.

There are no restrictions limiting glazed areas on doors that are not required to be fire-rated. Glass used in doors should be tempered for safety reasons. Large sheets of glass used in doors should be tempered and laminated. Glazing in doors is available in several configurations:

- As a single sheet
- As true divided light, small, individual panes of glass separated by mullions and muntins
- As imitation divided light (lattice of mullions and muntins that pop into the window frame on one or both sides)
- As a lattice of mullions and muntins that is installed between two panes of insulated window

CHAPTER 25

Hardware

Door Locks and Latches

Door lever and knob hardware is described first of all by function. There are entrance doors, passage doors, privacy doors, and closet doors; there are active hardware sets that latch or lock and dummy hardware sets that are stationary for pulling the door open. Doors are left-handed or right-handed. The hardware can be described in a ranking from the simplest to the most complex.

Roller Catch

In the hierarchy of locking and latching, the simplest latch is a magnetic or roller catch. There is no actual latching, just a catch to hold the door in a closed position. These doors are operated with a "dummy" hardware set, just the stationary levers or knobs (pulls) and no retractable latch, or moving parts. The pull hardware looks like a latch set but does not operate a latch.

Passage Set

The next simplest setup is the passage set (Figure 25.1). The passage set does not lock. It can always be operated by manipulating the lever or knob from either side. Latch sets will be either a cylindrical (Figure 25.2) or interior mortise (Figure 25.3). The door prep for these two types will be different because the cylindrical latch requires a very slender passage from the handle to the edge of the door (Figure 25.4a), but the mortise requires a large cavity (Figure 25.4b).

FIGURE 25.1 The passage set has no lock. Levers on either side can always operate the latch. *Baldwin set photographed with permission of Clark and Barlow Hardware.*

FIGURE 25.2 The cylindrical latch set by Von Morris.

FIGURE 25.3 Mortise latch set by Von Morris.

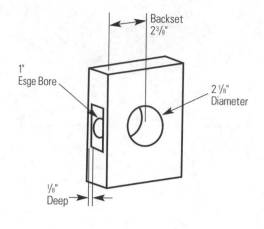

FIGURE 25.4 The boring or routing of the door will be different for the cylindrical latch set (a) from that for the mortise latch set (b). The backset information is independent of the type of boring.

Privacy Set

Privacy sets are the next step up in security (Figure 25.5). They are typically used for bathroom and bedroom doors. The knob or lever will operate the latch from either side unless the outside lever is locked by a push button on the inside. When the inside button is depressed, the lever or knob on the outside will not operate the latch. The privacy latch may be overridden on the outside in a couple of different ways. There may be a small knob or lever on the escutcheon plate, a trim collar between the door knob or lever and the door (Figure 25.6) that pulls out or a hole in the outer knob, may allow for a small object (like an unfolded paper clip or bobby pin) to be inserted to trip the lock and unlock the door. This is called the emergency release.

Storeroom Door Locks

Storeroom door locks always require keys to operate, and the latch is always operable from the interior side (Figure 25.7).

Entrance Door Hardware

Entrance doors (Figure 25.8) have a handle, lever, or knob, a lock that is keyed from the outside, and a turn knob (single cylinder) or another key on the inside (called double cylinder). In addition to the lock that disables the latch, an entrance set will usually have a dead bolt.

FIGURE 25.5 This cylindrical latch set from Von Morris has a privacy button that will be exposed on the escutcheon plate when the set is installed.

FIGURE 25.6 The release for the privacy lock may be a button or a small hole so that a slender object can be inserted to trip the lock.

FIGURE 25.7 The storeroom door locks with a key for safekeeping of the stored products, but the latch on the interior side is always operable.

FIGURE 25.9 The storefront set uses a key in the inside and outside of the door; this is permitted because the door is always unlocked when the shop is open for business. This lock would be selected for a glass door.

FIGURE 25.8 The entrance set provides the most security from intrusion. It has a key on the exterior side and a turnknob on the interior. The mechanisms, from the top down, are the dead bolt, the latch, and push buttons, which immobilizes the latch from the outside. The two circles in the dead bolt are free-spinning cylinders that inhibit an intruder from sawing through the dead bolt because the cylinders would roll against a saw blade and not be sawn through.

Storefront Sets

Storefront sets operate with a key on each side (Figure 25.9). Because the door is always unlocked when the shop is open, the safety concern about restricting exit is not present, as it is for other occupancies, where the door might be found locked by people inside and no key in the lock. This condition requires a sign adjacent to the door stating, "This door to remain unlocked during business hours."

Locks, like latches, may be cylindrical or mortised in (see Figures 25.2 and 25.3). Cylindrical locks sit in a round hole bored on the face of the lock stile. Backsets are the distance from the edge of the door to the center of the bore for the spindle or turn piece. Backsets are usually 2-3/8 inches or 2-3/4 inches on mortise or tubular sets for interior doors.

Cremone Bolts for French Doors

Cremone bolts for French doors (Figure 25.10a) stabilize one leaf of the two-leaf pair. You can imagine that if the doors were simply latched together and neither side was locked in place, the door could be opened easily by pushing between the two doors. One side must be secured in order to keep the doors shut. This is sometimes accomplished with a flush bolt (Figure 25.10b), but the cremone bolt is the traditional way of fixing one leaf of a pair of French doors. When the bolt is thrown, it may be received into the threshold, the

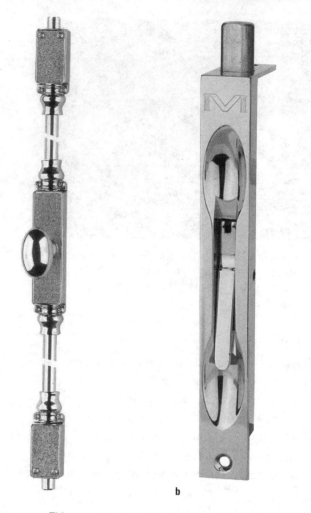

a   b

FIGURE 25.10 This cremone bolt from Von Morris (not shown at full height) throws a pin at the top and bottom into the strike in the floor and the head jamb. This bolt is operated by a knob, but cremone bolts are also available with levers that may be easier for people with limited dexterity to operate. If there is a transom window in the jamb, strikes can be surface-mounted to the mullions above. A pair of French doors could have a cremone bolt on each leaf or a flush bolt on one leaf and a cremone bolt on the other (a). The flush bolt from Von Morris would be used in the edge of a door and would throw the lock bolt into the head jamb or the floor. A strike plate would be installed to receive the bolt (b).

jamb, or into a catch mounted on the face of a mullion above.

Panic Door Latching

Panic devices are used for the rapid egress of a person from a building and feature a latch or latches that can be operated by a push bar or rail. They are required in assembly, education, day care, and some health-care and hazardous occupancies. Panic devices are also known as exit devices and come in several configurations based on application. The most common is the rim exit device; it mounts on the surface of the door and

latches into a surface-mounted strike on the door frame or mullion (Figure 25.11). Another type of exit device is the mortise type. It is similar to the mortise lockset in that it has a lock installed into a pocket on the edge of the door and is activated by the push rail or outside trim (Figure 25.12). The third and fourth types of panic devices incorporate vertical rods that allow the door to be latched at the top and bottom. This is ideal for pairs of exit doors where a center mullion may not be desirable. The surface vertical rod panic device mounts to the surface of the door with the vertical rods exposed (which is why it is described as "surface"). The concealed vertical rod exit device contains the rods, which connect the push and rail with the top and bottom latches within the door, thus concealing them from view.

Dogging function means that the latch and push bar can be held in the retracted position so that the door can be opened and closed quietly in presentation and performance spaces. This might be done with a hex key (standard), with a key (cylinder dogging), or electrically (electric dogging). The pushbar will have a lock cylinder in it for cylinder dogging. The pushbar may protrude more if operating the latch and be flatter to the door if dogged by adjustment on the device. Manual dogging is not allowed on fire-rated doors because the door is required to remain closed and latched even if something falls against it. Pressure on the bar itself must be the only action that releases the latch.

Other options for panic bar hardware include electric locking and latching functions, which can be controlled in a variety of ways (card readers, punch codes, remote controls, and buzzer systems). Delayed egress functions require that the pushbar be pressed for three seconds to initiate an alarm sequence that will allow the door to open thirty seconds later. This hardware is for situations where security and egress requirements indicate that egress must be easily allowable but theft or hazard indicate the need for restricting egress. Good examples of such spaces would be a museum or the birthing area in a hospital. The alarm function alerts occupants and security personnel. Integral alarms are available that sound when the pushbar is depressed and continue until reset by a special key.

Electronic Locking Devices

Electronic locking (Figure 25.13) is an attempt to avoid the conflict of safety, convenience, and security in high-traffic situations where numerous people with legitimate access come and go frequently. The problems of convenience and security are experienced by institutional and hospitality businesses as staff, tenants, and customers need to access the building. The various features of these sometimes very sophisticated locking devices must be reviewed product-by-product to ensure that the numbers of codes and tracking options coincide with your design program needs. The preference of battery over wired options should be discussed with your client. Even if you do preliminary legwork and recommend optional models for the client (or the client's designated decision-maker), you must work toward full client participation in this selection. The more complicated the item is, the more diligent you must be to fully inform your client to ensure a good fit between their needs and expectations and the product specified. Card readers, sequence or combination number codes, and fingerprint readers are some of the keyless options available.

Door Closers

Door closers (Figure 25.14) are common in commercial installations, frequently used in order to meet fire codes. Door closers do just what you would expect: They pull the door closed any time there is insufficient counterpressure to hold it open. It is not uncommon to see the door closer overridden with a rubber wedge holding the door open for reasons of function. This common, though illegal, practice underscores the need to factor in all code requirements at the early programming stages so convenience and safety are not at odds with each other on a daily basis. If it is anticipated that a fire door will need to be held open, there are specialty door closers with hold-open features that connect to the fire alarm and will close upon activation of the alarm.

Door closers are very adjustable, allowing for speed and force in the motion of the door. Most full-feature commercial closers have four

FIGURE 25.11 Panic hardware allows the latch to be released simply by leaning against it. Fire code requires that certain doors be self-closing and latching but easily released in case of an emergency where panicked people might not be thinking clearly. This version has the system exposed on the face of the door. *Image of Yale hardware courtesy of Assa Abloy.*

FIGURE 25.12 This diagram shows a door similar to Figure 25.11; the hardware is concealed within its body and routed along its length to provide passage of the vertical latching. *Image of Yale hardware courtesy of Assa Abloy.*

FIGURE 25.13 There are varying configurations of keyless locks that employ different technologies for ascertaining permission to enter. This lock requires users to punch in a number code.

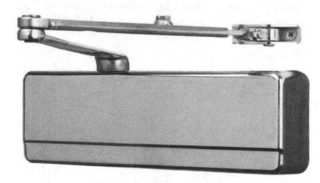

FIGURE 25.14 Door closers are required equipment on fire-rated doors because they must close and latch themselves. This Sargent door closer would be mounted at the top of a door.

adjustments: spring adjustment, closing or swing speed, latch speed, and backcheck.

Spring adjustment affects the entire cycle of the door closer movement and is used to size the closer for the particular door. Closing speed controls how fast the door closes to approximately 8 inches from the closed position; the latch speed controls the speed of the door during the final 8 inches of door swing. Latch speed adjustment is critical for door latching. Backcheck engages at approximately 70 degrees of the door opening cycle to prevent the door from slamming into

whatever door stop device is being used. These adjustments allow a door to be properly controlled during its entire opening and closing cycles.

Manual hold-open arms may be available with the door closers, but these cannot be used on doors in fire-rated partitions. These door closers will hold the door open if pushed wide enough. If opened less than this critical point, they will close the door normally. Spring hinges may be used to provide a similar function, but they do not control the door. They simply close the door.

Hinges

Hinges are the attachment between door and frame and they may be mortised, surface, or a combination of the two. Hinge selection is based on several factors such as door weight, frequency of operation, door material, frame material, door thickness, and aesthetics.

The mounting of the hinge is described by its relationship to the door.

- Full mortise—mortised into door and jamb
- Half mortise—mortised into door, surface on jamb
- Half surface—mortised into jamb, surface on door
- Full surface—surface-mounted on both door and jamb

The types of hinges that might be specified are described below.

Butt Hinge

There are two types of butt hinges (Figure 25.15). *Loose pin* hinges have a pin that can be removed from the barrel to demount the door. *Fixed pin* hinges have a pin that cannot be removed from the barrel.

Pivot Hinge

Pivot hinges may be located at the top, bottom, and sides of the door. Pivot hinges are single acting or double acting; double-acting doors swing both directions in an opening while single action will swing open in one direction, either in or out.

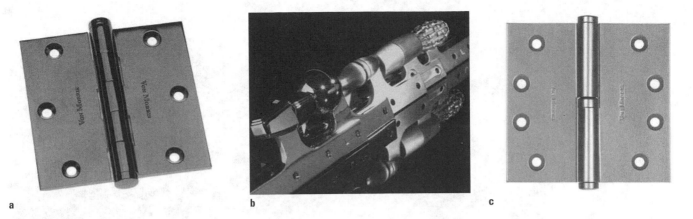

a   b   c

FIGURE 25.15 This five-knuckle hinge (a) has a fixed pin through the barrel. This olive knuckles hinges (b) demonstrates the options to the five-knuckle barrel; its simple cylindrical shape is replaced by smaller, elegant "olives" cast in forms to coordinate with other hardware in the line. Ball-bearing hinges (c) are engineered for greater weight-bearing. You can recognize a ball-bearing hinge by the alternating large and small knuckles on the barrel. A ball-bearing hinge is not available with a removable pin. *Hinges by Von Morris.*

Swing-Clear Hinge

Swing-clear hinges (Figure 25.16) will clear the door opening and allow the door to open to a position that leaves the entire door clear of the opening when open to 90 degrees.

Spring Hinge

Spring hinges have adjustable tension to close the door to maintain the fire rating. These hinges will be steel because brass hinges will melt at too low a temperature to provide enough resistance to fire. They close the door as a door-closer would, but they have no adjustability for varying sweep and latch speeds.

Wide Throw Hinge

Wide-throw hinges (Figure 25.17) are used where it is necessary to open a door 180 degrees around a large reveal.

Continuous Hinge

Continuous hinges (Figure 25.18) are for high-use or high-abuse situations. Continuous hinges are also selected if a lot of weight must be supported.

Electric Hinge

It is sometimes necessary to transmit electric power to an electric lock or exit device mounted on a door (Figure 25.19a and b). The best way to do this is to use an electric hinge, which trans-

FIGURE 25.16 A swing-clear hinge by Stanley allows a door to entirely clear its opening.

FIGURE 25.17 Wide-throw hinge by Stanley.

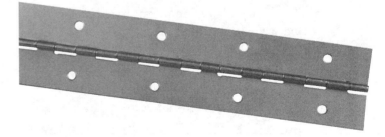

FIGURE 25.18 Continuous hinge by Stanley.

mits power from the door frame to the door through the hinge. Electric hinges may have as few as two wires or as many as 12 wires for connection to different devices to enable various features. Some of these electric hinges are available with a modular-type connector, making the door, frame, and electrified hardware "plug and play."

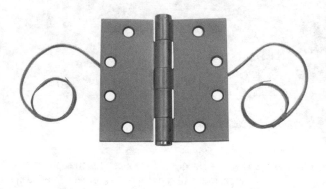

a   b

FIGURE 25.19 Electric hinges (a) allow low-voltage power to reach the door leaf to operate electric locking, provide feedback on conditions, and drive motor-driven accessories, such as electric blinds. The wiring (b) is sometimes secured by mastic, and the hinge itself is not electrified but simply holds the wires that transmit from jamb to door leaf. *Hinge by Stanley.*

Finishes

Typical finishes for hardware are brass (bright and satin), chrome (bright and satin), nickel (bright and satin), stainless (bright and satin), statuary bronze (bright, oil-rubbed, and satin), and antique nickel/pewter.

Clues to quality include the following:

- *Weight of assembly*: Light versus Heavy is Cheap versus Quality. Some convex shapes are "hollowed out" or concave on the back rather than solid. This material-saving approach makes a piece of hardware feel cheap.
- *Plating*: Number of coats on plated pieces. Quality plating has at least three coats. Check the reflection of the piece: The surface of good plating is smooth and even.
- *Finish*: Run your hand over it to check the edges. They should be smooth and even and somewhat softened. Burrs, sharp edges, and any bumpiness of plating are indications of lesser quality.

The quality differences will be more apparent with the passage of time when low-quality door levers sag and knobs loosen up and jiggle, and repeated adjustments will not correct the problems. The finish of cheap hardware becomes scarred as a single-plated coat is scratched instead of acquiring a patina (patina describes scratches that are only surface scratches and additional plating still covers the base material). This is not to say that economy choices will never be selected, but use them for light use or temporary situations. Also, look to the Builders Hardware Manufacturers Association (BHMA) for standards for testing hardware to various quality levels. BHMA-certified hardware offers some assurance that products meeting minimum standards have been thoroughly tested and certified to meet the needs of your clients. See *www.buildershardware.org* for more information.

CHAPTER 26

Drapery

You will orchestrate many issues of style according to your design program. Basic categories of soft goods that you will use or combine might include drapes, curtains, toppers (both hard and soft), custom fabric shades, and manufactured blinds (not technically soft goods but the function is strongly related). The drapery workroom will also fabricate simple furniture items such as upholstered headboards and will upholster walls.

The distinctions among these various soft goods are sometimes loosely defined because there are items that resemble more than one category. Drapery is often assumed to mean (although it does not necessarily mean) treatments that draw open and closed via rigging controlled by a pull cord or motor. Drapery and curtain are terms sometimes used interchangeably although the implication is that curtains are simpler than drapes and have nonmechanical hardware. *Café curtains*, for instance, cover only the lower half of the window and are not strung on movable rigging. They are often assumed to include a companion valance of some sort. *Dress curtains* are stationary panels that frame the window opening but do not draw across it. Toppers such as swags and jabots or valances are softly constructed decorative drapery treatments of fabric, often combined with other coverings (drapes, shades, blinds, etc.). Shades refer to fabric or other textile constructions that are understood to draw up and drop down, although some manufactured window coverings operate differently.

Fitting the Window Treatments to the Space

A simple draw drape on a traverse or other rod could be specified with a written specification alone, but most window treatment designs are best communicated with drawings that show the treatment in plan and elevation (Figure 26.1) with all pertinent dimensions, alignments to architectural features, and information to the installer. Included in the dimensions are the height, the treatment in relation to the floor or window frame (including the drop of a swag or jabot), and the width of the treatment, including stackbacks. The depth of a multilayered treatment or a treatment where the projection would become an issue (bay windows, drapery pockets, or any close proximity) should be shown on the plans. The location of the controls should be noted on a plan view; the control wand for the blinds and the cord for the blinds or the drapes should also be shown on a plan view.

The plan view that you forward to the workroom will show the depth of the treatment and the anticipated size of the stackback; the location of the pull cord or wand will be noted along with the correct location of floor vents, switch plates, and other service controls to communicate the relationship between the treatment and controls.

FIGURE 26.1 Even a simple drapery construction like this one should be drawn to scale to check the proportions of the stacked panel widths and the height of the rosettes, which determine the drape of the side curtains.

Depth of the Treatment

The depth of the treatment from the wall out will be greatly influenced by the number of layers. Estimate 6 inches of depth for each layer of custom soft goods so that the layers do not drag excessively on adjoining layers or the wall surface as the treatment moves to open and close. Consult the manufacturer's stack chart for purchased shades and blinds. Some woven grass and bamboo Roman blinds require up to a foot of depth projection to stack up. This can eliminate them from consideration in a situation where two corners meet or for a bay window. A lambrequin, cornice, or valance adds a couple of inches more to the depth. Show all these layers in your plan view so you can confirm furniture locations and fully comprehend the scale of the 3-D treatment in location. Sometimes it's quite a massive presence. If the drapery will retract into a pocket, there should be room at the front and back so the fabric does not drag and snag.

Width of the Stackback

The *stackback* is the width required for the open drapery to stand, either off the glass covering wall space or on the glass covering part of the window. It is typically one-third the width of the entire treatment but you can control for some variation. There are a few factors influencing the size of the stackback. One is the fullness. Typical minimal fullness for multipurpose fabric (medium-light drapery weight) is 2.75, meaning you will need to multiply the finished width of the treatment (window plus stackback) times 2.75 to have enough fabric to pleat. To look at it another way, if your drapes are made up out of 54-inch-wide fabric, each 54-inch-wide fabric panel will be only 19.63 inches after it has been pleated (54 inches divided by 2.75). Heavier fabric can look acceptable with 2.5 times the width; that is fortunate if the stackback is getting too wide, because heavy fabric needs more room to stand. So the second factor influencing the size of the stackback is fabric weight or the hand of the fabric. The number of pleats and kind of pleats also contributes to how tightly the treatment can stack. You can adjust the fullness and the number of pleats independently of each other. Fewer, fuller pleats can reduce the stackback without making the drapes look skimpy.

Lining will add to the bulk of the stacked treatment; lining and interlining (as is irresistible for taffeta and other thin solids) doubles the contribution of the bulk from lining. The kind of pleat selected also contributes to the stackback (Figure 26.2). The pleat style shown in Figure 26.3 is so fat (the goblet is usually even stuffed so it holds its shape over time) that you should really only consider it for stationary panels. They just need too much stackback for most locations.

Size and Mounting Location

Your elevation drawing should show the size and mounting location of the treatment in relation to the window height and width. It will clarify the width of the overall treatment in relation to wall space available, door and window casings, and height relationships to crown molding details. The mounting height can best be determined on elevation showing all casings and moldings indicated in correct scale.

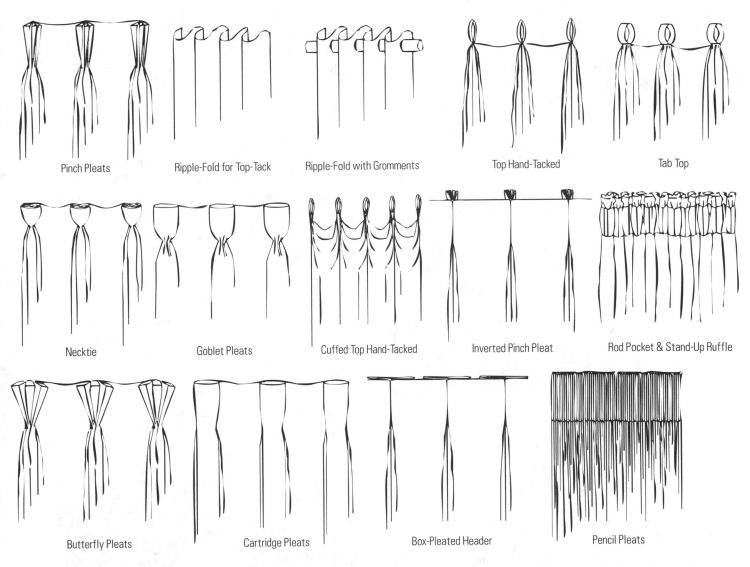

Pinch Pleats

Ripple-Fold for Top-Tack

Ripple-Fold with Gromments

Top Hand-Tacked

Tab Top

Necktie

Goblet Pleats

Cuffed Top Hand-Tacked

Inverted Pinch Pleat

Rod Pocket & Stand-Up Ruffle

Butterfly Pleats

Cartridge Pleats

Box-Pleated Header

Pencil Pleats

FIGURE 26.2 Various pleating styles have different requirements for the amount of stackback and will alter the one-third rule of thumb (see the section Estimating later in this chapter).

Location and Type of Control

Also on your plan view will be the control location and type. The location of a wand at the leading edge of the drapery panel or a pull cord for the rigging at the outside should be indicted on your plans so that the workroom and the client can comprehend the logistics of getting behind furniture to reach the wands or pull cords.

Accommodating HVAC

Heating, ventilation, and air-conditioning vents are located at windows to mitigate infiltration of cold and hot air. As a result, drapery panels might blow around in the forced air. For new construction, the vent location can be shifted slightly to accommodate the drapery location. In existing

FIGURE 26.3 The goblet pleats in this drapery designed by Tracy Hickman of Chicago are hand-tacked to rings on a wooden pole so this treatment would be drawn by hand. The stuffed goblets in the header prevent the treatment from stacking up tightly. *Design by Tracy Hickman.*

buildings, the vent will be in place and the drapery designed to accommodate the vent location.

Measure the exact location and size of floor vents when you do your site measure for rooms that may get drapery. For new construction, you will note the depth of treatment and then locate the floor vents. Yes, you must sometimes plan your window treatments a year in advance of installation. For a multilayered treatment, the vent may be located farther away from the window in order to avoid having the drapery blowing in the forced air current. Don't forget to communicate this information regarding the best location for floor vents to both the architect and the contractor. A single-layer treatment will stand forward a minimum of 4 inches, a double will stand forward a minimum of 6.5 inches, and if the vent is on the ceiling, any additional top treatment will have to be factored in to allow 3 more inches.

Location of Switch Plates

Switch plates are often located near terrace doors. If the drapery treatment planned for terrace doors will require a stackback, it will be preferable to have the entire stackback amount on the wall to allow the drapery to clear the open door completely. For new construction, the light switch can be precisely located beyond the stackback. Unless the distance is specified, the builder is likely to locate the light switch so close to the door opening that the plate will fall behind the drapery. In existing construction, the client may have to decide whether it will be a nuisance to reach behind the drape to operate the switch. Of course, the switch box can always be moved at an additional expense.

Hardware

There are a multitude of choices for drapery hardware. Basically, drapes can traverse on a track rigged with cords to open and close them with a full cord or can hang from a rod and be pulled by hand. Usually a wand is hidden behind the leading edge of a drape so the client doesn't need to tug on the fabric when moving the drapes. Decorative options for hardware with rigging are

limited, and if traversing drapes are desired, you might select one of the hollow-back estate rods or plan to cover the economical white traverse rods with an architectural or soft-goods detail. You might adhere a piece of millwork trim to the face of the traverse rod or cover it with a valance or cornice, for instance. Drapery headers might be pleated, requiring one kind of hanging system, or ripple-fold, requiring ripple-fold hardware. Some treatments are stationary (that is, they do not move). These treatments can be hung on a rod or mounted on a board.

Lining

Linings, when supplied by the workroom, will be a standard lining in white, black, or ivory, a blackout lining, or a thermal lining (Figure 26.4). Interlining (a fabric of a variable weight sandwiched between the face fabric and the lining) can be used to give a treatment more body or better thermal properties if necessary. You can also

FIGURE 26.4 Lining options at Baird's Decorating Services drapery workroom.

supply a special lining or interlining if your treatment calls for it. White or ivory became a standard to accommodate the exterior presentation of the building and because it does not alter the color of the treatment when the light shines through it. If the face fabric has a strong color, it may be apparent from the outside when the drapery is closed at night and lights are turned on inside. If you are supplying your own lining, remember that the seams on the lining should line up with the drapery seams, so ideally you purchase the same width as the face fabric or wider and then pay the labor charges to have the workroom cut it to width.

A matching or special contrasting lining is often specified for a treatment where the lining will show (at the leading edge of a tie-back, for instance) (Figure 26.5). This special lining will usually be sent to the workroom given that it is not a stock lining product. This is a tricky option, and it would be a good idea to purchase a couple of yards of all fabric to be used and hire the workroom to make a large sample to confirm results.

Dress Curtains

Dress curtains are stationary panels that look like functional draperies (Figure 26.6). You might use them if your client would like the softening look of draperies but the window does not require covering or the cost of drapes is too high. You can elect to cover the window with a shade and install stationary panels, which require less fabric, less labor cost, and no rigging, saving labor and fabric requirements. Make sure that the dress curtains have sufficient width to maintain attractive proportions. This can be determined with a scale drawing or even more quickly with a to-scale sketch. Remember that after side hems, a 54-inch-wide panel pleats to less than 20 inches. This looks skimpy on windows wider than 2-½ or 3 feet. Because dress curtains are not meant to draw they are often detailed with a tie-back (Figure 26.7).

Top Treatments

Top treatments may be combined with drapes, curtains, or shades, or they may stand alone.

FIGURE 26.5 This pencil-pleated drapery panel has a decorative lining at the leading edge so that when it is drawn up in the tie-back and the back of the panel is exposed, the lining revealed is also a facing fabric. In this case, it is contrasting but it also could have matched the face.

These treatments may be soft or hard. Soft top treatments include valances and swags (Figure 26.8). The difference between these two soft goods is that swags are understood to mean a top treatment that drops gracefully in the center and is often cut on the bias (Figure 26.9). A valance is a short piece of fabric cut on the grain (Figure 26.10), usually consistent in its height (called the drop), but it may be cut with a shaped bottom edge.

Top treatments also include upholstered cornice boards (Figure 26.11), lambrequins, and cantoneers, which are often constructed of plywood or another engineered substrate and padded and covered with fabric. They usually have a complementary relationship to the architecture as they transition from structure to window treatment,

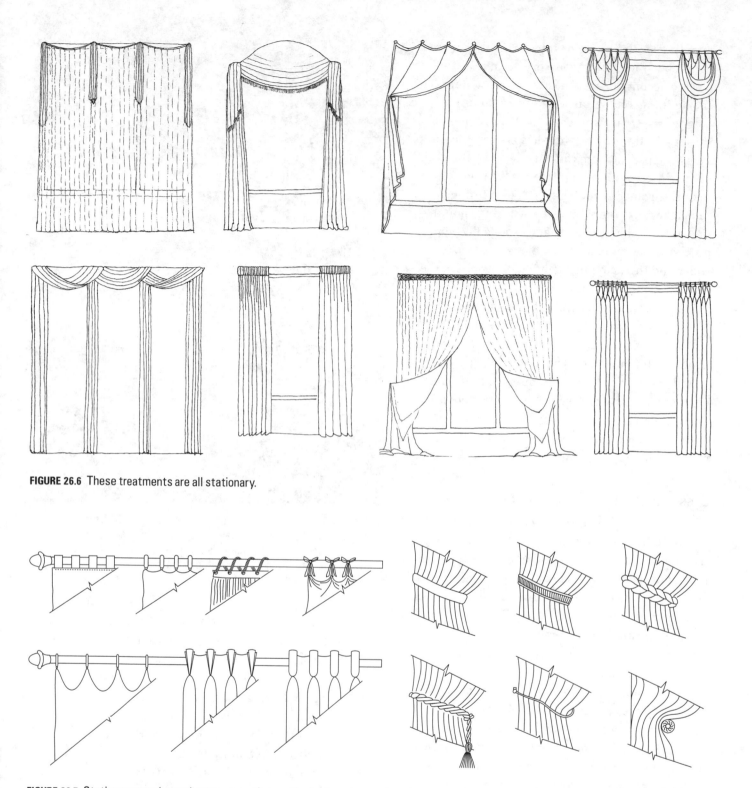

FIGURE 26.6 These treatments are all stationary.

FIGURE 26.7 Stationary panels need not move so they can be fastened to a pole or be supported in others ways that would not allow movable panels to function. This allows for more decorative options. Tie-backs are used with stationary and movable panels and must be unhooked before closing. There is an art to arranging the drape after it is tied back. Some clients are inclined to fuss with the drapery after it's been tied out of the way, so plan for very simple presentation if you expect the client to rearrange the drapery. In addition to fabric tie-backs that the workroom will make, you can specify a metal J-hook or rosette to hold the panel back.

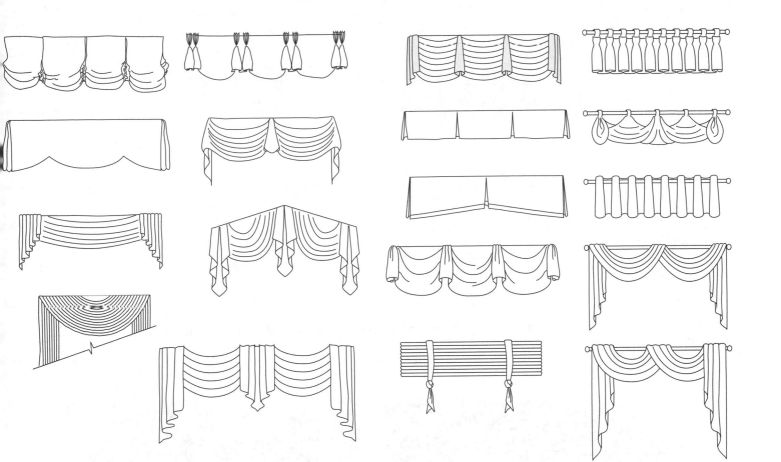

FIGURE 26.8 These soft treatments may hang from a board but are constructed of lined fabric panels.

FIGURE 26.9 (ABOVE) This custom treatment designed by Art and Design in Chicago, Illinois, employs stationary side panels with tie-backs, a swag at the top with a jabot centered on it, and cascades at the sides. The difference between the cascade and the jabot is that the jabot has folds along both sides while the cascade has a folded edge along one side.

FIGURE 26.10 (RIGHT) This custom valance, designed by Tracy Hickman of Chicago, Illinois, features a braid appliqué in the form of a Greek key and finishes a manufactured grass shade product.

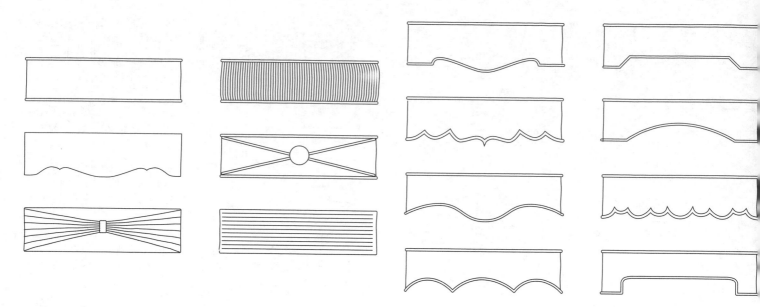

FIGURE 26.11 In contrast to valances and swags, the cornice board is constructed of plywood or another engineered wood product; it is then padded and upholstered in fabric.

FIGURE 26.12 This cornice board, designed by Joan Schlagenhaft of Mequon, Wisconsin, conforms to the structure with a rectilinear outer form, but the softening shape of the lower edge forms a transition from clean line to opulent tradition.

FIGURE 26.13 This lambrequin, designed by Deutsch Parker of Chicago, Illinois, is inside-mounted in a deep window recess. Lambrequins span the transition between architecture and furnishings and provide an opportunity to change architectural perceptions.

but they are sometimes used to lend a little architectural interest to spaces that are lacking in detail; for example, they might be shaped to provide an arch in a space that is too rectilinear. Cornice boards (Figure 26.12) cover the top of the window, lambrequins (Figure 26.13) cover the top and some portion, or all, of the sides, and cantoneers frame the window completely on all four sides.

Door Panels

If drapery treatment is covering a door, it must stack entirely off of the door or be mounted to the door leaf if the door is to remain operable (Figure 26.14). It is not a good idea to rig up a tie-back, J-hook, or other means of causing the panel to clear the door because your client may not use it. Your design has to handle that detail, no matter how committed your client seems to be to maintaining the panels without tears and soiling. Fabric window coverings can be mounted to the door if drapery stackback cannot be accommodated by architecture.

Shades

Custom fabric shades (Figure 26.15) are constructed in a variety of crisp (Figure 26.16) and soft styles (Figure 26.17). They may be lined or unlined.

Bedding and Pillows

Among the many kinds of items that you will have constructed out of fabric or covered in fabric for jobs are headboards (Figure 26.18) and upholstered box springs, pillows, and bedding. It's a good idea to sketch these items to scale, during the planning stage, to confirm proportions and sizes. A sketch with fabric identified for each area clarifies the details for the client and the workroom and locates multiple fabrics, if used for the construction. If a spread has piped seams, a banded edge, and a contrasting backing fabric, it doesn't hurt to confirm everyone's understanding of where those four different fabrics will be positioned in the final construction. The same can be true for pillows. When you

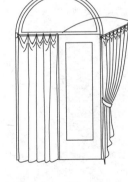
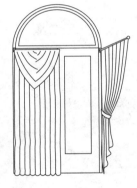
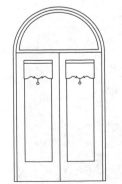
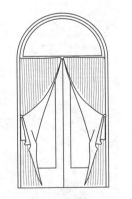
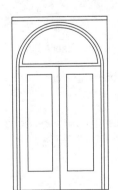

FIGURE 26.14 Doors present a special challenge. The most successful treatments clear the door when open, so the door is operable without damage to the drapery.

FIGURE 26.15 A variety of shade styles are available from tailored to fanciful. Custom shades can be designed to satisfy most design programs.

FIGURE 26.16 (ABOVE) This flat roman shade with a custom valance and appliqué was designed by Susan Ferris of Lake Bluff, Illinois. The tailored nature of this shade will "grow up" with the young boy who occupies this room.

FIGURE 26.17 (RIGHT) In contrast to the tailored shade, this one, designed by Tracy Hickman, demonstrates the softer, more feminine end of the spectrum of custom shade designs.

forward these sketches with your request for a deposit to the client and with your purchase order to the workroom, include swatches keyed to the sketch. It is a good idea to identify on the swatch which side is to be the face (even if it is obvious). It is very labor-intensive (therefore expensive) to pick the seams apart and flip the fabric right side out—if it can even be done.

The drapery workroom is also a resource for upholstered walls (Figure 26.19). If fabric is to be paper backed and glued to the wall, that work will be sent to the paperhanger. If the walls must be padded out and upholstered, a drapery workroom will be hired.

The Process

The design of soft goods requires that you be both a designer and a decorator. The two camps sometimes seem to be so sharply drawn that those who prefer to think of themselves as competent designers are almost embarrassed to admit to their intuitive side, and decorators who are very comfortable in the visceral skill of simply knowing "when it's right" go soft on the mechanics. Drapery is an arena where you need both sides of your brain just to navigate the territory.

Let's just imagine that the design program for the restaurant of our health club project calls for elegant drapery and then trace the development of a drapery treatment from consideration to completion. Let's notice that the restaurant has exterior windows on two sides (Figure 26.20) and is located in a climate with brutal seasonal temperature extremes. We know we can specify insulated, low-E glass for starters, but now we need a versatile treatment that will diffuse the sun, block the sun, and shield the diners from the howling winter extremes on snowbound nights.

You will need to design the treatment to have a diffusing layer (maybe shades, or sheers?) plus your drapery. Whatever you select will have some depth and projection to it. How much will this diffusing layer add to the drapery? It may add 4-6 inches for a roller shade, and for roman grass shades, it could add 8-13 inches, plus the drapes at 4-inch projection. Consider how to handle the treatment in the corner where the two window

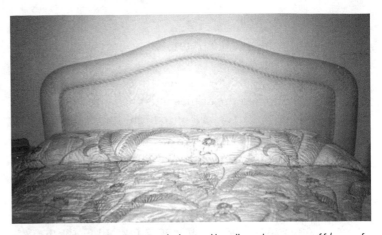

FIGURE 26.18 Because custom-upholstered headboards are one-off (one-of-a-kind) products, unlimited shapes and sizes are possible. A simple construction includes a wooden frame that is padded and upholstered and possibly trimmed, as this one is with a rope cord. *Courtesy of Baird's Decorating Services, Chicago, Illinois.*

FIGURE 26.19 This upholstered room, installed by Baird's Decorating Services of Chicago, Illinois, unifies the room and drapery. After the painter completes the painting of the grilles and access panels (they will be removed and painted off site) to match the fabric color, the backgrounds will be further softened. Notice that the drapery panels are still "tied up" at their bottoms. This installation was just competed and the pleats must be trained for about a week, so the fabric is getting a memory lesson.

walls meet if the treatment projects 14 inches into the space.

How will the drapery affect your lighting plan? When the drapes must be closed against the cold, you will want to highlight them in a way that creates psychological warmth without claustrophobia. How will you accommodate the HVAC? The floor vents shouldn't blow the drapes up on the diners in a billowing nuisance! But if the floor vents are too far from the windows, the windows may frost up and possibly "glue" the drapes to the frost, causing a water stain when the sun comes up. These drapes should be lined and interlined against the cold, so they will be heavy. It would be very convenient to open and close them with the flick of a switch, so you'll need to add information to the electrical plan and locate the place in the wall cavity where you can position the motors to drive each of the three rod lengths. You may require an outlet behind the stackback for each pair of drapes to use a motor.

You will need to look at the plan to follow what's next. Let's take a look at the south wall with the single window unit on it. We see that the architect has given priority to the structure from the *outside,* balancing the wall space next to the column and centering the window there. But what happened inside when the window unit was balanced on the columns on the outside? You ended up with an unbalanced elevation with the door off-set of visual center on the inside because of the elevator location (notice the width of the wall left and right of the windows). Let's trace this common scenario to its conclusion, just to understand some issues that should be confronted.

If you plan for equal stackback on each side of the window, you will have 4 feet of glass exposed on the elevator side when the drapes are open and 5 feet 10 inches of glass exposed on the other side of the door—not ideal. The alternative might be to even up the amount of glass on each side (Figure 26.21), which is not great either because the difference in the width of the drapery panels will be large enough that even nondesigners will notice. Instruct the installer to put the split off-center by a couple of inches, and top-tack the treatment onto the carriers (the small rings that hang from the rigging) so you can omit a little bit of fullness

from the stackback by reducing the number of pleats. We can set the traverse so that it doesn't open as wide on the side opposite the elevator, leaving more equal amounts of glass exposed on each side.

The combination of these three decisions (omit the pleats, off-set the split, and adjust the rigging) will probably give you a more symmetrical presentation. If this were a square corner, you might also arrange the adjacent drapery on the west wall to meet the face of the south drape instead of meeting in the corner, which would further reduce the wider panel width on the corner side.

The drapery can now serve to balance an elevation that was unbalanced at the outset, solving a potential aesthetic problem by adjusting measurements.

Now that the design has been confirmed, you can do a takeoff (estimate yardage required—more about that later) and contact the fabric vendor to reserve yardage and request a cutting for approval. Most fabric houses will hold yardage for a week or two without an order. This will give you time to get a precise quotation from your workroom (which must take its own measurements) with the fabric requirements spelled out and receive the cutting to confirm that fabric on hand does not vary from the original memo sample that you picked up at the showroom. If you will purchase for your client, you will now issue a proposal and a request for deposit. If the finished drapes in the health club restaurant are 10 feet and you use plain fabric without a repeat, this installation would require about 130 yards of fabric, so inquire about a quantity discount (anything over 50 yards is likely to qualify for bolt price versus cut price).

Estimating

Labor estimates are best collected from the workroom, although you may be able to base some rough estimates on previous similar work for purposes of planning only.

Fabric estimates can be roughly figured from yardage charts available from workrooms or by formula from the dimensions of the item to be produced and the dimensions of the goods from which the piece will be produced. A drawing of

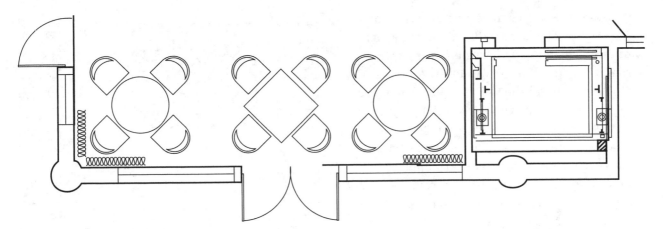

FIGURE 26.20 This is the situation regarding the drapery in the restaurant at the health club before adjustments are made to accommodate the architecture.

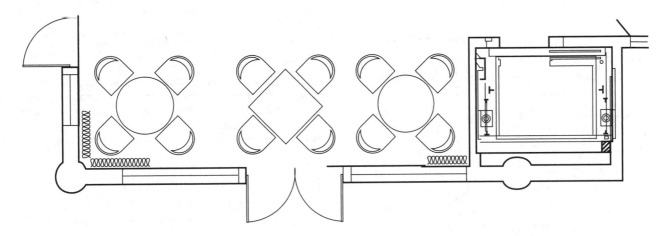

FIGURE 26.21 After some adjustments are made to the installation instructions, the presentation of glass on the left and the right side are more equal.

how the item will be constructed will help you to visualize the material needs.

Charts

Many workrooms estimate off of charts for simple constructions and your workroom will probably share a photocopy of its chart.

Formulas

There are formulas for simple constructions such as drapes and dusters, but the easiest way to estimate is to visualize how the items are constructed.

The Strip Method

The most accurate way to determine the amount of yardage for a price comparison is to calculate

the length and number of panels required to construct the drapes.

Reference a drawing or sketch with the dimensions of the drapery, pinch pleat, ripple fold, box pleat, or other, and account for the following amounts *working in inches.* For purposes of estimating, figure that the drapery will extend minimally 4 inches up from the top of the window opening and 4 inches out from the side of the opening, so include those amounts in your height and width dimensions.

WIDTH The finished width will minimally include the width of the window. If, when the treatment is open, the stackback is to cover part of the window and not be located on the wall space beyond the window, you need add nothing to the finished width of the window dimension for the stackback.

If you want the drapes to be entirely off of the window when open, you will add the stackback width to the window width when estimating yardage. One-third of the window width is usually a good estimate for the total stackback (not each side), so multiply the window width by 1.33 to add the stackback to the finished width.

Add side hems (1-½ inches double hem, so 3 inches each edge), returns, usually applicable (where the drapery bends around from the face of the drape to the wall), and overlap (where the drapes meet and overlap at the center when closed). A standard for returns and overlaps is 3 inches each, which equals 12 inches total. This number will increase if the return must be deeper. Add 4" for overlap.

Multiply this dimension by the fullness (two times for heavy fabric, and three times or more for lightweight fabric; standard weight is 2.75). This is your total width, which you divide by the width of the fabric to get the number of panels required. Round up to the next full number and add an extra panel (for controlling seam locations so they end up inside pleats). If you come up even (no fractions of panels), make sure that all seams can be hidden in the pleats or folds, not on the outside face of a pleat or on the flat between two pleats.

To recap, width of window times 1.33 (stackback) plus 12 inches (double side hems for a pair) plus 12 inches (returns and overlaps) times fullness equals total width. Dividing the width of the fabric into the width of the window treatment and rounding up to the next full fabric width gives the required number of panels.

LENGTH Measure the finished length of the treatment including the distance above and below the glass. Add doubled hems and headers (4-6 inches, depending on the fabric, to equal 8-12 inches total) to get the panel length of plain goods. Divide that length (the cut length) by the vertical repeat. If you get a fraction, round up to the next full repeat. For example, if you divide the length by the vertical repeat and get 7.5 repeats, round up to 8 repeats. Then multiply the vertical repeat by the number of full repeats. This is your new cut length. What you are doing here is allowing for

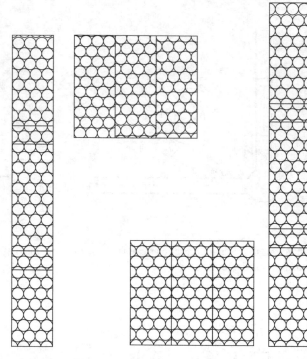

FIGURE 26.22 If you ordered the same yardage of a patterned fabric as for plain goods (left), the pattern would not match, and the drapes would appear as shown in the center top. If you purchased additional yardage and cut the goods as shown on the right, you would be able to achieve a pattern match (center bottom).

full repeats on every panel so you can match the pattern from one panel to the next (Figure 26.22). You may want to add another repeat so you can start the cut where you want (the amount cut from the bolt for the order ahead of yours may have left a partial motif and you might prefer a whole one).

To recap, determine the finished length of the drapery from the mounting hardware to the bottom of the hem. Add 8-12 inches (depending on weight of fabric) to that for double hems and headers. Round up for the repeat by dividing the cut length by the vertical repeat, and round up to full repeats for the new cut length. Add a repeat if you feel it is necessary.

QUANTITY Multiply the number of panels required by the panel length and divide by 36 to convert from inches to yards. Add 6 inches for straightening fabric in case it was not cut straight at the mill.

Estimating a Duster

For estimating a duster on a bed, you will need to know the length and width of the box spring and the drop to the finished floor. The design of the duster will influence the yardage. A full, shirred duster will need more fabric than a tailored duster that has only inverted kick pleats at corners. If you want the finished fabric to be used on the decking (the top of the duster, which is covered by the mattress except for the small amount that shows at the edges), you must add yardage for that. You will want to determine whether you can *railroad* the fabric (run it sideways to avoid seams). If the fabric has a definite up-down direction or if the same fabric is being used on drapes, you cannot railroad. Which sides of the bed will the duster cover? A daybed needs only two short sides and one long side; a bed typically needs two long sides and one short side. If there is a bed frame, the construction details must be known before the duster can be finalized.

Qualifying Installers and Fabricators

Find prequalified installers by word of mouth. Interview fabricators and installers, and review their work and their standard specifications. Ask them how long they have been in business. Review of their standard specifications should include quality construction and attention to detail.

For example, for drapes:

- The workroom is to take all of its own measurements.
- All fabric is to be inspected with bright light shining through it before it is cut, ideally when it is received at the workroom. If the fabricator waits until it is time to cut the fabric before inspecting it, you will have lost valuable time for getting replacement goods in hand if the goods are flawed.
- They always construct double hems and headers 4-6 inches deep.
- They blind-stitch hems.
- 1-½-inch double side hems are standard.
- All seams are serged and overlocked.
- All corners are weighted.
- Lightweight fabrics have beaded weights in the hem for improved draping.
- Pleating of multiple-width fabric should always conceal seams.

- Draperies are to be fan-folded for transport and to be steamed and tied on site.

It is preferable for the supplier to have its own workroom and its own installers, but successful relationships can be maintained as long as the supplier always assumes full responsibility for its subcontractors.

Other Window Treatments

In addition to custom fabric, window treatments and coverings include manufactured shutters, blinds, and shades.

Shutters

Shutters are custom constructions that must be measured after the mounting has been determined. They are bulky treatments unless you can inside-mount them, so plan for them as if they were an architectural component in the room rather than a window treatment, and consider how they can be integrated into the architecture. If the site has complicated architectural construction at the windows, it is a good idea to meet the installer at the site or review the plans if there is no site to visit, work out the mounting details, and write your request for bids after you have the installer's input.

Good shutters are constructed with the same considerations that you would give to cabinet doors. They have the added complication of needing to be light and slender like cabinet doors but having large size like a room door (which we can accept as an even bulkier component than we'd like to see on the windows). As with cabinet doors, the stiles must be a minimum 2 inches wide on their faces and 1-¼-inch thick for stability. The joints are ideally a slotted joint construction (like mortise and tenon). They should be kiln-dried hardwood for a transparent finish but could be an engineered wood product for paint. In high-moisture situations (e.g., pool houses exposed to a lot of weather conditions and not always controlled with the same tenacity as the air inside the main house) you may want to consider vinyl. Vinyl has standard sizes, and you will adjust the opening or framing to accommodate the standards. It is crucial that you purchase shutters from shops that specialize in them. Materials for shutters include the following:

- *Engineered hardwood* This offers a great surface for paint; molded edges are crisp and surface is smooth.
- *Alderwood* This is a good choice for paint and stain applications.
- *Basswood* This is a good choice for stain and acceptable for paint; it does not have a high surface hardness.
- *Poplar* This is a less stable wood than the other choices.
- *Polys, PVCs, cellulars, vinyls, hollow fills, vinyl clad* These choices are suitable for use in high-moisture situations, but they may discolor and sag over time in hot, south-facing windows.

Blinds

Your supplier or installer is likely to represent product from many manufacturers. Because this product is considered to be something of a commodity, the manufacturers rely on proprietary colors and textures as well as quality specifications to differentiate among the many product offerings. Most manufacturers offer a couple of different price points so that blinds that will not be handled by the end user on a consistent basis don't have the same rigorous specs as blinds that they will adjust frequently. These blinds will not cost as much as blinds with superior materials and rigging. There is a quality difference, and you do get what you pay for. I notice that my installers have their favorites and their opinions don't align with any single product, so while you should comply with the installer's recommendations to some extent (they are the ones who have to stand behind the product), there is probably no need to compromise your design program to meet the installer's quality preferences. There is very likely a product that satisfies everyone.

Options that you will encounter among blinds manufacturers' offerings include width of slats; kind of control (cords, continuous pulley, motorized on a battery, or hard-wired); decorative considerations such as color, surface, decorative tapes, special valance profiles to conceal the mechanics at the top of the blinds, the option to locate controls left or right, and vertical (vertical blind) or horizontal vanes, among other choices from specific manufacturers.

Shades

Numerous manufactured textile window coverings can be designed as flat roller shades, pleats and woven and nonwoven honeycomb constructions, which can draw up or down (or both).

Installation of Shutters, Blinds, and Shades

After a review of manufacturers' product specifications, you will select the product and determine the mounting type (inside, outside, on door or window frame). The control type and location and accessories required may limit your selection so the design should be finalized in tandem with product selection.

Meticulous installation and quality of service are the primary factors distinguishing good installers for blinds and shutters. These manufactured products are produced by others, so the evaluation of the quality of the shades, blinds, and shutters is separate from the evaluation of the installer. Installers with experience are better than novices at solving problems presented by the site. It is a good idea to meet your installer when the measure is taken to review site conditions and likely installation configurations for any except the very simplest installation.

CHAPTER 27

ELectricaL Devices

The designer's typical responsibility for electrical devices is usually focused on location and confirmation of its function. It will primarily be planning the location of equipment such as computers, audiovisual equipment, phones, and alarm sensors to meet the unique needs of the project. These needs for equipment will be discovered during the programming phase, and the location of equipment will be determined. The power requirements of the equipment will be discovered by reviewing the cut sheet describing each piece of equipment, enabling you to key the correct receptacle to the plans and schedules. The location will also drive the selection of the device. In wet locations, such as at kitchen sinks and bathroom vanities, a GFI (ground fault interrupt) or GFCI (ground fault circuit interrupt) device is required by code. The electrician will install the various devices indicated on your plans, the simplest of which are electrical outlets. The outlets may be "hot" or switched (connected to a light switch). The outlets may be a combination device such as an outlet–switch combination.

Electrical Receptacles and Devices

Different quality grades of electrical receptacles are available. Standard grade is for household or common receptacles. Specification grade is a quality upgrade from standard. Industrial grade refers to higher-rated receptacles—up to 60 amperes—and may allow for wider blades and alternate blade configuration.

Hospital grade implies all that industrial grade offers plus requires special safety features pertaining to the device itself, as well as grounding, nonflexible raceway, and wire characteristics. In pediatrics wards, tamper-resistant features and covers are also mandated. The receptacle must also indicate required features; for example, tamper-resistant receptacles must display TS and be orange with a triangle on isolated ground (Figure 27.1).

Electrical devices include the two-blade grounding prong that is most common, as well as other configurations serving many different power needs. The idea is to make it impossible to plug a device into an outlet that does not meet its need perfectly. The diagram in Figure 27.2 shows a few of the many straight-blade, nonlocking configurations. Also available are twist and lock connections that prevent removal without a deliberate two-step operation.

Devices refer to both power and data, and since both are frequently required at the same location, they are also paired together. Devices are housed in boxes that may be flush-mounted on walls (that is, recessed into walls), surface-mounted onto floors or walls, or installed through floors, walls, or furniture tops and sides (Figure 27.3).

Electrical Wiring

The types of wire and the way they are configured are indicated on the plan for the electrical system.

FIGURE 27.1 This twist and lock outlet is orange with a green triangle, as required by hospital codes.

Electrical Wiring Configurations

An approach to wiring that is becoming widely preferred for sophisticated electrical schemes is called structured wiring. *Structured wiring* allows multiple locations on the job to access a single device, rather than installing duplicate devices in several locations.

Structured wiring implies a wiring configuration, as well as the kind of wires being run. Previous to the influence of structured wiring, wires would travel from device to device (outlet to outlet, sconce to sconce) in a layout called a daisy chain. Wires would meet each other in junction boxes and the two ends would be capped together, securing the contact that allowed electricity to flow. Structured wiring is also called *home-run* (Figure 27.4) because each location has a unique path back to the panel and is not dependent on a connection made at a previous junction.

In Figure 27.4, notice that the convenience outlets that ring the room, installed in or just above the baseboards, are daisy-chained, and the circuit runs from one to the other. The structured wiring outlets at the computer, phone, TV, and video equipment and the outlets that operate motorized drapes all spring from the central wiring plate. Both methods might be employed in an installation in this way.

	15 Ampere		20 Ampere		30 Ampere		50 Ampere		60 Ampere	
	RECEPTACLE	PLUG	RECEPTACLE	PLUG	RECEPTACLE	PLUG	RECEPTACLE	PLUG	RECEPTACLE	PLUG
125V [1]	1-15R	1-15P								
250V [2]		2-15P	2-20R	2-20P	2-30R	2-30P				
125V [5]	5-15R	5-15P	5-20R	5-20P	5-30R	5-30P	5-50R	5-50P		
250V [6]	6-15R	6-15P	6-20R	6-20P	6-30R	6-30P	6-50R	6-50P		
277V AC [7]	7-15R	7-15P	7-20R	7-20P	7-30R	7-30P	7-50R	7-50P		
347V AC [24]	24-15R	24-15P	24-20R	24-20P	24-30R	24-30P	24-50R	24-50P		
125/250V [10]			10-20R	10-20P	10-30R	10-30P	10-50R	10-50P		
3∅ 250V [11]	11-15R	11-15P	11-20R	11-20P	11-30R	11-30P	11-50R	11-50P		
125/250V [14]	14-15R	14-15P	14-20R	14-20P	14-30R	14-30P	14-50R	14-50P	14-60R	14-60P
3∅ 250V [15]	15-15R	15-15P	15-20R	15-20P	15-30R	15-30P	15-50R	15-50P	15-60R	15-60P
3∅Y 120/208V [18]	18-15R	18-15P	18-20R	18-20P	18-30R	18-30P	18-50R	18-50P	18-60R	18-60P

FIGURE 27.2 A National Electrical Manufacturers Association (NEMA) chart shows the various outlet configurations for ensuring that the correct power supply is paired with the correct device.

FIGURE 27.3 When the presence of the outlet is not constantly required, it can be elegantly concealed from view, as with these products by Doug Mockett.

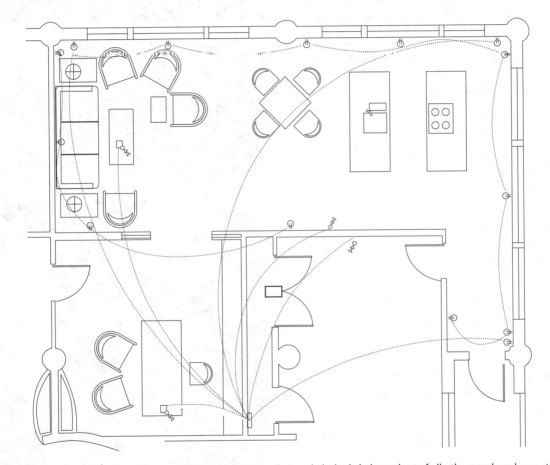

FIGURE 27.4 Structured wiring allows for *granularity*, which means that each device is independent of all others and can be controlled independently.

Electrical Wires

Not only the configuration but the actual wire for phone lines is a little different from electrical wiring. When designing the electrical layout for spaces you are working on, you will encounter the need for category- (CAT) numbered wiring. CAT-numbered wires are twisted pairs that afford better protection against interference for carrying data. The different categories indicate how much information the wiring can handle. For instance, CAT3 (Category 3) wiring is the minimum for phone lines. CAT5 and CAT5e wiring (Figure 27.5) are common for data lines. CAT5e has the same megabytes per second capability as CAT5, but it has some enhanced function built in, making it slightly preferred. CAT6 is the current highest

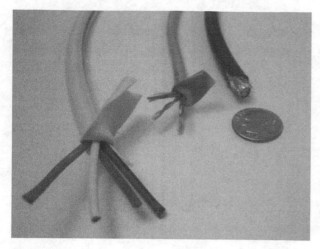

FIGURE 27.5 When observing progress at the job site, look for bundled cable (left) for computer and TV locations. This contains two structured wires and two CAT5 wires. At phone locations you may see CAT5 wiring (center). At TV locations and wherever video is required, look for shielded cable (right); this will have a fine mesh of metal wire inside the outer sheath to protect the video stream from interference.

FIGURE 27.6 Numerous devices have unique connectors. Baumeister must have a wide array of connectors on hand as it configures commercial and smart house installations.

standard to be considered for "normal" functions. Wire and cable are fitted with different connector ends, which allow them to communicate with various devices (Figure 27.6).

Video equipment uses shielded cable (see Figure 27.5), which further minimizes interference. The cabling should be isolated from other wiring (because of interference), 6 inches away from alternating current (electrical wires), 12 inches away from motors and wiring from motors, and 24 inches away from fluorescent lights. Combo cable strands referred to as "bundles" (see Figure 27.5) that combine wires and cables frequently find themselves used as companions for various multimedia applications.

Opinions vary about the sense in using bundled cables. In jurisdictions that require all wire to be protected by conduit, it may be difficult to pull stiff, bundled cable through conduit, and the electrician will install conduit larger than the typical ¾-inch size. Larger diameter conduit may be preferred even if a customized assembly of wires and cables is to be pulled.

Communicating the Plan to the Electrician

You may be responsible for planning all outlet locations or simply the ones required for a known function, leaving the electrician to install any additional convenience outlets that would be

ID	FROM	TERM	TO	TERM	C5	RG6	BNDL	14/2
1a								
1b								
1c								
1d								
2								
3								

FIGURE 27.7 Structured wiring schedule.

required to meet code. You will review the locations at the job site. You will review outlets and devices that are to be positioned inside cabinetry, along with all other outlet locations if you are doing job-site observations. You'll confirm distances and relationships to the furniture plans.

The structured wiring diagram and schedule would be produced by the wiring designer. As the interior designer on the job, you may review the diagrams prior to wiring to confirm that all the equipment locations that you have planned will be wired. Video is RG6; speakers use wire designated by two numbers separated by a slash, such as 14/2, but they are mostly cabling options, and you may want to review the diagrams with the wiring designer to confirm all locations. The diagrams will likely have information in a table format, as shown in Figure 27.7. The columns may be in different order but the information they typically contain is as follows:

- ID: Each cable should have its own identification number. Bundled cables will have several functional cables contained in them, and each cable in the bundle may have its own ID. For example, if cable #1 were a bundled cable, then the structured wiring designer might break it down, possibly as shown in Figure 27.7–with 1a, 1b, and so on. It may also be the case that bundled cable will be identified with a key or note describing the contents of the bundle but be given a single ID designation.
- The FROM column: This is the origin of the cable—the power source end. It may be the infrastructure distribution panel (IDP) or the central wiring plate (CWP) or some other desig-

nation indicating from where the cable will be pulled.

- The TERM column: The TERM column following FROM is the termination at the origin and destination. The bare wires will be fitted with some kind of connector cap that allows them to slot into the panel or become a jack or port on the destination end so that equipment can plug in. The panel and equipment specified will determine the kind of termination to be fastened to each end of the cable.
- TO: TO is the destination of the cable. It may consist of a room abbreviation (CONF or LR) or room number and be accompanied by the outlet or device. The TERM column following TO is the termination at the destination.

There will be several columns listing the kinds of cables used on the job. In the column below the heading is the length of that kind of cable for the location/destination noted by row. These tables are usually in a spreadsheet format so the cable lengths can be added up, indicting the amount of each cable that will be used on the job.

There may be additional columns for initials or check marks as the work progresses. Column headings may be PULL to indicate who pulled the cable through or when. TEST will indicate that the cable was tested, TRIM will say who applied the terminators or when they were added, and TEST following TRIM will indicate that the cable and trim together had been tested.

It is common to control lights, fans, and window coverings with switches, but it is uncommon to control other electrical devices that way. These device controls and light switches will be coordinated as you select the manufacturer and color to be used for switches, outlets, and jacks.

The planning process for electrical equipment and devices typically occurs alongside lighting planning. The plans are sometimes referred to as power/voice/data plans. Planning would ideally be thoroughly complete and all equipment specs known at the rough electrical stage. Even though not all jurisdictions require conduit for sheathed cable and wires, it is difficult to pull the cable through wall cavities after drywall is on. If there are still decisions to be finalized and it is anticipated that additional cable will be required, the structured wiring installer may install *pull cords*. These sturdy cords are pulled through the site as the cables would be and are fastened securely at each end. If equipment is later added to the job, cable is tied and taped to the pull cord, and the pull cord is drawn out the destination end, pulling the new cable through with it. In jurisdictions where it is required that all wire run through conduit, rigid conduit of a generous diameter is installed "empty" in the wall cavity, just to allow for the future installation of as-yet-unknown technology.

It is possible to retrofit existing spaces with these devices to control new equipment purchases, as long as there are not too many tight bends along the route from the home-run panel to the end point. If the retrofit job in an existing space becomes too invasive (Figure 27.8) with too many openings required, a wireless system could be considered. There are radio frequency systems to address many popular technologies.

FIGURE 27.8 Grand Home Automation installs special wire racks to cradle the wires required for the various devices in the installation to communicate with one another.

CHAPTER 28

Lighting

Lighting design is an interior design specialty that requires a high level of technical expertise. An interior designer with a more general practice might want to call upon such a specialist to create the desired aesthetic and functional results in a complex project. However, even generalists need at least a minimal understanding of lighting to integrate the lighting plan—their own or a specialist's—into the design of an interior space.

For the health club project, assume that the lighting plan has been designed. Your job will be to specify the lighting fixtures, which professionals refer to as *luminaires*. They essentially include the lamp, the housing, and the trim; some luminaires require other parts as well.

Lamps

The centerpiece of the luminaire is the lamp; it is responsible for the general characteristics of the light, which may be modified somewhat by the fixture. The *lamp* is the bulb or envelope surrounding a specially formulated gas or vaccume and containing either a filament or electrodes to produce an electric arc, depending on the type of lamp.

The envelope may be clear, inside frosted, or soft white (which is coated to diffuse the brightness of the filament). Some lamps have an integral reflector to control the direction of the light. Color may be added by the use of tinted glass, enamel coating, or fused color filters. There may be special coatings to prevent glass shards from scattering if the lamp is broken.

The base allows the lamp to be connected to the electrical supply (through the fixture). It also holds the filament in position. The power required influences the size of the base. For example, a small candelabra base is used for low-wattage lamps; the medium screw base is used with midrange wattages; and the Mogul base is for 300 watts or more.

Lighting characteristics delivered by lamps are described in the following terms:

- *Foot-candles, lux, or lumens* all refer to the amount of light. The use of foot-candles as a descriptor is being replaced by lux and you will likely encounter both terms. One foot-candle is roughly 10.76 lux; both terms describe the amount of light falling on a surface, indicating the amount of light available for seeing objects. This is differentiated from lumens, which are simply the amount of light available from the lamp, independent of any calculation for distance as is required for foot-candles and lux.
- Color is described in degrees *Kelvin*, which is a metric system that uses the same size degree as Celsius but sets absolute zero as the zero mark, which is equal to -273 degrees on the Celsius scale, and -459 degrees on the Fahrenheit scale. When reviewing the Kelvin rating of various light sources, you will notice that the lower numbers look warmer.
- *Color Rendering Index (CRI)* measures the ability of the lamp to render color accurately. The CRI uses incandescent lighting as the standard,

which is set at 100; any number above 83 is considered acceptable for habitable spaces (excluding spaces such as warehouse and storage rooms, which can acceptably drop below that number). The light color of many lamps becomes more pronounced at lower light levels. Visit a lighting store to see the relative quality and brightness of various lamps before finalizing your specification if you are not familiar with the differences.

- *Beam spread* describes how widely the lamp disperses the light, and it varies from a wide flood (WFL) with a wide beam spread to the VNSP designation for very narrow spot. To realize the importance of beam spread on performance, consider that the available photons are like a pat of butter; the wider you spread them out, the thinner they are applied. The 50-watt WFL will not be as bright upon landing as the 50-watt VNSP.

- *Quality* of light or characteristics of the light emitted can be described as sparkly, diffuse, crisp, pointed, or rich (enhancing depth). Other considerations can also be used to describe light's characteristics, such as *drop-off* (the light may fade out from the edges of the beam or produce a sharp edge).

Lamp function distinguishes one lamp from another, including the way the lamps light up, how much power they need, and their shapes, which influence light distribution.

How Lamps Light Up

There are two common ways of making a lamp light up. One is to burn a filament, as in an incandescent lamp (such as the common pear-shaped lightbulb or MR16). The other is to "excite" gases with an electric arc, as with a fluorescent lamp or a lamp with "vapor" in its name. Lamps that burn thanks to excited gases need a ballast (discussed later in this chapter); make sure when ordering that you are getting this necessary part. You should also ask how noisy it will be because some of them hum.

Families of Lamps

Incandescents (Figure 28.1) include par, R, halogen, and general-purpose lamps. Fluorescents include compact fluorescents, as well as fluorescent tubes.

HID includes metal halide, sodium vapor (yellow/orange—not for spaces where color counts), and mercury vapor (green/blue SAA) lamps. Newer technologies include LED and fiber optics.

INCANDESCENT The incandescent category includes regular incandescents in various shapes (A-lamp, flame shape, round tube Lumiline, etc.), R-lamps, par lamps, and halogens. Fixtures typically take one or two kinds of lamps; they are not universal in their acceptance of lamps. There are various bases on lamps, including screws, pins, posts, and prongs. All incandescents "burn" a filament.

Contrary to popular belief, there is seldom an actual vacuum in these lamps, although oxygen is absent. "Regular" incandescent lamps will probably have nitrogen or argon, both of which create a good environment that allows the tungsten filament to glow without flaming to destruction. Some soot still burns away and is deposited on the inside of the envelope.

Halogen gas burns hotter and allows for molecular transportation of tungsten molecules, which have become soot on the envelope, back to the filament. This process extends the life of the lamp, but the lamp must occasionally be burned at full intensity (rather than just dimmed) in order for this to occur.

Krypton is a large molecule that is inefficient at transmitting heat, so it converts more of the available energy into light than into heat. A combination halogen and krypton gas is common. Xenon is actually a halogen-xenon combination. Because xenon is more expensive than halogen, lamps that contain xenon in addition to halogen are called xenon (to clarify the price point). Xenon does not require the bulb to burn as hot.

Higher-wattage lamps are more efficient than lower wattage lamps. For example, one 100 A 19-watt lamp produces more light (1710 lumens) than four 25-watt lamps (840 lumens); one 150 A 21-watt lamp gives more light (2780 lumens) than two 75-watt lamps (2360 lumens).

Generally speaking, incandescent lamps:

- Do not require a ballast
- Have a warm color appearance with a low Kelvin number and excellent color rendering (CRI 100)

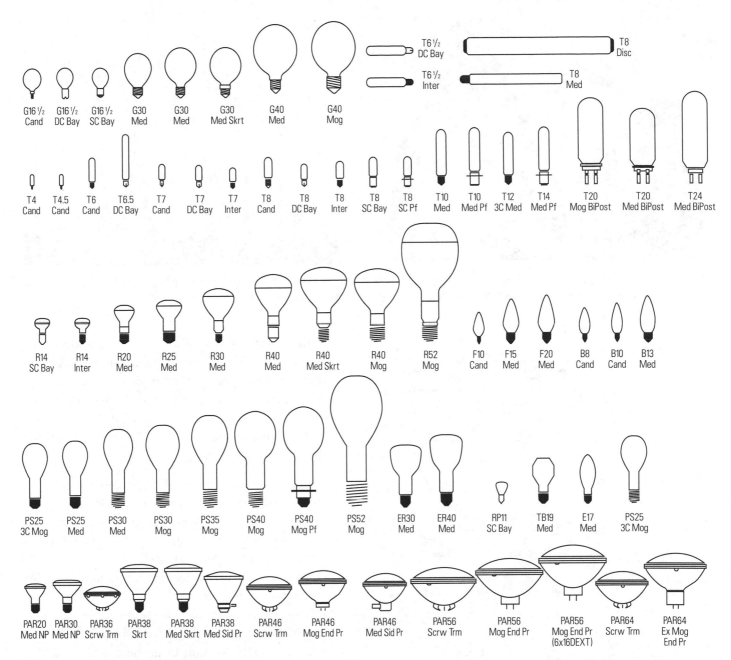

FIGURE 28.1 Incandescent lamps may enclose a vacuum; other kinds of lamps contain gases such as halogen and xenon. Their names are derived from their shape. They may be low voltage or line voltage.

- Are a compact light source
- Require only simple maintenance because of a screw-in Edison base
- Are a less efficacious light source than fluorescents
- Have a shorter service life than other light sources in most situations
- Have a filament that is sensitive to vibrations and jarring
- Can get very hot during operation
- Have a continuous spectral distribution

Incandescents must be properly shielded because incandescent lamps can produce direct glare as a point source. They require proper line voltage because line voltage variations can severely affect light output and service life.

FLUORESCENT Fluorescent light sources have a discontinuous spectral distribution. Discontinuous spectral distribution, as diagrammed in Figure 28.2, renders the degrees Kelvin as an *average* of wavelengths in a discontinuous spectrum. This means that two lamps

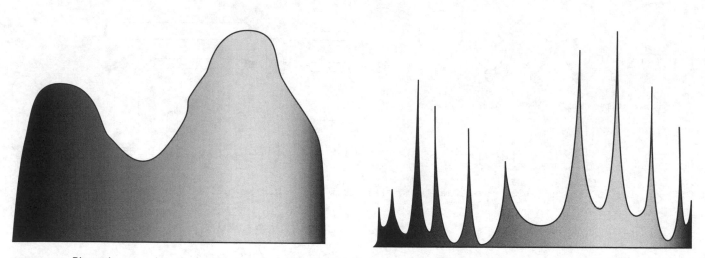

FIGURE 28.2 Discontinuous and continuous spectrum have the same Kelvin temperature, but the quality of the light will not be the same because the Kelvin rating of the discontinuous fluorescent source is an average of all the peaks in the illustration.

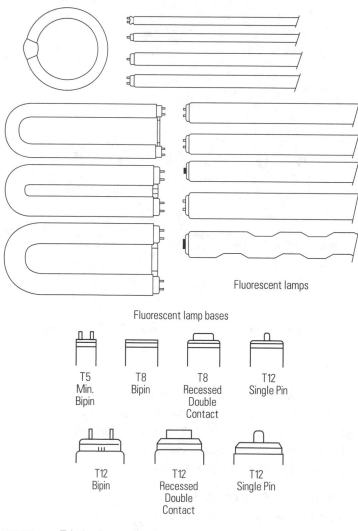

Fluorescent lamps

Fluorescent lamp bases

T5
Min.
Bipin

T8
Bipin

T8
Recessed
Double
Contact

T12
Single Pin

T12
Bipin

T12
Recessed
Double
Contact

T12
Single Pin

FIGURE 28.3 Tubular fluorescent lamps require specific fixtures to meet size and pin configuration requirements. The correct lamp should be available in a variety of Kelvin ratings with a range of quality in color rendering ability (CRI).

with the same Kelvin temperature, say 2800 K, may be visually different, with one looking yellow and one appearing somewhat pink. The differences between one manufacturer's phosphor cocktail and another's accounts for the difference.

Fluorescent lamps (Figure 28.3) have the following characteristics:

- They need a compatible ballast. All fixtures installed indoors must use a Class P ballast that disconnects the ballast in the event it begins to overheat; high ballast operating temperatures can shorten ballast life.
- Low temperatures affect starting unless a "cold weather" ballast is specified.
- They are available in a range of color temperatures and color rendering capabilities.
- They have low surface brightness compared to point sources like incandescents.
- They operate cooler than incandescent lamps.
- They operate more efficiently than incandescent lamps.
- Ambient temperatures and convection currents have an effect on light output and life.

A variety of "color" or relative "warmth" options are available, and it is important to see the lamp under consideration if you are not familiar with the output. You could describe the general color families as "blue," "white," "yellow," and "pink," noticing that warmer Kelvin ratings are yellow and pink when the light strikes a white surface. Warmer colors tend to feel "more natural" to end users, but there is a perception that a higher Kelvin rating (whiter light) improves depth perception. This is a consideration with fluorescents because they are a diffuse, shadowless light source, and acuity at edges and on textures may be compromised as we lose the crispness that sharper shadows can deliver. You could consider that you end up with "warm fuzzies" (an exaggeration for purposes of illustration) versus richer depth. Your design program will indicate what Kelvin rating is most congruent with your overall design scheme.

The CRI of fluorescent lamps is a tricky judgment because of the discontinuous spectrum. If a light source is weak in a particular wavelength, the color that would be shown by that specific wavelength will be muted or absent. Overall CRI may be good, but one fabric in your scheme may still go flat. It is a good idea to confirm all color selections, viewing them under the lamp that you intend to use.

The lamp identification is a combination of letters and numbers. For one common system, the identification begins with the letter F for fluorescent, followed by the number of watts, then lamp shape and size. For example, F32T8 can be translated as F = Fluorescent, 32 = Watts, T = Tubular in Shape, 8 = Diameter in eighths of an inch, so in this case the lamp has a diameter of 1 inch.

Compact fluorescents (Figure 28.4) are miniaturized fluorescents, often with an integral ballast (magnetic or electronic) and a screw-type base. Some are modular, so base and lamp can be separated. If a fluorescent lamp is not modular, the ballast is thrown away with the lamp when it burns out.

When planning to use a compact fluorescent in place of an incandescent (they are designed for this purpose), remember that the fluorescent version is usually slightly bigger than the incandescent, so confirm that the fixture will conceal the lamp as expected for viewing and cut-off angle (the ability of the fixture's design to hide the lamp from most viewing angles). The relationship to cones and baffles, which direct the light and screen the interior of the housing from view, may be different from that for incandescent lamps, so light control may not be as anticipated. Color temperature

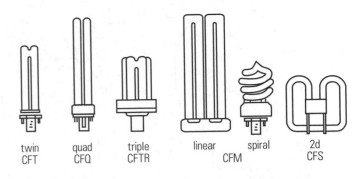

twin CFT   quad CFQ   triple CFTR   linear CFM   spiral   2d CFS

FIGURE 28.4 Compact fluorescent lamps are energy-saving alternatives to incandescent sources. The light quality will not be the same when switching from incandescent to fluorescent. Fluorescent lamps can be used in socket fixtures designed initially for incandescent lamps, but they may not perform the same as in fixtures designed for fluorescents.

noted may rely more on "pink" than on "yellow" light quality, so color rendering will not be identical from one to the other. If fluorescent lights are frequently turned on and off, they wear out faster than they would otherwise. Use fluorescents only where they will be left on for at least half an hour.

The lamp identification for compact fluorescents is similar to that for other fluorescents in that it is a combination of letters and numbers. The identification begins with the letter CF for compact fluorescent, followed by the shape of the lamp. The various shapes are twin parallel tubes (T), four tubes in a quad configuration (Q), three tubes (TR), square-shaped (S), and multiple or miscellaneous (M). The shape will be followed by the number of watts, then the base configuration. Information about the color rendering and Kelvin temperature may also be included. For example, a lamp designated CFT9/G24D-2/827 is a compact fluorescent with twin parallel tubes of 9 watts; it has a two-pronged base, a CRI of 80 and burns at 2700 degrees Kelvin.

GAS-DISCHARGE LAMPS Gas-discharge lamps include sodium and mercury lamps, metal halide lamps (Figure 28.5), and self-ballasted lamps that can be screwed directly into incandescent fixtures. They:

- Require a ballast
- Have light output that's not affected by ambient temperature, although low ambient temperatures can affect starting, requiring a special ballast
- Are a compact light source

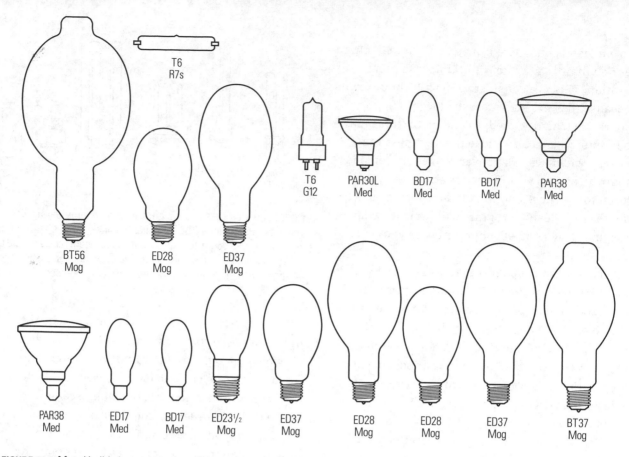

FIGURE 28.5 Metal halide lamps are powerful and energy-efficient while delivering acceptable color rendering for commercial environments.

- Have high lumen output
- Are a point light source
- Portray a range of color temperatures and color rendering abilities, depending on the lamp type
- Provide long service life
- Are highly efficacious in many cases

Because they sometimes require some "warm-up time" when power is interrupted, gas-discharge lamps cannot be immediately relit. To overcome the inconvenience caused by this wait time, some luminaires contain a halogen backup that remains illuminated until the HID lamp restarts. Color can vary when the HID lamps are dimmed.

The best color rendition in this group comes from metal halide. Kelvin temperature ranges can be generally 4200 to 3200 for some mixed-vapor metal halide options, which is a visually pleasant range. Designation of the lamp is slightly different than for other lamp types—the M for metal halide precedes the wattage. An MV designation indicates multivapor (GE and Phillips). Sylvania uses an "M" designation. Envelopes can be clear or coated.

Metal halide lamps have a variety of strengths, including the following:

- Designed for general lighting applications
- Relatively long lamp life
- Interchangeable with mercury lamps in many applications
- Concentrated source easily controlled by special fixture characteristics
- A bright crisp white light
- Twice as efficient as mercury lamps and six times as efficient as incandescents with 65–115 lumens per watt
- Fairly good color rendition (70 CRI) for use on sales floors, where lots of light is required and good color rendition is desirable

Metal halide lamps also have some weaknesses:

- Short life compared to other HID lamps (6,000 to 20,000 hours, depending on size and manufacturer)
- Different lamps must be used for base-up

versus base-down burning configurations (they can point only one way).

- Horizontal operation may severely reduce lamp life.
- Require a ballast
- Some lamp types require two to five minutes to warm up before giving full light output and 10 minutes to cool down. Others have instant restart capability.
- Color may vary from lamp to lamp (color shift).
- Many wattages require operation in enclosed fixtures because of the risk of lamp breakage upon failure.

LIGHT-EMITTING DIODES An emerging technology that holds a lot of promise is that of *LED, light-emitting diode lighting*. It offers the following advantages:

- Low heat
- Long life—50,000 (white) to 100,000 (colors) hours compared to 1,000 hours for a standard lightbulb
- Efficiency
- Easy control for changing display
- Variety of color effects
- Small size for tight applications
- Safety—very low UV and infrared (IR) radiation
- Durability—no filament to break or burn out
- Extreme durability due to protection afforded by being built inside solid cases, unlike incandescent and discharge sources
- Ability to be designed to focus its light because of its solid package
- Emission of light of an intended color without the use of color filters that traditional lighting methods require. This is more efficient and can lower initial costs.

Incandescent and fluorescent sources often require an external reflector to collect light and direct it in a usable manner.

However, LEDs also have some disadvantages. Manufacturers are still working to improve the quality of white light, even though great gains have already been taken to solve this earlier problem. Color rendition is rapidly improving, and precise control is possible and depends on the phosphor "cocktail" the manufacturer uses.

LEDs fail by dimming over time, rather than burning out abruptly as incandescent bulbs do. LED performance largely depends on the ambient temperature of the operating environment. Operating LEDs in high ambient temperatures may result in overheating of the LED package, eventually leading to device failure. Adequate heat sinking is required to maintain long life.

Currently, they are more expensive in terms of lumens per dollar than more conventional lighting technologies. The additional expense partially stems from the relatively low lumen output and the drive circuitry and power supplies needed.

FIBER OPTICS Fiber-optic lighting can fall into either category—filament burning or excitation of phosphors—or neither, depending on how you look at it because the illuminator (the light source) can be any light source. The light emitted via fiber optics is "clean," that is, it does not have the heat of an incandescent source nor the UV rays of a fluorescent source.

The benefit offered by fiber-optic systems is that the illuminator is remote from the fixture. This has advantages for environments where protecting the fixture is important (such as underwater) and where heat gain from a luminaire is undesirable (such as environments that are not easily vented). Fiber optics are also preferred for highlighting items (in museums, for instance) that may be damaged by the ultraviolet rays generated by some lighting systems because fiber-optic systems can be designed to deliver no UV rays. The fiber-optic system is comprised of three essential parts: the illuminator, the cable, and the fixture or port. Accessory items can be added for special control or effect.

Other Parts of the Luminaire

Although the lamp is the essential defining part of a luminaire, it cannot function without some sort of housing, and some lamps require or benefit from a ballast, a transformer, or other accessories.

Housings and Trims

The housing and trim compose the part of the luminaire that many people refer to as the fixture

(Figure 28.6). It may be recessed, surface-mounted, pendant, or portable. After selecting the lamp that will best serve your installation, there will be *hundreds* of holder options. These are sometimes further divided into housings and trims to allow for very precise control over lighting quantity and effect. The hierarchy in your selection process is to first select the lamp, then the trim, then the housing. The lamp provides the general light quality, which is slightly modified by the trim. The trim (Figure 28.7a-h) may also serve to conceal or display the lamp. The housing may accommodate accessories such as lenses and filters. The housing is most essentially the container into which the trim and lamp are installed. By the time you have selected the lamp and trim, the housing is often a given.

Ballasts

Ballasts are required for fixtures that produce light by exciting gasses, such as fluorescent and HID fixtures. Ballasts may be electronic or magnetic. Electronic ballasts are more sophisticated and are more successfully paired with dimming controls. Fluorescent ballasts include rapid start and instant start.

FIGURE 28.6 The housing of a recessed light is completely concealed when installed. New construction housing will be braced against joists while remodeling housings are smaller and supported by the ceiling surfacing material. One housing model may hold a variety of trims.

RAPID START (RS) An RS ballast heats electrodes while initiating a starting voltage across the lamp. This process reduces the voltage needed to start the lamp, but the electrode heating continues after starting and consumes additional power. For this reason, rapid start systems consume more energy than instant start systems. Rapid start ballasts contribute to longer lamp life.

INSTANT START (IS) An IS ballast supplies a higher starting voltage without heating the electrodes. This shortens lamp life somewhat but also reduces energy consumption, which offsets the slightly shorter lamp life.

Transformers

Low-voltage lighting, such as some halogen sources and LEDs, requires a transformer to "step down" the voltage from line voltage, which is 120 volts, to low voltage, which generally is 12 volts. Transformers might be integrated right into the fixture or purchased separately. Occasionally, you will be able to locate a remote transformer in a nearby, concealed area (in a closet, for instance) and have no visible transformers within the lighting assembly. Electronic transformers must be well ventilated and are limited to 300 watts. Magnetic transformers are very reliable and may be fitted with debuzzing coils to reduce noise that they may otherwise generate. You must select the proper dimming equipment to use with either electronic or magnetic transformers.

Accessories

Accessories are used to further control light quality (Figure 28.8). They are specified to direct the light beam, control the spread, filter unwanted characteristics (such as UV light and glare), screen the lamp from view, and alter the color of the light presented, among other benefits.

Often, the fixture itself must have finish or accessory parts specified or ordered separately. Sometimes, the height or drop of a pendant fixture must be specified. Some fixtures can be either wall- or ceiling-mounted or mounted horizontally or vertically. You must specify in your instructions to the electrician how it will be

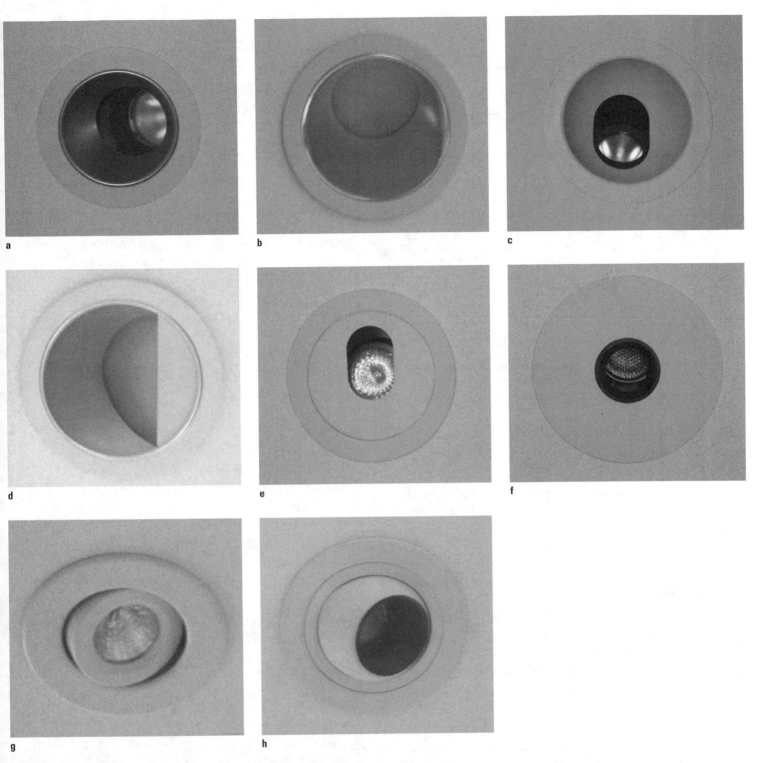

a

b

c

d

e

f

g

h

FIGURE 28.7 The trim is the portion of the recessed ceiling luminaire that we see; it conceals the housing and modifies the quality of the light beam. A fairly deep housing (a) limits direct glare (a term used when the light source if visible) but will also restrict beam spread. A matte or haze cone (b) minimizes the visual impact of the fixture in either a light-on or light-off situation. A fully recessed adjustable fixture (c) will allow for a smaller angle of adjustment but will be visually most similar to direct downlights used in the same area. A wall washer (d) is fitted with a spread lens to throw the light farther. When the ribs on the lens go side to side they spread the light up and down. When the ribs on the lens are vertical, they spread the light in a horizontal direction. A recessed fixture (e) has a slot aperture trim that directs and controls the light while minimizing the size of the opening. It would be selected to direct the light toward an object to accent it. A small aperture trim (f) also controls the beam while minimizing the visual impact of the lighting equipment. The lamp-holder portion of a fixture is adjustable on a gimble ring (g). Because the light source is below the ceiling plane, it will be more effective at throwing light to the sides. Careful positioning will be required to avoid direct glare because the light source is visible. The eyeball fixture (h) was the original adjustable light and even though designers prefer to minimize the visual impact of the lighting equipment, the ability of this fixture to throw light sideways while concealing the light source is still unmatched by more recent developments in lighting design.

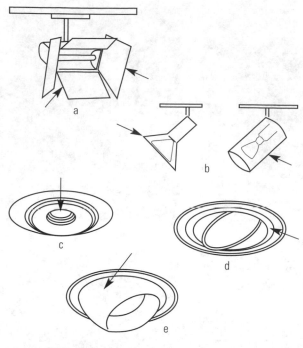

FIGURE 28.8 Examples of accessories for luminaries: (a) barn door shutters, (b) extension hoods (right) and cowls (left), (c) pinhole rim, (d) gimbal ring, and (e) eyeball.

hung. Sometimes, a fixture that is intended for a ceiling application can be wall-mounted and a fixture that is intended for a wall-mount can be ceiling-mounted. Check with the manufacturer to make sure that the fixture is rated for that kind of installation so you do not void the warranties if you deviate from standard.

Decorative Fixtures

Fixtures that are recessed behind surfaces (walls, ceilings, and floors) do not allow for the same wide beam spread as do fixtures that are actually within the space. Surface-mounted, projected, and suspended fixtures deliver a wider "throw" for the light. The needs of the job functionally and aesthetically will influence your selection. Fixtures are designed to be mounted and to deliver light in a number of ways.

Fixture types include the following:

- *Surface-mounted* (Figure 28.9) on walls or ceilings may direct light up, down, and/or out through perforations or diffusers.
- *Suspended* downlights (Figure 28.10)—fixture is hung below ceiling plane and directs light down; drop is quite variable, from a few inches to several feet

- *Suspended, indirect*—fixture is hung below ceiling plane and directs light upward; the drop is quite variable here as well.
- *Track lighting* (Figure 28.11a and b) is considered to be architectural lighting, although it makes a strong style contribution to the space. The description as relating to the installation includes voltage, number of circuits, mounting, size, and finishes.

Retrofitted and *custom* fixtures will always require even more intense scrutiny than manufactured fixtures. For custom fixtures, determine what kind of light and control you need; consider the dissipation of heat and the blocking of glare as well as the appropriateness of materials under consideration.

For a retrofitted fixture, you will have to assess how to get electricity to the location of the lamps. If the armature is solid instead of hollow, the wiring will have to be run along the outside of the fixture, then be drilled up through the bobesche (the shallow, bowled cup that prevented wax from dripping down from antique chandeliers that burned wax candles, and is now used decoratively on electric chandeliers). Figure out how to make the wiring unobtrusive.

Consider whether lamps should be shielded and how should this be accomplished. Evaluate

FIGURE 28.9 Surface-mounted fixtures include any fixture that is not recessed into the ceiling (it will be mounted to a recessed junction box) and does not hang from a stem, wire, or chain. Even a short stem would qualify as a pendant.

FIGURE 28.10 A suspended downlight will have a stem, wire, or chain from the lamp holder to the canopy, which conceals the junction box in the ceiling. Whether the length of the suspension is a few inches or several feet, the fixture will still be categorized as a suspended fixture.

the finish to determine whether plating or replating is called for.

If the fixture is to be assembled from various parts, can they be successfully adhered to one another by welding (the behavior of old metal is not always predictable) or will they have to be screwed (sometimes the unknown metal composition is brittle)? Technology in materials was not always consistent, and sometimes old metals cannot be safely welded or drilled, so the base metal must be clearly identified to ensure it will allow for successful plating or welding, These are all considerations that will have to be addressed at some point, and you will probably have to consult with a workshop to answer some of them.

It is widely expected that lighting fixtures will be UL listed (tested and confirmed safe by Underwriters Laboratories). This is not always possible. In the case of a custom fixture or retrofitted luminaire, the next best thing to a UL listed fixture is a fixture made out of UL-listed parts. If

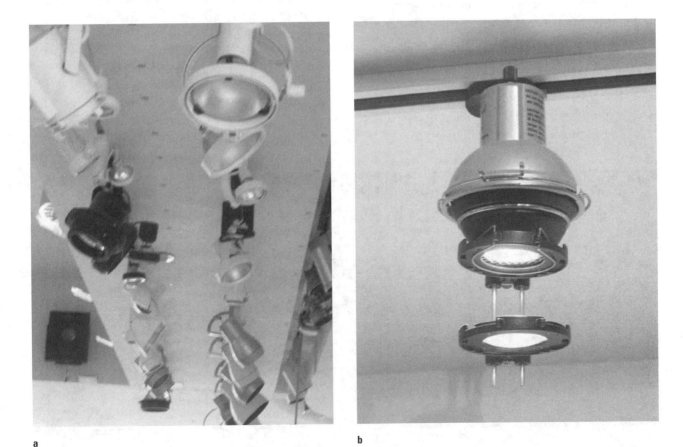

a   b

FIGURE 28.11 Suspended uplights provide indirect lighting that emits a pleasant ambient light. Some suspended fixtures provide uplight and downlight (a). This fixture has two layers of lenses modifying this light quality (b).

a fixture must be certified, it must be submitted to Underwriters Laboratories for inspection. This takes time and money, so use this option judiciously when designing custom fixtures. The prototype will be destroyed during testing. It is often a condition in insurance policies that fixtures be certified as safe, so work with experienced workrooms to bring an antique back into service or build a custom fixture.

Switches

In addition to wall switches and dimmers, a fixture might have a switch on it. A door may have a switch button in the frame to turn the lights on when the door is open. Jamb switches are popular for closet lights. There are motion detectors that turn the lights on when someone enters the room and daylight sensors that automatically adjust the amount of light relative to the amount of natural light present. Photo and motion sensors turn the lights on when it is dark and someone is moving in the space. There are time clock switches, and emergency response switches that will automatically turn all lights on at full wattage in response to fire-safety systems. There are dimmers that look like a toggle switch, touch dimmers that respond to contact with your finger (you just hold your finger on them until the light level you want is reached), in addition to the

rotary and toggle and slide dimmers (Figure 28.13a-c) with which you are likely familiar.

Lights can be switched and dimmed from two or more locations. Switches, along with other electrical devices such as outlets and jacks, are available in a limited number of colors. White and ivory are common and some companies offer brown and black. At least one company offers a small range of other colors. The plate or cover can often be painted—just purchase a metal cover intended for paint. You may want to coordinate fan controls with the switch so all switches look the same.

Computerized controls make managing multiple "scenes" easier; master control panels can operate any light on the system and allow lighting systems to interface with security systems. Radio signal systems are available for retrofit situations; hard-wired systems are convenient for new construction. Both allow for one important advantage related to lamp life. When a lamp is operated at 90 percent of its possible output, the life of the lamp is doubled. The maximum brightness can be set to 90 percent on the system to extend the life of all lamps.

Responsibility for Planning

Trained interior designers produce lighting and electrical plans and documents for purchase of lighting equipment. Because lighting is a very

a   b   c

FIGURE 28.13 Dimmer switches may have an on/off rocker switch and a slide dimmer (a and b) or a slide that controls both the on/off and dimming functions (c).

complex specialty, many interior designers prefer to collaborate with a lighting professional on large, complex jobs that have the budget for such an expert. On smaller and less complicated jobs or jobs with small budgets, you may find yourself with responsibility for the lighting design and specification.

Managing the Lighting Plan and Specification

If you are not working with a lighting professional on a project and have full responsibility for the lighting design, you will also be responsible for managing the lighting selection and specification. This text is not to be understood as a replacement for in-depth lighting training, but rather to present the most elemental considerations for selection and specification of the lighting or lighting system. As with all areas of design, the solution flows from the design program.

IDENTIFY THE GOALS You will first identify the goals of the lighting design throughout the entire space. Start with a survey of the following:

- Desired light levels based on the tasks performed in the space
- Room size and dimensions
- Structural obstructions such as beams, ducts, and pipes, etc.
- Layout of furniture and obstructions (such as partitions or tall panels in a commercial space)
- Room and object surface colors and reflectances
- Special concerns such as safety and security
- Hours of operation
- Assessment of normal operating conditions
- Possibility or known existence of abnormal operating conditions
- Cleanliness of the area during operation
- Maintenance schedule
- Availability of daylight and daylight management
- Lighting budget

SELECT FIXTURES Generally, the best way to select a fixture is to start with the kind of light you want. Then discover the light source that delivers the light with the characteristics your project requires. Finally, select from the luminaires that use that lamp.

You will briefly assess the needs of the design relative to the characteristics of the lamp. Evaluate the efficiency of the source in terms of cost of the entire assembly (meaning the lamp and all fixture parts). Consider operation cost and energy relative to heat buildup, as well as flexibility in case of future changes. Sometimes, a general ambient light scheme is more efficient than one that locates fixtures with a strict relationship to furnishings that may be moved in the future. Evaluate the energy load, produce plans, prepare schedules and specifications for purchase. Interact with suppliers and tradespeople to implement the design.

As you finalize your selection, you will assess these characteristics of the fixture:

- Quality of the construction
- Applicable code restrictions
- Style (including functional as well as visual characteristics)
- Cost

MANAGING THE BUDGET Define the budget and quality level of lighting equipment that the project can afford. If the budget allows for builder's grade, there is little likelihood that a professional lighting designer will be engaged. If you must use modest-quality equipment to meet budget needs, you don't have the funds for special services and you won't get the best work from the lighting designer anyway as control options will be limited.

Commercial grade is the next quality level up, and specification grade is the highest quality. There are tangible differences from one grade to the next, so don't imagine that you are saving money without any compromise when you elect to use lower-grade equipment. The differences between commercial grade and specification grade are more clearly realized over time, and you may want to mix grades selectively. For example, if your client has a budget indicating commercial grade but is likely to have a changing art program that will require periodically re-aiming the lights in the corridors, you may specify commercial grade throughout but specification grade for the artwork lighting. With commercial grade, the fixtures that will be handled frequently will be of a quality to withstand re-aiming. Another aspect of the improved grade is that the optics will likely be a bit better, so the artwork will be enhanced. It is possible to see the difference in the showroom if two similar fixtures of different grades are displayed within the same area. Sometimes the difference is obvious (more glare delivered by the commercial grade, for instance) and sometimes it requires a closer look (perhaps you will notice the even quality of the light at the edges of the beam versus ragged edges where the beam of light falls on a surface).

WORKING WITH ELECTRICIANS AND VENDORS As you progress through the process toward installation, you must follow a process. It will begin with programming, plans, and selections; proceed to bids, contracts, and installation; and end with inspection.

Communicating Your Design Drawings with standard lighting symbols, keys, and terminologies are most easily understood by all parties involved in the project. Refer to and use established symbols whenever possible, and always provide a "key" legend to avoid miscommunication.

Any fixture that gets attached to the architecture requires that information be given to the electrician. Provide all information that you have about the fixture, including mounting instructions. Describe the location—vertical as well as horizontal dimension—as they apply. Relay all relative alignments and clearances, and key the switching or show the circuitry. Call particular attention to any special instructions, such as a special J-box (Junction Box) size or shape. If extra bracing is required, detail that for the carpenter and electrician.

Include a furniture plan in the instructions to the electrician. The exact location of some of the fixtures will have to be shifted because of joist locations or location of services (plumbing pipes, ductwork, speakers, and so forth). The electricians will have a better idea of your intentions if you provide them with a furniture plan, as well as a lighting plan. The housings are usually put into place but not piped (conduit can be run later) before the HVAC tradespeople come in. If the lighting housings will not be installed before the HVAC tradespeople move through, critical light locations may be made unavailable by duct routes. You might ask the electrical contractor to fasten aluminum pie plates to the lighting locations so there can be no dispute about where ductwork can go because the lighting locations can be known even without the housings in place.

Special Conditions Plenum ceilings are suspended ceilings in which the air space between the suspended ceiling surfaces and the ceiling deck actually functions as part of the air-handling system. There are special plenum-rated fixtures that satisfy fire-rating issues. There are also air-handling light fixtures that can eliminate the need for having a lot of air-handling vents on the ceiling surface. Whenever you encounter a commercial space that has a suspended ceiling, you need to find out (1) whether it is a plenum ceiling, and (2) what the structure of the ceiling system is. Light fixtures that are to be integrated into the ceiling system have to be compatible with the type of support structure.

Codes affect all structures to some degree. Your electrician is responsible for installing equipment that meets code restrictions, but you should have enough general knowledge to develop code-compliant configurations and specifications. There are several building classifications, each subject to different requirements; for multipurpose buildings, you may have to get in touch with the building inspection department of your jurisdiction to ascertain correctly which codes apply to your project.

A general understanding of the kind of electrical service available (the primary and secondary service) will help you make good design decisions and communicate with tradespeople. Primary service comes *to* the building. Secondary service distributes the power *within* the building.

Collecting Bids The electrical contractor and lighting supplier (who may be the same "entity") will need to know the scope of the job, this will be conveyed in your plans, drawings, and specs. Your information will include any custom constructions (such as light valances), which information will also be given to the carpenter.

Some information contained in the bid documents will be stressed in the walk-through. Detailed drawings will show any construction that must be assembled to hold and/or conceal lighting equipment. For example, cove lighting must hold and direct the light and allow for changing the lamp, so there can often be no alteration to the plan on the construction of the cove or the function of the system will be compromised. This is an instance in which three or more tradespeople (carpenter, drywaller, and electrician) will contribute to the construction and must coordinate their work to accommodate the requirements of each trade's work. This type of construction is ideally discussed in the walk-through with all involved tradespeople present.

The electrical contractor should have a copy of the plans and specs. Walk through the job site (if possible) to answer all questions that the contractor might have relative to the site and also to point out anything that you believe could be a complication or question. An on-site walk-through may not always be possible (e.g., new construction), in which case you will schedule a meeting for a focused review of the plans.

Ordering Always check the lead time for fixtures; any fixtures that will have to be installed by the electrician (which means all except the portable lamps) will have to be on the site at the time the electrician is there doing work. If the electrician finishes everything else and leaves the job, the installation of that single fixture could be very expensive. Sometimes a fixture must be in place in order to close on a building. If a fixture that is very much preferred by your client is going to hold up the closing, you may want to purchase an inexpensive temporary fixture. Any electrical fixtures purchased by your firm will, of course, have to ship to somewhere, so ask the contractor where to send them. If the electrician cannot receive and store them, ship them to your warehouse until it is time to install. Do not ship fixtures to the job site unless there is a confirmed procedure for receiving and logging them in and a locked storage area in which to house them. Fixtures laid in an out-of-the-way place on the job site grow legs and run away.

Installing On the building side of the installation, accommodations will be made for the fixtures, the most obvious being the electricity to be provided. In addition to that, consider the possible need for any of the following:

- *Special J-box size or shape.* For instance, if the backplate or canopy of a fixture is especially small, an octagon or a switch box must be required, with special attention given to the blocking for attaching the fixture if the fixture can't hang on the box itself.
- *Extra bracing.* This may be required to stabilize a fixture with moving parts during the installation, when the fixture must endure the extra stresses of being tugged on and manipulated. Heavy chandeliers also need extra bracing, which is often provided by wooden blocking installed between the joists at the fixture location.

Often, the fixture itself must have finish or accessory parts specified or ordered separately. Sometimes, the height or drop of a pendant fixture must be specified.

Managing the Records over Time After you have carefully devised the lighting scheme and selected the best lamps for the job, it might be disheartening to see changes occur during construction, when services are routed through lighting locations, or over time, as the maintenance staff relamps with the wrong manufacturer's product. Print labels that read, "NOTICE: Re-lamp only with [X]. Lamp ordering code is [X]," and affixing them inside the housing at a location that will become visible when relamping. This way, the integrity of your lighting design will not be destroyed by improper lamping.

WORKING WITH A LIGHTING SPECIALIST The lighting specialist will have a good understanding of the nuts and bolts of lighting assemblies, performance of systems, and product availability. As the project designer collaborating with the lighting designer, you will be responsible for programming in collaboration with the lighting designer, and you will assess his or her proposed schemes. Your likely role in the process is to prevent any error in addressing client and project needs. As the project designer interacting with a lighting designer, you must understand and approve of all suggested schemes and equipment, as well as any proposed custom construction. As the project designer, you need to assess another professional's plans for the following reasons:

- You are very familiar with the client's wishes and the demands of the project. You have drawn up the design program and devised the design concept, so you are in a position to assess the proposal for fitness to the function and aesthetics of your design. This includes fixture style, as well as the quality and distribution of light emitted.
- You are responsible for the locations of lights relative to your furniture arrangements, locations proposed for artwork, and other features that will be affected by the lighting plans.
- You have planned for multiple scenarios related to procedural flow and use of the space over time, so you can best evaluate the completeness of the schemes for all functions and times.
- You have selected material and color schemes that will be affected by the characteristics and color temperature of the lighting used.
- As the "hub" of the project, you are in communication with and orchestrate the work of other people involved in the project.

You may begin the process of working with a lighting professional like this after the design program is roughed in. You will convey to the lighting specialist the following information:

- List the activities and tasks that will occur in the space and where exactly in the space they will occur.
- Point out objects and architectural elements that should be emphasized. Lighting attracts the eye and should be used to reinforce a focal point or distract from an unfortunate element in the space.
- Define the mood and style of the space. Convey your programming for the various schemes that you envision.

- If you foresee any problems related to the lighting or interface between lighting and other constructions or systems, bring them up at the outset so they can be properly investigated.

Using Drawings and Sketches Take to-scale drawings to the first meeting; the plan set is unlikely to be complete at this stage, so sections and elevations may be lacking detail, and plans may be sketchy, but that should not be a problem as long as room sizes (including ceiling heights) and orientation are known, and functional assignments have been established for each space.

The lighting designer may suggest equipment that requires certain architectural constructions, such as slots, coves, trays, or surface-mounted equipment that must be drawn to scale to communicate its impact on the space. The architectural drawing will remain your responsibility, but the lighting designer is likely to dictate size and details, often communicated by sketches. The designer's sketches are likely to be accompanied by lighting manufacturers' CAD drawings or cut sheets for you to incorporate into your drawing.

Checking the Progress of the Lighting Design As the work progresses, you will be responsible for double-checking the locations of lights relative to your furniture arrangements, locations proposed for artwork, and proposed use of the spaces. Review fixtures selected relative to their use by mentally walking through the space (as suggested in the lighting information sheets in the checklist section of the CD). The correct attitude here is that you are still responsible for the outcomes, even though you are willing to defer to the expert. The qualified lighting designer will maintain a posture of being responsible for outcomes as well. The client is well-served when two professionals are communicating well with each other, both take their responsibilities seriously, and both have the program and client in mind.

CHAPTER 29

Plumbing

It is a good idea to have a basic understanding of plumbing. Aside from verifying location, you are unlikely to have responsibility for checking the plumbers' work, but for purposes of sensible planning and communicating with tradespeople, you must have some comprehension of plumbing configurations.

Construction Related to Plumbing

Among other things, you should know that plumbing fixtures have a stack that goes down for sewage and up through the roof for venting. These venting locations should be remote from any windows, roof decks, skylights, and fresh air inlets—for obvious reasons.

It is relatively difficult to relocate fixtures in a remodeling job because of waste and vent locations. Supply is easier to relocate because water arrives under pressure, so you can push it fairly far. Waste pipes are not so easy to move because waste moves out, thanks to gravity, so a slope must be maintained down to the vertical waste pipe. Moving a toilet often requires ripping up the floor or the ceiling in the space below—easier done when the same person owns all adjacent levels than in a commercial or condo/apartment scenario.

Sometimes simply removing a fixture requires tremendous effort. For example, replacing a tub often necessitates removing the surrounding wall to some extent, freezing the tub with dry ice to make it brittle enough to break

with sledgehammers, and carrying the fragments out. Access to shut-offs, motors, and steam generators and special heater units for spas and steam showers is required, so any additional equipment required for the new selection must be located to allow for access.

Sometimes your plans will call for difficult measures, but you will at least be able to demonstrate that you are aware of the complexity and feel that the result will be worth it. As a practical matter when designing, keep in mind that grouping water and waste pipes either horizontally and/or vertically is often a way to economize with no compromise to the material scheme.

Renovation Projects

For bathroom or kitchen renovation and repair, a person authorized to make decisions should be available via phone (if not on the site) if something unforeseen comes up, like hidden parts that have deteriorated or were not properly installed in the first place. These kinds of unforeseen problems are often not discovered until the walls are opened up, and they usually conflict with your plans or budget in some way.

Collaborating with the Plumber

When these unexpected conditions arise, the plumber will make recommendations but is unlikely to continue working if additional costs are not approved by someone authorized to do so. The timetable cannot be delayed because of indecision or inaccessibility. Tradespeople are often scheduled very tightly, and you don't want the plumber to leave for another job site because a decision was unobtainable; this would affect the schedules of all the tradespeople who follow the plumber's work (and wreak havoc with the schedule and final completion date—which would be pushed back exponentially as each subsequent tradesperson had problems with the new schedule).

Adding Fixtures and Extra Fittings

A typical ½-inch branch line can serve a tub/toilet/shower situation, but if additional fixtures are added (second sink, bidet) or additional fittings are planned (rain shower, body sprays, multiple showerheads), the supply should be upgraded to a ¾-inch or even a 1-inch line to be on the safe side. The same holds true at the other end of the process when sizing drains.

When tying into existing waste lines, confirm their size if you are adding more fixtures or fittings to the area. Multiple water outlets are popular in showers now, and an existing 2-inch drain will most likely have to be upgraded to a 3-inch drain to handle the extra water. A 3-inch drain or two 2-inch drains are recommended if a curbless shower pan is being planned for a universal design solution.

The flow rate for all fixtures likely to be used simultaneously should be tallied and compared to the existing hot water heater capacity. For safety reasons, many people prefer to set the temperature of their hot water heater below scalding. This safety precaution would have to be circumvented if the total capacity of the outlets exceeded flow rate times length of showering and shaving time.

But wait—it doesn't end there. More fittings mean more hot water and more hot water means more steam. We don't deal with ventilation as part of this topic, but don't forget to address that equipment, too.

Selections

Selections of plumbing fixtures are affected by codes and safety issues, which should be addressed in the early planning stages, as well as by the preferences and the needs of the primary users.

In addition to safety as mandated by code, consider this: The bathroom is one of the most dangerous rooms in the house because of accidental falls. Some of the elegant details that people like (sunken or platform tubs with steps, for instance) should be carefully assessed before becoming part of the design because they can be too dangerous in many circumstances. Slip resistance and ease of entering and exiting the tub should be investigated.

Although the concept of ADA compliance and universal design is outside the bounds of this topic and is too large to include conveniently in this information about material and people resources, the topic must be addressed here because it influences selections in bathrooms. Codes mandate mounting heights of sinks and toilets (measured to the top of the seat). There must be a shield or snood or shroud over the waste pipe of the sink so that a pipe heated by pouring hot water through it cannot burn someone. Handheld showerheads are very convenient at tubs and showers. When designing for all users, including the disabled, consult code and universal design guidebooks to ensure that your designs and selections meet requirements and suggestions for use by everyone.

Accommodating Client Wants and Needs

Ideally, the height of vanity cabinets and kitchen sink counters should be determined to suit the primary users. In the case of bathrooms, it is easier to accommodate taller and shorter users with your design. In kitchens, the counter height, and therefore height of plumbing fittings, is influenced by the height of appliances. Even though the sink base can easily be made taller or shorter than standard, the logical practice of putting the dishwasher next to the sink indicates the height of the counter immediately adjacent to the sink; other practical issues such as a continuous work surface and ease of cleanup restrict flexibility here. The approximate ideal of having the bottom of the sink at one inch above the user's wrist can be somewhat accommodated in a standard counter height by carefully selecting the depth of the kitchen sink bowl.

If a custom fixture is required, the possibility of a testing the product may vanish altogether, so you may ask the fabricator to produce a mockup of the characteristics contributing to comfort. This is especially important for custom tubs; the cost of the mockup will undoubtedly contribute to the price of the tub.

When planning a custom tub, check out the depth, the height of seats and molded arm or headrests, pitch of the back and the bottom, the curve of the edges, the location for handrails and special fittings such as soap dishes, as well as any specific issues that made a custom tub necessary for the location in question. A client should test any large tub by actually climbing in, testing the slope of the back, the length of the tub (shorter people have no place to brace their feet to keep them from sliding under the water as they relax in a long tub—which is not very relaxing at all).

For a custom shower (a very common situation), the width and length for the number of persons using the shower, the height and pitch of the seat and backrest, and the precise location of outlets (body sprays, handheld showers, etc.) can be fine-tuned to the end users.

Specification

Standard manufacturers' fixtures often offer options with respect to materials, colors, accessory parts, and specific configurations (left-facing or right-facing, for instance). Information must be conveyed carefully in order to ensure that the proper item is delivered. Different manufacturers' specifications are organized differently. Some manufacturers sell multiple items under a single item number to make it easy to include all the parts required for function (showerhead, controls, and diverters, for example). Other manufacturers sell each item separately.

When you are specifying for purchase by others, you may be able to rely on the supplier to assume responsibility for ensuring that all required parts are ordered; when necessary, fixture parts must be ordered separately. For example, sink pop-ups (or baskets) are ordered with the faucet, not with the sink, and often have to be specifically and separately ordered or you will have no means of blocking small objects from falling down the drain or filling the vessel with water. Trims and roughs are ordered separately and sometimes trims and handles come separately if more than one option is available (such as cross-handles or lever handles).

As you prepare a cost comparison, send your tally of parts to your supplier or the manufacturer's sales staff to be reviewed for completeness. When plumbing items are to be bid competitively, contact the manufacturer—not one of your suppliers—for confirmation of the parts list. Your supplier will be disinclined to break the individual parts out for you out of concern that you may forward the parts list to a competitor, making it too easy for the competitor to bid. If you intend to place the order with your preferred supplier, you can forward information to that firm alone for its bid, in which case you may not need the individual parts listed.

Plumbers frequently prefer to order the fixtures and fittings. They may charge more for their labor if you do not allow them to order, partly because their job costs will rise if any part is missing and partly because they may offset some of their labor bid with a markup on sales.

Sinks and Tubs

Kitchen sinks, lavatories (bathroom sinks), and tubs are manufactured in a variety of materials, sizes, colors, shapes, and styles. All of these factors affect the selection and installation of the fixtures.

Materials

The materials from which sinks and tubs are made include metals, stone, and other natural and manufactured materials. Some of these materials are used for plating or coating. The nature of the material allows for choices of finish and surface texture. Figure 29.1 and 29.2 show examples of sinks made from a variety of materials, and Figure 29.3 shows one of the materials used for tubs.

FIGURE 29.1 Decorative painted designs are available in custom patterns as well as in standard colors and patterns, as in this one from Kohler.

FIGURE 29.2 Many materials can be used for sinks and tubs. Glass and stone bowls are popular for vessel sinks, such as this glass vessel sink by Decolav.

METAL Stainless steel is often used for kitchen sinks and bar sinks. Some styles are applicable to lavatories as well. The difference between bar sinks and lavatory sinks, which are similar in size, is that bar sinks have a flat bottom (so glassware can stand in there) and lavatories have a curved bottom.

Stainless steel is measured by gauge; higher numbers represent thinner materials than lower ones. In better sinks, 18-gauge stainless steel is used. The higher the nickel content of the stainless, the less water-spotting your client will experience. Polished stainless steel sinks are often nickel-plated and polished because nickel will more easily attain a higher polish than stainless. Stainless is easy to care for and will not chip, though a thinner-gauge stainless can dent if subjected to forceful impact. Brushed and satin textures can be cleaned with abrasive cleansers without damage. Many stainless steel kitchen sinks come with a sprayed-on sound-deadening coating on their undersides. If your job site will have multiple stainless surfaces (sinks and appliances from

FIGURE 29.3 Stone tubs are rare and opulent, and freestanding models such as this tub, which is carved from a block of stone, are the most preferred style. Tub is by Stone Forest.

several different manufacturers), each surface will have a slightly different appearance because of texturing and content. If you believe your clients will focus on that, you should prepare them for this likelihood (a secondary sink or faucet).

Other metals that are common in sinks are brass, which can be lacquered or unlacquered or plated in a variety of other metals. Nickel, chrome, and "pewter" (which is often a chrome with a slightly pigmented lacquer to darken the surface) are metals used for plating. Brass, bronze, copper, and silver are used for plasting and can oxidize unless sealed with lacquer.

Occasionally, a small nick in the lacquer will permit the metal to darken from exposure to air and water. This oxidation, once started, can continue under the lacquer, requiring that the sink be stripped to expose the metal for repolishing of the oxidized area before resealing it. The entire sink must be polished if a portion of it requires polishing because the surface quality could vary between the factory-finished area and the repaired area. Polished finishes will show water spotting and metal sinks are often specified with a hammered or satin finish to lessen the need for constant maintenance.

Enameled cast iron fixtures are heavy and tough. Enamels allow for a wide range of color, have a high gloss, and can tolerate abrasive cleansers. They will chip from forceful impact. They cost more than other options but will be serviceable for decades. Make sure the carpenter is made aware of the weight of these tubs when filled with water (and one or more persons, depending on size), especially in the case of remodeling an upper-story space into a bathroom.

Enameled steel is lighter and a little bit more likely to chip than cast iron. Enameled steel has somewhat more "flex" than iron and usually has a thinner coat of enamel than cast iron; this property makes enameled steel fixtures vulnerable to chipping from sharp impact and when they do, they may rust. The heavier the gauge of the metal (lower numbers), the more durable they will be. They are somewhat similar to cast iron, but their forms are less rounded-looking, and they are a little bit noisier. They have less thermal mass than cast iron, so the water cools off faster. They have

the same durable enameled surface at a lower price point. Enameled steel is very resistant to chemicals.

People sometimes complain that these tubs are "tinny"-sounding. This can be alleviated to some extent by packing insulation up under these tubs to muffle the hollow sound and possibly slow down heat loss.

OTHER MATERIALS Tubs coated with FRP (fiberglass-reinforced polyester) are lightweight and inexpensive. Polyester scratches, and some manufacturers suggest waxing these tubs with a marine-grade wax if they become dull-looking after use. They are more prone to cracking than other materials.

Acrylic tubs are less susceptible to scratching or chipping than similar-looking gel-coat tubs but are more expensive. Acrylic is lightweight, with a slightly more matte surface than gel-coats. The nature of the material makes it a good choice for molded-in accessories (seats, soap dishes, handles). Tub and shower surrounds are available for a one-piece-unit look for the entire tub or shower area. Sometimes the vertical surfaces of these surrounds are a color-coordinated plastic, which is not as durable as acrylic. There are different formulations of acrylic and some quality differences. People like acrylic for tubs because of its light weight and lower cost. These tubs are "warm to the touch" compared to cast iron or enameled steel. Some cleaning chemicals will damage acrylic tubs.

Gel-coat tubs look like acrylic and have many characteristics in common with acrylic, but they are not as durable. Clients can anticipate a 10- to 15-year life span with normal use. They have a fiberglass structure, and the better-quality fixtures and surrounds will have multiple layers of fiberglass. A foam core may also provide some heat and sound insulation.

Acrylic, fiberglass, and gel-coated tubs can be resurfaced on-site, but the process will not correct stress fractures. The spraying process takes about a day. Slip resistance can be added. Warranties vary, but may range up to five years. The resurfacing process will save up to three-quarters of the cost of a new fixture.

Soft tubs are a foam-cushioned tub with a tough protective shell. This is a unique, proprietary material and is being used by only one manufacturer. The four-layer surface is flexible and durable.

China sinks are used primarily in bathrooms. They have properties similar to those of glazed tiles. Like glazed tiles, they may have decorative painting. They will chip if struck forcefully. They have a very durable surface that can withstand cleaning by abrasive cleansers. They come in many colors and do not discolor over time, as some plastics will when exposed to hot water.

Glass is hard and durable, and resists chemicals, but it can chip if heavy objects fall on it. Transparent glass sinks require more maintenance to keep them looking clean than will other textures and patterns. Different formulations of glass yield slightly differing properties and lead glass is preferred for sinks.

FIGURE 29.4 The versatility of concrete makes custom configurations very feasible for solving unique design programs. This installation uses concrete sinks by Two Stones Designs.

Stone, often marble, is used for plumbing fixtures offered in more limited selections as standard and for custom fixtures. The cost of such fixtures is high, and the fabrication of custom fixtures requires careful selection of the proper fabricator. Markings in the stone that will be seen on the sink's surfaces will not be uncovered until the fabrication is complete. Matched pairs are difficult to achieve because of variations in stone, but matched pairs are seldom a real necessity. When considering this material for a bathtub, remember that stone is very good at soaking up and holding heat. The holding heat part is very good, but the heat will be coming from the bathwater, so initially some of the heat from the hot water will go into heating up the tub. This is true for all tub materials, but thinner materials require less heat than stone does to get warm. In a stone tub, your clients may have to run their bathwater a little bit hotter than they'd actually like to soak in so that it will have some heat to lose to the stone. Stone tubs are often slab constructions, unlike sinks, which are often carved from a block.

Concrete is a good choice for integral sink/counter applications (Figure 29.4) and for custom tubs. The form can be easily controlled during fabrication for just the right length, support, height, and shape. It must be sealed, and many fabricators seal with a water-base urethane before shipping. Like stone, concrete has good thermal mass, but the bath will have to be run a little hotter so some heat can be given up to heating the tub. Initially, there may be extra maintenance involved with the installation of a concrete tub. The fabricator may suggest that the tub be waxed frequently in the beginning of its life. The fabricator will suggest appropriate products based on the sealer used in the shop.

Composites are solid material, so burns or small spots of permanent damage can be sanded off. The vessel can be molded continuously with a countertop or tub/shower surround.

Composite quartz and granite contain actual quartzite or granite chips embedded in resin. They are usually 70–90 percent stone. These composites are very durable and heat- and scratch-resistant. Composites are color-through materials available in many colors. Composite granites are especially heat-resistant and some can withstand temperatures of 500 degrees Fahrenheit.

Installation

Sinks can be undermounted, overmounted, integral with the countertop, tiled-in wall-mounted, or pedestal (Figure 29.5a to f). One toilet manufacturer makes a toilet with a small sink built into the top of it so that the water used for hand washing is reused in the next flush. If the sink is under-mounted, confirm that hangers are included. Let the plumber know if he or she must supply the hangers at installation.

Sinks may be predrilled for faucets. A single hole is drilled for a center-fit faucet, which has a single unit for controlling temperature and

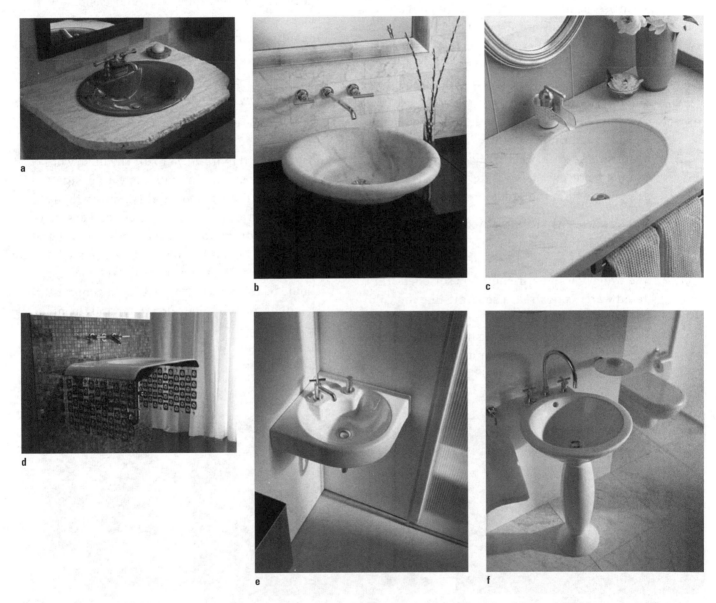

FIGURE 29.5 The most-used installation methods for sinks include drop-in (a) and vessel sinks (b), as shown here with Kohler products. These are simple installations with the surrounding surface supporting the sink. The vessel sink height must be considered and the countertop lowered to compensate for the height of the bowl, which also requires a wall-mounted or deck-mounted faucet taller than that of a drop-in. The undermount sink configuration (c), as shown here by Kohler, has clips holding it to the underside of the countertop. These clips are separate items from some manufacturers, so make sure they are included in your order. Wall-hung sinks like this one from Kohler (d) and this corner sink from Duravit (e) are supported off of the wall. The supporting wall must be braced if necessary to support not only the sink but the addition of any reasonable, if nonrecommended, weight, such as a child getting a sponge bath in a large sink. Pedestal sinks (f) are considered a classic configuration even in a modern form, such as this one from Duravit. Consider adding additional surface near a pedestal sink.

dispensing water. Single-hole designs, as well as 4-, 6-, 8-, and 10-inch spreads, are typical for predrilled sinks. A 4" spread faucet has the spout and controls arranged on a "platform." Wider spread set faucets have handles and spouts that are separate from one another. An 8-inch spread is very typical. The water-carrying tubes are often flexible within a range of around 8 inches.

KITCHEN SINKS Avoid small (12 × 12-inch) sinks, even as second sinks; the drain does not accept a disposal and they are so small that water will splash out when there are items inside them. Round sinks are smaller than comparably sized square or rectangular sinks and they require deck-mounted faucets.

Double-bowl sinks, when undermounted, will splash water on the counter if the faucet is swung from sink to sink. The saddle between the sinks should be recessed, but water will still splash if it's poured onto the saddle.

ACCESSORIES AT THE SINK Accessories often located near the sink include a soap or lotion dispenser, a hot water dispenser, and occasionally, if the water for an entire house is softened or if filtered water is desired, a separate line for (cold) drinking water (Figure 29.6a to c). Even if all dishes are washed in the dishwasher, a drainboard is still convenient for draining fresh food after washing it. All such accessories should be

noted on your plans and the hidden portions (filtration, heaters, containers for soap and lotion) must be accommodated in the sink base cabinet.

High-rises require a vacuum breaker, sometimes called an air gap, if there is a dishwasher. It is usually installed on the countertop between the sink and the dishwasher. It is often possible to get permission to install the air gap in the sink base. It will stand up on a pipe sticking up out of the bottom of the cabinet. It will occasionally "leak" small amounts of water and suds. If installing a sink in a corner, make sure the front edge maintains the normal 2 or 3 inches from the front edge of the counter so the client has comfortable access.

TUBS Tubs are usually constructed for freestanding, drop-in, corner, or three-sided alcove installation (Figure 29.7a to d). The luxury of incorporating a custom tub into your design comes with extra responsibility. Rather than select features, you must consider and design them. In addition to considerations about the tub itself, there are issues to investigate related to the structure. The floor under the tub location should be reinforced if necessary to support the weight of the tub filled with water and the number of bathers it is intended to accommodate. You may want to hire a structural engineer to check this out.

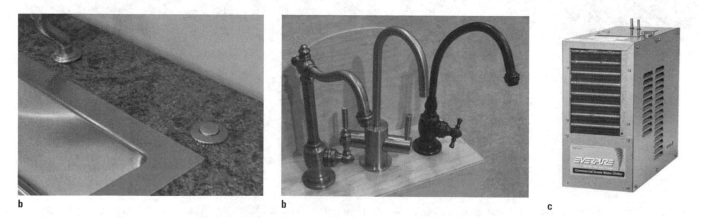

b   b   c

FIGURE 29.6 Accessories are often desired near a sink (or tub). An air switch (a) for a garbage disposal or a whirlpool tub controls electric motors without danger of electrical shock. Instant hot, chilled, or filtered water faucets (b) are often placed near kitchen sinks for convenience. Unlike a soap or lotion pump next to the sink, hot and cold water dispensers have additional equipment that must be accommodated nearby, often in the cabinet under the sink. This Everpur chiller (c) is a commercial unit; smaller units are available for residential use. Confirm all equipment sizes during the planning stages to ensure fit. This gets especially tricky when multiple accessories (chilled and filtered water taps, a garbage disposal) are all required at the sink. *Photographs by Alana Clark.*

a

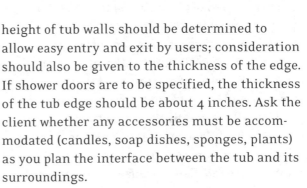

b

c

d

FIGURE 29.7 This freestanding concrete tub from Sonoma Stone (a) will require a floor-standing faucet as shown here. Custom tubs require special planning but allow for nonstandard characteristics, such as the deep soaking basin here. The drop-in tub (b) requires a deck surround to support it. A more successful design allows for room on all four sides for both overmounted surrounds, where the flange sits on the tub deck, and undermounted models, where the tub deck covers the flange of the tub. The safest way to enter a deck-mounted tub is to sit on the edge and swing your feet in. Do not feel compelled to provide a step, which only provides a slipping hazard. This tub is by Kohler. Corner tubs (c) seem very spacious. This Kohler tub requires a wall on two sides. This Kohler alcove tub (d) has an integral apron (the vertical part spanning the height of the tub), so it would not have to be ordered separately. Always confirm that the apron is included so you don't receive a drop-in when you were expecting an alcove. This tub is a very common configuration that requires walls on three sides.

Ideally, the clients should mock up distances and posture in the presence of the fabricator. Include space around each bather, the angle of the back slope, location of jets relative to each bather's location, the height and curvature (if any) of back support, and the location and height of any armrests and "foothold" features (to keep bathers from sliding down into the tub farther than they want to). The height of tub walls should be determined to allow easy entry and exit by users; consideration should also be given to the thickness of the edge. If shower doors are to be specified, the thickness of the tub edge should be about 4 inches. Ask the client whether any accessories must be accommodated (candles, soap dishes, sponges, plants) as you plan the interface between the tub and its surroundings.

FIGURE 29.8 Whatever you select as your material or configuration for the tub, consider the slipperiness of the surface, especially if the tub doubles as a shower. Some manufacturers offer slip-resistant surfacing on their tubs, as Kohler has done for this tub.

Surfacing material should be slip-resistant (Figure 29.8), have low absorbency (less than .6), a smooth surface, and resistance to stains and cleaning chemicals. The assembly must ensure a watertight installation. Water softeners sometimes restrict the flow of water, so select one with a high flow rate.

If stone is under consideration for a custom tub or shower, suggest that the client soften the water and wipe the stone down after use to minimize the formation of mineral deposits on the surface. Use smooth, impervious surfaces, light-colored stones, or a stone with a coloration that's similar to water deposits (reddish in areas with some iron in the water, whiter where the water is very hard). The idea is to keep mineral deposits from showing. Honed surfaces will deflect light similarly to mineral deposits. If a polished stone is selected for maintenance reasons, consider using smaller-size pieces (tiles) in the bottom of any vessel used for showering (people are standing and moving rather than semiprone and stationary), so the grout lines will provide more slip resistance. This strategy implies that the tub and shower should be different vessels because people generally do not like to sit on tiled surfaces (to avoid the dreaded grid-butt phenomenon).

Stone and concrete should be treated with a subsurface repellent because even granite, which is very hard and impervious, will darken as capillary action in the stone's internal structure pulls water below the polished face. Specify a matte sealer to alter the appearance of the stone as little as possible. Specify a color-enhancing sealer to deepen and enrich the color presentation. If you are considering a honed surface, request a matte sample and a color-enhanced sample for comparison with your other material samples for the space.

Whirlpool Tubs

Whirlpool tubs move water through jets that are traditionally located at feet and back locations (four-jet models) and also one on each side (six-jet models). The number of available jets seems to be restricted only by the need to maintain enough surface to mount them stably. Whirlpool tubs are often acrylic or fiberglass, although some cast iron models are available and some enameled steel may also still be available.

The motors commonly used in these tubs operate by a couple of different technologies. Brush-driven motors are inexpensive and are found on "builder"-grade models. They are noisier and are said to have shorter life spans. An induction motor is a step up in price. Some of these models offer more than one speed, allowing for more control over the characteristics of the stream delivered. Adjustable jetted outlets combined with the various motor speeds allow for a more customized stream.

The rule of thumb for evaluating the hot water heater that will serve the whirlpool is that the capacity of the heater should equal two-thirds the capacity of the tub. If the water heater available is not large enough, the choices are to increase the size of the hot water heater, install two water heaters, or specify a tankless water heater along the supply line. If the whirlpool will be used for an extended period of time, you should also specify an in-line heater, which maintains the temperature of the water. However, this is not the same thing as a tankless water heater, which provides hot water on demand. If an in-line heater is used, it will require a 240-volt power supply, even for motors of less than one horsepower.

Supporting the tub is another consideration.

Many codes require that the motors be controlled by timers. Many models are available with timers, but if the model selected does not have a timer and local code requires one, a wall timer can be specified.

Locate the pump, activator switch, and timer switches on your plan (most codes require electric switches to be 60 inches away from the tub). An air switch on the tub may be available; this is safer and more convenient because air pressure, not electricity, activates the switch so there is no danger of shock, even when the switch is pressed with a wet hand.

The pump and heaters must be *accessible* for maintenance. It is possible in some cases to install a remote pump up to 60 inches away and no higher than the highest jet (2 inches below the waterline) and no lower than the suction fitting. The preferred location is under the tub with access through the apron or through the wall of an adjacent closet.

Sanijet makes a pipeless whirlpool tub with each jet having its own motor. This addresses client concerns about infectious bacteria and dirt remaining in the jet pipes, while still allowing for water jet technology that some people feel is superior to air jet technology for massaging sore muscles. Consumers can clean each outlet without the need for special chemical flushing, which may be required when cleaning piped models.

Whirlpools force water through jets to massage; air jets push heated air out through jets. The air jet technology is quieter, and the motor can be remote from the tub; water is not recirculated through a piping system, so there is no danger of long hair getting sucked into the intake from the tub and pulling someone's head under water or even just clogging up the works. Bath salts and oils can be used with air jets (no bubble baths, though, because these can reportedly whip up enough foam to fill the bathroom). There will be less standing water in circulating pipes that would require special maintenance for cleanliness. Some models blow air through the tubes after the tub has drained to clear water that falls into the air tubes during and after operation.

For people who can't make up their minds regarding air or water jet technology, there are manufacturers offering both systems in a single fixture.

For a custom whirlpool, jets should be precisely located and all at least 8 inches below the surface of the water. Motor locations should be accessible, as should the in-line heater (water will cool off initially in large stone, concrete, or tiled tubs). Between the drawings and the written documentation, everything about the tub should be spelled out.

Spas also recirculate the water, but they come in larger sizes and the tub is not drained after each use, so chemicals are used to keep the water from "coming alive."

Typical North American housing construction supports 40 pounds per square foot. One gallon of water weighs 8.33 pounds.

Showers

Prefabricated shower pans are typically made of terrazzo, gel-coat, or acrylic (Figure 29.9). They can also be custom-built and surfaced with tile or stone. You can specify that they be cast out of concrete. Surrounds are tiled or stone clad on

FIGURE 29.9 A prefab shower base simplifies construction issues related to leak-proofing the shower area. This model by Duravit is a space-saving angled unit. Because of the angle, it seems more open and larger than its footprint might imply.

one-piece units. High-tech integrated units that offer several water delivery options and steam showers are available.

Environments that simulate wind and rain and also offer heat, steam, sauna, whirlpool, and speakers for music have specific plumbing, electrical, and venting requirements.

Configuring the Shower

Consider the following points when configuring the shower:

- The showerhead should be located so the spray is directed toward the body, not toward the face and hair. The rough placement is approximately 72–78 inches above the finished floor.
- If multiple users of varying heights use the same shower, consider a slide bar so the height of the shower spray can be adjusted.
- Controls should be located to allow a person to turn the water on without standing under the spray.
- The size of the shower should allow the user to step out of the spray and adjust the temperature.
- A seat or at least a footrest should be provided. A seat should be a minimum of 15 inches deep and 16–19 inches high. The location of the seat should provide the user the option of being in or outside of the shower spray.

Steam Showers

Steam showers come as integrated units or can be custom-built. Sometimes the regular shower in a bathroom doubles as a steam shower with a transom window above the door. The transom should be installed so that it sheds condensation into the shower when open instead of into the room. As with whirlpools, the generator units must be accessible.

The closer the steam generator is to the unit, the better, so search for a nearby closet in which to locate it or select an in-wall unit that can fit between studs. There will still be an access panel, so an unobtrusive location is still preferred.

Plan to build the steam shower, as any shower, out of cement board or you will need to detail for a built-up cement mortar on lath. On top of

this, there will be a moisture barrier (heavy plastic or a painted-on barrier). The surface will be covered with material that is heat- and moisture-resistant. For steam showers, it is important to select nonporous surfacing. Tile, especially nonporous porcelain or glass, nonporous stones, and cement (with a nice finish) are safe choices, but other materials can be used with the recommendation of the manufacturer. Steam showers have prolonged exposure to moisture, so do not use any material that is degraded by water and high heat. (For example, DuPont currently does not approve Corian products for use in steam showers.) Use waterproof substrates and sealants. Crackle-finish tile is sometimes discouraged for steam showers. The joints between the walls and floor, between the seat and walls, and between seat and floor are often caulked to prevent moisture penetration as much as possible because steam can penetrate small voids. Installers refer to these unmudded, caulked joints as "expansion joints."

Place a seat away from the steam nozzle so your client will not be burned by an unexpected burst of steam. The location of the nozzle should be as out of the way as possible. For aesthetic reasons, you may be tempted to locate it with other fittings (in line with the showerhead or handles), but consider the heat rising from that location and be sure it's not too close to the handles or other parts that people will touch.

Specify a completely enclosed unit with a vapor-proof door and an operable transom that's installed so that the condensation runs down into the shower pan when open. If it is only for steam baths, the transom may not be necessary because the client will never want the steam to escape while the unit is in use, unlike a shower where the client may want to release the steam while showering.

While planning the design of a steam shower, remember that people use them to relax, so you must include a seat in the plans. To ensure comfort, you may want to slant the back, starting immediately above the seat and extending up to 20–24 inches, like a park bench. Mock this up with your client, and consider transitioning from slant to vertical at the user's shoulder height. Slant the backrest a minimum of a 1:3 pitch for lounging. This minimum slant feels very straight up and down. A slope of 1:5 begins to feel like leaning back. Because users will be sitting and leaning against these surfaces, you might want to warm them with a radiant heating system.

Condensation dripping off the ceiling is another consideration but is not easily solved. If you slant the ceiling to try to prevent condensation drips, it must have a pretty dramatic slope to be effective. The water drops tend to cling to a gentle slope; if you have a tile ceiling, they are likely to roll just to the grout, then drop from there. If you do find a way to induce the water to roll across the ceiling before dropping, you can plan the slope to deliver water away from the seat.

Consider installing electric radiant heat in seats and any surface subject to condensation.

Steam showers typically reach 120 degrees Fahrenheit; saunas are limited by law (in the U.S.) to 170 degrees Fahrenheit. Saunas are usually sold as complete units assembled on site parts from rather than being custom-built. Saunas take up more room than a steam shower would require. The most popular material for prebuilt saunas is cedar. It is resistant to decay, does not transmit a lot of heat (so it doesn't feel as hot to sit on), and cleans easily. Design seating so people can relax sitting or lying down.

Shower Fittings

The two main parts of a shower system are the valves and the outlets. Drains and other parts complete the system. Showers are central to the luxury bath today. Tubs are usually visually prominent in the bathroom, but the shower is more important to daily function. The trend today is to install multiple outlets in both new construction and remodeling. There are two factors to consider here: One is flow rate, and the other is water pressure. Water pressure pushes the water through the fittings, and flow rate is the capacity of the fittings, that is, how many gallons per minute they can deliver.

Valves

The valve is the entry point of water into the system. There are pressure-balanced valves and ther-

mostatic valves. A pressure-balanced shower valve is designed to compensate for changes in water pressure if someone flushes the toilet or runs the hot water tap. A pressure-balanced valve uses either a diaphragm or a piston mechanism to balance the pressure of the hot and cold water inputs. These valves keep water temperature constant within plus or minus 2–3 degrees Fahrenheit, but they do this by reducing the flow of water through either the hot or cold supply. Most are able to reduce water flow to a mere trickle if either the hot or the cold water supply fails.

Where both flow and volume control are important, a better (although more expensive) choice is a thermostatic valve. These valves will maintain water temperature within a degree or two of the set temperature, but they also have ¾-inch inlets that can pour water through multiple shower outlets, maintaining supply and temperature simultaneously. For instance, they can supply a showerhead, hand shower, and three or four body sprays. If your system will contain more outlets than this, consider specifying a 1-inch pipe supply and another thermostatic valve. These valves are required in new construction in many jurisdictions.

The volume-control valve dials the amount of water delivered into the system up from "off" to "full-on." The diverter valves do not turn the flow on or off; instead, they divert incoming water to one of multiple outlets. This means that the diverter will chose one or the other. If your client prefers to use body sprays *or* a rain showerhead, the diverter can take the place of one thermostatic valve. If your client wants the option of using the rain shower *with* the body sprays, then the diverter is not sophisticated enough to allow for that. It is an on/off switch for the two fixtures attached to it.

Both temperature and pressure-balanced valves can be set for the preferred temperature control. The range from 70 to 110 degrees Fahrenheit is considered to be the broad comfort zone. Not all valves work with all outlets (showerheads, handheld showerheads, and body sprays), so confirm compatibility during the selection phase.

Outlet Types

The three outlet types—showerhead, handheld showerhead, and body spray—have a variety of differences. A showerhead is fixed in its location, which is typically above eye level, if not above head level. A handheld showerhead is exactly what its name implies. It may be installed on a slide bar so that its height in the holder is adjustable or it may be stored on a bracket with a fixed location and used in place or removed and held in the hand (Figure 29.10). Handheld showers, when used as the only showerhead, are positioned higher, as high as a showerhead would be. When used in conjunction with a showerhead, a handheld shower is usually between waist and shoulder level (especially if it's being accessed from a seated position on a bench in the shower). Body sprays are in fixed locations positioned between shoulder height and knee height, usually used in multiples, creating a "human car wash" effect (Figure 29.11).

There is a federally mandated limit of 2.5 gallons per minute for 80 pounds per square inch of pressure (or 2.2 gallons per minute for 60 pounds per square inch of pressure) for showerheads. Although it is illegal to remove these governors, suppliers will very nonchalantly discuss flow rate "with" and "without" restrictors. These flow regulators are very easy to remove, and they often are. This all-too-common practice is a sign of a failure to specify properly. Spray options, aerators, and good maintenance of the system as a whole should allow for the desired result without circumventing the law and good conservation practices.

Each of these outlets is available in a number of spray-quality options. Manufacturers refer to champagne spray (lots of bubbly air), massage (forceful), pulsating (variable and forceful), and needle (for stimulating the skin), among others.

When multiple outlets are used, you will have to specify enough diverters or volume controls to regulate water delivery to each outlet. Usually, one control is planned for each showerhead (handheld or fixed) and one is planned for every three body sprays. Individual volume controls for each item or group of body sprays are usually preferred. Don't forget that when planning for the simultaneous use of multiple outlets, you should consider upgrading to a 3-inch or a pair of 2-inch drains.

FIGURE 29.10 This shower system by Herbeau exposes plumbing pipe for decorative effect, allowing us to see the route the pipes travel to connect all the parts. Recall this image when you are planning a recessed soap niche centered where you can see the vertical pipe supplying the showerhead. This shower does not need another spout and diverter to switch the water from a tub faucet to the showerhead, so the exposed plumbing is simple and elegant for a vintage-looking installation.

FIGURE 29.11 Rainbars, as shown here, and body sprays are auxiliary outlets and are typically used along with showerheads. Multiple outlets may require more water and larger drain capacity, so calculate the gallons per minute in the early planning stages.

Toilets

Toilets are made of vitreous china or stainless steel (Figure 29.12), both of which are impervious to chemicals. One-piece and low-profile units are generally more costly.

Flushing

All toilets must be of low water-use (1.6 gallons per flush) design. Water-saving toilets can flush by means of gravity-fed, wash-down, vacuum-assisted, pressure-assisted, electrohydraulic, dual-flush, or flushometer flushers.

GRAVITY FLUSH TANK Water is poured into the bowl and out through the S-shaped trapway, and waste is siphoned out of the bowl. Some gravity flush tanks require two flushes to clear the bowl.

WASH-DOWN TOILETS Large trapways are paired with a small waterspot (the surface area of the water left standing in the bowl after flushing). Thanks to the big trapway, wash-down toilets are less likely to clog than other toilets, but they sometimes do not clean the bowl surfaces as well.

VACUUM-ASSIST The vacuum-assist flush is similar to the gravity flush but has two tanks within the toilet tank that hold only 1.6 gallons of water combined. When the toilet is flushed, a vacuum is created that boosts water into the bowl with a more efficient flush.

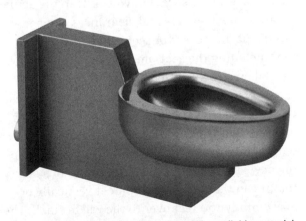

FIGURE 29.12 Stainless steel is now a readily available material for high-style plumbing fixtures, but the original stainless steel toilets were available only in styles designed for prisons, which are an exceptionally hard-use environment. This toilet by Bradley has a streamlined, one-piece industrial design that will remain sound even if abused.

PRESSURE-ASSIST Compressed air in the tank propels water to the rim and siphon jet, creating a powerful flush. These flushers are louder (and more expensive) than gravity toilets, but are known for clearing the bowl with a single flush.

ELECTROHYDRAULIC Electrohydraulic toilets are the latest in high technology. They use electric motor(s), pumps(s), and controllers to assist the flushing action by monitoring and controlling the flush and dictating the exact discharge from the tank into the bowl. These tankless units have offered product designers additional freedom in designing toilets.

DUAL-FLUSH Dual-flush toilets have two buttons, one that flushes using less than 1.6 gallons per flush for liquid waste, the other using the full 1.6 gallons per flush for solid waste. Some dual-flush toilets are wash-down models.

FLUSHOMETER VALVE These are the flushers that you see in public restrooms. An external valve is connected directly to the pressurized water supply line so water arrives in the bowl under greater pressure (Figures 29.13 and 29.14).

Toilet Forms

Toilets are either floor-mounted or wall-mounted. Some models have tanks; some have other ways of pressurizing the water for flushing. Other models with tanks have the tank hidden in the wall (Figure 29.15). It is common for the tank to remain exposed.

Toilets with attached tanks are described as one-piece or two-piece units (Figure 29.16). Two-piece toilets are usually lower in cost than one-piece styles. This is because if a manufacturing defect is found in one part of a two-piece unit, the other part of the unit is still usable. If a one-piece unit has a manufacturing defect in one half or the other, the manufacturer must scrap the whole toilet. The sleekness of the one-piece unit is often enough of a selling point to override the additional cost.

Tank liners, available from a few manufacturers, solve the sweating tank problem in spaces that are not strictly heat- and humidity-controlled. There are also some DIY after-factory kits

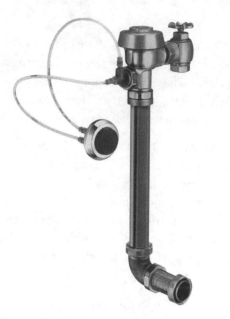

FIGURE 29.13 The flushing valve of this Sloan Flushometer is entirely concealed within the wall. The Flushometer replaces water pressure, otherwise created by the toilet tank, with a pressurized delivery system to help clear the bowl. Although this model is concealed within the wall, other models are exposed.

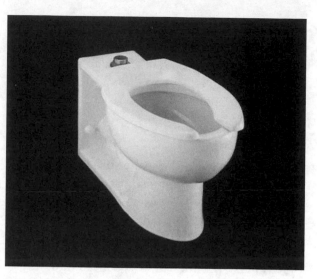

FIGURE 29.14 A toilet that is served by a valve, such as an exposed Flushometer, may have a rear spud like this model from Kohler. If the valve were concealed as shown in Figure 29.13, the spud would be at the back, where the toilet connects to the wall.

FIGURE 29.15 This toilet has a water tank hidden in the wall. The activation panel on the wall is large enough to function as a cover plate, which, when removed, allows access for adjusting the tank. The tank is installed between the studs in the wall and covered over with wall surfacing.

designed to insulate the tank. Another suggestion is to deliver hot and cold water to the tank. The temperature cannot be regulated like on a faucet tap, but this technique will warm up the water in the tank enough so that the tank will not sweat as it warms up to room temperature.

Toilet bowls are described as rounded or elongated. Elongated bowls are often preferred for their more comfortable contours, but they are about 3 inches longer from front to back than rounded versions, so if you are working with a tight space, make sure that you draft in the actual length so door swings and clearances can be evaluated. To meet ADA requirements, the rim (not including the seat) must rise to 16-½ inches AFF (above finished floor).

A related product is a problem-solver for residential clients wishing to add a bathroom to a location that is not plumbed. This unit from Saniflo (Figure 29.17) is a macerating and pumping device that can "blenderize" waste to a slurry that it can then pump up to 9 feet vertically or horizontally 100 feet over to the waste stack. The same pump can also handle the gray water (from sink and shower) along with the waste, as long as the gray water travel path maintains a proper slope down to the unit. For those very mindful of water conservation, the company also has units

FIGURE 29.17 Saniflo makes special equipment that permits for the location of toilets in places that might otherwise present plumbing problems. This in-the-wall unit improves the success of pumping wastewater traveling up out of below-grade bathroom locations.

that use the gray water from the hand basin to flush the toilet. Check your local building codes for possible restrictions.

Bidets

The bidet (Figure 29.18) resembles a toilet, but unlike a toilet, its function is for cleaning, as with the sink and tub, rather than for simply disposing of waste. The user sits on the bidet facing the water outlet (the faucet-using styles are the most popular) and soap and water are used to clean more thoroughly than can be accomplished by wiping with toilet paper.

The different ways of delivering water into the bidet include a "regular" tap, a vertical spray up out of the bottom, filling the bowl under the rim like a toilet, or a horizontal spray.

In addition to simple rinsing, bidets are sometimes used for sitz-baths, which are often recommended for medical conditions such as urinary tract infections and hemorrhoids. They can also be used for washing feet after running barefoot in the yard and for icing down a bottle of wine for that romantic soak in the whirlpool.

Urinals

Urinals are often made of the same vitreous china required to meet code for toilets, but code does not apply in the same way to urinals; they

FIGURE 29.16 One piece toilets, such as this one by Toto (a), have the base and tank molded as one unit. These are preferred by some people for easy cleaning of the exterior and for aesthetic reasons. Two-piece units, such as this one (b), also by Toto, are more economically priced than one-piece units; this is because of production issues and not because of quality concerns.

FIGURE 29.18 The bidet has proven to be more than a fad, and this model by Duravit is one of a few available configurations. This rimless bidet has a horizontal spray. What is missing from this lovely promotional shot is a convenient soap and towel holder.

may be made of steel, stone, china, or any practical material. Models include floor- and wall-mounted urinals for a single user or a trough style that accommodates multiple users. The floor-mounted models are not as good at protecting their surroundings from splashing as wall-mounted urinals. Flushing technologies include wash-down, siphon-jet, and blow-out. The wash-down is the quietest and requires a ½-inch supply line. The siphon-jet requires a ¾-inch supply. The blow-out requires a 1-¼-inch supply. The waterless urinal requires no water because it does not flush; a special configuration in the bottom and a replaceable cartridge seal in odors.

Faucets

Faucets, like most shower fittings, simply deliver water into the fixture. Spray features and styles vary. Quality faucets are entirely made of metal—with the exception of special lever handles—and may, furthermore, be plated with other metals.

Materials

Brass is a durable, long-lasting metal alloy that holds up to heavy use. Brass faucets are costly initially because the material itself is costly. It may be a solid brass fitting or a brass coat applied over a base metal. Brass is a common base for other plated finishes.

Chrome plating is extremely hard and does not oxidize. It is electrochemically deposited over nickel-plated base metal.

Plastics are not as durable as other materials and are difficult to plate unless they are "plating grade." They can be damaged by sand and silt in the line. Color matching is difficult because of differences in gloss and light reflection off of real metal pieces and plated plastic ones. Plastics can be attacked by petroleum-based products.

Copper is softer than brass and prone to corrosion and scratching.

Finishes

Finishes are similar to the metal finishes described in Chapter 12 and will be plated or baked on.

- *Lacquer* is attacked by water and needs to be dried after each use.
- *Epoxy* is stronger but can be scratched by abrasive cleaners. Epoxy coatings are used to create a colored finish. They are baked on to provide even coverage and protection.
- *Gold plate.* Use only heavy (13–50 millionths of an inch) gold-plated fixtures in a bathroom, never gold flash or gold wash, which can wear out in three to six months. Never expose gold plate to abrasives or acids.
- *Nickel* is used for plating because of its resistance to oxidation and deep rich luster.
- *Pewter* is an alloy of tin with brass, copper, or lead added that is very soft. "Pewter" is a term that usually refers to the appearance of pewter, rather than the actual metal. Pewter finishes are usually chrome or nickel with a darkening overglaze of lacquer.

Textures

Faucet textures can be polished to mirror-quality brightness. A brushed finish is created with a wire wheel that leaves a soft linear texture. Matte surfaces are created by a sandblasting process using fine glass beads.

Styles

Faucets come in a variety of styles and finishes. Many are plated on brass. Many metal finishes can be found among the standard offerings; if you shop enough different manufacturers, you can probably find the style that you want in the finish that you want. If not, order the style faucet that you want in brass and have it stripped and plated by a local plater.

Plumbing hardware is often coordinated with door and window hardware. The brass/chrome dilemma has been neatly solved by the number of manufacturers who offer faucets in a combination of brass (or gold) and chrome (or nickel).

Quality is wide-ranging, and poor quality can be a nuisance. Some low-end faucets have chrome-plated plastic parts. The weight, scale, and quality of the finish (how smooth and clear is your reflection for polished faucets, how consistent is the texture of the finish from part to part for satin or brushed) all indicate the quality of the faucet to some extent.

Whenever possible, stick to manufacturers who have a proven record of quality. Some very expensive specialty plumbing hardware is actually not as well engineered as less costly alternatives. It pays to become familiar with the performance of fixtures over time.

The finishes available are generally the same ones available for metal sinks. Plating is critical for faucets to a greater extent than for sinks. People wearing rings will scratch the plating of faucet handles so the number of times the piece was dipped into the plating bath is important.

Water conservation paired with function analysis indicates that the ideal flow rate is 2.2 gallons per minute for kitchen faucets and 1.5 gallons per minute for bathroom lavatory faucets. Tub fillers deliver as much as 10 gallons per minute and showerheads (handheld, rain, and stationary wall fittings) with flow restrictors deliver about 2.5 gallons per minute (usually 7 or 8 GPM with flow restrictors illegally removed). Body sprays usually deliver less than a gallon per minute.

Many faucet/control combinations are available(Figure 29.19a-h). Some faucets come with built-in accessories, such as pull-out sprays for kitchen faucets (Figure 29.20a and b), numerous aerators for introducing air into the stream or eliminating splashing, and dual-spray options. The faucet should deliver the water far enough into the bowl so that it is not splashing on the side of the bowl nor should the faucet/bowl pair cause the user to splash on the deck. It is a good idea to draft these relationships to scale on your plan to check several features. One thing that this confirms is that the water is delivered into the bowl close to the drain; it also confirms there is enough room between the handle and the back-splash to operate the faucet. This is especially

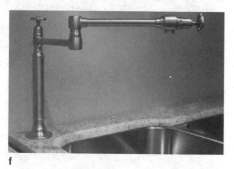

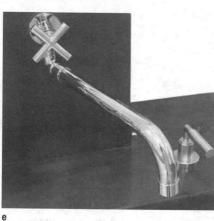

a

b

c

d

e

f

g

h

FIGURE 29.19 Numerous configurations are available for faucets that address all manner of needs in the kitchen, bar, and bath. The center lavatory set (a) is a typical configuration. There are three holes drilled below the integral deck supporting the control handles and the spout. A single-hole lavatory faucet (b) will have a single hole drilled in the sink or countertop. A single-lever, two-hole faucet, such as this Lacava model (c), allows for one-handed control of water temperature and volume. A bridge faucet (d) mixes the hot and cold above the deck. If your client would like an additional hand spray, you must confirm with the manufacturer that it can be provided. Not all bridge faucets can have a mixture of hot and cold because the hand spray must be connected to the system after the two are mixed. Pot fillers are used most often at the cooktop to make water immediately available when cooking and to fill big (and when full, heavy) pasta pots. A wall-mounted pot-filler (e) provides only cold water. Wall-mounted faucets are available with single hot/cold controls or two controls. Pot fillers are also available as deck-mounted versions (f). Freestanding tubs like vessel sinks, have special height consideration (g). Most standard tub sizes are easily accommodated by standard manufacturer offerings, but if you intend to customize the tub size, as with a custom option like the one shown in Figure 29.7, you must confirm that the height planned can be provided by the manufacturer. A vessel sink (h) stands taller than most other sinks. Not all vessel faucets work with all vessel sinks, so check for height compatibility. *All images except (c) photographed by Alana Clark with permission of K&B Galleries.*

important if a 1.25-inch/3-centimeter stone splash is specified because that is the material that you used on the counter. These clearances can get a little bit tight.

Faucets and hand-spray combinations are common in kitchens and at large tubs. If a pull-out or separate handheld spray device is present, you may be required to install a separate vacuum breaker or check valve. This will prevent a hose lying in a sink full of dirty water from drawing contaminated water into the pipelines, contaminating the freshwater source.

For cooks who use large pots, the gooseneck spout is another alternative to the pull-out spray. A gooseneck spout leaves ample room under the tap for rinsing. It lacks the spray angle flexibility the pull-out spray provides.

Factors Contributing to Costs of Plumbing Fixtures

Custom fixtures, premium colors (nonwhite), and special finishes (custom plated locally to match your submitted sample) all contribute to cost without a corresponding jump in quality. Materials used in fabrication affect cost (enameled steel is cheaper than cast iron or china, for example). Design factors such as location affect cost; grouping fixtures is more economical than dispersing them in all directions. Leaving them in or close to their current location when remodeling is more economical if it does not compromise the final design.

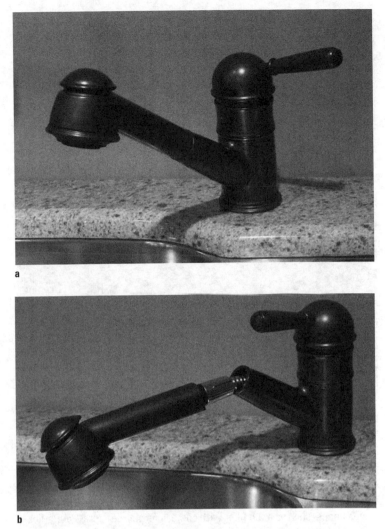

a

b

FIGURE 29.20 This pull-out portion hand spray is designed for use in a kitchen. It has a control button on the allowing the user easy, one-handed control while washing and manipulating with the other hand; this is a more convenient configuration than those with the control at the lever only. Hand sprays are available for tubs and showers also, but they are not integral to the main water outlet as shown here. *Image by Alana Clark with permission of K&B Galleries.*

a

b

Other Plumbing Fixtures and Fittings

There are special fixtures and fittings for penal institutions, commercial specialty scenarios (restaurants and darkrooms are two examples), and other customized scenarios (Figure 29.21a and b). Not all plumbing fixtures are actually plumbed. Chemicals used in some basins (like film-processing locations) may not legally be introduced to wastewater collection systems, so drains lead to collection tanks instead of sewers.

FIGURE 29.21 Specialty plumbing fixtures meet a variety of commercial and unique needs, such as a tub filler with companion pull-out spray (a). Perlick offers a number of configurations to meet a variety of needs and code stipulations. Unique program requirements can be met by standard offerings. A hand laundry sink by Jentle Jet (b) functions as a sink and as a special washing machine for hand-washable laundry.

CHAPTER 30

Fireplaces

When a client wants the plans for a space to include a fireplace, the interior designer is usually consulted for the location and size of the firebox opening. For our health club project, we will assume that the design aspects of logical focal points and traffic patterns, which the interior designer would certainly take into account when determining the location of the fireplace, have already been considered. In addition to design aspects, the designer should be aware of some technical aspects of fireplaces when specifying a new fireplace, considering the value of an existing fireplace in a new scheme, or making any modifications to an existing fireplace.

Fireplaces are strictly governed by code, and because requirements vary among jurisdictions, it's important to review the local codes. Noncombustible surrounds are defined for the structure surrounding the box on all four sides, including the opening. The hearth (the floor surface immediately outside the firebox) is always mandated as noncombustible and its size is specified by code. If the entire floor in the room is a noncombustible material, you may still be required to delineate the hearth area permanently so flammable rugs or furniture will never be positioned within that space. You may have to install a contrasting noncombustible material at the limits of the minimum hearth area to satisfy code in some jurisdictions. If you have a decorative mantelpiece that projects forward of the opening, you will have to increase the size of the required noncombustible surround proportionately to the projection. The more a combustible mantelpiece sticks out, the wider and taller the surround must be.

Kinds of Fireplaces

There are two categories of fireplaces that you might specify for your project: custom-built masonry or prefabricated units. Custom-built fireplaces are practical only for new construction situations because they require *footings* (like foundation walls). The ground must be excavated below the frost line and footings poured before the masonry fireplace and chimney (usually brick) can be built on it.

Custom Masonry Construction

Fireplaces can burn wood or gas. Wood burners are sometimes equipped with gas starters, so even if your client intends to burn wood, you may have to plan for gas lines and a gas key, which resembles a big wing nut that is turned to open the gas valve. Decorative gas keys can be specified for a less utilitarian aesthetic. The mason will size the flue based on the volume within the box and the size of the opening (Figure 30.1). Many proportions are allowable. Typically, the deeper the box, the shorter the height. Many fireplaces have a rectangular opening that is shorter

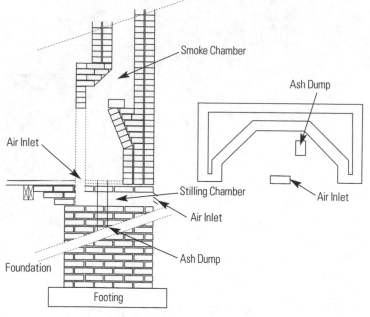

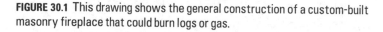

Parts of a Masonry Fireplace

FIGURE 30.1 This drawing shows the general construction of a custom-built masonry fireplace that could burn logs or gas.

than it is wide. Rumford fireplaces have an opening that is as tall as it is wide, which is allowable because the depth from front to back is shallower.

The location of the chimney projecting beyond the roof will dictate the chimney's height. Usually, the chimney will stand above any adjacent ridgeline to eliminate the possibility of back-draft, which would draw smoke into the room. When suggesting a fireplace location, check out the exterior elevations for the location and appearance of the chimney.

Prefab Units

Prefabricated fireplace units can be distinguished from one another by their venting systems. The three types available are the direct vent, B-vent, and ventless fireplaces. Pre-fabs are more akin to appliances than to architecture so you may look ahead to the possible future replacement of the unit. Hopefully without extensive damage to it's enclosure or surround.

DIRECT VENT A direct vent fireplace vents to the outside vertically or horizontally (Figure 30.2). A direct vent uses a high temperature glass panel to seal off the burn area of the fireplace from the

interior of the home. This means that you will also specify the doors that are required for this unit. Because 100 percent of the combustion air comes from outside the home, a direct vent gas fireplace will not affect the indoor air quality of your client's home. Because no air from your client's home is going up the chimney, a direct vent model is roughly 70 percent efficient. Sometimes the exhaust is boosted out with a blower, so confirm the need for electricity after selecting the model to use so your plans and instructions to the installer are complete. Direct vents can be vented vertically or horizontally through an exterior wall.

B-VENT The B-vent (sometimes called natural vent) fireplace must be vented vertically. These fireplaces use the air in the room to support com-

FIGURE 30.2 This prefab direct-vent fireplace is designed to heat the air in a room. The vents must remain unobstructed, so no decorative surround can be applied over the vents or the fireplace will not heat the room. The direct vent fireplace is not to be confused with the ventless fireplace. Heating a room is a feature that could be available with vented or ventless units. This fireplace happens to be a direct vent, so a permanent glass panel covers the opening.

bustion in the firebox. This is important in new construction or well-insulated homes that are tightly built, where fresh air is not leaking into the house. The fire burns oxygen, and your clients also breathe oxygen, so they may want to open a window slightly when they use the fireplace.

VENTLESS "Vent free" or "ventless" (Figure 30.3) should actually be called "room-vented" because the by-products of gas combustion all spill back into the room. The single largest by-product of the gas combustion process is water vapor. Oversizing or overuse of a "vent free" fireplace can lead to excess moisture in a well-built, tightly constructed home. Excess moisture can contribute to the growth of mold and mildew inside the home.

Many codes prohibit the use of ventless fireplaces in bedrooms and bathrooms and require oxygen sensors that sound an alarm if oxygen falls to 18 percent or less of total air composition. California prohibits their use entirely. If you are specifying a ventless unit, make sure the location is not near a high-traffic area or draft (check HVAC supplies, in particular). These fireplaces burn with the damper closed, so there is no updraft to entice the heat and by-products up the flu; consequently, there is nothing to counter a room draft pulling the heat and by-products in the direction of the draft.

Because ventless fireplaces (Figure 30.4) burn with the damper closed, they are more efficient as contributors to the ambient room temperature. People with sensitive noses can smell the fuel, so carefully consider their use in small, enclosed spaces, where the odor could possibly collect and concentrate to "smellable" levels.

When you are specifying a ventless fireplace or a log kit for one, you will specify a special ventless log kit.

Altering an Existing Fireplace

A common client request is to convert a fireplace from wood to gas or gas to wood. Wood fireplaces can be easily converted to burn ceramic logs as long as there is an ash dump to bring the gas lines through. If there is no ash dump, the gas

FIGURE 30.3 This ventless fireplace comes ready to set in place and hook up to a gas line, as do all prefab fireplaces.

FIGURE 30.4 This ventless fireplace is fitted out with a small fireback, which is a metal panel traditionally used to reflect heat into the room. Because this unit uses the air in the room for combustion, the glass is optional.

lines can be broken through the side or back of the box.

If a gas fireplace was installed as such, it cannot be converted to wood. However, a wood fireplace that has had gas logs installed into it can be converted back to wood burning. Here are some hints on identifying whether a fireplace was originally wood- or gas-burning:

1. If the doors are fixed closed, it is almost surely just gas-burning.
2. If it has wall switches or remote controls, it is also likely gas-burning only.
3. If there is a damper that can be closed in the upper part of the firebox, it might be wood-burning.
4. If it has a large-diameter chimney, more than 8 inches round, it is probably wood-burning.

Another frequent request is to turn a one-sided fireplace into a two-sided one. This is rarely successful. The flue size is determined based on the size of the opening and the size of the firebox. Even though the box size stays the same, you now have doubled the opening size, and the fireplace will not draw properly. If the flue is generous for the existing box, it may work to install a brick platform in the bottom of the firebox to raise the fire up while shrinking the interior volume of the firebox. This is preferable to installing tall grates (which also *sometimes* solves the problem of soot in the room) because grates are portable and could be replaced with shorter grates in the future.

Accessories

The decision about a screen or door should be made early in the design of the fireplace so that the mounting and details can accommodate the selection. This is not a critical decision for the function of the fireplace, but the screen or door (especially the door) will be better integrated into the design if its details are planned along with the fireplace details.

Other fireplace accessories include andirons, firebacks, and tools and tool stands. *Andirons,* also called firedogs or chenets, hold logs or support a grate or log basket. *Firebacks* reflect heat and light into the room. A fully appointed fireplace includes firedogs, grate, fireback, and tools in a stand.

INDEX

abaca carpeting, 119*f*

abrash, in handmade rugs, 133, 134*f*

acid stain, 51, 99

acoustics, 39-46

  characteristics of sound, 43-44

  doors and, 221, 222

  managing sound, 42-43

  and noise reduction, 42, 46

  rating and measuring sound, 40-42

  and soundproofing, 45*f*

acrylic carpeting, 118

acrylic finish, for concrete, 153

acrylic paint, 180

acrylic surfaces, 168, 191, 192

acrylic tubs, 275

ADA. *See* Americans with Disabilities Act (ADA) codes

adaptability, 34

adhesives, for laminates, 191

aggregate

  in concrete, 51-52

  in terazzo, 161-66

alkyd paint, 182

allergens, and carpet, 126

aluminum, 76, 83, 201*f*

American Society for Testing and Materials. *See* ASTM International standards

Americans with Disabilities Act (ADA) codes, 15, 17, 272, 286

annealed glass, 86

anodizing, of aluminum, 83

antique flooring, 96-97

antiques, assessing, 209-10

architect, 8, 30

area rugs, 131-42

  See also carpets and rugs

  care and maintenance, 140-41

  custom made, 137, 139, 141-42

  handmade *vs.* machine-made, 131-32

  kinds of, 134-40

  orientals, 134-37

  patterns in, 134-35, 136*f*, 137*f*, 138

  rag rugs, 138-39

  repairs in, 133-34, 135*f*

  selection criteria, 132-33

arm styles, upholstery, 215*f*

Arzurug (organization), 136-37

ASTM International standards, 30, 37

attenuation, of sound, 42, 43*f*

Avery Boardman Furniture, 212-16*f*

balance match, of veneer, 106, 107*f*

ballast, for lighting, 258, 259, 262

ballpark estimates, 12-13, 174

bamboo flooring, 97

banquettes, 213

base styles, in upholstery, 215*f*, 217

bathroom safety, 272

  See also showers; toilets

bathtubs. *See* sinks and tubs

beam spread, in lighting, 256

bedding and pillows, 241

  bedduster 246-47

  headboards, 241, 243*f*

bidding process, 5, 27

  for carpeting, 130

  lighting, 268-69

  for painting, 177

  reviewing bids, 22-24

  for stone work, 73

  for upholstery, 216

  wood paneling, 111

bidets, 287, 288*f*

blinds, 234, 248

blueprint matching, of veneer, 109

book match, of veneer, 106, 107*f*, 108*f*

box match, of veneer, 106, 108*f*, 109

braided rugs, 139

brass and bronze, 76, 81, 275, 288

  in terazzo installations, 164, 166

brick, 55-62

  coatings for, 57-58

  colors and sizes of, 56

  finishes for, 56-57

  mortar joints in, 58-59, 58*f*

  orientations for, 59-60

  patterns (bonds) for, 59-60, 61*f*

of carpeting, 124
of materials, 34
of wallcoverings, 171
Dutch bond, in brick, 60, 61f
dyeing
See also color
of carpeting, 123-24, 136, 142
of concrete, 50, 51f

echo, 41f, 43. See also acoustics
edging, 150f, 157f
See also wood trims
for glass, 91
for stone, 70-71f
electrical devices, 249-54
whirlpool tub, 280-81
wiring, 249-52
electric hinge, 231, 232f
electrician, communication with,
9, 252-54, 268
electrohydraulic toilet, 285
electronic locking, in doors, 228,
229, 230f
enamel finish, 178
for glass tile, 153
for metal, 83, 223, 275
end match, of veneer, 106, 107f
energy costs, 34-35
in window glazing, 86
engineered stone, 161
engineered wood, 198, 204, 248
See also medium density fiberboard; particleboard
English bond, in brick, 60, 61f
Environmental Protection
Agency (EPA), 35, 36
epoxy coatings, 181, 289
epoxy grout, for tile, 159
epoxy resin matrix, 161, 163, 165
estimates. See budgets and estimates

fabric
See also drapery; upholstery
panels, 174, 176
railroaded, 212, 247
wallcoverings, 168-69
faucets, 17, 277-78, 288-91, 290f
faux bois (wood grain), 182, 184f

felted rugs, 139, 140f
ferrous metal, 75-76. See also
steel
fiber, for carpeting, 117-19, 126
See also specific fiber
fiberboard. See medium-density
fiberboard (MDF)
fiberglass backing, for stone, 73,
74f
fiberglass doors, 223
fiberglass tubs, 275
fiber-optic lighting, 261
fiber pads, for carpet, 126
film-formers
for brick, 57
for concrete, 53
finishes
for brick, 56-57
for cabinetry, 201-2, 207, 208
concrete, 49-51
enamel, 83, 153, 178, 223, 275
faucet, 289
flame resistance of, 16-17
gloss level of, 99, 156, 202
hardware, 232
lacquer, 75, 202, 275, 289
for metal, 75, 80-81, 83, 84, 223
polyurethane, 99, 100, 147, 153
for sinks and tubs, 274-75, 276
wax, 83, 97-98, 100, 147, 148f,
202, 276
for wood flooring, 97-100
of wood paneling, 110
firebacks, 295f, 296
fire/flame resistance, 16-17, 293
doors, 224
in glass, 87
in walls, 178, 179f
fireplaces, 293-96
hearth area, 293
mantles for, 116f
venting styles, 294-95, 295f
fire-safety codes, 16-17, 293, 295
panic door, 228, 229f
flame resistance. See fire/flame
resistance
floor cloths, 138
flooring
See also carpets and rugs

ADA codes for, 18
bamboo, 97
cork, 97, 101, 145, 147, 148f
laminated, 95-96, 101, 144
resilient, 143-50
substrate for, 101-2, 157-58,
164
terrazzo and stone composites,
161-66
wood, 93-102
fluorescent lamps, 256, 257-59,
259f
flushing, of toilets, 285, 286f
foam padding, for carpet, 126,
126f, 127
foam padding, in upholstery, 212
foam underlayment, in floors,
101-2
foil wallcoverings, 169
foot-candle (light measure), 255
formaldehyde, 102, 202
frequency of sound waves, 44
fresco, 182
furans, 36, 159

gas-discharge lamps, 259-60
general contractor
communication with, 24-25
hiring and qualifying, 21-22
responsibilities of, 9
and waiver of lien, 23
glass, 85-92
block, 88-89, 89f, 90f
in doors, 223, 224
mirrors, 90-92
panels, 92
production of, 85-86
properties of, 86-87
sinks, 274f, 276
in terrazzo aggregate, 162f
tiles, 153, 154f
types of, 87-90
glazed tiles, 156, 157f
glazing, 182, 184f
overglazing, 207
gloss level
of finishes, 99, 156, 202
of paint, 181
gold plating, 81, 289

fluorescent lamps, 256, 257-59, 259f

gas-discharge lamps, 259-60

incandescent lamps, 256-57, 257f

LEDs and fiber optics, 261

lighting specialist, 269-70

luminaires (fixtures), 255, 261-66, 267, 269

metal halide lamps, 260-61, 260f

recessed ceiling, 263f

light switches, 266, 266f

light transmittance, of glass, 86

lime plaster, 178

limestone, 64f, 68, 69f

linen carpeting, 118

linen glaze technique, 182, 184f

lineoleum flooring, 143

lining and interlining

for drapery, 234, 236-37, 237f

for wallcoverings, 171, 173

liquidated damages, 24

local materials, 34

low-embodied energy, 34

lumen (light measure), 255

luminaires (light fixtures), 255, 261-26

See also lighting

decorative, 264-66

housing and trims, 261-62

leadtime for, and installing, 269

recessed ceiling, 262f, 263f

selection of, 267

lux (light measure), 255

management. *See* project management

mantlepieces, 116f

See also fireplaces

manufacturer, and specs, 32

marble, 65, 66-67, 67f, 71

chips, in terazzo, 162, 164t

masonry fireplaces, 293-94

matching, of veneers, 106-9

material schedules, 20f, 26-27

matrix binder, in terazzo, 161, 163, 164-65

medium-density fiberboard (MDF), 150, 174, 190

as baseboard, 115

for cabinets, 195, 196f, 204

as substrate for veneer, 102, 103

melamine resin, 189

metal doors, 223

metal halide lamps, 260-61, 260f

metal laminates, 199-200, 201f

metal leaf, 182

metallic paint, 182, 183f, 185

metal plating, 81-82, 84, 232, 275, 288, 289

metal(s), 75-84

See also specific metal

alloys of, 75, 76

anodizing of, 83

cast, 75, 77-78, 78f, 79

coatings for, 76, 82-84

extruded and spun, 78, 78f

ferrous, 75-76

finishes for, 75, 80-81, 83, 84

forming, 76-80

judging quality in, 84

kinds of, 75-76

nonferrous, 76

oxidation of, 75, 76, 81, 82-83, 185, 275

pipes and tubes, 78-79

salvaged, 80

in terazzo installations, 164, 165f, 166

toxic, 36

weaving and welding of, 79, 79f, 81f

metal sinks, 274-75

metal tiles, 154, 155f

methenamine pill test, 16

millwork trim, 113-16, 187

mirrors, 90-92

modified closed specs, 32

modular carpet tiles, 122, 129f

moisture control

See also water-resistance

in floors, 93, 122, 149, 150

molding. *See* wood trims (millwork)

mortar joints, in brick, 58-59

music, reverbation of, 43

Mylar films, 90, 169

National Electrical Manufacturers Association, 250f

National Ornamental and Miscellaneous Metals Association (NOMMA), 78f, 80, 80f

needlepoint rugs, 140f

nickel, 75, 76, 82, 84, 274, 289

Noise Reduction Coefficient (NRC), 42, 46t

See also acoustics; sound

nontoxic materials, 35-36

nylon carpeting, 117-18

oil-based paint, 180

oil finish, 100, 202

olefin carpeting, 118

onyx (stone), 69, 70f

open (descriptive) specifications, 26-27, 31-32, 204

oriental carpet, 134-37

owner-build, 6

oxidation

in metallic paint, 185, 187

in metals, 75, 76, 81, 82-83, 275

in wood, 93

padding

for carpets, 125-27, 127f

foam, 126, 126f, 127, 212

in upholstery, 211-12, 216

paint, 180-82, 186, 187-88

See also coatings; primers

painted concrete, 50-51

panels. *See* glass panels; wood panelling

panic door latching, 228, 229f

paper trail, 27

paper wallcoverings, 167-68, 171, 173

parquet flooring, 96, 97f

particleboard, 102, 150, 190, 195

parties to project, 5-10, 29-30

patinas, for metal, 83

patterns